MASTERPIECES

EARLY MEDIEVAL ART

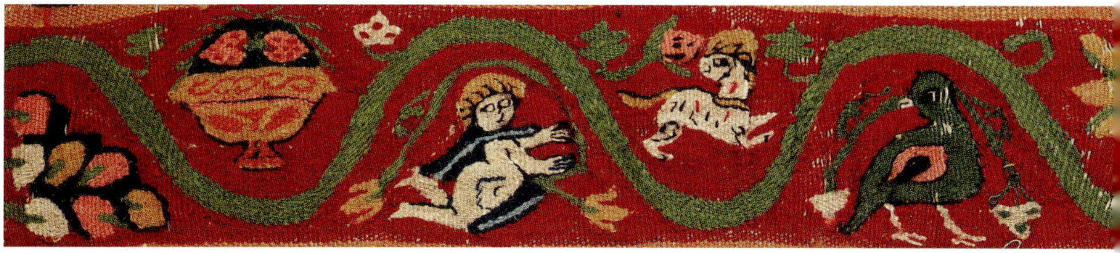

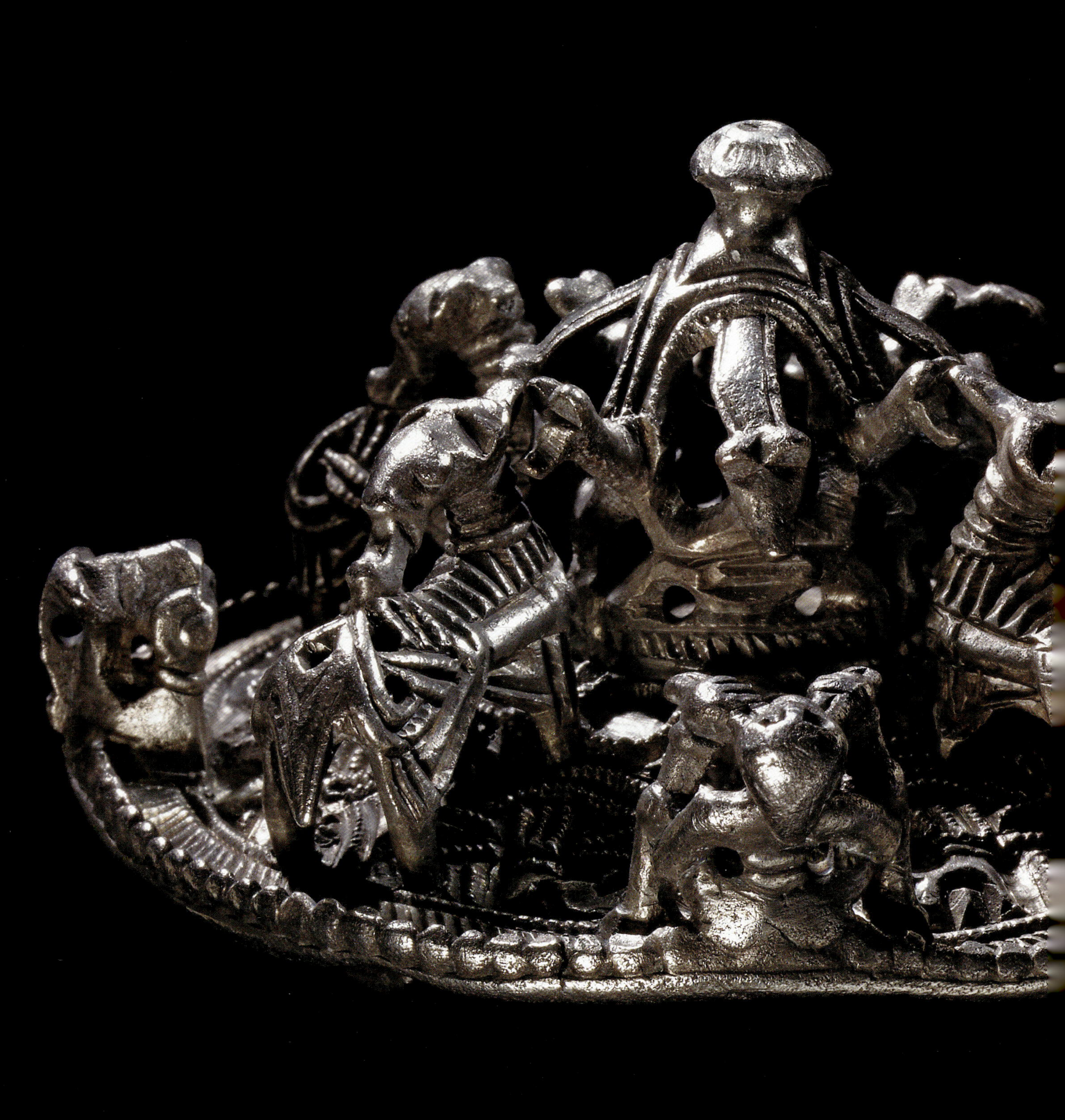

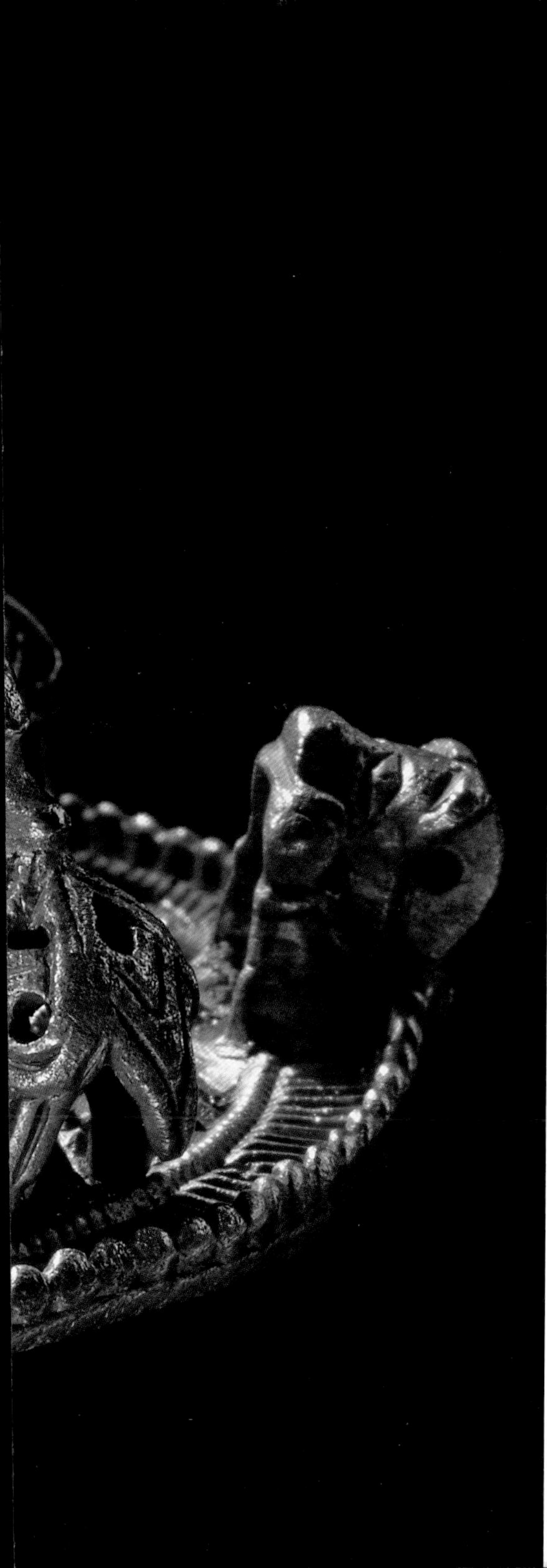

MASTERPIECES

EARLY MEDIEVAL ART

SONJA MARZINZIK

THE BRITISH MUSEUM PRESS

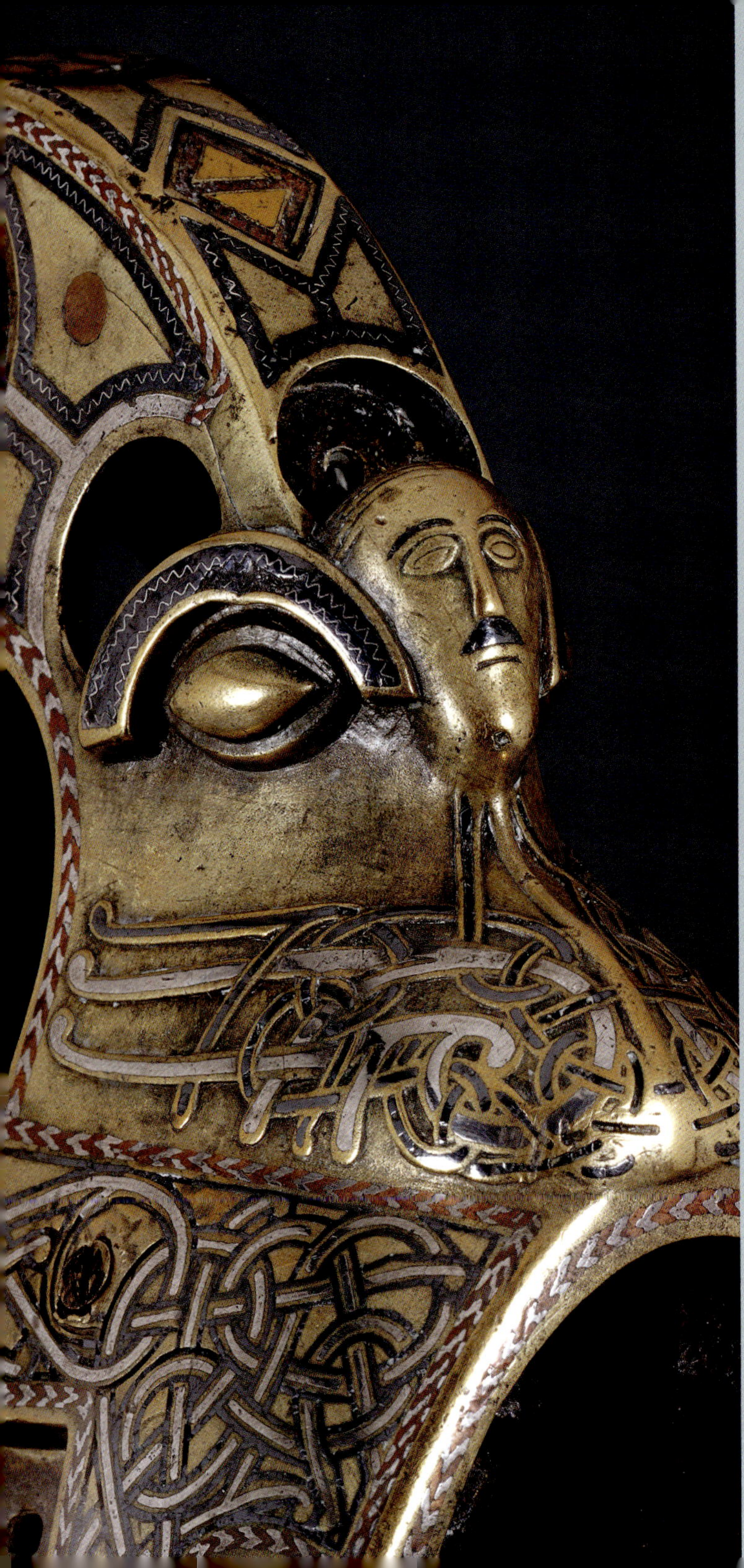

For Sir Paul and Lady Ruddock
with thanks for many years of
generous encouragement

CONTENTS

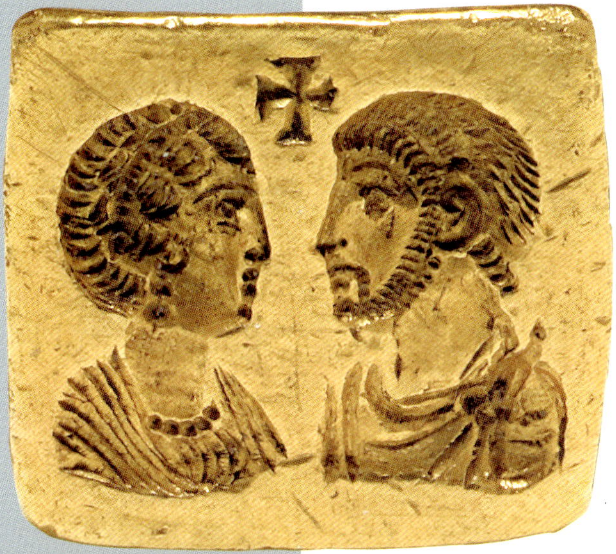

ACKNOWLEDGEMENTS

A great many people have contributed to this work and I am particularly indebted to my former colleagues Sue Brunning, Leslie Webster and Barry Ager. Further invaluable assistance came from Richard Abdy, Roger Bland, Stefanie Friedrich, Rupert Gebhard, Martin Goldberg, the Harrers, Michaela Helmbrecht, Richard Hobbs, Joachim Huber, Thomas Kiely, Beverley Nenk, Elisabeth O'Connell, James Robinson, Harald Schulze, St John Simpson, Niamh Whitfield, Gareth Williams, Jonathan Williams and Sue Youngs. Haneesha Melwani, Lluis Tembleque and Rosie Weetch were indispensable in resolving all manner of detailed questions, and Marion Archibald, Renee Massarrello and Griffin Murray generously granted permission to refer to their unpublished works.

I could not have wished for a more supportive and patient editor than Sarah Faulks. At the British Museum Press, I would also like to thank Rosemary Bradley, Naomi Waters, Felicity Maunder, Kate Oliver, and the book's designer Andrew Shoolbred.

Wonderful new photography was taken by Saul Peckham, while the various specialists in Conservation Section ensured that all the objects looked at their very best. The use of both published and unpublished analyses carried out by Science Section greatly enhanced my research. Graphic work came courtesy of Craig Williams, and Axelle Russo as well as Katie Anderson helped with the picture research.

An essential research visit to London and Oxford was made possible through the kind hospitality of Roberta Marchesin, Katy and Charlie Tee, Charlotte Behr and John Yarnold, as well as Jason and Charvy Narain-Zerdin.

To all these colleagues and friends my warm thanks for their support and inspiration.

Munich, 5 November 2012

PREFACE

This book is a companion to the new gallery at the British Museum displaying objects from the late Roman world to the early Middle Ages dating from between AD 300 and 1100. Neither the redisplay of the gallery nor this publication would have been possible without the generosity and enthusiasm of Sir Paul and Lady Ruddock. Their wide interests take in this period, which is now seen not so much as the end of one era, but as the transition to another which helped shape Europe and the Mediterranean into the world we know today. There is no doubt that the changes and transformations involved with this were painful, coming with their fair share of violence and disruption.

However, the continuities of social, cultural, artistic and even legal structures are considered to be at least as important as the discontinuities. In particular the lasting influence of the Roman Empire, be it the old city of Rome in the West or later Byzantium in the East, is reflected in many pieces in this volume.

The late antique and early medieval collections of the British Museum are among the finest and most comprehensive known. While the concept of art primarily for aesthetic pleasure had been well known in antiquity, other aspects, such as the use of art to display status or for the expression of political ideas and religious beliefs, increased in importance in the post-classical world. Beauty permeated everyday life and personal adornment, in the form of brooches, buckles, textiles and jewellery, was a prime focus of artistic expression. Refined decoration, precious materials and exquisite craftsmanship continued to command a great deal of appreciation.

Starting with the richness of the late Roman world both inside the empire and beyond its borders (Chapter 1) and moving into the Byzantine era (Chapter 2), we encounter the successors to the Romans in the north. The Anglo-Saxons (Chapter 3) are notable for their exquisite artistry, while objects from the Migration Period to the Holy Roman Empire (Chapter 4) take the reader through all of northern Europe and beyond to the Mediterranean and the Black Sea. The Vikings in Scandinavia and the British Isles, as well as their neighbours in the Baltic and central Europe, are the focus of the next chapter (Chapter 5). The volume concludes with some of the most stunning art from the period, crafted in the Celtic sphere (Chapter 6).

Each entry draws on numerous sources and the Further Reading section is a good starting point for those with a deeper interest. Contextual maps and a glossary of techniques, styles and other terms discussed in the text can be found at the back of the book.

Isidore of Seville wrote in the seventh century that 'there are three genres of "literary works"....The first kind are extracts...in which things that seem obscure or difficult may be outlined in brief summary....The second kind are homilies...which are delivered before the public. Third are tomes...which we call books or volumes.' To some degree this publication covers all three of Isidore's categories and it is hoped that readers will enjoy the journey through time and space presented here.

1 THE LATE ROMAN WORLD

(THIRD TO SIXTH CENTURY AD)

By around AD 400 the Roman Empire (**Map 1**) had endured almost a century of continuous political turmoil and wars along its borders. And yet its cultural output was unbroken. With the strengthening of Christianity, which in AD 313 had been made a legal religion by the emperor Constantine (AD 306–37), and the comprehensive prohibition of pagan rites under Theodosius I (AD 379–95) by AD 392, new impulses and iconographies were joining the artistic repertoire.

From a modern viewpoint the emergence of Christian art may look like a major event, especially as it established some visual conventions which are still valid today, such as the depiction of the Cross and the Crucifixion of Christ (**15**). Yet rather than being something completely new, Christian art was in many ways a natural continuation and development of late Roman artistic styles and practices. Up to the late fourth century, for example, the same workshop might have produced sculpture, fine metalwork or glass with pagan themes, mythological scenes or Christian imagery (**3**), depending on what a customer required.

Detail of a late Roman elephant ivory diptych, possibly AD 402 (**13**)

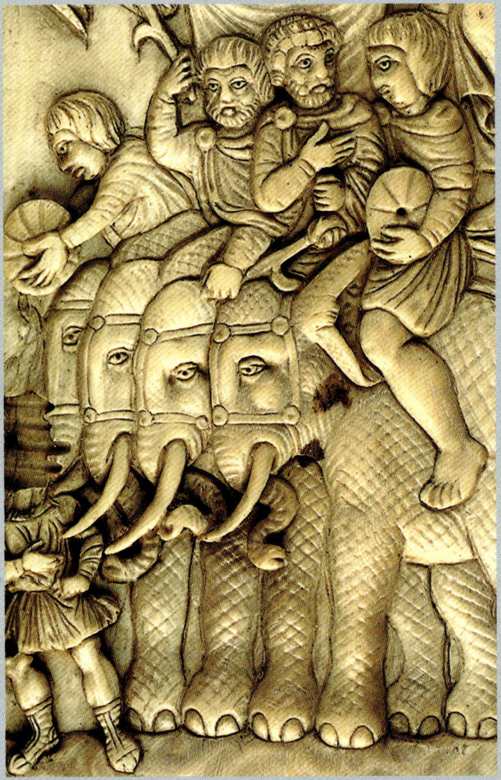

Art was made for pleasure, prestige and commemoration, but sculpture, portraiture on coins, epigraphy and architecture in particular were also deployed for political ends, propagating approved notions of the state and imperial authority. In the same way, religious art of this period served not only for individual contemplation, but also played a role in providing a focus for communal ritual and promoting the faith. It, too, could serve as an expression of social or political views (**13**).

The influence of the Roman Empire did not stop at its borders. For centuries, there had been contacts across these borders, and Roman luxuries and trade wares were exported far and wide. Glass and metal vessels, pottery, jewellery, dress accessories and Roman coinage arrived abroad through trading, raiding or as diplomatic gifts (**16**). Despite border skirmishes and all-out wars, 'barbarians' – those who did not speak Latin – served in the Roman army and could rise to the highest offices. Mercenaries returning from the Roman army brought goods as well as customs and ideas back to their homelands. Access to prestigious objects and their redistribution are likely to have influenced the social structure of local societies and their elites. Concurrently, the styles and techniques of Roman art had an impact on traditions outside of the empire, which assimilated some Roman elements into their own artistic practices. For instance, Mediterranean interlace patterns, which were popular on mosaics, contributed to the genesis of Germanic animal interlace. Furthermore, late Roman military metalwork was often decorated with chip-carving, a technique which was taken up enthusiastically in fifth-century Scandinavia where it was used to perfection on female jewellery. Remarkably, the same military buckles and belt fittings also seem to have inspired Celtic craftsmen, resulting in new and hybrid metalwork (**19**).

But goods did not just travel in one direction. Slaves, timber, furs, metal ores and wild animals for circus games, to name but a few, were imported into the empire. Precious commodities, such as amber from the Baltic coast, ivory from Africa (**13**), pepper from India and gemstones such as garnets from Sri Lanka, were much sought after as well.

The Roman Empire was formally divided into an eastern and western part in AD 395 in an attempt to make the enormous territory more manageable. A myriad of reasons, including internal power struggles, external conflicts and economic difficulties, contributed to the eventual demise of the western half. In AD 476 Romulus Augustus, the last Roman emperor in the West and himself the son of an usurper, was exiled by Odoacer, a Germanic military commander, who had risen high in the Roman army. Odoacer took control of Italy until AD 493, when he was murdered by Theoderic the Great (AD 493–526), who established the Ostrogoth rule there (**83**). While its art lived on, the political entity of the Roman Empire in the West had ended. It was succeeded by numerous Germanic kingdoms, which carried some of the Roman traditions forward into the period now known as the early Middle Ages (Chapters 3 and 4).

1 THE LYCURGUS CUP

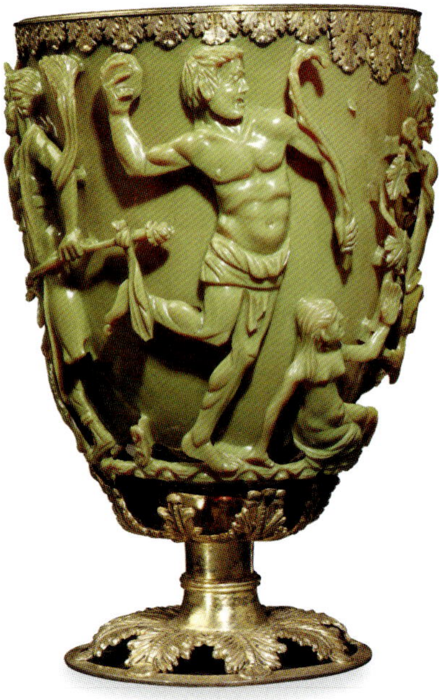

Roman
Unknown findspot
Cup *c.* AD 290–325
Foot and rim fittings *c.* 1800
Total height 15.9 cm
Acquired with a contribution from The Art Fund
1958,1202.1

Perhaps one of the most wondrous glass vessels to have survived from Roman antiquity is the Lycurgus cup. Its glass wall, which was originally about 1.5 cm thick, was cut away using rotating wheels, leaving behind a delicate network of relief and freestanding ornament. In addition, those parts of the glass which feature figures were partly hollowed out from behind to enhance further the astonishing properties of the glass. While it is an opaque, glossy green under ordinary conditions, it glows a purplish, translucent red when light shines through it. The cup was not fire polished, as was once thought, but mechanically finished, confirming the immense skill of the glass cutter.

The image on the right shows the figure of the Thracian king Lycurgus captured by vines, as seen from the inside of the vessel. Lycurgus had attempted to kill the maenad Ambrosia, who was part of the entourage of the god Bacchus, but she was transformed into a vine. On the near side of the cup, the angry god is seen striding towards the scene. As the light in the photograph is directed away from Bacchus, he is a more opaque shade of green, with slightly translucent red overtones. The view on the left shows one of the god's outraged followers about to hurl a stone at Lycurgus.

It was probably by accident that Roman glass workers discovered that red tones and colour changes could be created by adding minute quantities of gold and silver to the molten glass mass. Recent scientific analysis has demonstrated that the colour effects result from the development of silver-gold nanoparticles, which are finely dispersed in the glass. The right production conditions would have been difficult to control and the technique does not seem to have lasted beyond the fourth century.

Such glassware must have been extremely rare and precious. A letter supposedly written by the emperor Hadrian (AD 117–38) mentions gifts of cups which change colour, marking them out as suitable presents among the very highest circles of late Roman society.

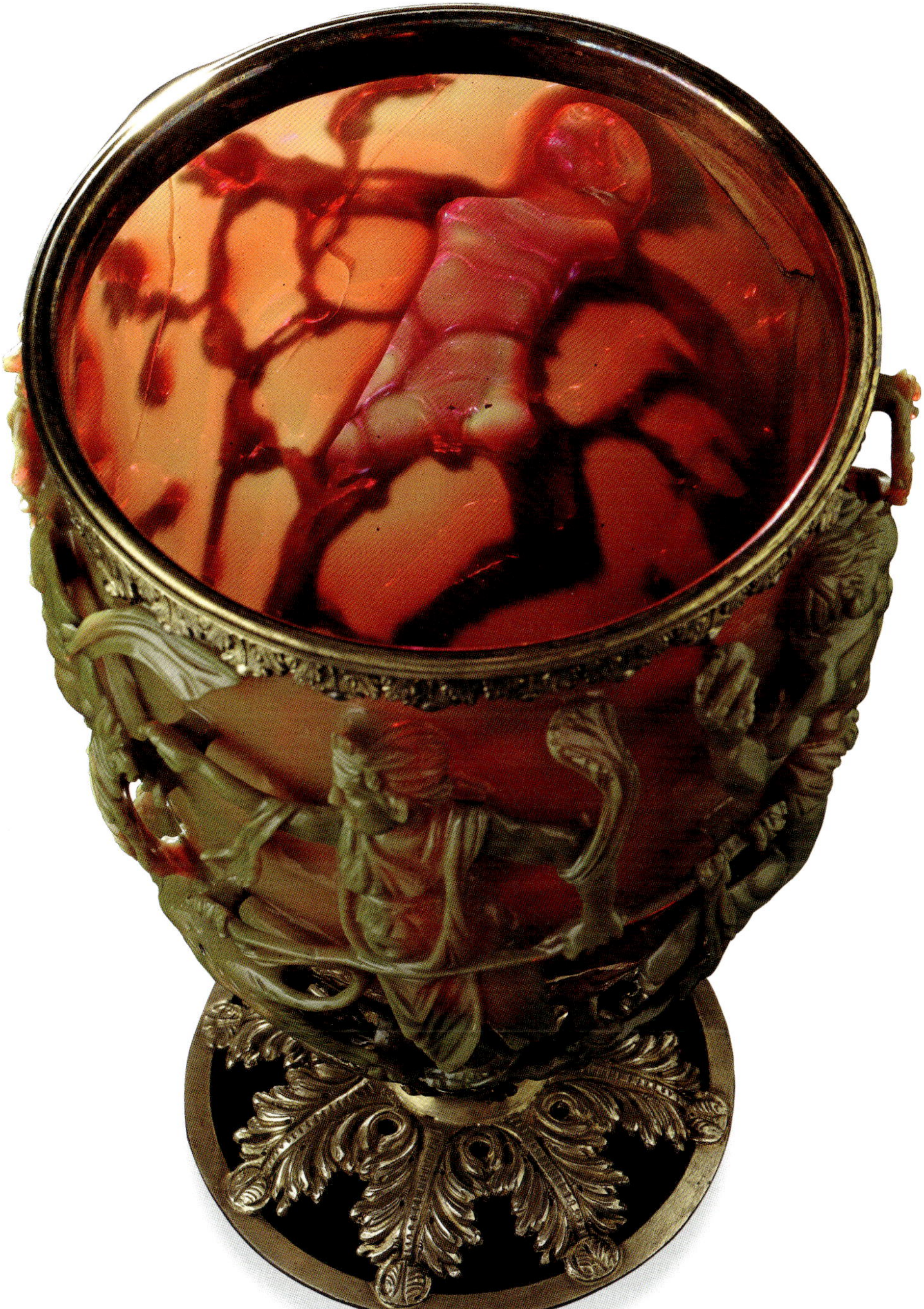

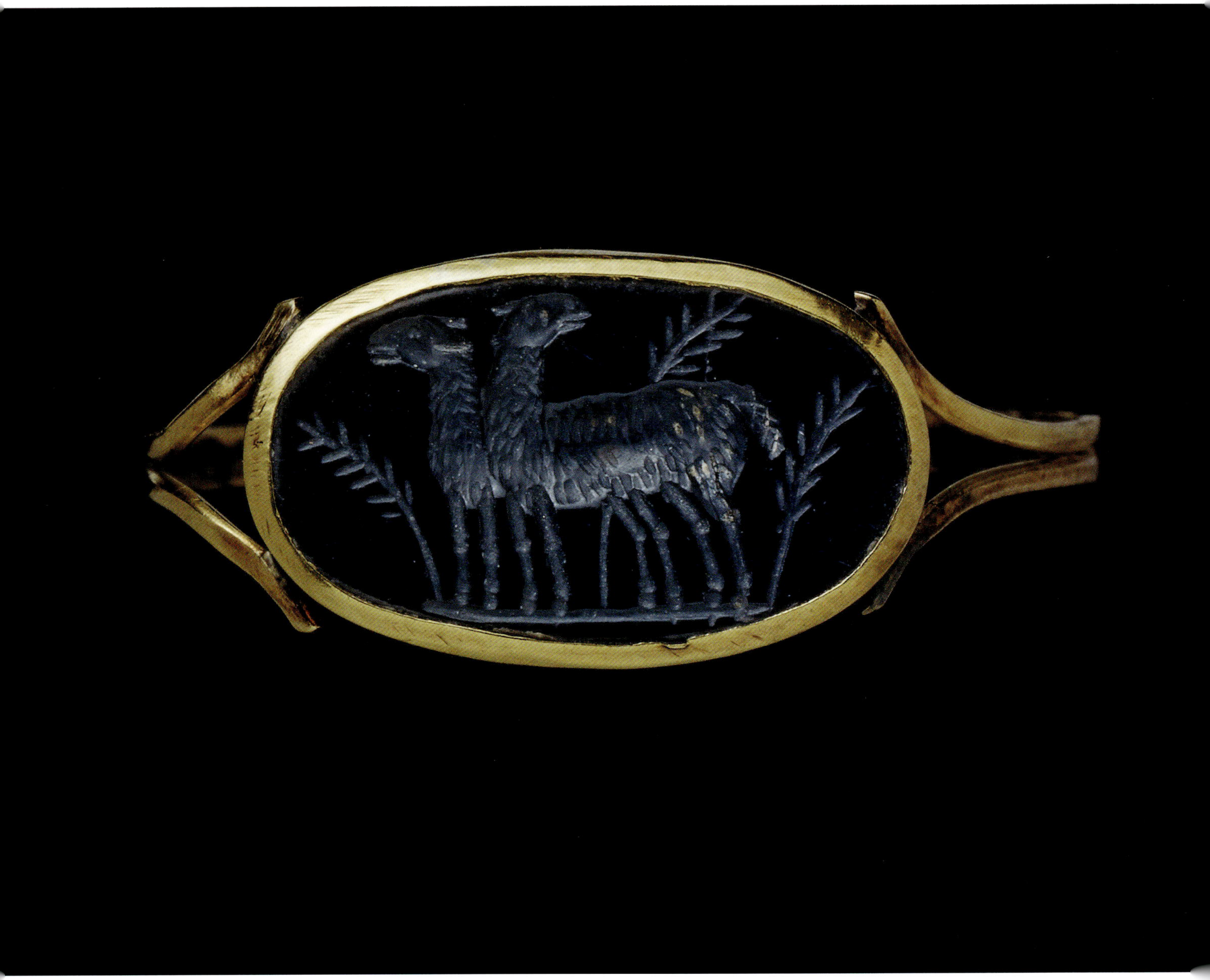

2 JASPER INTAGLIO

This intaglio or gem has often been described as early Christian. Two sheep are shown, surrounded by what appear to be palm branches. They are engraved into a green jasper gem, now set in an eighteenth- or nineteenth-century gold finger-ring. The detail of the animals is beautifully observed, their coats rendered through small scoops of the engraving tool; even their hooves are finely modelled. The gem was employed for sealing documents as it could be impressed into heated wax.

Certain images were considered suitable for explicitly Christian finger-rings (**22**): fish, fishermen, anchors and doves were, for instance, deemed to be appropriate in an influential second-century text. Sheep were not mentioned, and yet the motif of the Good Shepherd was the second most widespread after the fish for gem-set rings in the third and fourth century. The shepherd is usually shown as a young man wearing a short tunic and carrying a lamb across his shoulders, a composition called *kriophoros*. On other gems in the British Museum, he is also depicted surrounded by sheep. The scene is found in many media, including frescoes in catacombs and images moulded or impressed on oil lamps.

The image can be read as a reference to the episode in the New Testament where Jesus likens himself to the good shepherd who would give his life for his flock (John 10:1–18), or another passage which refers to the shepherd who carries home the lost sheep (Luke 15:3–7).

But caution is advisable when offering an interpretation, as shepherds and bucolic scenes were already popular Roman themes before the birth of Christ (**11**). On rings which are definitely Christian, the *kriophoros* is often accompanied by other explicitly Christian symbols or inscriptions. The sheep here are shown with palm branches, a possible allusion to Christian martyrs whose emblem they were. But the iconography is unusual and the gem may have had no religious meaning at all. It exemplifies how stylistic elements common in late antiquity were naturally adopted into the canon of Christian expression to the degree that their significance is sometimes ambiguous.

Roman
Unknown findspot
Gem probably 3rd century AD
Ring 18th or 19th century
Length of intaglio 1.4 cm
1856,0425.20

3 THE PROJECTA CASKET

A sea dragon is ploughing through the waves, carrying a *nereid* or sea nymph on his back, who reclines gracefully while holding a gilded festoon (**32**) in her hands. A chubby *erot* is cavorting in the water, stretching his arms out towards her, while a dolphin splashes to the right. The gilding on the scarf blowing around the nymph adds to the liveliness of the silver relief, creating an almost painterly impression. This playful scene unfolds on the lid of one of the most magnificent surviving pieces of Roman silver which was intended to be used as a container for toiletries. The three other sides of the lid also depict mythological sea scenes, showing the goddess Venus and her companions, while the lower part of the casket displays imagery relating to bathing and beautification.

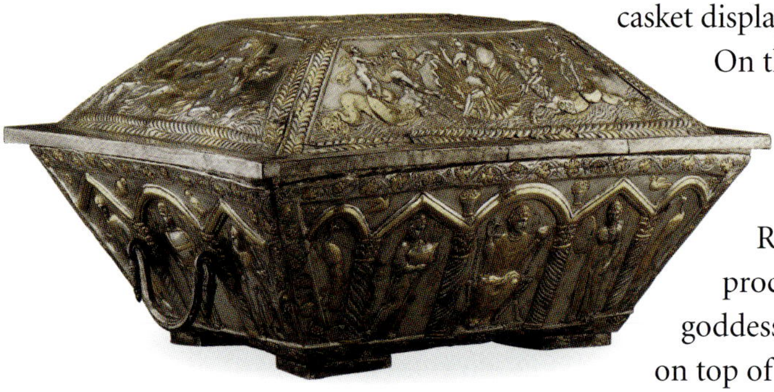

On the front of the casket a lady is shown pinning her hair while a servant holds up a mirror to her. She is also seen in a procession, in which a casket just like this one is being carried. The narrative that unfolds seems to refer to a late Roman wedding: the preparations of the bride, the probable procession to the groom's house, the imagery relating to the goddess of love and her retinue, and finally the wreathed medallion on top of the casket showing the lady and her husband (**17**).

An inscription around the lid addresses the bride and groom directly: 'SECVNDE ET PROIECTA VIVATIS IN CHRI[STO]' – 'Secundus and Projecta, live in Christ'. It may seem contradictory that the casket, most probably a wedding gift, uses pagan imagery alongside a Christian admonition, but the allusion to a mythical setting for marriage would not have struck a contemporary viewer as odd. In fact, Christian scenes may have been considered inappropriate for something as mundane as a toiletry container. The casket therefore illustrates perfectly how a late antique workshop could have provided luxury goods for customers of different faiths, but in a style that was understood by all.

An eminent Roman named Projecta died on 30 December AD 383 and it is probable that this casket once belonged to her. It was discovered with other silver items (**4**) in 1793 which are now collectively known as the Esquiline Treasure.

Roman
From Rome, Italy
c. AD 330–80
Width 55.9 cm
1866,1229.1

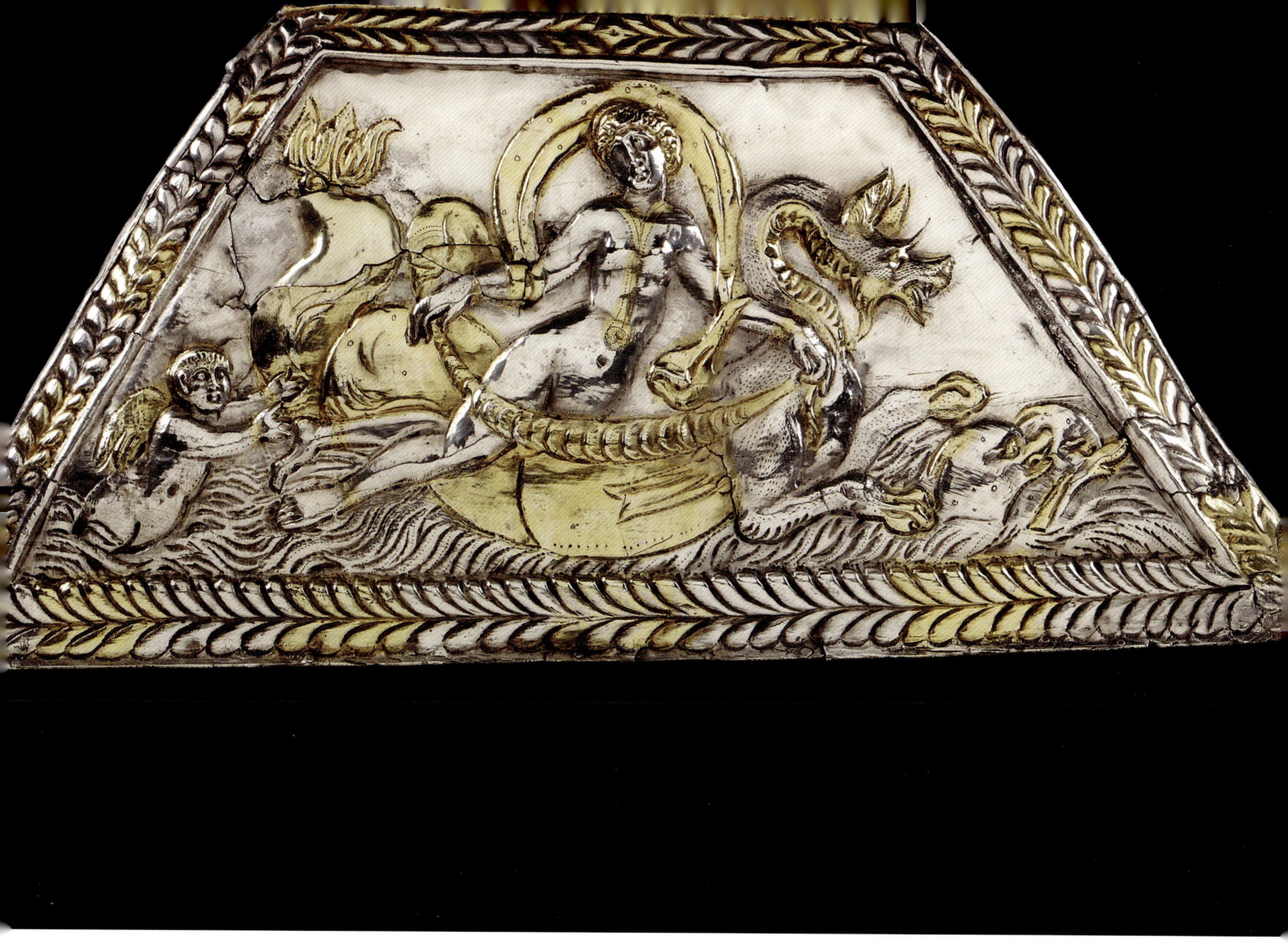

4 FIGURE OF ALEXANDRIA

Both the Greeks and later the Romans personified cities in the form of goddesses. This goddess, representing Alexandria, is from a set which also depicts Rome, Constantinople and Antioch, the great centres of the Roman Empire. All four figures wear elaborate clothing and hold various symbols, and are seated on rectangular sockets which are open at the back. These sockets reveal the function of the statuettes as ornaments that capped the ends of the horizontal frame of a type of sedan chair. A pin and safety chain on the socket ensured that the figures could not slip off. A hinged openwork leaf below the feet of each figure would have swung when the chair was being carried.

This personification of Alexandria, the foremost city in Egypt, is shown wearing a long, belted garment and mantle together with boots. Her complex headdress consists of a crown with turrets, walls and gates, while one of her feet rests on a ship's prow. All of these are references to Alexandria's defences and the significance of her harbour. The fruit and sheaves of grain in the figure's hands allude to the rich harvests of Egypt and the exports of grain which were of great importance to the empire. The precious material and detailed workmanship, which enlivens the figures' clothing and ornament through fine punch work, indicate that they were made for a person of standing. Moreover, groups of city personifications were associated with the emperor and high-level members of the administration.

Workers discovered the figures together with large silver containers, other chair fittings, flagons and dishes while digging at the foot of the Esquiline Hill in Rome in 1793.

Due to inscriptions on some of the objects, it has been suggested that the owners of the treasure came from the powerful Turcii family. Notably, one member of this clan, Secundus, was married to a woman named Projecta from AD 379 to 383 when she passed away. They may well be the couple addressed in the inscription on the Projecta Casket (**3**), which is also part of the Esquiline Treasure.

Roman
From Rome, Italy
c. AD 330–80
Height 19.0 cm
1866,1229.24

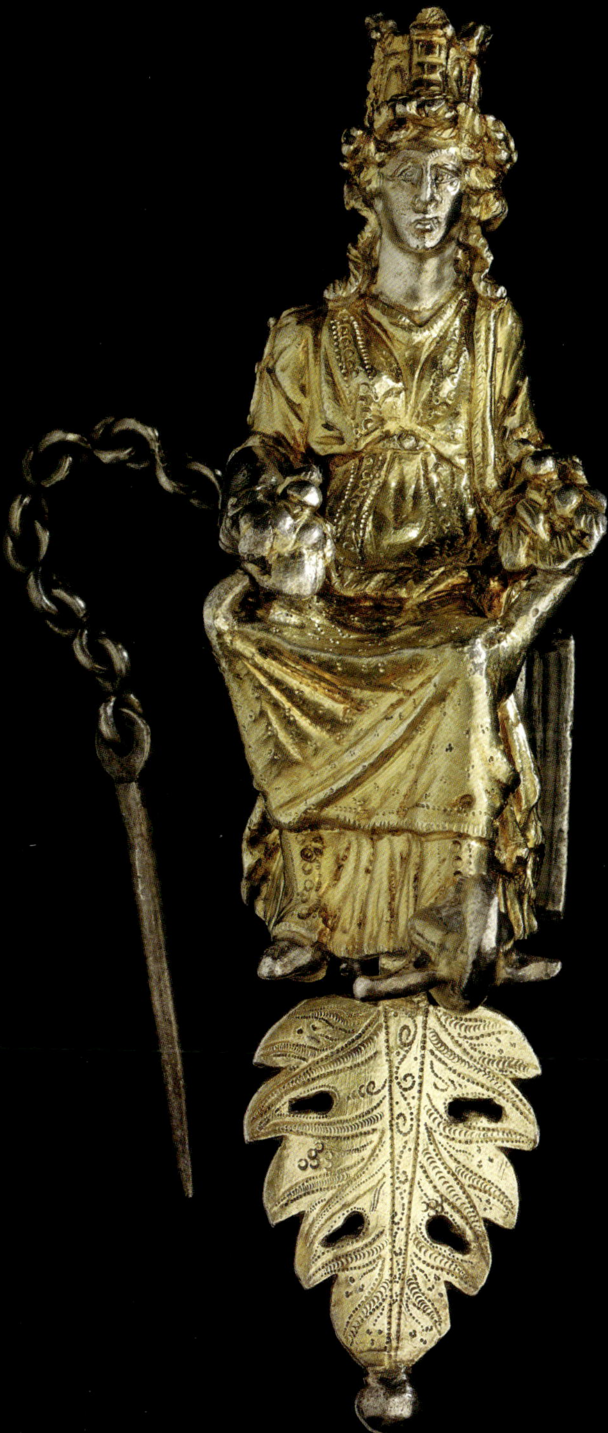

5 OPENWORK PLAQUE

A rider is galloping along at full speed while steering her mount alongside a running lioness. A tree is visible to the left and floriate designs are set in each corner. Details are accentuated by the finest engraving and stippling, decoration made by fine dots. The hunting scene is placed against a background of *opus interrasile* or pierced work (**8**, **34**), forming a floral scroll and cable pattern design.

Pierced work was created by various techniques of perforating, cutting, drilling or chasing a thin gold sheet with a selection of different tools. Depending on what method or combination of techniques was chosen, the resulting openwork might have a rather flat appearance or show a very subtle relief effect, as in the plaque here.

Up to six different metalworking techniques have been identified from the third to seventh century. It appears that this variety was motivated more by economic concerns than by craftsmen's skills, aesthetic criteria or a desire to simplify work processes. *Opus interrasile* was not only attractive, but also had the benefit of being cost-effective in its use of gold, while looking sumptuous at the same time. Notably, the technique first became popular during the third century when the demand for luxurious jewellery had to be reconciled with economic strictures.

On the reverse, another plaque with a pierced work pattern replicates the floriate corner design of the front in rows. The fairly chunky beaded upper border is threaded onto a gold pin that appears cut at either end. It is unclear how the plaque would have been worn, but it was certainly a high-class piece of jewellery.

The plaque was found with six gold coins and some further gold jewellery (**6**) in the province known as Asia Minor during this period. At close to eighty-seven grams, the plaque equalled the weight of around fifteen gold *solidi*. Considering that an ordinary soldier would have earned approximately four to five *solidi* a year, and that many people had to survive on about three *solidi*, this sets the contents of the hoard into perspective.

Late Roman/early Byzantine

From Asia Minor, modern-day Turkey

4th century AD

Height 5.1 cm

Bequeathed by A.W. Franks

AF.332

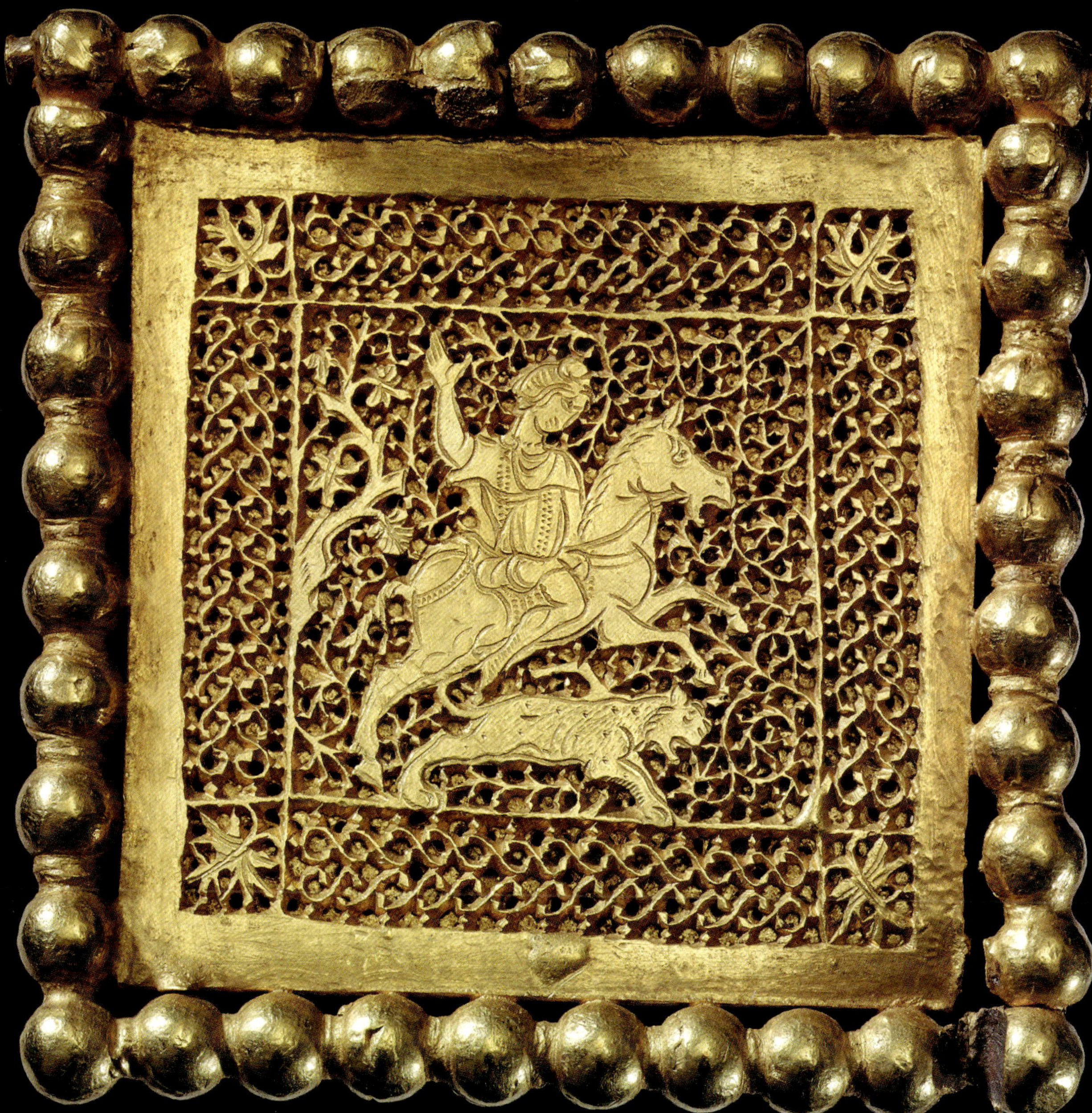

6 BELT FITTING

The same hoard which contained the superb *opus interrasile* plaque (**5**) also included two highly unusual belt fittings. Both are made from gold and composed of a central portrait medallion, with a substantial beaded frame and six hollow petal-shaped elements at the top and bottom. Large rivets on the back would have allowed the fitting to be mounted onto a belt strap, which probably had further mounts like the present one.

A young man wearing a cloak gathered with a prominent crossbow brooch (**17**) on his right shoulder is shown on the medallion. He is set against a nielloed background and his body and clothing are reserved in gold with any outlines also nielloed. The artist almost seems to have sketched the design, which has the character of an impressionistic ink drawing, demonstrating that he was an experienced and accomplished goldsmith.

This style is reminiscent of the busts of the young men and women shown on the band of a late Roman marriage ring also in the British Museum (**14**). The portrait also echoes the roundels with depictions of young men found on late antique luxury silverware and on the most exclusive types of crossbow brooches.

The other fragment from the hoard is clearly from the belt buckle itself, as it still contains part of a hinge. Its portrait would therefore have been at the front and centre of the belt, which is only appropriate as it presents the bust of a ruler characterized by a nimbus or halo and an imperial brooch (**94**). The likeness of the young man on the present fitting is anonymous, as are those on the ring mentioned above, and this type of image follows the model of the ageless ruler portrait found on jewellery. It seems that the portrait of the well-to-do young man – as illustrated by his large crossbow brooch – was seen as a symbol of success and social standing. It is therefore possible that these depictions represent propitious allegories, in the same way that *erots* (**3**) and *genii* or pagan spirits of the seasons had been used in the past to herald good luck.

Late Roman/early Byzantine

From Asia Minor, modern-day Turkey

4th century AD

Maximum width 3.5 cm

Bequeathed by A.W. Franks

AF.334

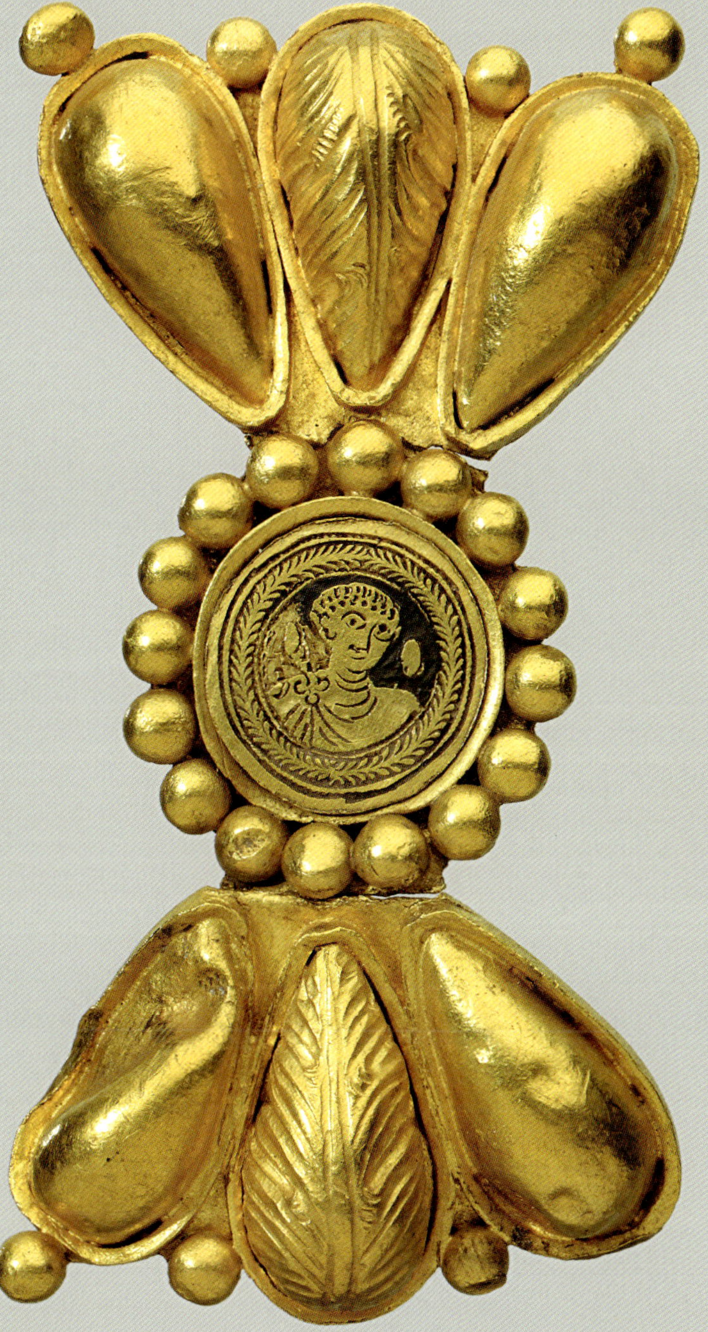

7 BOWL WITH GOLD MEDALLIONS

Originally this bowl, of which only fragments now remain, would have had a magnificent appearance. It is likely that it was a gift for New Year's Day or some other special occasion, though it was discovered in a sarcophagus in the late antique cemetery near St Severin's Church, Cologne. Whether the bowl was made in Rome or the Rhineland is uncertain.

The gold-leaf designs were applied to the exterior of the bowl and then a hot blob of blue or green glass was used to seal them in. In some places the coloured glass does not quite cover the gold leaf, leaving it exposed. Twenty small medallions are still present on the two fragments in the British Museum, illustrating a selection of popular scenes from the Old Testament, as well as Christ with a staff in his hand, identifying him as the miracle worker. Adam and Eve are also depicted, covering themselves after eating the fruit from the Tree of Knowledge, as well as Abraham preparing to sacrifice his son Isaac (**26**). Several other scenes concern the story of Jonah and the great fish.

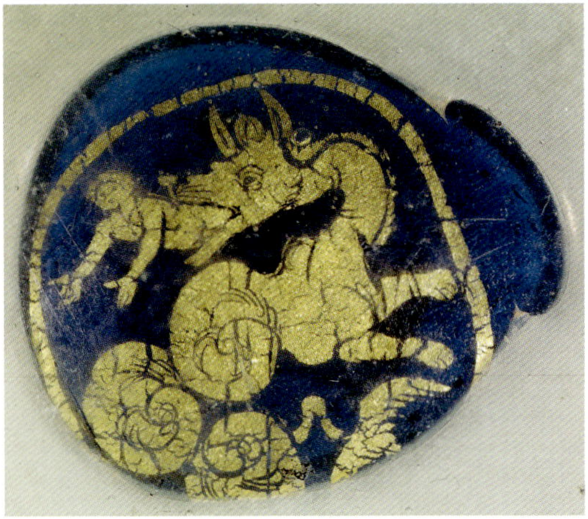

The roundel illustrated on the right shows a ship being rowed across the sea, with a dolphin swimming alongside it. Perhaps things are already not going well, in accordance with the Old Testament story that Jonah had disobeyed God's command and as a result when he took a journey at sea, a storm ensued and he was thrown overboard to pacify it. Jonah was swallowed by a giant fish and spent three days and nights praying in its stomach, after which God forgave him and the sea monster spat him back out onto land. This moment is captured in the medallion shown on the left. As this episode mirrored the Resurrection of Christ on the third day, it was often depicted on sarcophagi.

Other medallions have been found set into the plaster that sealed the cubicles in which the dead were laid to rest in Roman catacombs. Larger portraits of individuals cut out of the bottom of gold glass vessels were, however, more common. Another roundel from the present bowl is kept in the Landesmuseum at Bonn, near Cologne.

Late Roman
From Cologne, Germany
Second half of the 4th century AD
Length of whole fragment 16.8 cm
1881,0624.1

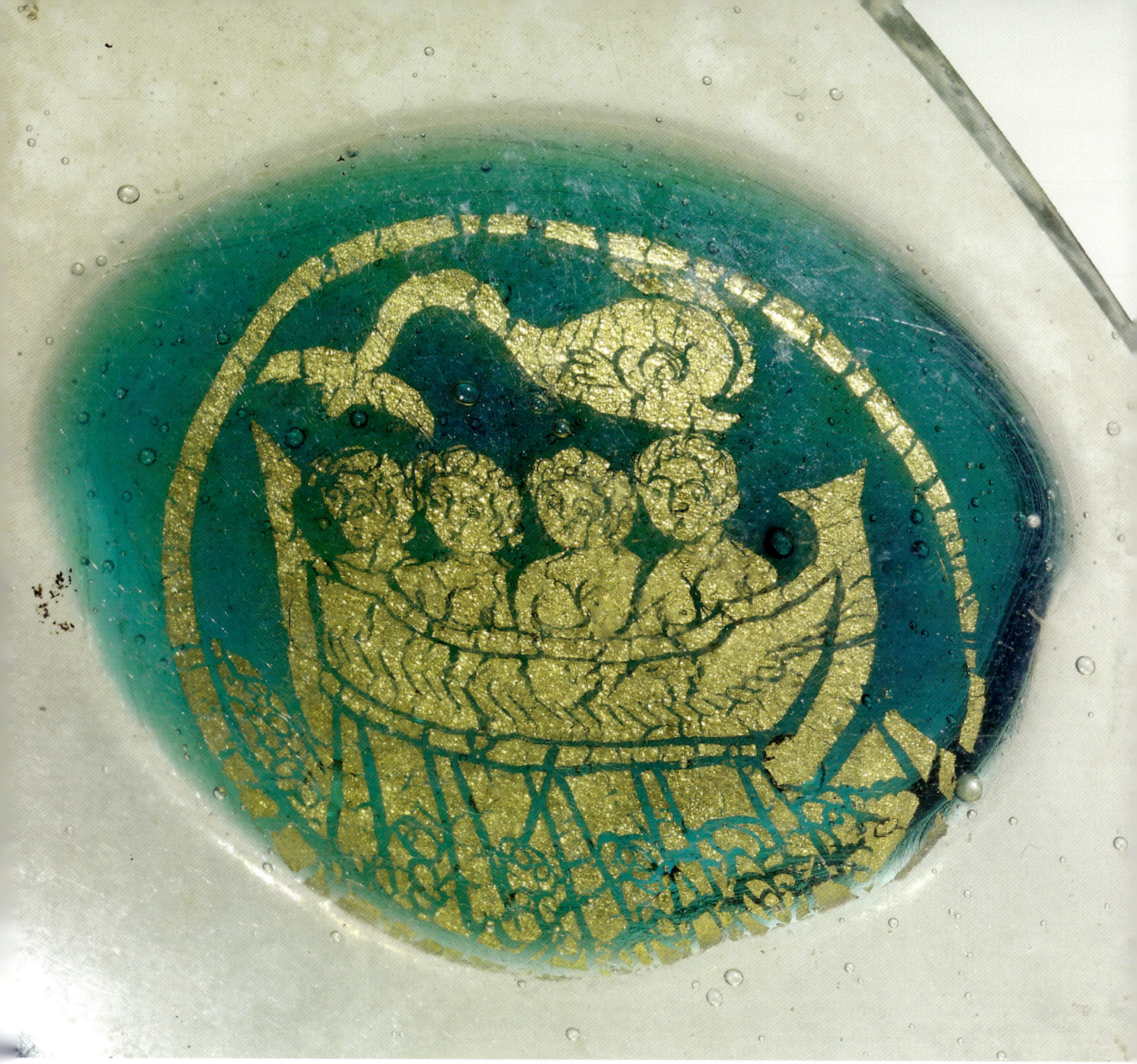

8 COIN PENDANT

This ostentatious pendant displays at its centre a gold medallion, a double *solidus* of Constantine the Great (AD 306–37). It shows the emperor in profile, with a diadem, cuirass and *paludamentum*, the imperial military cloak. Constantine is identified by the surrounding Latin inscription, while another inscription on the back of the coin names Sirmium, in modern-day Serbia, as the minting place.

A delicate, hexagonal pierced work or *opus interrasile* (**5**, **34**) frame provides the setting for the coin. Six three-dimensional busts with highly individualized features are integrated into the floral openwork. Despite the different ages, hairstyles and attires of these portraits, their identities have proven elusive. However, the youth at the top left may represent Bacchus due to the vine leaves and grapes in his hair. The female next to him could then be Ariadne, his consort. If this is correct, the other busts may also be gods or mythological figures.

The solidity of the busts and their half-turned aspects reflect contemporary trends in imperial portraiture without the seriousness of expression commonly found in these works (**23**). The floral openwork lends further lightness to the composition.

Since at least the third century, exclusive gifts such as the Constantine medallions were integrated into sumptuous jewellery. This not only allowed the wearer to display his position as a member of the circle of high-ranking officials, but also to express his loyalty to the ruling house. The outstanding quality of the frames created for the imperial medallions suggests a link to court jewellers. As similar *opus interrasile* work has been found in the Rhineland, it has been suggested that this was made in a workshop at Trier, one of Constantine's centres.

The pendant illustrated here is one of several in various American and European collections, all probably from one necklace. The mint date of the coin is AD 321, but on the basis of stylistic comparisons with the busts, which also occur elsewhere on jewellery and other types of metalwork, a date in the later fourth century has been proposed for this pendant. This is supported by an almost identical example found in a hoard in Libya together with coins that were buried in AD 388 at the earliest.

Late Roman
Unknown findspot
Last quarter of the 4th century AD
Width 9.2 cm
1984,0501.1

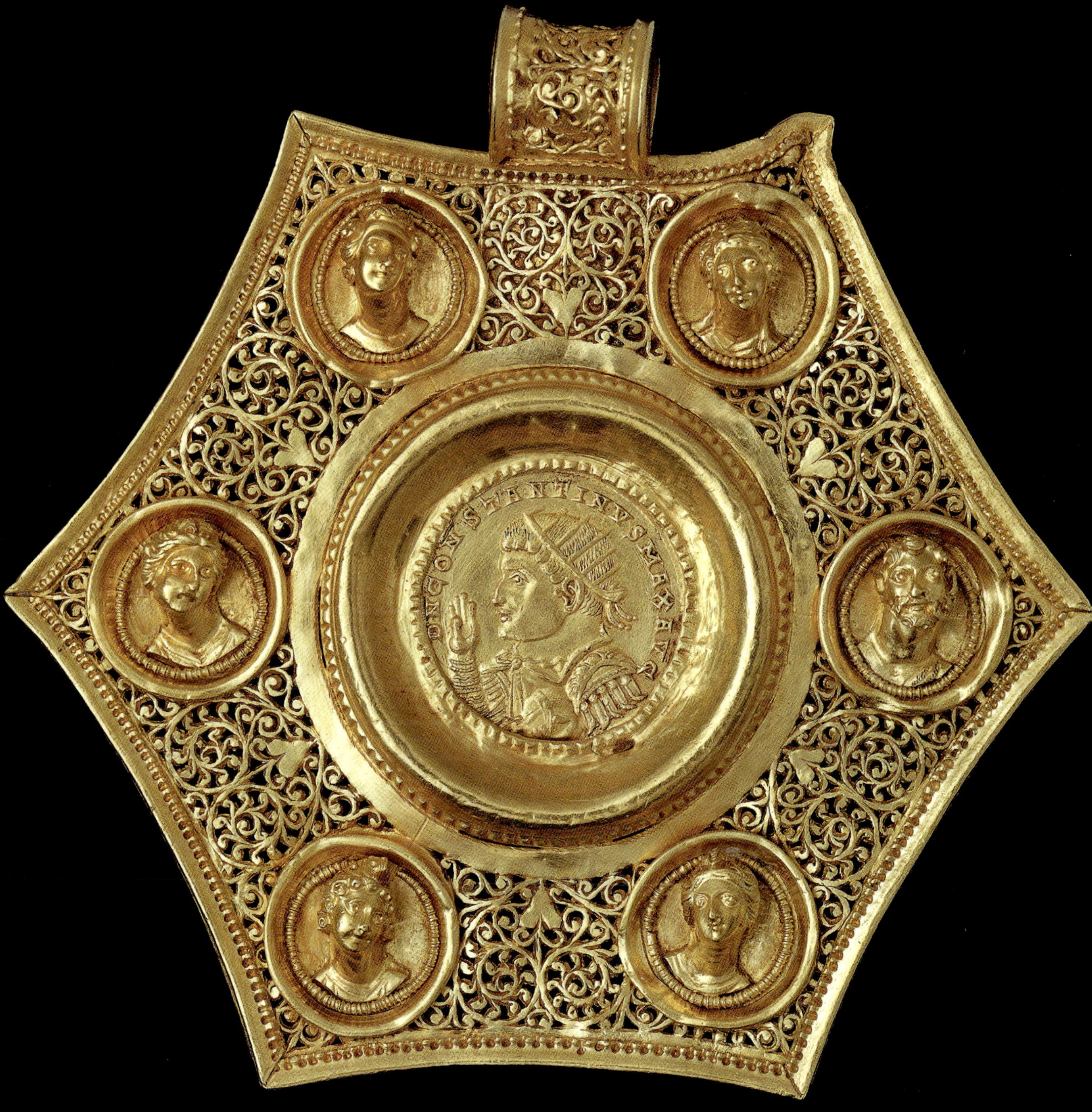
DN CONSTANTINVS MAX AVG

9 SHIP'S FIGUREHEAD

The ambiguity of cultural backgrounds and the general currency of styles, tastes and techniques in late antiquity are perfectly exemplified by this massive wood carving from the River Scheldt. On a long neck sits a beaked head with a gaping maw full of sharp teeth. A tenon at the lower end shows that the sculpture was once fitted upright at a slightly forward angle into a larger structure, most probably a ship's prow.

Its fierce aspect and bulging eyes suggested to earlier scholars that this was a 'barbaric' piece and from the late 1930s onwards it was considered to be Viking. But was it? The intricate lattice on the creature's neck is an enlarged version of the chip-carving found on late Roman, high-status, silver-gilt metalwork (**19**). For instance, both a strap-end from the late Roman hoard at Traprain Law, Scotland, and a sword scabbard fitting from Trier, Germany, feature miniature versions of the deep, inverted pyramids. The niello inlay on these pieces is paralleled by the carved ledges framing the lattice ridges on the figure's neck. The figurehead was probably once painted, mirroring the multicoloured nature of late Roman metalwork. On the left is a detail of a late third-century gold medallion of Constantius Chlorus (AD 292–306), father of Constantine the Great, showing an indubitably Roman boat with a very similar animal figurehead.

BELOW:
Detail of an electrotype copy of the 'Arras' medallion
B.11477, Dept of Coins and Medals

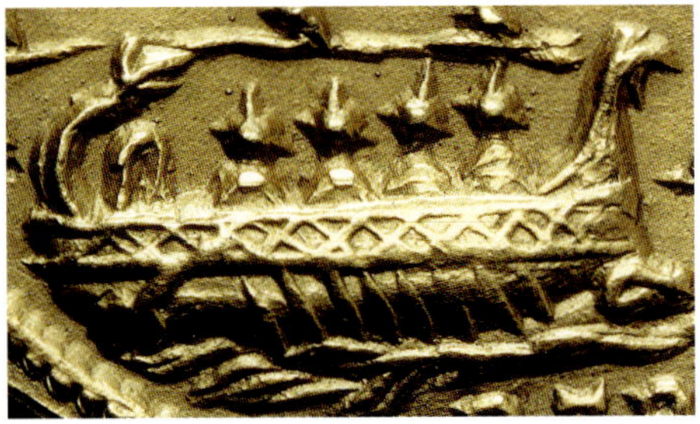

Eventually a small sample was taken from the figurehead and Radio Carbon (C^{14}) analysis at the British Museum Research Laboratory yielded a calibrated date of AD 400–615 for the oak wood. Therefore, nothing spoke against a late Roman date and the style of the chip-carving does support a date in the late fourth or early fifth century.

The huge popularity of chip-carving and other late Roman art styles and techniques, as well as the mixed cultural milieu does mean that there are many possibilities as to who made the figurehead. It could have been Gallo-Roman craftsmen, or Germanic craftsmen settled in northern Gaul and employed by the Romans, or even Germans who were influenced by Gallo-Roman boat-building traditions.

OPPOSITE:
Late Roman or Germanic
From Appels, near Dendermonde, Belgium
Probably late 4th to early 5th century AD
Height 149.0 cm
Acquired with contributions by The Art Fund and Christy Fund
1938,0202.1

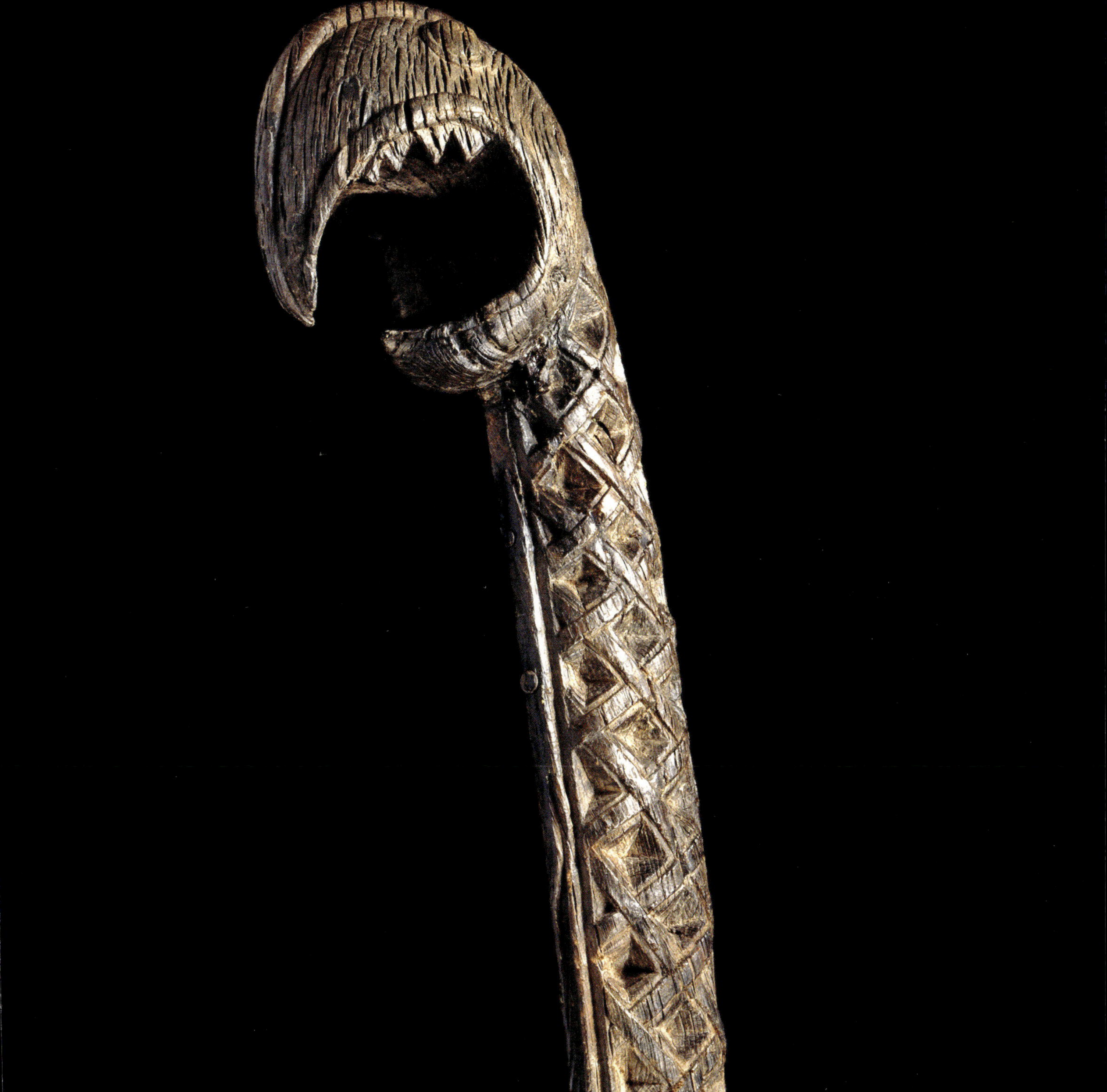

10 LIDDED BOWL

Late antique plate is often highly ornate, with cast and chased ornament and beaded rims, like several other pieces from the so-called Carthage Treasure (**11**). Parcel or partial gilding and niello inlay were popular too, as seen for instance in the Kaiseraugst Treasure from Switzerland or the Traprain Law Treasure from Scotland.

The present bowl is, however, the opposite of these styles. It captivates the viewer with its deceptively simple design and clear lines. The broad, vertical surfaces were achieved through even hammering. The ensemble is very practical, as the cover could be used as a dish, with its tubular handle acting as a foot ring. The form already prefigures Byzantine dinner services, and parallels have been found in Serbia and Italy. It has also been suggested that these new, plainly executed covered varieties of silver were influenced by Sasanian designs from the Persian Empire. This raises the additional question of whether the bowls were associated with new table manners or ways of preparing food, as their rim profiles indicate that they were not meant to be drunk from.

This bowl, together with two additional examples in the British Museum and one in the Louvre, forms part of the Carthage Treasure, which is divided between the two institutions today. Thirty-two pieces of silver tableware, including ornate plates, spoons, bowls (**11**) and some gold jewellery, are still extant, but it is unclear when the find was made and whether it is complete, as all the pieces passed through private hands before reaching the two museums. The British Museum's pieces were acquired in 1897.

With the help of various documentary sources the findspot has been narrowed down to the Byrsa Mound, also known as the Hill of St Louis, in Tunisia, where in antiquity, a large civic building stood. It is not known why the objects were hidden, but it is possible that the owners tried to save them before the sudden conquest of Carthage by the Vandals (**79**) in AD 439.

Late Roman
From Carthage, near Tunis, Tunisia
End of 4th to early 5th century AD
Height 11.4 cm
Bequeathed by A.W. Franks
AF.3280

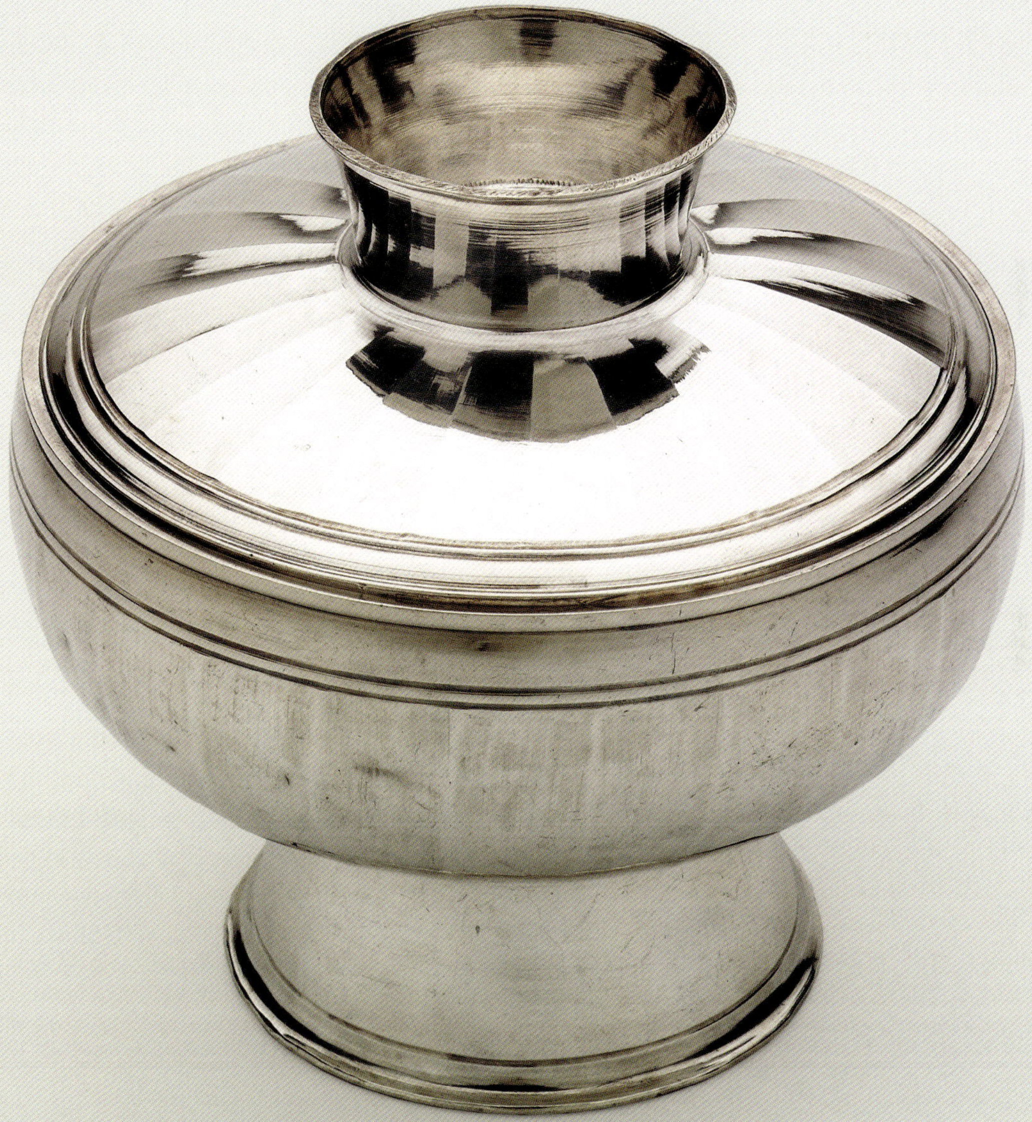

11 SILVER BOWL

Late Roman
From Carthage near Tunis, Tunisia
End of 4th to early 5th century AD
Diameter 17.5 cm
Bequeathed by A.W. Franks
AF.3275

A broad, decorated rim with a pearled edge surrounds this bowl from the Carthage Treasure (**10**). Bucolic relief scenes are the theme and the central medallion displays a vision of rural idyll. A shepherd is leaning on his crook, while his dog and a ram look up to him as he points to the right. There is some generic greenery visible behind them, just as foliage and delicate floral sprigs are interspersed with the scenery unfolding on the rim.

Here, four more shepherds are shown, leisurely reclining in various modes. Some are accompanied by dogs, while grazing sheep and goats lend the proceedings a peaceful air. A tower is visible in the background, perhaps suggesting a city. Four large profile busts are placed along the rim. Opposite each other, the heads of two satyrs are recognizable by their wild hair, beards and strong foreheads. The carefully delineated hair of the two females is held up by strings of pearls, with a ponytail pulled up at the back, a style which was fashionable in the fourth century.

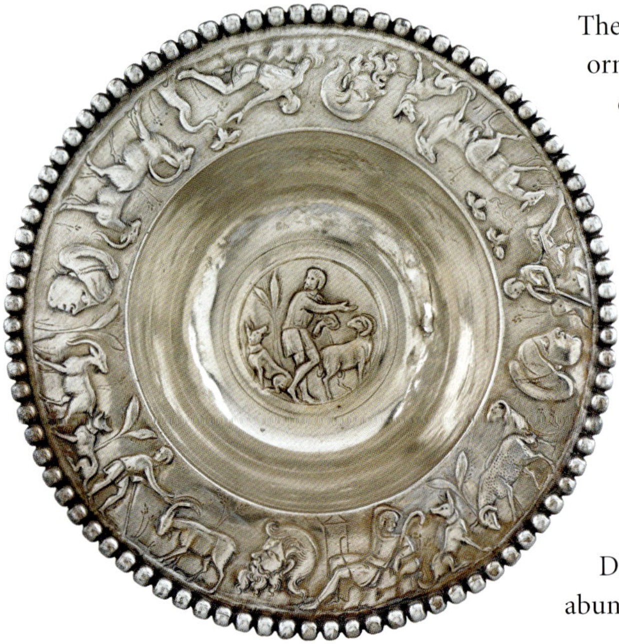

The plate is noticeably worn, with some of the engraved and stippled ornament only faintly visible and several of the faces almost reduced down to the eyes, which were originally the parts most deeply set. Ornate plate with beaded rims was found in most, if not all, Roman hoards from the fourth and fifth century. The classical style of this bowl suggests a date in the late fourth century. This could be confirmed by the inscription on another plate from the Carthage Treasure which mentions the Cresconii, an influential North African family with several members holding high offices in the imperial service at this time.

The gentle, playful mood of the decoration on this plate reflects the general fondness for bucolic scenes since antiquity (**2**). Such settings represented a carefree state of happiness, and the satyrs and young women, perhaps maenads or followers of Dionysus, were possibly meant to emphasize notions of fertility, abundance and good fortune.

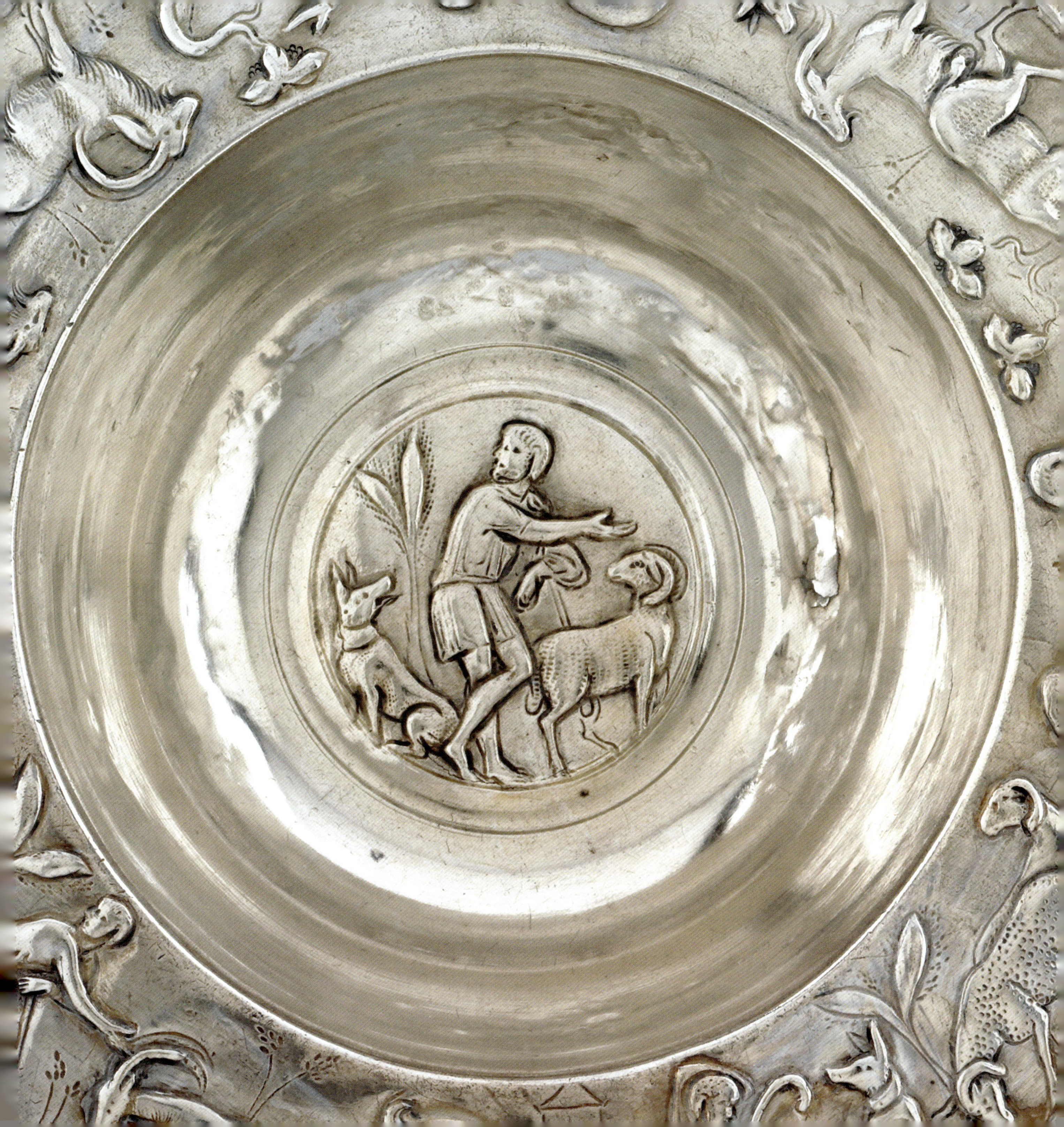

12 BRIDLE CHEEK-PIECE

Horses from Spain were famed in antiquity and they played an important economic and prestigious role on the large estates of the Hispanic gentry during the fourth and fifth century. They are depicted on mosaics and murals, often in the context of the hunt, a favourite late antique pastime (**5**, **16**, **79**). Decorative horse tack has been found in some quantities, including cheek-pieces, which prevented the bit from being drawn sideways out of the horse's mouth when one of the reins was pulled (**132**).

The present cheek-piece and its pair are examples of rather elaborate circus or hunting scenes. Other known designs included geometric patterns, heraldic animals, inscriptions and Christian symbols. On the left a man is leaning forward, linked to a four-legged animal by a spear which has been thrust into its chest. The stance of this hunter is reminiscent of the lion hunter on a Byzantine buckle from Algeria (**79**). This creature has a short mane and it has been suggested that it might represent a lion or a wolf. It is also beleaguered from the other side by a small dog biting its hind leg. The dog is followed by a second hunter, who is crouched low, and his legs are joined with those of the first hunter.

The detailed openwork is a masterpiece of copper alloy casting. Melted bronze is prone to cooling quickly when poured into the mould and so getting all the small channels to fill up is testament to the craftsman's skill. After it cooled, the piece was worked over and detail was added by engraving and sharpening up the cast parts of the ornament. While both this piece and its pair seem to have been made from the same model, they show minor differences due to the results of the casting process. A costly piece of horse tack such as this would have been in keeping with the fine horses and social cachet of any Hispanic landowner, whether he was of Roman, or later, Visigothic descent.

Late Roman
Unknown findspot, probably Spain
4th to 5th century AD
Height including strap loop 9.2 cm
1990,0402.2

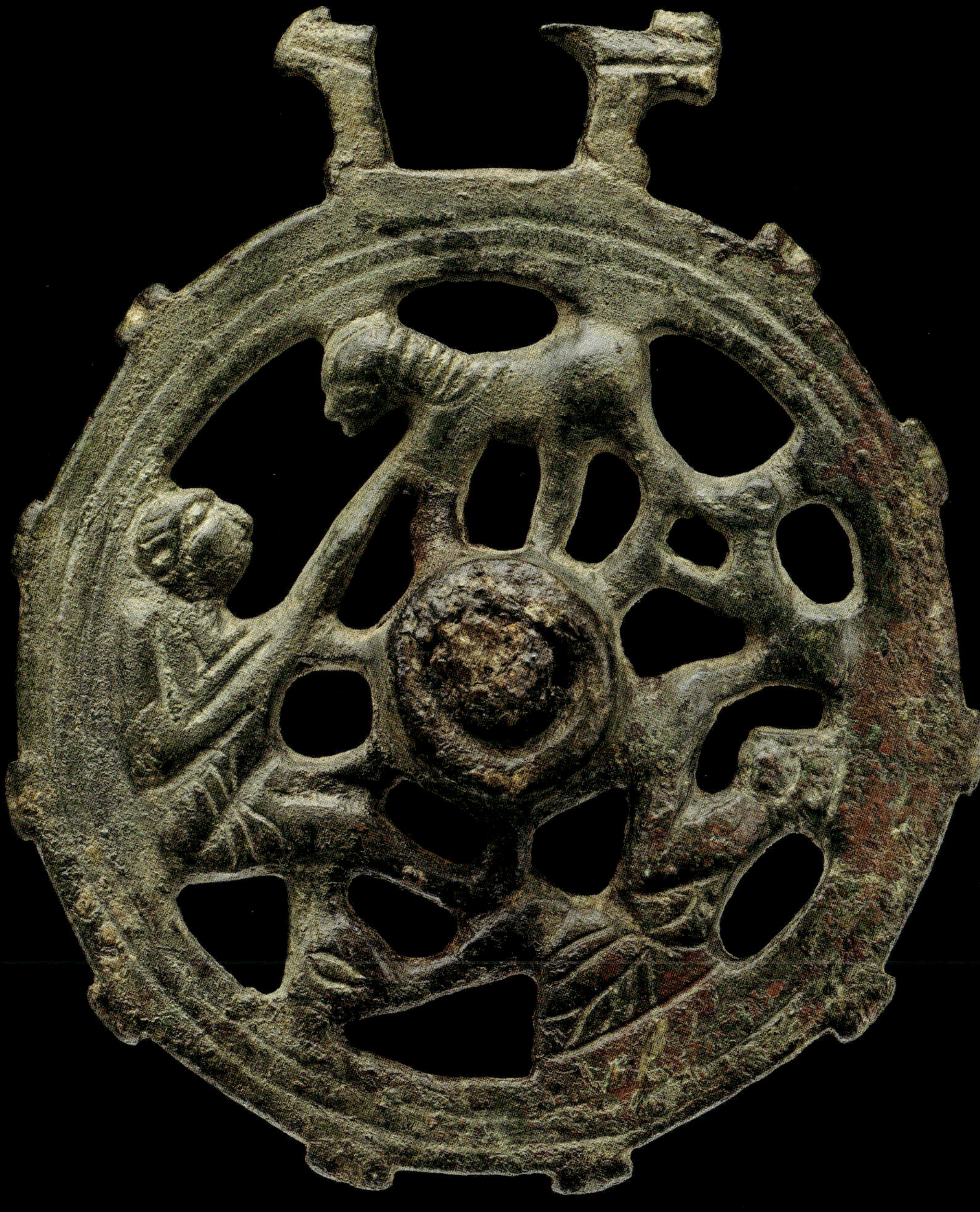

13 THE DIPTYCH LEAF OF THE SYMMACHI

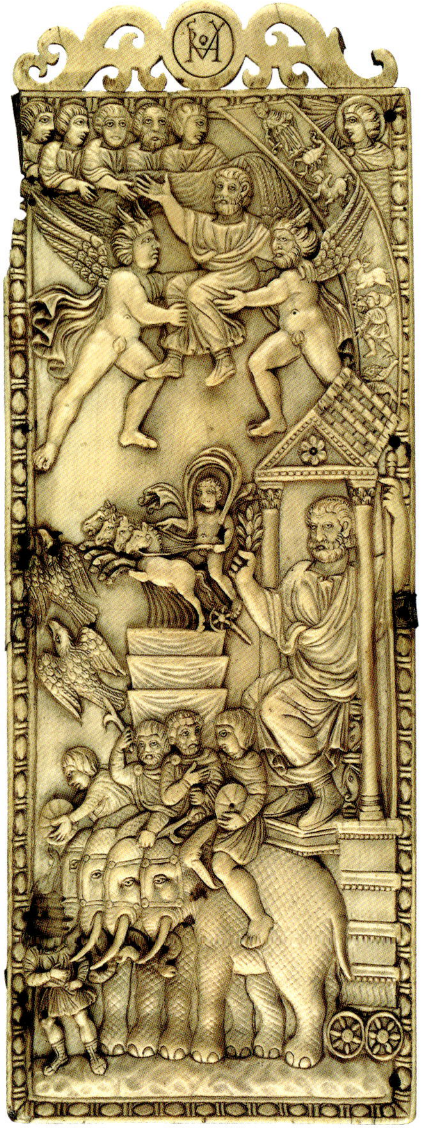

A complex sequence of episodes unfolds on the right wing of a carved elephant ivory diptych (**28**), the left part having been lost. The relief is given great depth through the incision of deep contour lines, demonstrating the excellent skill of the carver.

Four elephants are pulling an elaborate cart with an *aedicula* or classical style building atop. In the cart sits a bearded dignitary, draped in the senatorial toga, with a staff in his left hand and a sprig of laurel in his right. Above and behind this scene is a draped funeral pyre, crowned by a chariot drawn by four horses. The two eagles flying away from the pyre may represent the soul of the deceased. He is next seen being borne upwards by two personifications of the winds, identifiable by the wings on their heads and backs. Beyond an arch carved with some of the zodiac signs (depicted in the same way as they are today), five men who are possibly ancestral figures await him. Meanwhile, the sun god Helios, crowned by the rays emanating from his halo, looks on.

The narrative represents the transformation of this dignitary from a mere mortal to a god. Both his identity and the date of the panel are debated, and one school of thought has interpreted this scene as the deification of an emperor. However, the monogram at the top can be read as SYMMACHORUM, meaning 'of the Symmachi' family.

The events depicted may concern the death of a prominent member of the clan, Quintus Aurelius Symmachus, in AD 402. By this time, Christianity had been established in the Roman Empire. The overt paganism of the diptych could therefore be a proclamation of defiance by one of the leading pagan families in Rome. On stylistic and iconographic grounds, however, a new reading prefers to see the dignitary as the great-grandson of Quintus Aurelius, who was sentenced to death by Theoderic (AD 493–526) in AD 525/6. In this light, the image scheme of the diptych is considered a statement on what it meant to be a Roman and the values they stood for, rather than a declaration of pagan beliefs.

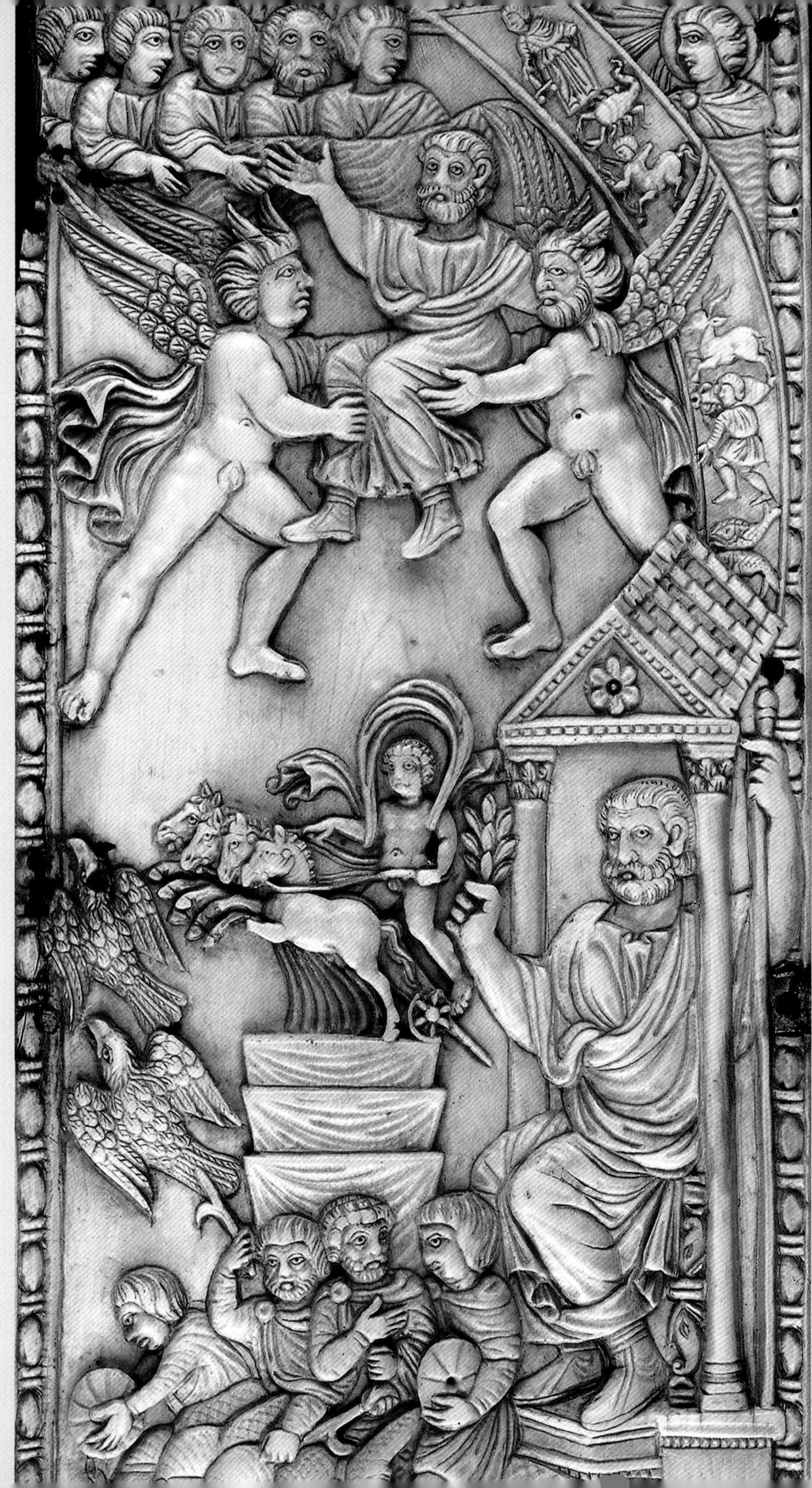

Late Roman
Unknown findspot
Possibly AD 402
Height 30.1 cm
1857,1013.1

14 MARRIAGE RING

A man and woman are gazing at each other on the square bezel of a golden finger-ring. This act of contemplation is taking place below the sign of the cross. The hoop of the ring is formed by seven medallions, the joins of which are cleverly hidden by small gold pellets.

The deep engraving of the piece, which could have served as a seal ring, is exquisite. The woman wears a mantle in fine pleats across the shoulders, her earrings and necklace are clearly visible, and her hair is artfully gathered up. The man is equally neatly coiffed and his cloak is held on the left shoulder by a crossbow brooch of a type common among late Roman civil and military officials of high rank (**6**, **17**). This handsome couple is surrounded by alternating identical male and female busts on the medallions of the hoop. They are depicted in a more fluid, impressionistic style of light engraving inlaid with niello.

The material, iconography and type of ring identify this as a marriage ring for someone from an elevated section of society. It may originally have been one of a pair and could have belonged to either a man or a woman. If the latter, its large size means that it would have been worn on the thumb.

While marriage rings had already come into fashion during imperial times, the prominence of the cross on this late Roman or early Byzantine piece is notable. Portraits of couples which included Christian iconography, for example on gold glass medallions (**7**), became popular from the late third century and may reflect a changing attitude to marriage. It was now considered a bond entered into before God, as opposed to a mere legal union, and thus considered indissoluble. This couple, contemplating each other within a circle of idealized men and women, and under the auspices of the cross, may be a clear statement of this new understanding.

Late Roman or early Byzantine

Perhaps from the eastern Mediterranean

Late 4th to early 5th century AD

Diameter 2.6 cm

Bequeathed by A.W. Franks

AF.304

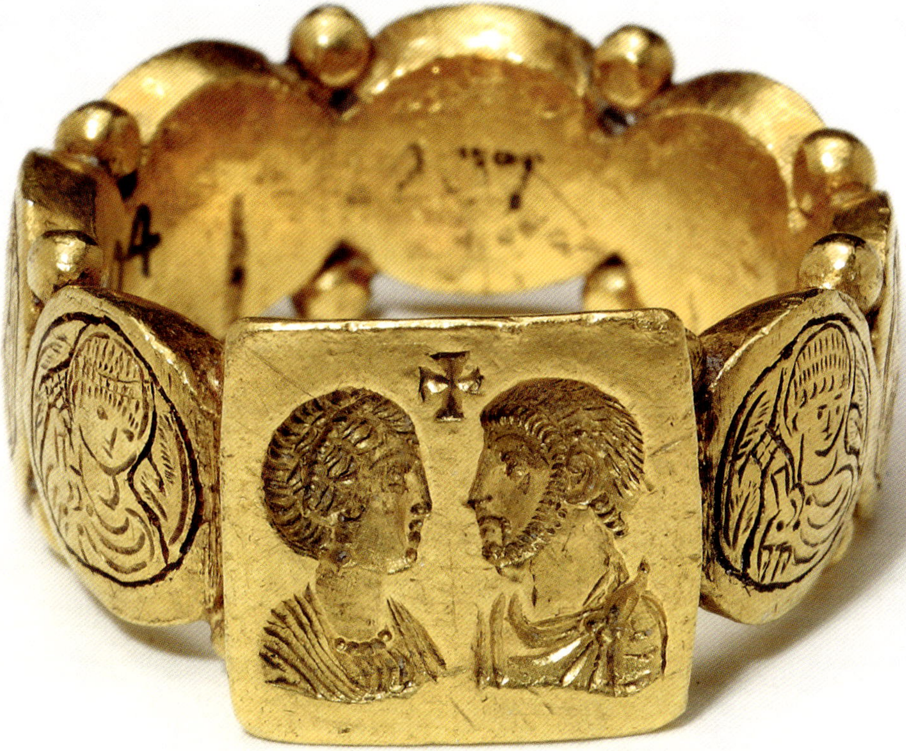

15 CRUCIFIXION IVORY

An ivory panel dated to the fifth century shows what appears to be the earliest surviving depiction of the Crucifixion in a narrative context. It is one of a series of four plaques telling the New Testament story of Christ being sentenced to death through to his demise on the Cross and reappearance to his disciples before his Ascension to Heaven. The illustrations are particularly close to the account presented in St John's Gospel.

On the present panel the events surrounding Christ's Crucifixion unfold. He is at the visual centre of the composition, already nailed to the Cross but by no means defeated and, as evidenced by his open eyes, very much alive. Christ is clearly shown as the victor over death, his power emphasized by his athletic build and upright posture. This body language would have been familiar to the late antique viewer as it followed known iconographies of imperial and sporting successes. Additionally, an abbreviated inscription at the top of the panel addresses Christ as 'Rex Iudeorum' or 'King of the Jews'. The later, medieval, emaciated and slumped figure of the Son of God, who gave his life to redeem mankind (**98**), is both visually and conceptually distant from the present ivory.

Three further figures feature in this scene. To the left of the Cross Mary and John, the favourite disciple, look towards the man on the right, whose raised hand once contained a spear. He represents the Roman soldier Longinus, who pierced Christ's side with a lance. Some seven hundred years later this moment is still an instantly recognizable part of the Crucifixion (**151**).

The narrative of the panel also takes us elsewhere to witness the death of Judas, who has hanged himself. The bag of money he received as a reward for betraying Christ spills at his feet. His shameful end provides a foil for the triumph of Christ over death.

The four ivory panels once formed the sides of a box, which may have held a relic or the consecrated Host.

Late Roman
Unknown findspot
c. AD 420–30
Width 9.8 cm
1856,0623.5

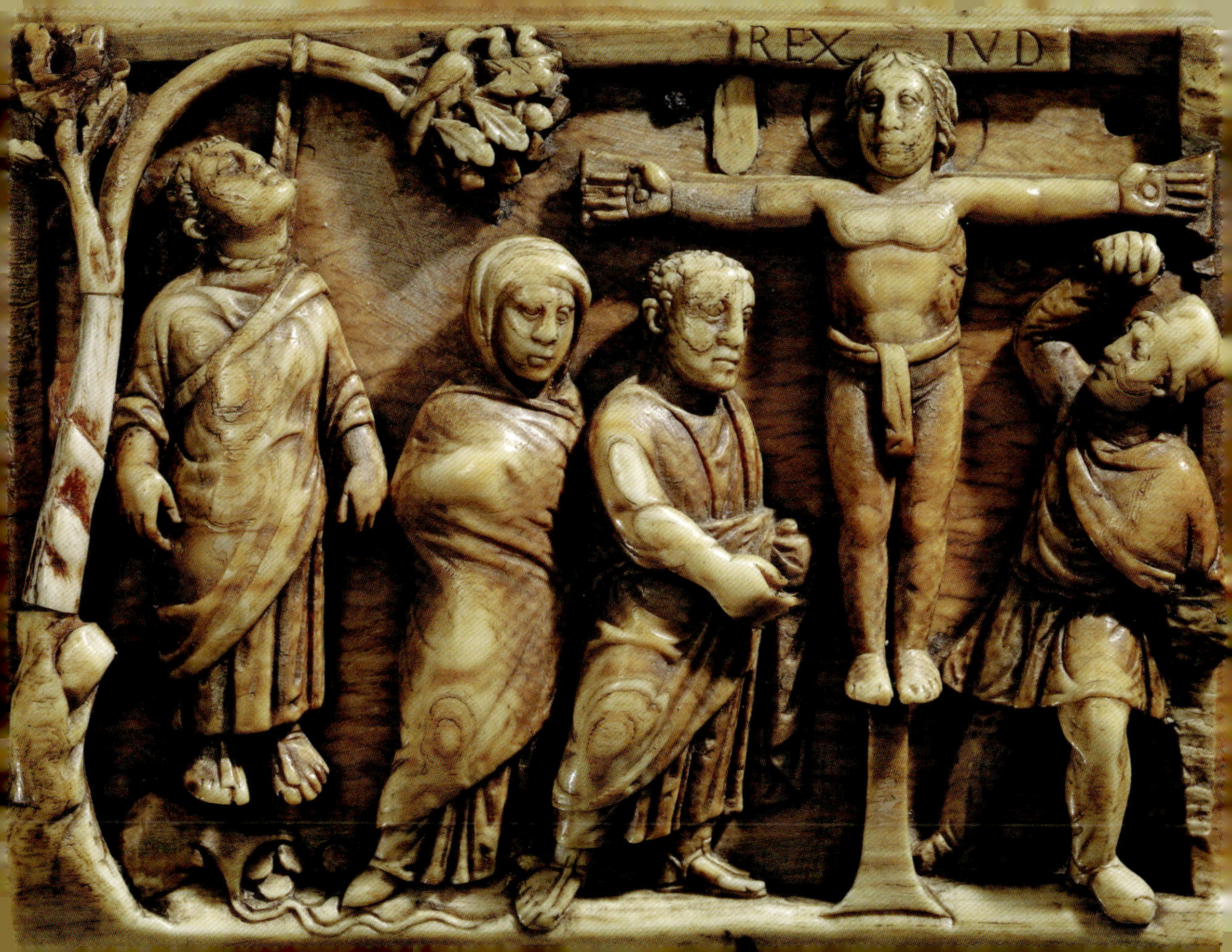
REX IVD

16 THE LEUNA GLASS BOWL

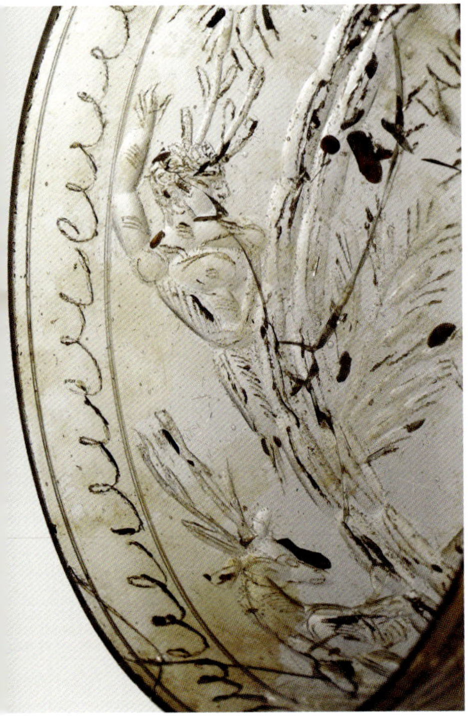

Roman
Found near Leuna, Germany
Second half of the 3rd century AD
Diameter 12.1 cm
Bequeathed by F. Slade
S.320

A small group of elite burials from third-century central Germany stand out from the mass of graves through the sumptuousness of the objects found within them. The men and women buried here were laid to rest in chambers with astonishingly rich burial goods. Although the Roman Rhine border was hundreds of kilometres away, these people seem to have enjoyed excellent relations with the empire and some of them may have held imperial military office. Apart from rich Germanic goods, the graves abound in fine Roman objects, including silver, glass and copper alloy vessels.

The present cut-glass bowl comes from the burial of a man who must have been a leader in his community, judging by both the Germanic and Roman riches he was interred with. One of two glass bowls from the burial, it is hemispherical and translucent, engraved with a scene from the myth of Artemis and Actaeon. The latter was a hunter who secretly watched the goddess as she bathed in the woods. Artemis discovered him, however, and turned him into a stag.

This is the moment the engraver has captured. Actaeon, whose name is engraved beside him, is seen twice: once as a man sporting antlers and then as a deer, while the goddess is shown turned away from both figures. The hunter's fate is sealed: his own hunting dogs, here represented by one hound braying at the feet of Artemis, will tear him apart. Fragments of a vessel showing Actaeon's death have been excavated at Dura Europos, Syria, and are thought to have been engraved by the same craftsman.

Glass such as this was precious even within the empire. Specially trained engravers worked lathes with rotating wheels and the glass was ground with the help of abrasive pastes. The techniques were probably not dissimilar to those employed in gem cutting. The repertoire of images encompassed pagan, Christian and Jewish themes. Hunting scenes, for instance, were very popular. As in the production of Coptic textiles (**33**), pattern or sketch books from which a customer could choose a design were probably used for glass vessels as well.

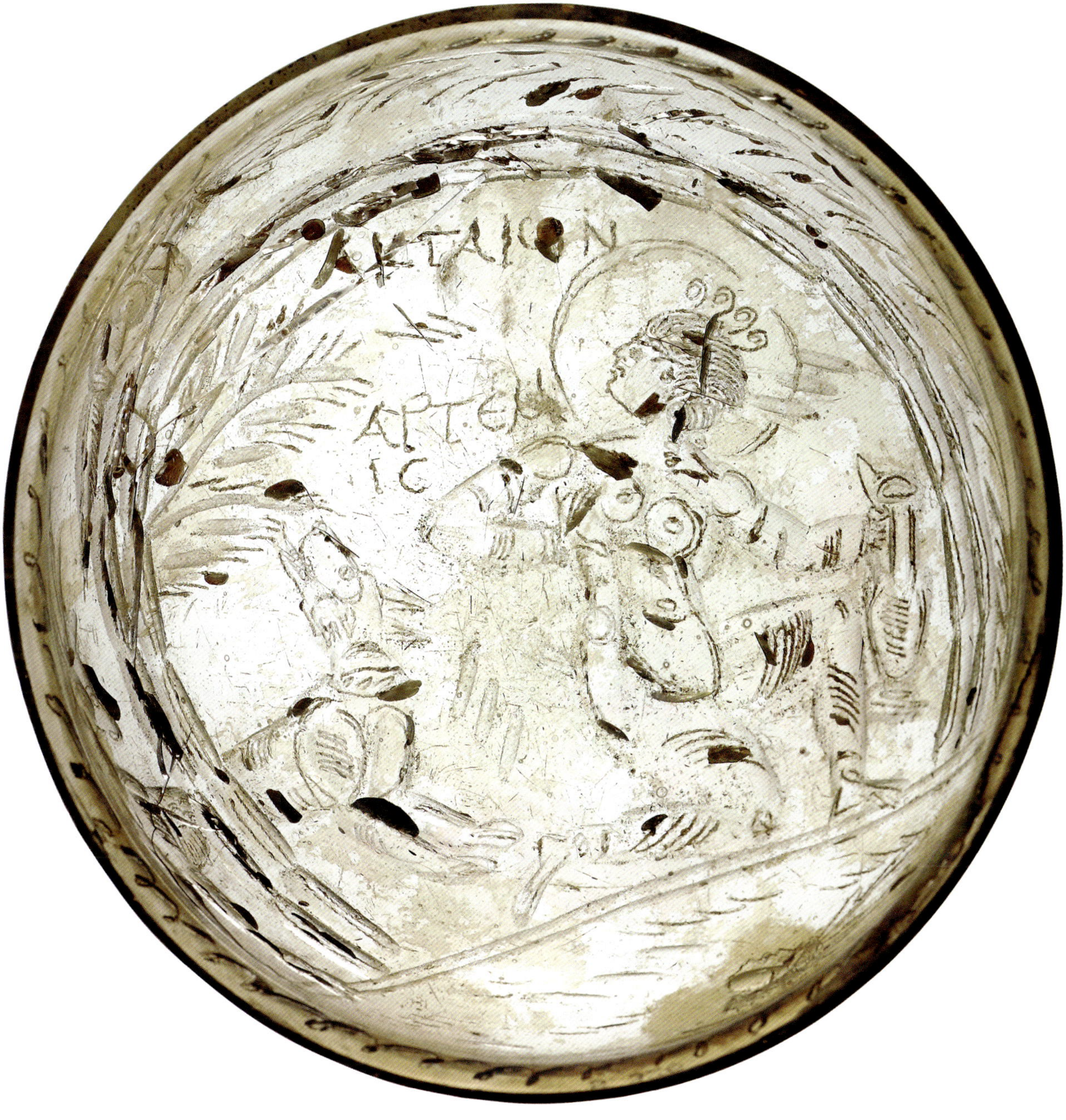
ΑΚΤΑΙΩΝ
ΑΡΤΕΜΙC

17 CROSSBOW BROOCH

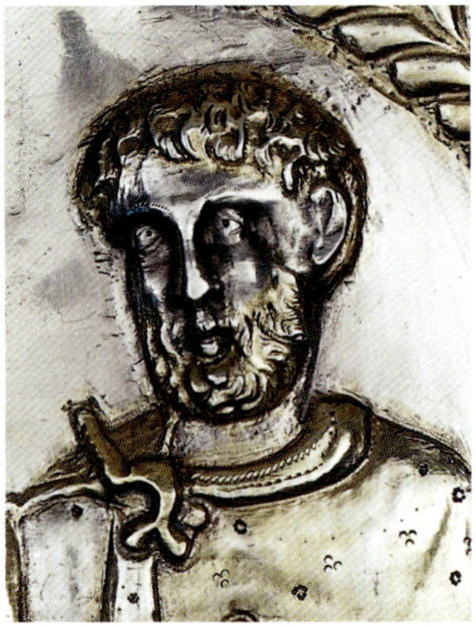

ABOVE:
Detail from the Projecta Casket
Roman
c. AD 330–80
1866,1229.1

OPPOSITE:
Roman
From Moray Firth, Scotland
c. AD 400
Length 7.9 cm
1962,1205.1

Far outside the Roman Empire, from where such brooches originated, this exquisite gold example was found in the Moray Firth area of Scotland. This type name is a modern term derived from its resemblance to the medieval weapon. The back ridge and sides of the bow display delicate niello triangles, while the foot is ornamented with lateral curled gold *peltae*. The three onion-shaped knobs are trimmed with beaded gold wire.

Such brooches are a late antique form, appearing towards the end of the fourth century and remaining popular into the middle of the fifth century. The appearance of this example places it among the latest types of crossbow brooches, which included some of the most precious. Pictorial evidence in Byzantine sources shows that similar forms were still worn into the sixth century. While early crossbow brooches are restricted to the Roman Empire, later forms have been found in the burials of Germanic and other leaders, as well as in a number of hoards associated with late Roman or early Byzantine elites.

Many precious objects, such as gold glasses, finger-rings and ivory carvings, as well as frescoes and mosaics, show men wearing such brooches. They are always depicted with the narrow end upwards on one shoulder. The detail on the left from the medallion on the lid of the Projecta Casket (**3**) portrays Secundus with his cloak clasped in this very manner. Generally these brooches, especially the precious types, were worn by military and state officials and reflected their office and standing (**6**, **14**). They were also awarded as signs of imperial favour to non-Roman allies, as in the case of the Frankish king Childeric (AD 457/8–82). This is the context in which this gold brooch from the north of Scotland should be viewed. It dates to around AD 400 and belongs to a slowly growing corpus of high-quality finds which demonstrate that relationships between the empire and the tribal societies and petty kingdoms beyond Hadrian's Wall were not always hostile. While raiding and trading certainly account for some of the coins, silver plate, copper alloy vessels, fine tableware and hacksilver found north of Hadrian's Wall, clusters of finds from high-status sites may have been associated with subsidies to client rulers, diplomatic links with friendly overlords or rewards for services to the empire (**19**).

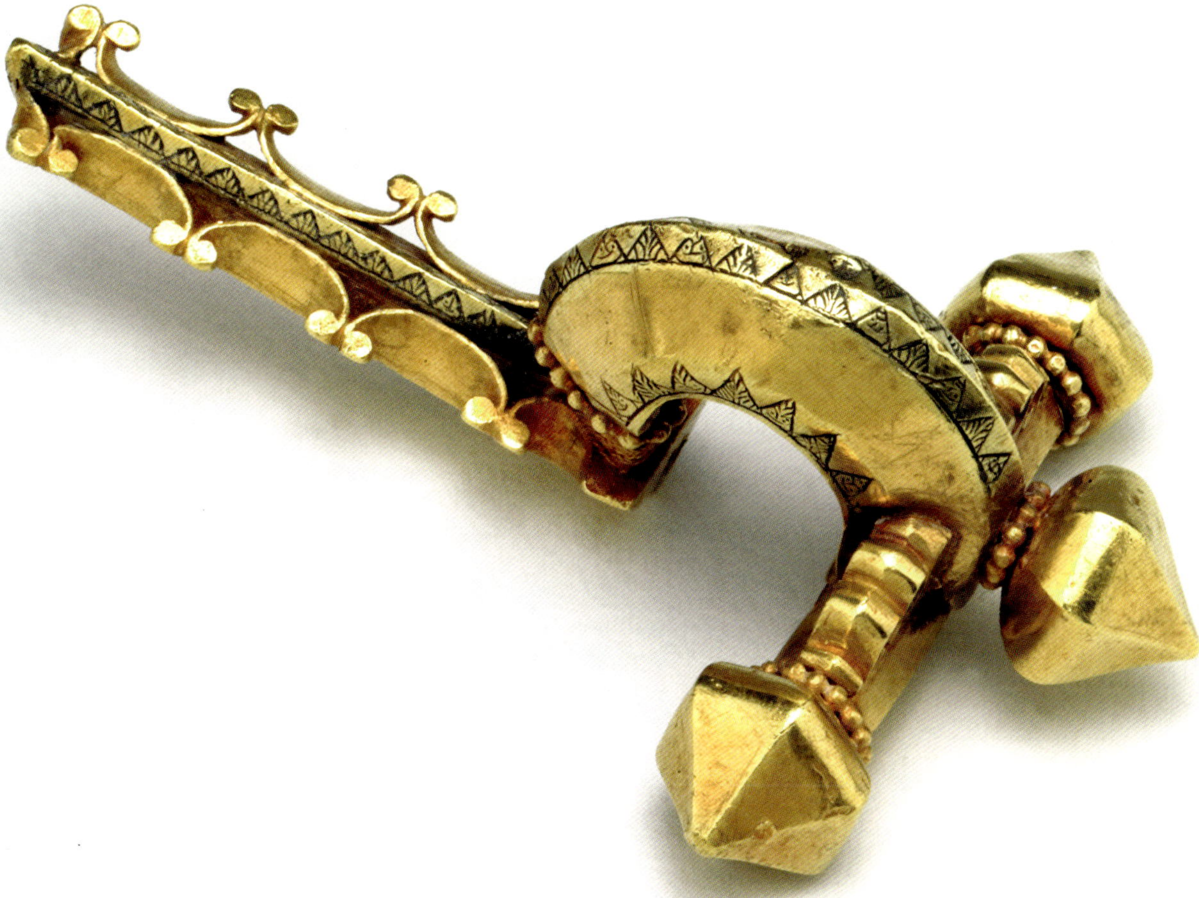

18 THE MUCKING BELT SET

Like the Sarre brooch, the Mucking belt set of decorative fittings is ornamented in the Quoit Brooch Style (**21**). Typical features are the sea creatures in shallow relief and the inlay of silver wire in the copper alloy body of the belt set. To create an even more sumptuous effect, parts of the decoration would originally have been covered with silver foil.

The late Roman roots of the Quoit Brooch Style are particularly evident in this example. The combination of the fittings follows the layout of an officer's belt, as it would have been worn in the field army or *comitatenses* on the Continent. The decorative motif of complex geometric patterns and the positioning of the sea creatures on the edge of the fittings are also a direct reference to military metalwork, while the curvilinear ornament engraved along the sides of the buckle harks back to late Roman art. Technological examinations of Quoit Brooch Style metalwork have indeed shown that it was made and decorated in different methods to those later used by Anglo-Saxon craftsmen.

The original appearance of the Mucking belt suite would have been splendid, with the once gold-coloured copper alloy setting off the silver to great effect. A belt suite of this calibre must have been special, and it is likely that many of those seeing it would have been aware of the Roman as well as military connotations. Interestingly, it was found in a burial without other grave goods, which according to anthropological examination may have belonged to a young man. Perhaps he was of Roman heritage, as in a Germanic burial one would have expected some weaponry, accoutrements or vessels (**39**) to accompany him. Equally he may have been of Germanic or mixed descent and his affiliation to Rome, whether through family ties or service in the army, was expressed in the way he was laid to rest.

In any case, the community at Mucking attracted settlers from many backgrounds. This is also reflected in its two cemeteries, which contained some of the earliest Anglo-Saxon material in England (**20**).

Late Roman

From Mucking Cemetery i, Grave 117, Essex, England

First half of the 5th century AD

Maximum width 4.80 cm

Donated by the trustees of the estate of F. W. Surridge

1970,0406.26a–e

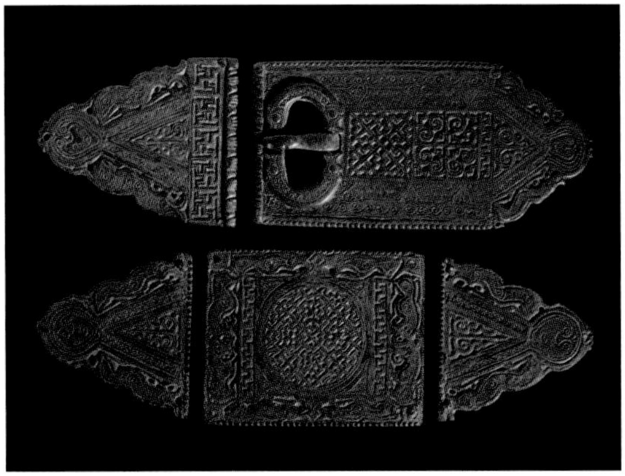

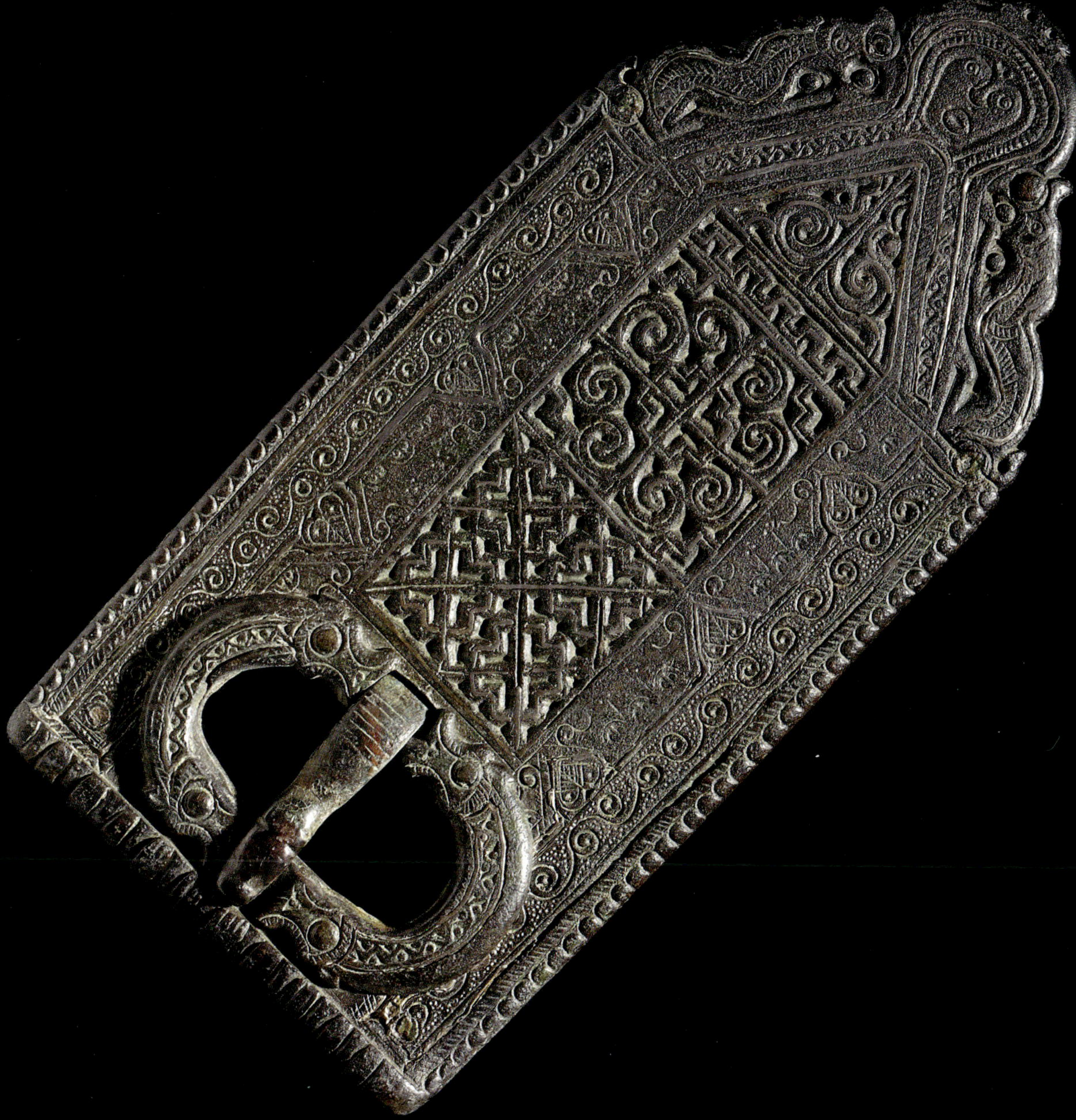

19 THE LONDESBOROUGH PIN

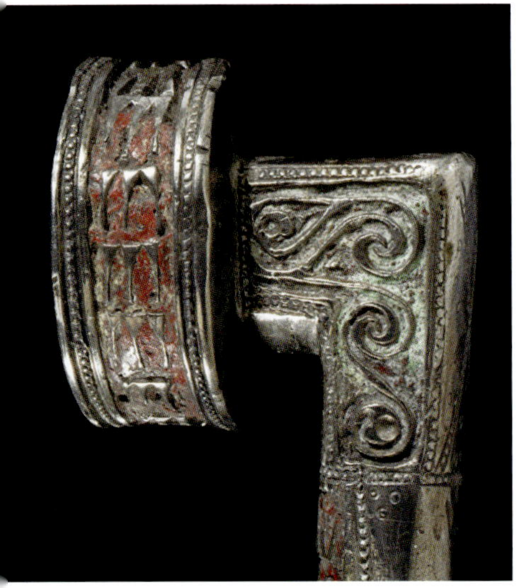

While the Romans had aspirations to conquer Scotland and Ireland, they were never absorbed into the empire. Yet Roman goods and ideas certainly reached them (**17**). Celtic mercenaries served in the late Roman army and large silver treasure, such as that from Coleraine, Northern Ireland, or Traprain Law, Scotland, are now seen as probably including accumulations of prize monies and awards which they brought back home. Roman gold and silver may, moreover, have been gifted to friendly tribal leaders. Consequently, there was an awareness, sometimes even an intimate knowledge, of everything from Roman plate and jewellery to furniture and mosaics decorated with framed and beaded panels, and filled with geometric or plant ornamentation.

Additionally, chip-carved military belt fittings were found among the hoards. The technique was derived from woodworking and the characteristic deep-cut relief with sharp, narrow ridges produced surfaces which are enlivened by the contrasts in texture and the play of light (**9**).

The Londesborough pin, along with a selection of other, high-quality dress pins (**124**) from the Celtic sphere, incorporates all these features. The upper part of the shaft is richly textured and divided into panels with beaded frames, filled with punched, drilled and carved ornament, some of which is clearly based on Roman scrolling vines and bunches of grapes. The drum-shaped head projects from the shaft and the right-angled join shows chip-carved spirals imitating a meander motif. They may once have been embedded in an inlay, just like the decoration on the pin head in red enamel (**135**). Some of the shaft panels were enamelled as well, and there may have been some niello inlay. The latter stems from late Roman metalworking traditions in Britain and it is likely that pins such as this one developed from there.

Outstanding craftsmanship and the use of silver, a metal which was rare in the Celtic regions at the time, mark out this pin, formerly in the Londesborough collection (**148**). It illustrates both the conscious adoption and adaptation of late Roman styles by Celtic elites as a means of status expression.

Celtic
Probably from Ireland
5th century AD
Diameter of head 1.9 cm
1888,0719.100

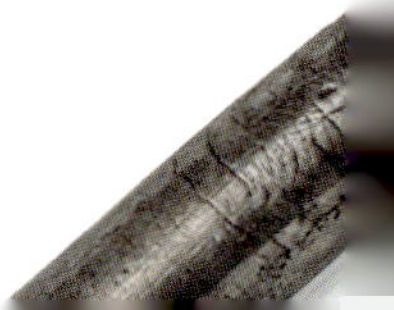

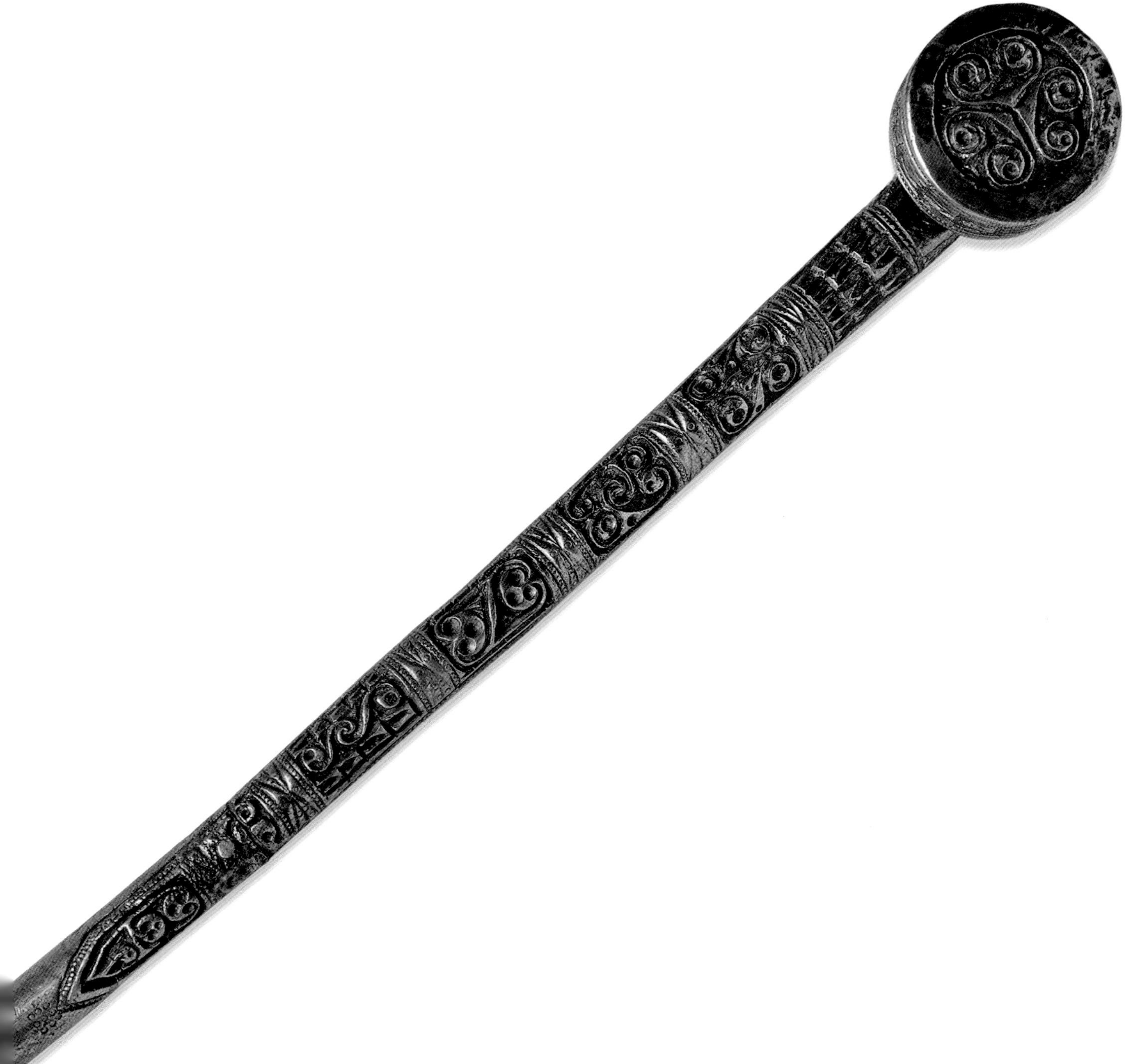

20 THE MUCKING CLAW BEAKER

One of the earliest examples of the strange vessels known as claw beakers comes from a cemetery at Mucking, Essex (**18**). These beakers are the most complex and memorable glass vessels of the early medieval period. Their voluminous protrusions – two rows of four claws – still show their ancestry clearly as this glass form was inspired by a rare Roman drinking vessel, the dolphin cup. Only a few such cups survive, but they all feature glass dolphins applied to the main body of the vessel. Strong echoes of the dolphins are still evident in the Mucking beaker. With time, the claws – or 'elephant trunks', as they are called in French and German – became increasingly more stylized and slimmer (**39**).

The production of claw beakers would have required extensive experience and excellent timing. First, the conical body was blown, and trails of hot glass were applied to it for decoration. The claws were then formed by fusing a blob of hot glass to the cooling vessel. The blowing continued and the claw was extended outwards, pulled down and fixed in an elegant little swoop. Each claw is hollow and connected to the main body of the vessel, which made for a nice visual effect when the beaker was filled, but it did mean that care had to be taken when drinking from it. The glass trails decorating the claws were applied last and indented with a blunt tool. The rim of this vessel was not smoothed, but when it had cooled completely, it was simply snapped off the blowing rod and ground slightly, leaving a comparatively sharp edge.

This is an early fifth-century technique of glass finishing. Additional grave goods in this female burial suggest that it took place in the first half of the sixth century, so the beaker must have been old by the time it was deposited.

The beaker had been placed by the head of the woman (**39**). Judging by the silver-gilt brooches she was wearing she must have been from one of the more affluent families in her community. This is supported by the fact that she also had a large rock-crystal bead, the sides of which had been painstakingly polished into facets – the only one to be found among the 745 inhumations and cremations from this cemetery at Mucking.

Anglo-Saxon

From Mucking Cemetery ii, Grave 843, Essex, England

Early 5th century AD

Height 20.5 cm

Donated by the trustees of the estate of F. W. Surridge

1970,0406.1675

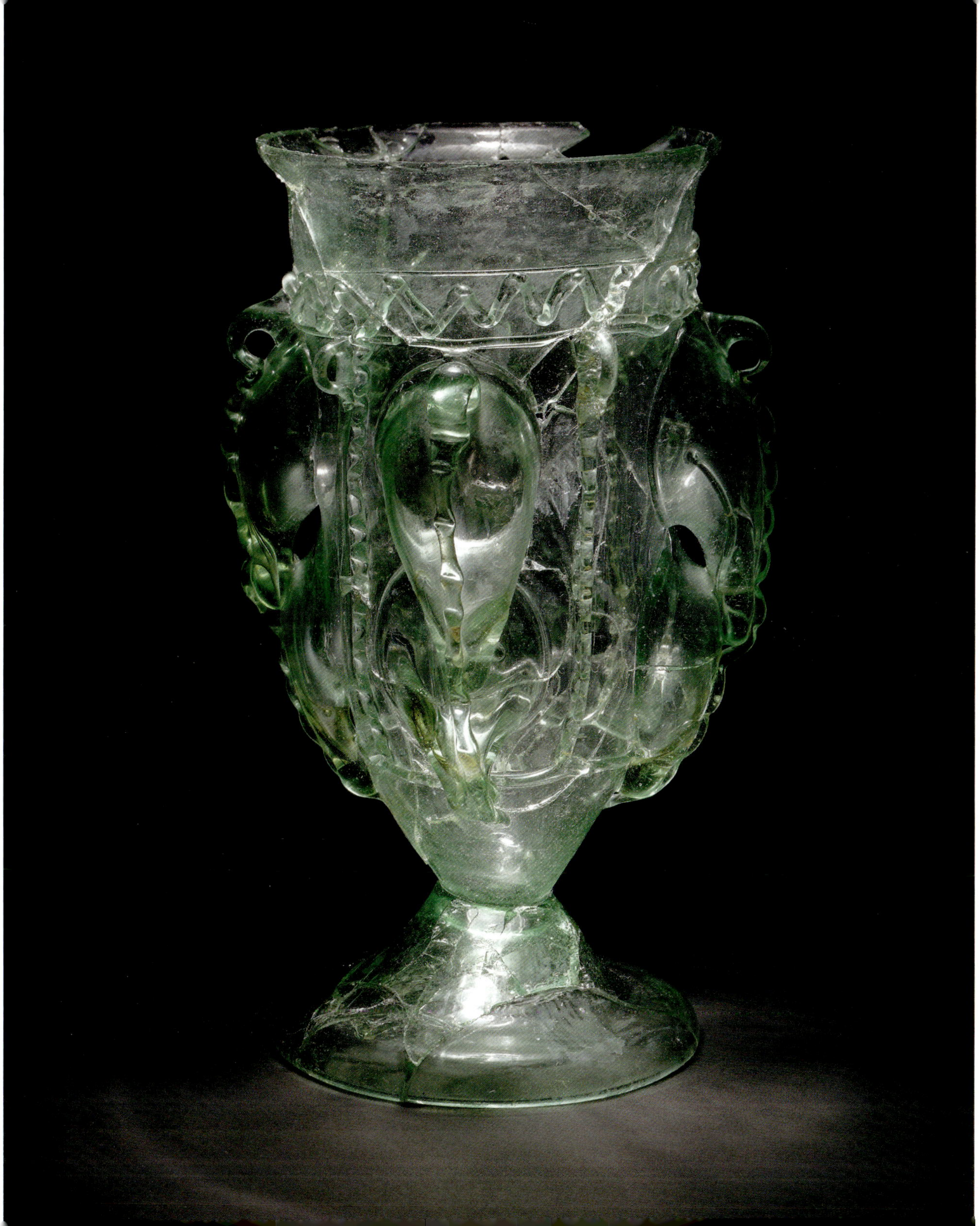

21 THE SARRE QUOIT BROOCH

Quoit brooches are named after the flat rings which were once popular in throwing games. The brooches' highly distinctive decoration gave its name to the Quoit Brooch Style, which is also found on buckles (**18**) and fittings. A broad annular band with a notch through which the pin is passed is a typical feature of these brooches, although the more complex pieces, such as this one, may possess an additional inner ring on which the pin slides.

This example from an Anglo-Saxon cemetery at Sarre is undoubtedly the finest of its kind. Made from gilt silver, it is decorated with two concentric processions of four-legged animals. The shallow engraving is beautifully detailed and precise, and is accentuated by plain sections in the ornament. What sets this brooch apart, however, are the three perfectly modelled, three-dimensional doves. Two perch on the brooch band and one is on the base of its pin; their maker has brought them to life through the careful application of punch marks to represent their plumage.

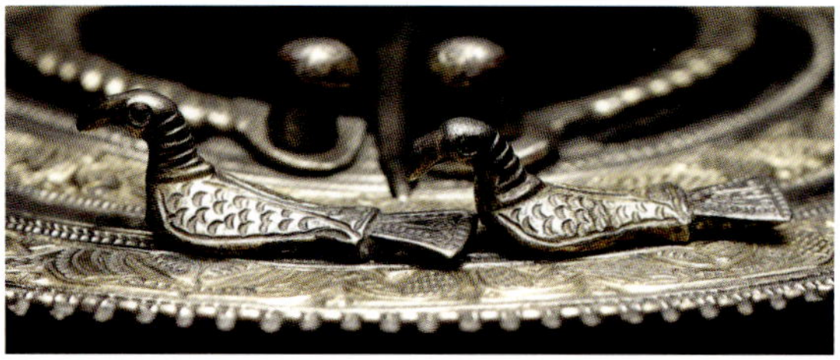

It was once thought that the Quoit Brooch Style was a Germanic fashion, but this is not supported by its distribution, the object forms it occurs on or the decorative techniques used on such metalwork. Rather, its ancestry lies among late Roman traditions, in particular the decorative styles associated with military metalwork, such as the belt suites which were emblems of rank or office. Moreover, the emergence of the style in the early fifth century and its short existence, ending as that century drew to a close, make it possible that there were only a few workshops, or perhaps even just one, which were fluent in late Roman artistic practice. This is supported by the imagery used, which is also found in various permutations on provincial Roman metalwork: friezes of animals, often quadrupeds or sea monsters, running or turning their heads back towards the next fantastic creature. The textured bodies are particularly distinctive, with the use of punch marks or engraved lines to imitate fur. A good parallel for this is a gold bangle from Hoxne, Suffolk, in the British Museum, which also features scenes of parading animals.

Anglo-Saxon
From Sarre, Kent, England
5th century AD
Diameter 7.7 cm
1893,0601.219

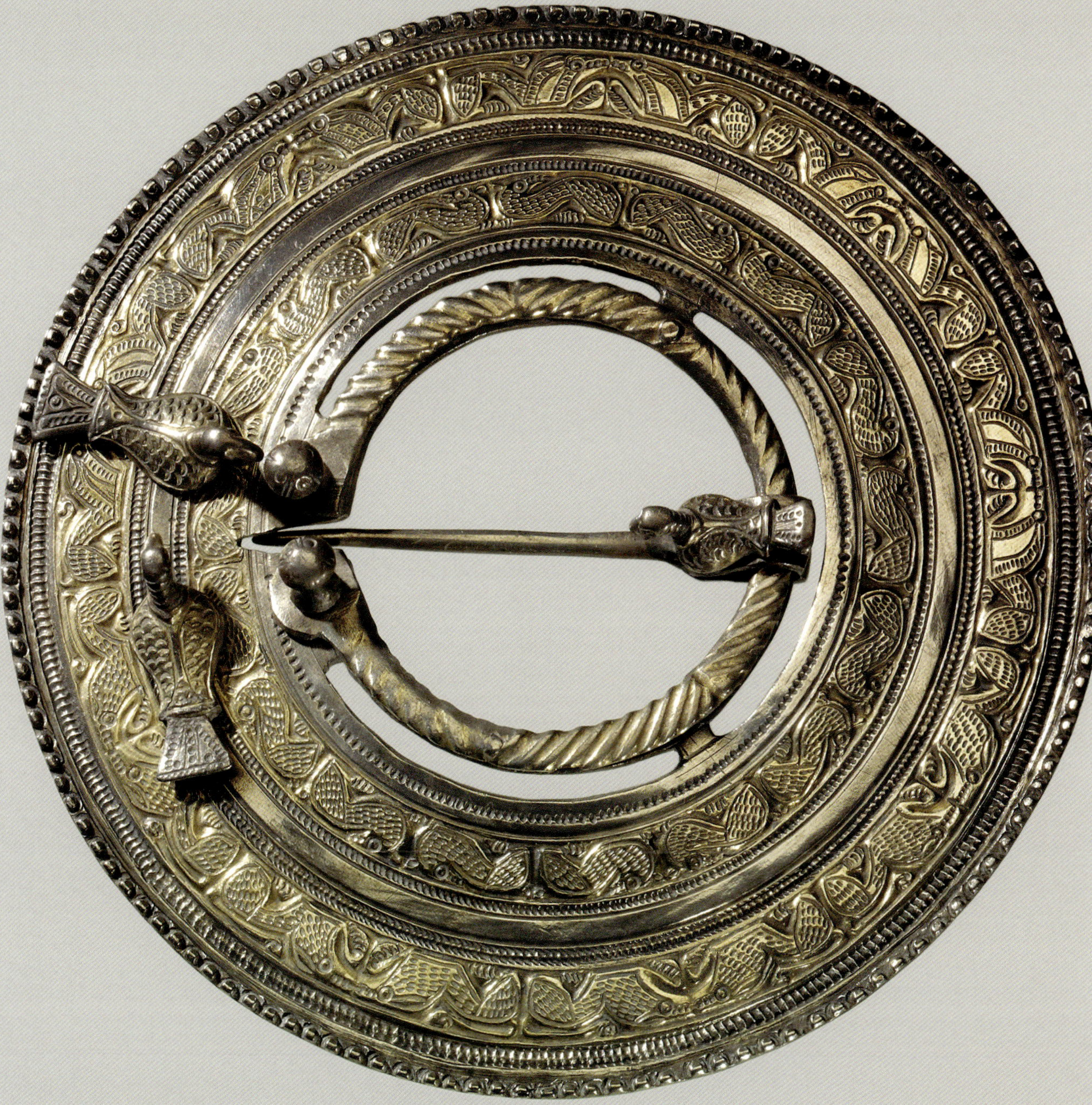

2 BYZANTIUM

(FIFTH TO ELEVENTH CENTURY)

When Constantine the Great proclaimed the ancient city of Byzantium as his new capital and then renamed it Constantinopolis in AD 330, would he have envisaged it becoming the centre of an empire that would last for over a millennium? It was certainly a calculated move to establish himself in the East, away from the old power centres and aristocracies of the West. He had chosen an ideal, strategic position on the straits of the Bosporus, from where access to the Black Sea and the Near East was easily controlled (**Map 1**).

Solidus of Justinian I, minted at Constantinople AD 527–65; Dept of Coins and Medals, 1904,0604.76

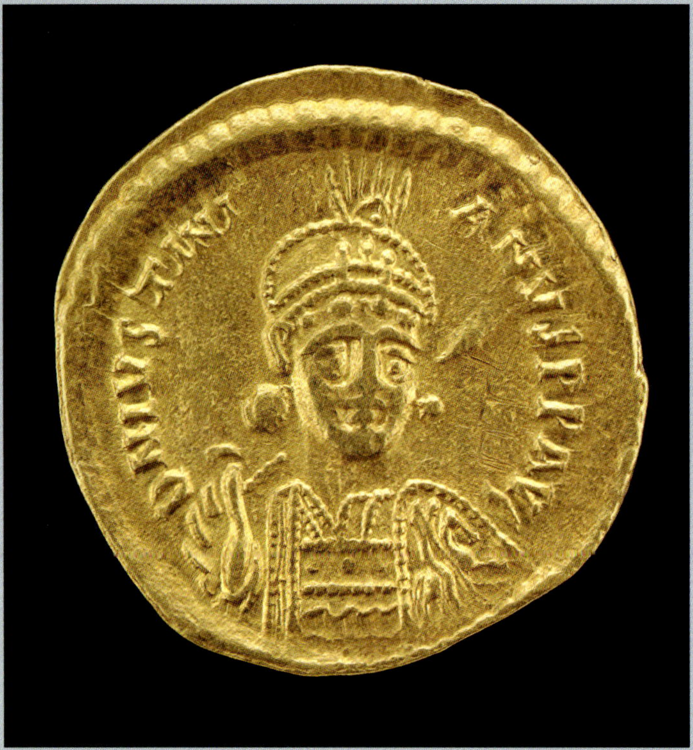

At this time the Roman Empire was still going strong. With the final demise of Roman rule in the West in AD 476, Constantinople remained as the capital of what today we call the Byzantine Empire. This is not a term that contemporaries would have recognized, as they saw themselves as *Romaioi* – Romans – and their culture as a natural continuation of ancient traditions.

Greek was the common language of the city and many of the empire's dominions. Under the long rule of Justinian I (AD 527–65) areas which had been lost to Germanic tribes, such as the Goths in Italy and Vandals in North Africa (Chapter 4), were won back. At its greatest extent the Byzantine Empire stretched from modern-day Algeria all around the southern and eastern shores of the Mediterranean, across the Balkans and on to Sicily and parts of Italy, southern France and Spain. However, the sway of Byzantine politics and fashions held even further afield. Luxury goods from the empire, such as silk, jewellery and silver plate (**10**, **35**, **36**), were deployed by the Byzantine emperors as diplomatic gifts or rewards for allies, as well as to pay off enemies. In addition, trade networks conveyed gemstones, copper alloy vessels (**49**) and spices over vast distances across the Mediterranean and beyond.

All these riches were highly coveted by people outside the empire, from the Avars to the Anglo-Saxons. The objects influenced local artistic developments and were sometimes imitated outright. Byzantine gold coinage, for example, was not only a model for the coins issued by Germanic rulers in the West (see facing page; **84**), but also served as the raw material from which jewellery and ornaments were crafted. In exchange, anything and anyone, from furs to foreign mercenaries, including the famous Viking imperial guard from the tenth century onwards, came to Byzantium.

The spiritual world of Byzantium was not without turmoil. Christian controversies blighted much of its early history and the great iconoclastic storms of the eighth and early ninth century led to the widespread destruction of artworks and architecture. This also affected the depiction of particular religious subjects in line with officially sanctioned iconographies. Nevertheless, the artistic achievements of gold and silversmiths, bronze casters, sculptors, painters, mosaicists, weavers, embroiderers and architects flourished in this period.

Despite its formidable military power, in the end the Byzantine Empire could not defend its holdings against the Germanic tribes in the west and the steppe nomadic and Slav peoples in the north. In addition, it steadily lost ground to the Islamic dynasties in the Near East and North Africa, especially from AD 630 onwards (**Map 5**). Aspects of Byzantine art and architecture nonetheless remained influential and are reflected, for example, in Slavic churches as well as major Islamic buildings such as the Dome of the Rock in Jerusalem and the Great Mosque at Damascus. On a smaller scale, continuities are visible, for instance in textiles (**33**), glass (**99**, **100**) and jewellery.

Christian crusaders captured Constantinople in 1204, but after a reconquest and final flowering of the city, it fell to Muslim armies in 1453. Increasingly known as Istanbul, it became the capital of the Ottoman Empire and today is still a key city in bridging Europe and Asia.

22 SIGNET RING

Like the late Roman marriage ring (**14**), this substantial gold piece is a signet ring, characterized by the deeply engraved design on the bezel. Its weight was equal to approximately 4.5 to 5.5 *solidi*, which was more than the price of a horse.

A youthful, beardless Christ sits facing the viewer, his left hand – which would have been his right in impressions of the seal – raised in a gesture of benediction. The hoop is formed of smaller, rounded medallions, each of which contains a standing male figure. They are all shown in classical, draped dress and each clenches a handful of fabric. It has been suggested that the figures may represent apostles. Moreover, eight-sided ring designs were thought to have apotropaic or evil-averting properties.

Early Christians were concerned with the appropriate choice of motifs for seal rings. In his writings, which stayed influential long after his death in the early third century, Clement of Alexandria set out which emblems were acceptable (**2**). As the wearing of precious metal jewellery was itself a contentious affair for Christians who were supposed to shun all worldly vanities, he specified that one gold seal ring could be worn by a woman in charge of a household or a man conducting business. Clement even proposed that men should wear the ring at the base of their little finger so it would not get lost easily.

Symbolic devices such as the fish, the Greek word for which was an acronym for Christ (**54**), the Good Shepherd (**2**) or the anchor, which represented the Cross as well as the spiritual security that the truly faithful enjoyed, were common. With the strengthening of Christianity's influence in the Roman Empire during the fourth century, explicitly Christian motifs became more common.

The quality and detail of the deep engraving is superb. Christ is seated on a cushioned throne with a footstool. These are signifiers of elevated status, derived from imperial iconography and still present, for instance, in the depictions of the Adoration of the Magi on a Byzantine medallion (**29**) and the Franks Casket (**58**), or on the Ottonian reliquary crowned by a figure of the enthroned Christ (**102**).

Byzantine

From Smyrna, modern-day Izmir, Turkey

Late 4th to 5th century AD

Height of bezel 1.5 cm

AF.288

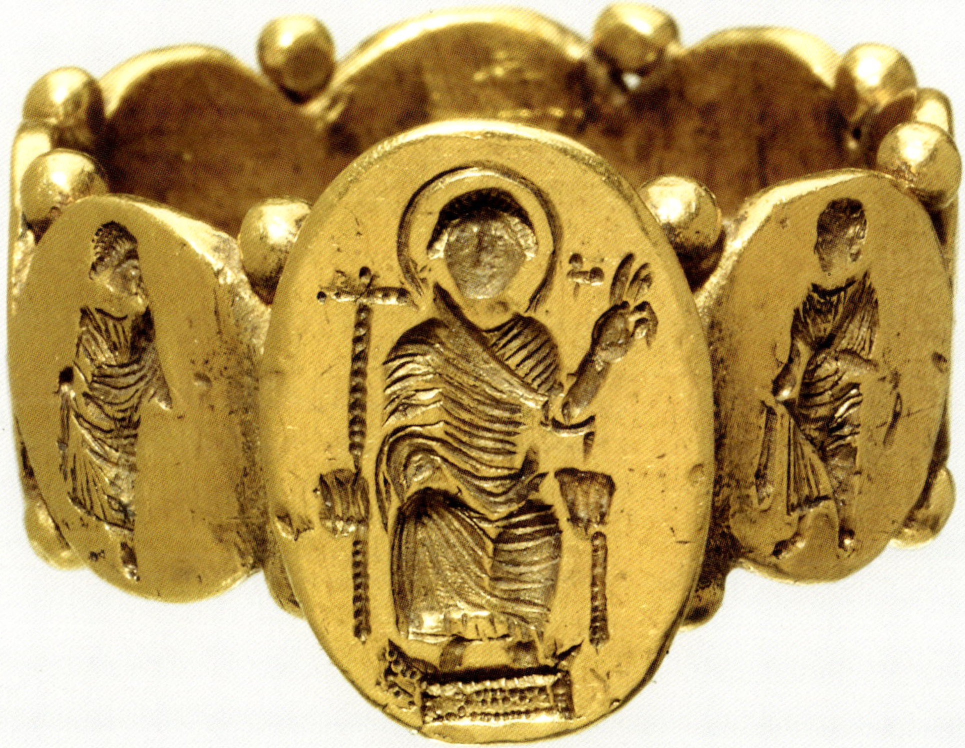

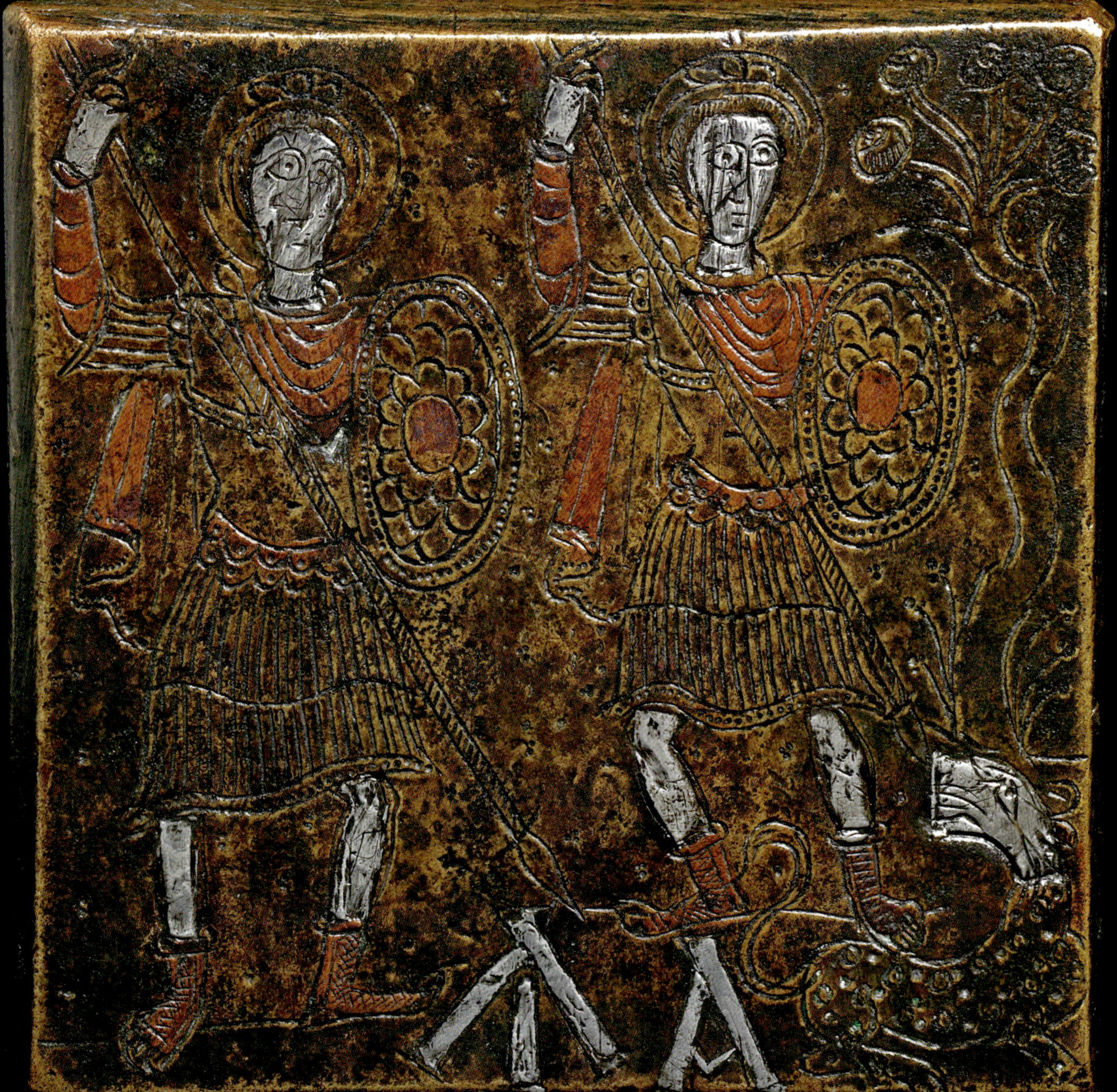

23 TRADE WEIGHT

Late Roman and Byzantine trade weights from around the third to the seventh century came in three materials: copper alloy, glass and lead. Those made from copper were usually simple squares or discs marked with their weight and perhaps some additional ornamentation, such as a cross. But more complex square examples with imperial iconography were also occasionally produced. On most instances, two imperial busts are presented inside a wreath. The present one pound weight, depicting two full-length figures in motion, is among the most elaborate of the type.

Each male figure is shown with a nimbus or halo, wearing a diadem and a military cloak or *paludamentum*, which is fastened by a crossbow brooch on the shoulder (**17**). Carrying a shield and brandishing a spear, they are both armoured in leather or metal with a cuirass to protect the upper body and an apron-like skirt or *pteryges* which reaches to the knees. The hunt, a favourite pastime of the elites, is the setting (**5**, **79**) and to the right of the scene, the hunters' spears are aimed at a leopard crouching beneath a tree. A polychrome or multicoloured effect is achieved by the pure, reddish copper inlay on parts of the shields and clothing, while the hands, legs and faces of the emperors and the leopard, as well as the denominational mark for one pound at the base, shine in silver.

The figures have in the past been described as military saints, but they are clearly identified as emperors by the cuirass and type of diadem they wear. Their inclusion on this weight would not only have lent it legitimacy, but may also have been a symbol of the unity of the empire after it had been divided into a western and an eastern half.

Late Roman/early Byzantine
Unknown findspot
Late 4th to 5th century AD
Length 6.9 cm, weight 324.0 g
1863,1228.1

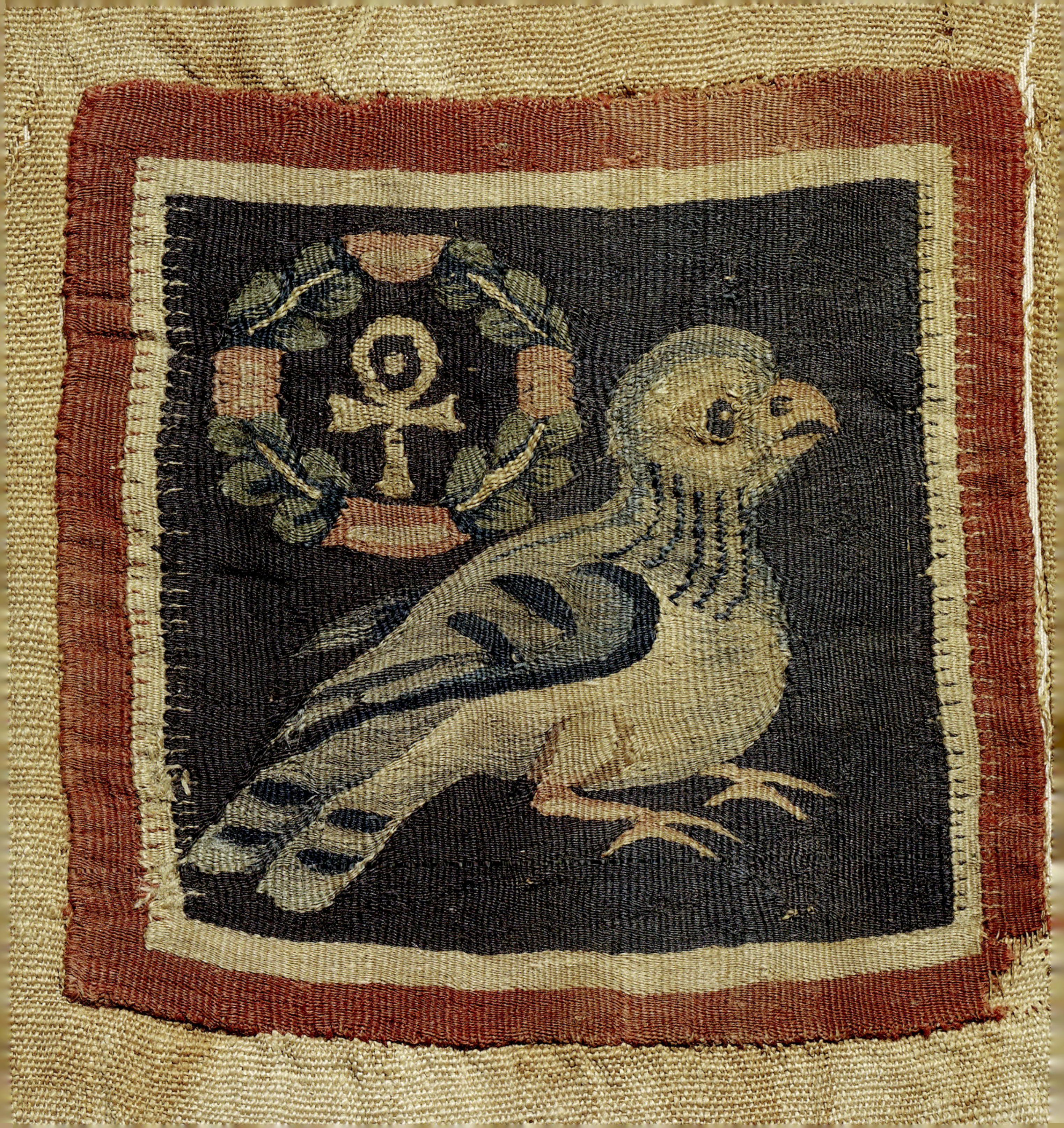

24 TEXTILE FRAGMENT DEPICTING A BIRD

On a dark background, a colourful little bird is perched. This decorative square known as a *tabula* was once part of a larger textile, perhaps placed alongside other bird panels also preserved in the collection of the British Museum. Whether this was a tunic, mantle or shawl, or alternatively a blanket or decorative hanging, is now impossible to say as this bird was cut out from his linen base cloth (**33**), suffering the same fate as many other textiles excavated in Egypt during the nineteenth and early twentieth century.

Textiles from Coptic – namely late antique to early Islamic – Egypt are among the finest known from antiquity. Preserved in the hot and dry climate, they form a vivid array of sometimes luxurious clothes (**33**) as well as furnishing fabrics (**32**).

From the second half of the fifth century, multicoloured single motifs, rather than whole scenes, became more popular through the influence of Sasanian silk textiles from Persia. As in mosaics and jewellery (**21**), lifelike images of various species of birds were depicted. Peacocks, quails and pigeons featured, sometimes even parrots. Eagles seem to have had a different significance, as they usually appear in a more stylized form, perhaps conveying heraldic connotations.

Birds could represent the immortality of the soul and this is the appropriate reading here as positioned prominently behind the bird is an *ankh*, a cross with a looped head. This sign had been used by the Egyptians to symbolize immortality long before the late Roman and Byzantine periods. The *ankh* is set inside a jewelled wreath, illustrating how its meaning had now blended with the Christian reverence for the Cross.

The whole textile is executed in the tapestry technique; the cream base cloth is a plain weave, while the decorative parts are created by interweaving coloured wool threads. This allows for subtle gradations of colour, and in the best pieces an almost painterly impression is achieved. Here these fine colour transitions have been employed to great effect, especially on the breast and wings of the bird, as well as to imply faceting on the gems of the wreath.

Coptic

Thought to be from Akhmim-Panopolis, Egypt

5th century AD

Width of decorative field 13.3 cm

1891,0509.78 (EA22868), Dept of Ancient Egypt and Sudan

25 THE BAPTISM OF CHRIST

The young Christ is standing naked in a river, while St John the Bapist reaches out from the left to baptize him. This composition incorporates the three manifestations of God that Christians would have believed in: the hand of God is seen releasing the Holy Spirit from Heaven, here represented by a dove, which holds out a baptismal bowl to Christ, God's incarnation on earth.

Baptism played a central role in the early Christian mind, as it was the way to achieve salvation through the symbolic washing away of sin. Depictions of the Baptism of Christ were therefore common in late antiquity, for instance on catacomb walls. Mosaics in some of the most lavishly decorated ecclesiastical buildings in Ravenna, Italy, such as the Orthodox Baptistery, dated around AD 458, and the Baptistery of the Arians, probably from the late fifth century, both illustrated this episode. In both cupola mosaics Christ is depicted naked, waist-deep in water, just as he is on the present ivory carving. Another shared feature is the presence of a bearded older male personifying the River Jordan, as seen in the bottom right corner here.

Lush hair and a rather androgynous body characterize Christ in all three depictions, which has been interpreted as a reflection of the all-encompassing nature of baptism: through this sacrament, the faithful are reborn in Christ irrespective of whether they are male or female. The choice of the male nude still follows classical traditions. The skill of the ivory carver and the mosaicists is highlighted by the fact that Christ's form is still clearly discernible through the water. The iconography and basic elements of this scene were preserved for centuries, although in general Christ's sex was no longer shown (**71**).

Recent conservation work has identified previously unknown traces of colour, which became noticeable during microscopic examination under UV light. Blue colourants were detected in the river area and the remains of black pigments were discovered on St John the Baptist's left sleeve as well as on the head of the personification of the River Jordan. Most exciting of all, tiny traces of probable silver leaf and gold specks have survived around St John the Baptist and Christ, which illustrate how this precious carving was once enhanced even further.

Byzantine
Unknown findspot
5th century AD
Height 16.3 cm
1896,0618.1

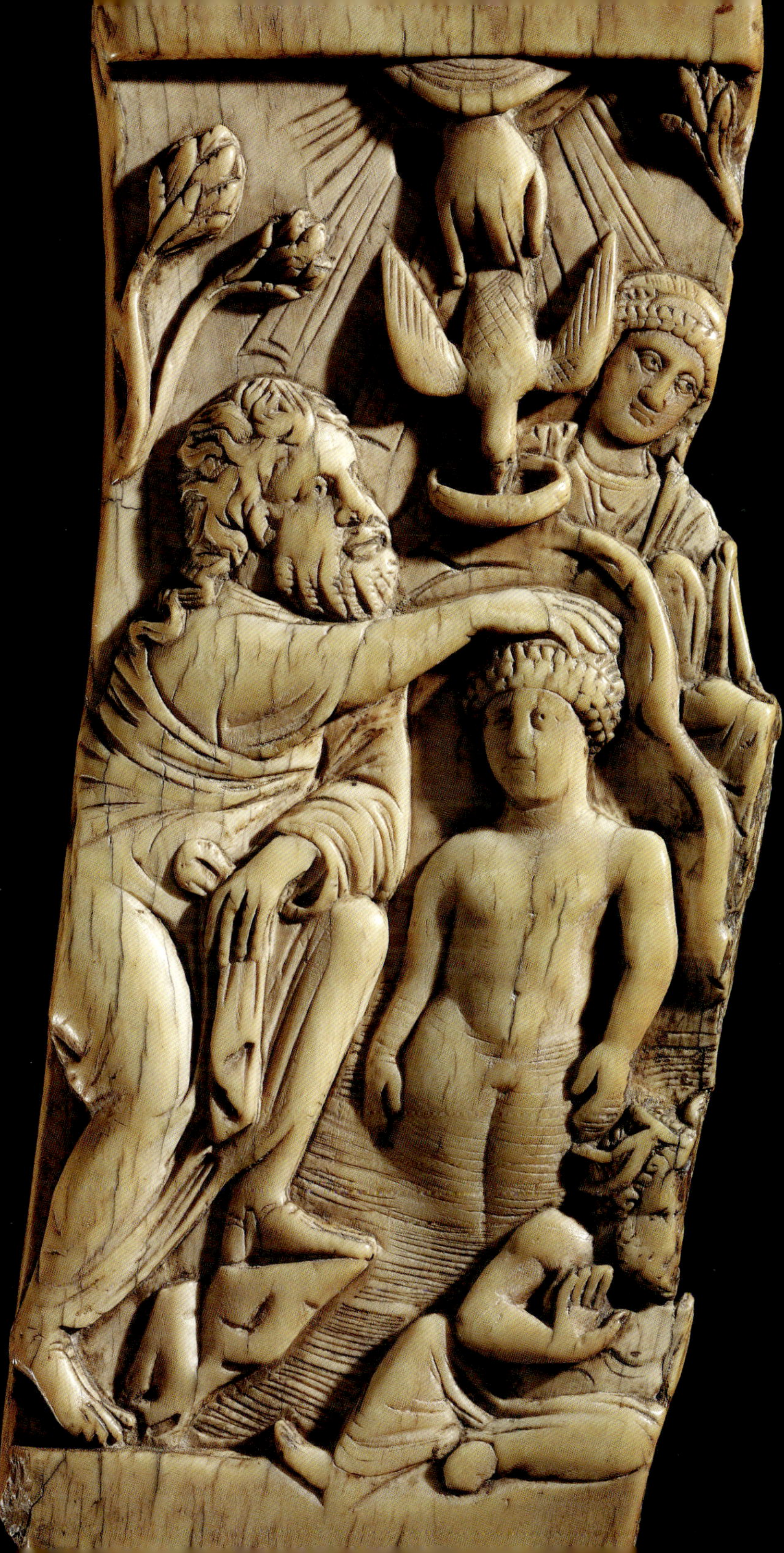

26 PYX

Originally, the Ancient Greek term *pyxis* simply signified a vessel made from boxwood. In antiquity, however, wood, ivory or metal pyxes served as a variety of containers. On an ivory diptych leaf in the Victoria and Albert Museum, London, for instance, a Roman priestess is seen sprinkling incense from a pyx onto an altar fire. The early Christian Church adopted the cylindrical container form, using it to contain the Host for the Eucharist, a practice which continued into the early medieval period (**95**, **111**).

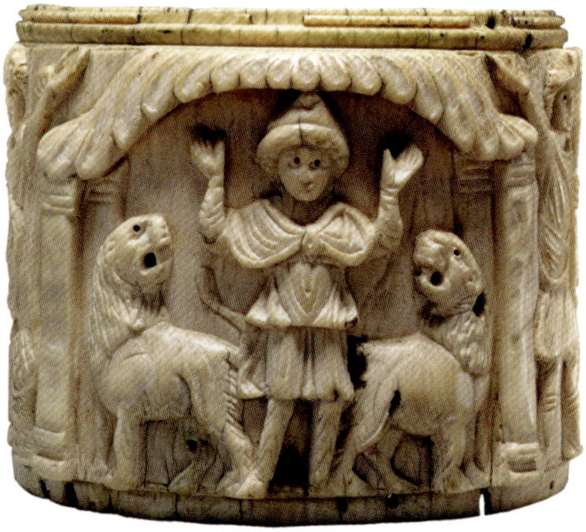

Two events from the Old Testament are displayed in deep relief carving on this British Museum ivory pyx. An angel is charging forwards and pointing towards a ram, which is looking up to the left. What both are looking at is not shown, but it would have been Abraham about to sacrifice his son Isaac. At that moment, Abraham heard an angel call out to tell him to stop. The ram, caught in a nearby thicket (here represented by a tree), was used as an offering instead (Genesis 22:11–13). The urgency of the situation is expressed in the figure of the angel who hastens towards the ram, his garments fluttering. The second scene on the pyx, illustrated here on the left, shows Daniel in the lions' den. He had been thrown in as a punishment for breaking a royal decree by praying to God, but the lions left Daniel unscathed and are here shown turning their backs on him. This took place in the Persian Empire and consequently Daniel is wearing a Phrygian cap and trousers.

These seemingly unrelated events are part of a complex theological allegory. Isaac represents Christ, whose sacrifice redeemed humankind; conversely, the figure of Daniel, who escaped mortal peril through his faith, stands for the redemption of humanity as a result of Christ's death. Both are eminently suitable motifs for a container central to the Eucharist, which is celebrated as a symbol of Christ's sacrifice.

Judging by its style, this piece is likely to have come from Syria, or perhaps North Africa. Ivory pyxes were often preserved in church treasuries so a comparatively large number of them have survived.

Late Roman or Byzantine
Unknown findspot
5th to early 6th century AD
Height 7.6 cm
Donated by A.W. Franks
1877,0706.3

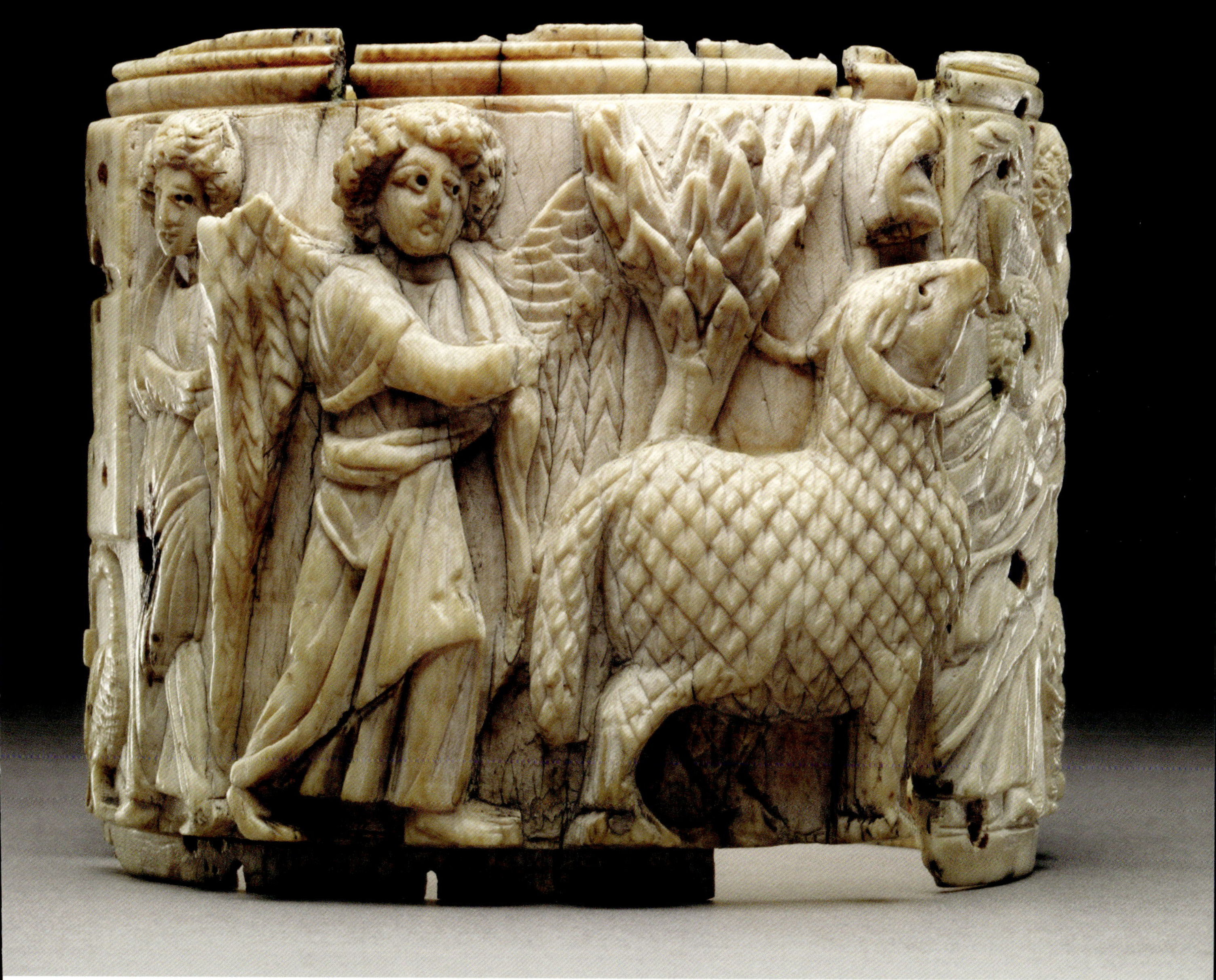

27 GRIFFIN OIL LAMP

Lamps deserve a special place in our appreciation of everyday examples of Byzantine material culture, whether they were for domestic use or the illumination of churches and palaces. A simple basic principle – namely a container for the fuel with an opening for the wick – was developed into a multitude of designs and adapted for carrying, placing on furniture or special stands, or for suspending from candelabra.

Many are decorated with Christian designs, like this one from the British Museum, and there was certainly a considerable need for the illumination of spacious church interiors. Constantine the Great, for instance, donated 169 lamps with a total of 8,730 individual flames to the church of St John Lateran in Rome. In addition, he made provision for the vast amounts of olive oil required to fuel these lamps.

The present lamp was not made for hanging, but for setting down on a custom-made stand. Its heavy copper alloy body fits neatly in the tradition of Byzantine bronze casting (**49**) and is distinguished from the majority of lamps by having two spouts. The elaborate handle is in the form of a griffin, with a sharp beak, small circlets for eyes, a long neck and a wavy mane (**36**). A cross crowns the beast's head, placed between its ears. Two further crosses have been inscribed on the body of the lamp with ring-and-dot punches.

In antiquity, the griffin was considered to be not only an exotic animal (**36**), but also a bearer of light and this meaning may have been carried through into Christian times. While a lamp like this one need not have come from a church, the frequent appearance of crosses on lamps certainly alluded to the epithet of Christ as the 'Light of the World' which is mentioned throughout the New Testament.

Byzantine
Unknown findspot
5th to 6th century AD
Length 16.5 cm
1850,0805.10

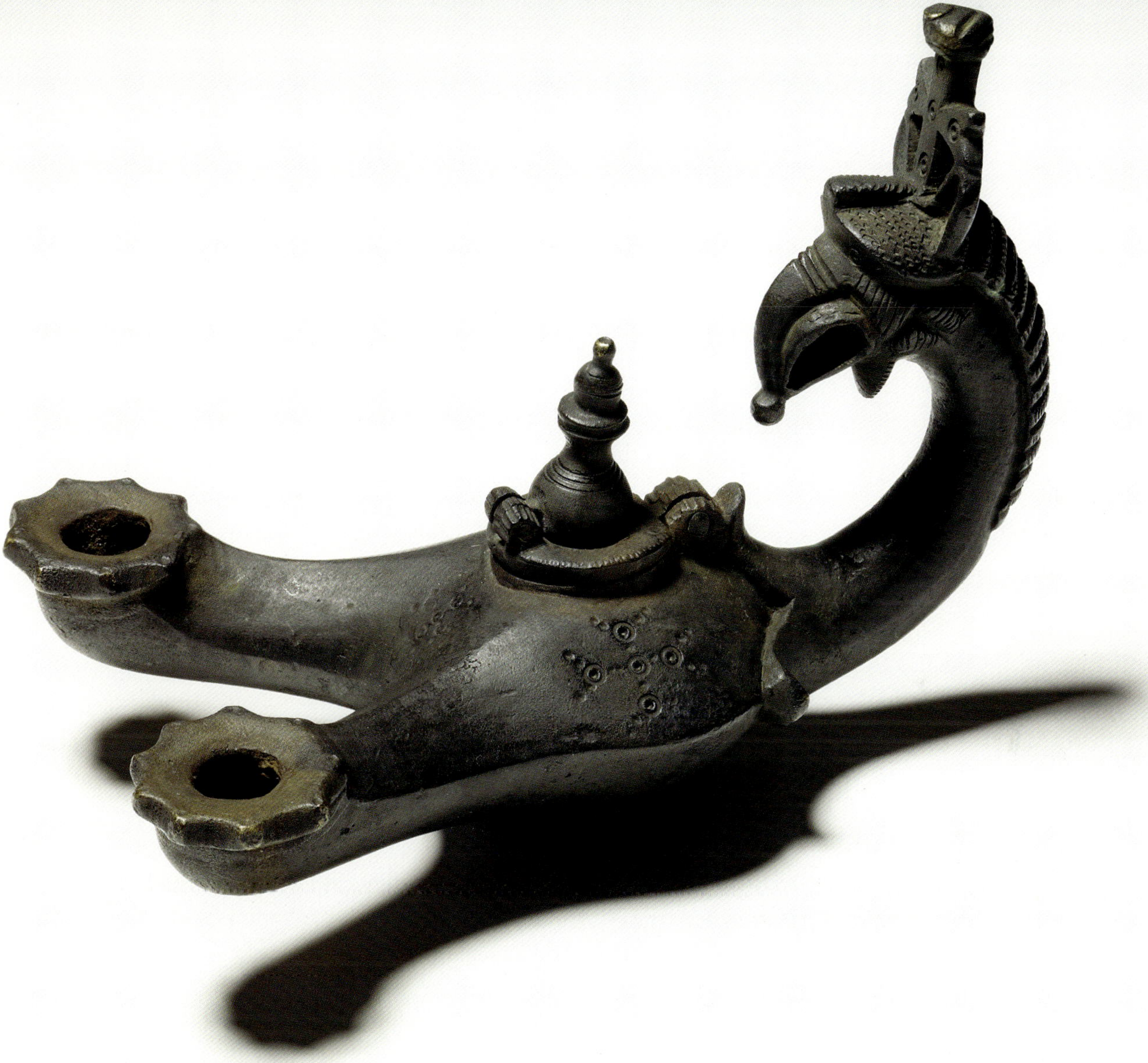

28 DIPTYCH LEAF OF AN ARCHANGEL

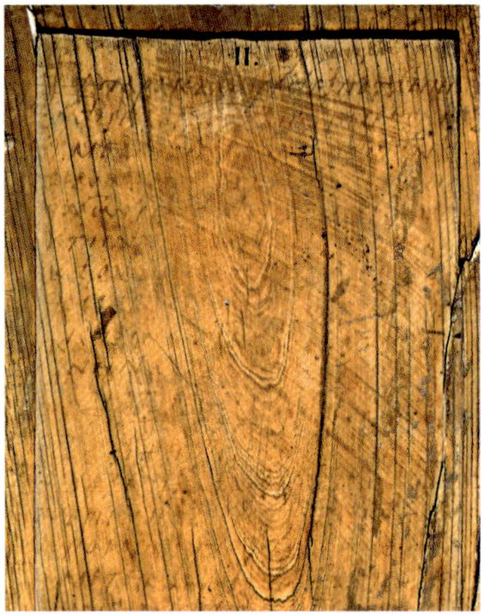

Byzantine
Unknown findspot
Second quarter of the 6th century AD
Height 42.8 cm
OA.9999

The Archangel Michael is positioned within a niche holding a long ceremonial staff in his left hand in the same mannered posture as the dignitary on the Apotheosis diptych leaf (**13**). A panel above him contains a Greek inscription which begins with a cross emblem. The texture has been rendered lovingly to delineate the draped fabric, the archangel's hair and feathers, and the intricate architectural ornament above his head. The ivory carving is of exquisite quality. This, together with the outstanding size of the panel, which is probably as large a piece as can feasibly be cut from an elephant's tusk, suggest that the imperial court at Constantinople was the likely setting for the diptych.

There has been much discussion surrounding the inscription. One proposed translation is 'Accept present circumstances, even understanding their origin'. This reading of the inscription in light of the imagery, which shows an archangel presenting a globe, signifying the world, crowned with a Christian cross, has been taken as a symbol of imperial rule and authority under divine sanction.

This interpretation would fit, for instance, with the accession of Justinian I (AD 527–65) to the Byzantine throne, which took place around the time the diptych is thought to have been carved. Notably during his reign, imperial iconography increasingly incorporated Christian aspects which promoted the idea of the direct endorsement of the emperor by Christ. It is likely that this large and outstanding object was used in court ceremonial.

The diptych seems to have had an afterlife in the seventh century, as faint traces of Greek notes on Syrian liturgy can be seen in the recess on the back. Originally the recess would have been filled with wax, into which messages could be scratched with a stylus.

This is not the only diptych leaf to have been reused in such a way. Another example in the British Museum, still comprising the majority of its two leaves, has the names of clerics, including two bishops from Egypt, and lay people inked onto the back. Such lists were recited during services to commemorate the dead.

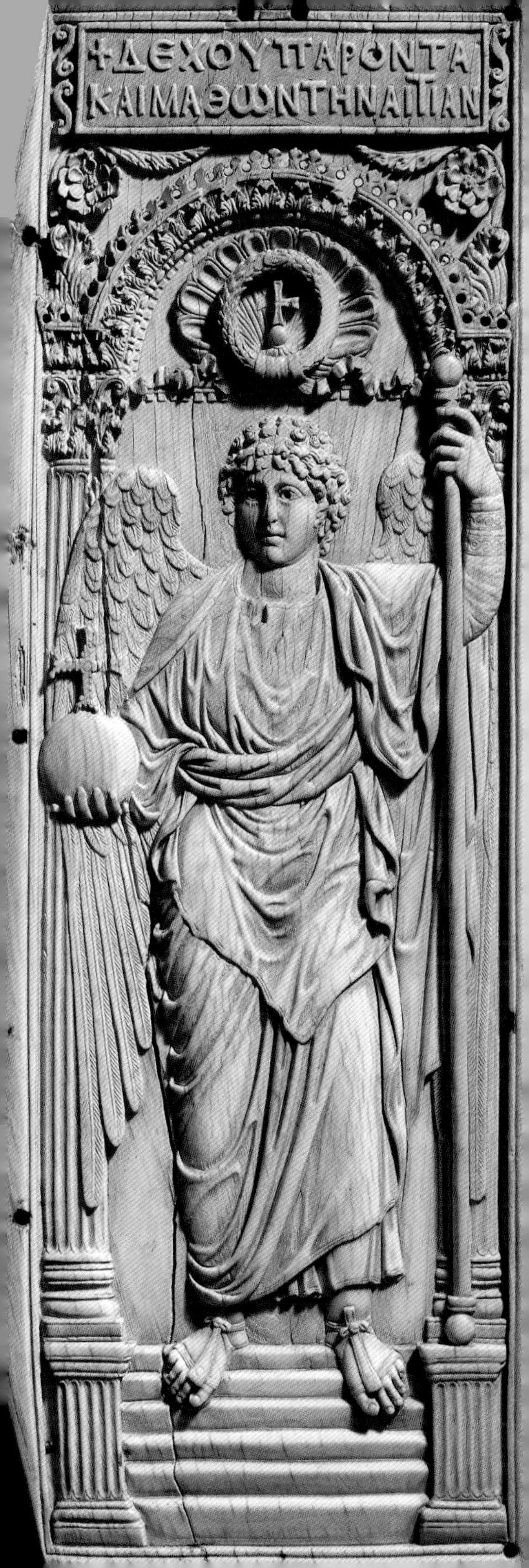
+ΔΕΧΟΥΠΑΡΟΝΤΑ
ΚΑΙΜΑΘΩΝΤΗΝΑΙΤΙΑΝ

29 GOLD MEDALLION SHOWING THE ADORATION

Byzantine pendants with religious scenes were known as *encolpia*, translated literally as 'on the chest'. They came in the form of pectoral crosses or medallions, such as the present example.

This medallion is composed of two discs of sheet gold which are set back to back, joined at the edges and framed with a beaded gold wire. Both faces contain scenes in repoussé from the New Testament and the loop is constructed in such a way that it could be worn with either side outwards.

The scene illustrated presents the three wise men approaching the Virgin with the Child seated on her lap. The Magi are identifiable by the gifts they carry and their Phrygian hats which denote their Eastern descent. Above them are both the star which guided them to the stable in Bethlehem and an angel gesturing towards the Virgin and Child. An inscription below the scene reads 'Lord protect the bearer. Amen', emphasizing how *encolpia* were believed to act as protective amulets.

The scene on the back shows Christ seated on a throne and being borne up to Heaven by four angels, while the Virgin and the twelve Apostles look on with gestures of awe and amazement. Thus the medallion frames the narrative of Christ's life, from his incarnation on earth to his Ascension.

This medallion is one of seven known examples which all depict scenes from the life of Christ. Stylistically they are closely connected to reliquaries and pilgrim *ampullae*, or containers, made in the Holy Land around AD 600, which were perhaps manufactured for wealthy pilgrims.

However, scenes such as the Adoration of the Magi had a far wider currency beyond the borders of the Byzantine Empire, acting as models for locally made religious jewellery, such as the disc brooch probably from Pannonia (**87**).

Byzantine
Unknown findspot
6th–7th century AD
Height including loop 6.8 cm
1983,0704.1

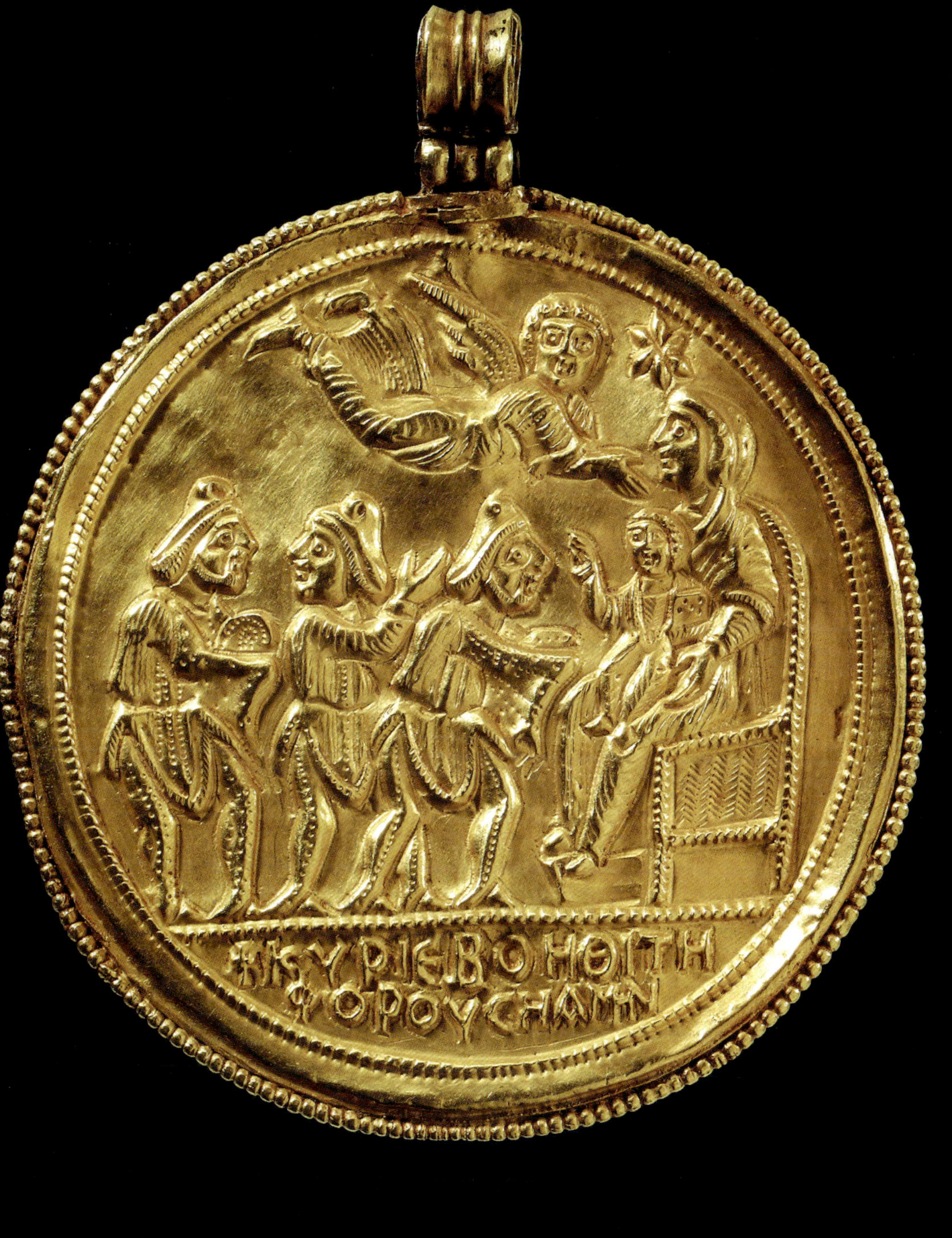
+ΚΥΡΙΕΒΟΗΘΙΤΗ
ΦΟΡΟΥϹΗΑΜΗΝ

30 *LUNULA* EARRING

Crescent-shaped or *lunula* gold earrings were phenomenally popular in the later sixth and seventh century. Although the design was originally conceived in the eastern Mediterranean, it spread quickly. The present example is from Crete, but such earrings have been found as far west as Italy and their northerly distribution extends to Bavaria, the western Carpathian Basin and, with a few pieces, even to the steppes of southern Russia.

While attractive and, apart from a handful of exceptions, always made from gold, they were relatively easy to produce and, due to their openwork nature, economical in the amount of gold required. In addition, the clear Byzantine connotations may have contributed to their popularity outside of the empire. Such earrings were, after all, tokens of exotic contacts.

Lunula earrings were made in many places, yet their appearance as well as the choice of decorative imagery is surprisingly homogenous. Four groups of motifs have been noted, all of which are related to Christian iconography. These themes are also found on other jewellery and remained a staple of the canon of Christian designs for a long time. Paired birds facing one another, as here, or positioned back to back either side of a floral motif or *kantharos*, were particularly common (**34**, **133**).

The present pair of birds are identifiable as peacocks by their elaborate tail plumage. In Christian contexts, they symbolize the immortality of the soul and therefore they are depicted, for instance, on sarcophagi or in catacomb paintings. Since late antiquity, the peacock has also been represented on a wide variety of jewellery (**34**). Both of the peacocks are feeding on a stylized bunch of grapes placed between them. This is an unambiguous reference to Christ as the vine, whose fruit nourishes the birds in the same way as the Eucharist gives spiritual sustenance to the faithful (**63**).

It has been proposed that these connotations of eternal life and salvation could be the reason why such examples are particularly common among the types of earrings which occurred in Mediterranean burials.

Byzantine
From Erythrea, Crete, Greece
6th to 7th century AD
Height 3.7 cm
Bequeathed by A.W. Franks
AF.347

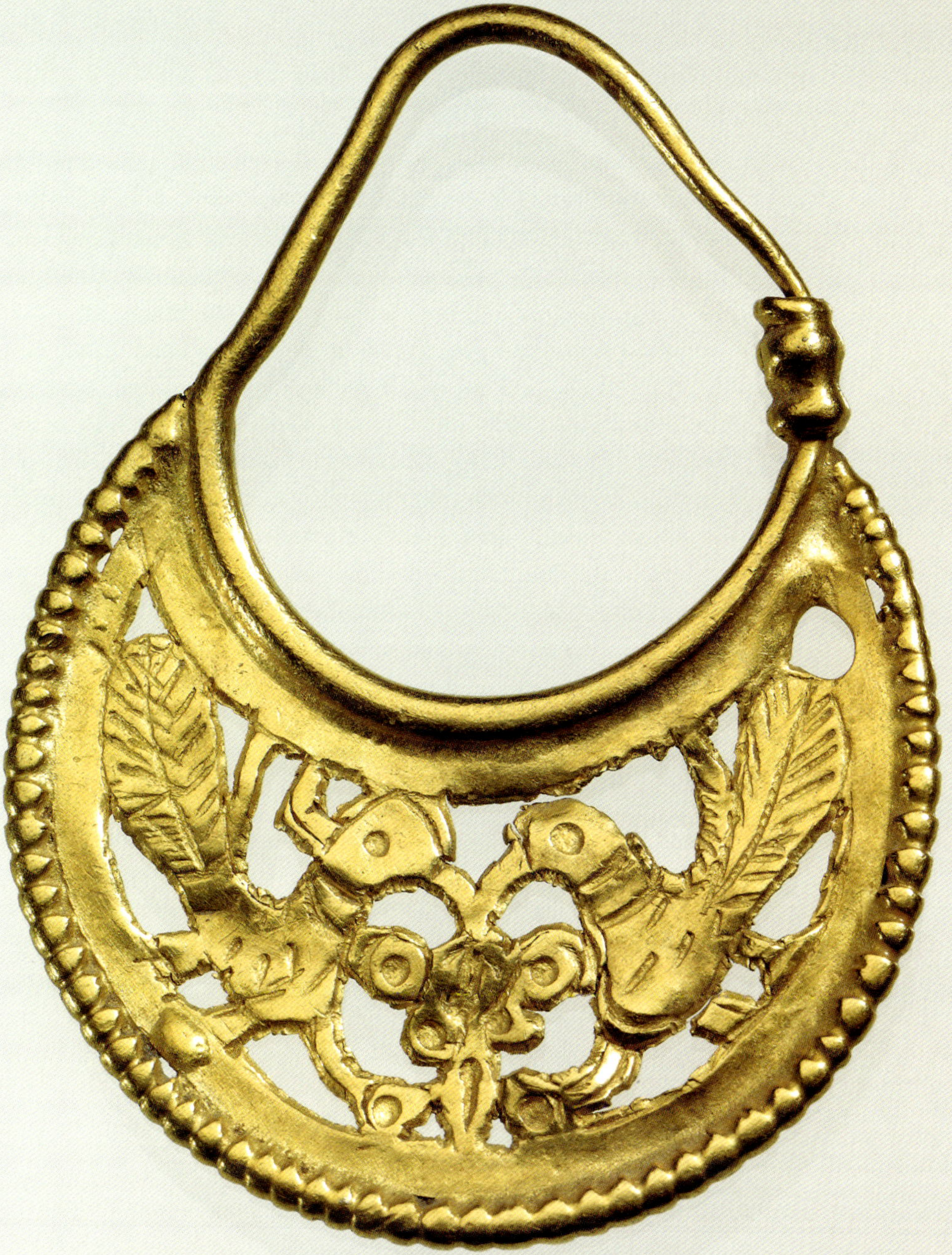

31 JEWELLERY

When a monograph on the so-called Asyut Treasure was published in 1918, it was thought to comprise thirty-two pieces of gold jewellery for both men and women, some of it also set with precious stones. Between 1909 and 1914 these objects were sold to four private collectors and today are in museums in Washington, Berlin and New York, as well as the British Museum.

But whether all these pieces really are from one hoard has recently been called into question. The necklace illustrated here is certainly part of the treasure, as grains of the same reddish sand found on eleven other pieces were present. However, doubts have been raised over the remaining objects, including the pair of earrings shown here and a golden body chain also in the British Museum. They exhibit typical characteristics of jewellery made in Egyptian-Byzantine workshops of the later sixth and earlier seventh century, so therefore fit into the period when the treasure was hidden, but their only other link to the treasure is the word of the dealer who sold all of the pieces. As it was a well-known practice to ascribe a famous findspot to an object in order to increase its value, the provenance of the earrings and body chain should be treated with caution.

This slight question mark in no way detracts from the intricacy of the necklace and earrings. Short lengths of gold chain alternate with pearls, dark green emeralds and gold medallions on the necklace. In addition, the round pendant contains drop-shaped sapphires, and the earrings feature the same array of pearls and precious stones. Several other pieces from the treasure are bejewelled in a similar manner. According to a law of the Codex of Justinian (Paragraph 11.12, issued in AD 529 and revised in AD 534), these exact combinations on particular types of jewellery and other objects were only to be used by members of the imperial family or the highest-ranking officials and their wives. Certain types, such as jewelled collars, were exclusive to the emperor and his close relations. Transgressions incurred high fines and, under certain circumstances, even resulted in the death penalty. This suggests that the jewellery known as the Asyut Treasure once belonged amongst the highest echelons of society in Byzantine Egypt.

Byzantine

Thought to have been found at Asyut, Egypt

c. AD 560s to 640s

Length of earrings 12.4 cm

Donated by Mrs Burns

1916,0704.2 to 4

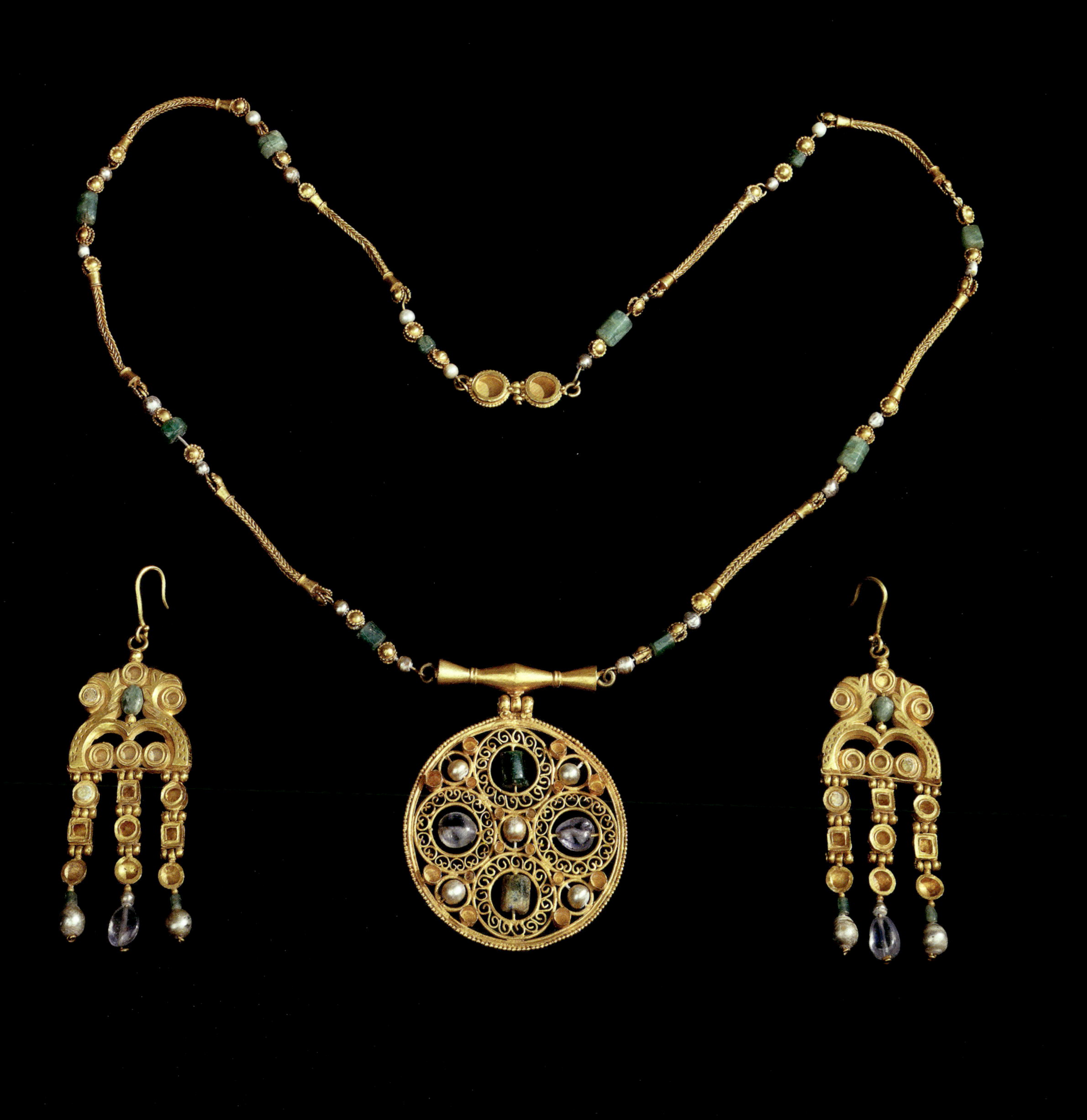

32 CURTAIN

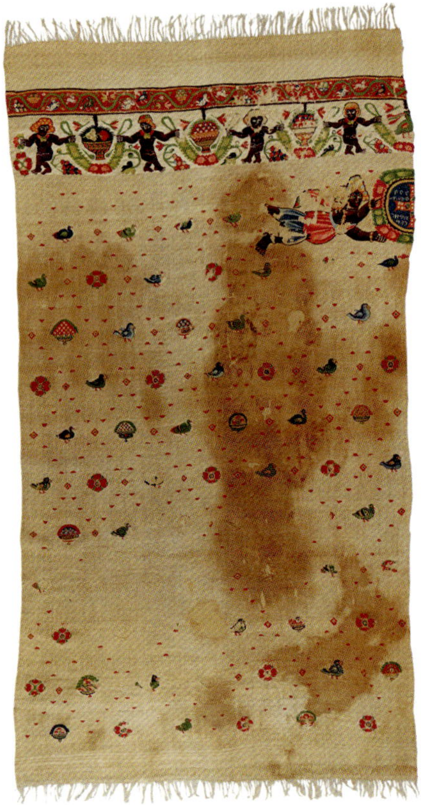

Coptic
Thought to be from Akhmim-Panopolis, Egypt
c. AD 600 (?)
Width of each curtain 145.0 cm
1897,0112.1352 (EA29771), Dept of Ancient Egypt and Sudan

Many spectacular textiles have been preserved as a result of Egyptian burial customs in practice between the third and ninth century. This cloth was used to wrap a body, which explains the elongated dark stain running its length. Written sources from the period convey a strong concern for appropriate burial in dignified clothing. Cushions could also be placed under the head and feet of the dead, and for those who could afford it, these textiles were highly decorated in the tapestry technique (**24**).

However, the fabrics of such textiles were not always new. Some garments were mended and the present textile was not made as a shroud, but as one of a pair of curtains. During the Coptic period, hanging cloths like these were draped over doorways and used as room dividers. On mosaics and ivory carvings (**96**) cloths are shown slung back to reveal interior settings. Indeed, the upper third of this curtain and its pair were sewn together, suggesting that the figurative bands at the top remained visible at all times, while the rest of the fabric could be tied back.

The stylized imagery is still brightly coloured. At the top, a vivid green vine scrolls its way between flowers, fruit, birds, leopards and sea nymphs or *nereids*. Below, a procession of dancing *erots* clasp festoons of leaves and blossoms (**3**) intertwined with bunches of grapes and surrounding baskets of fruit and flowers. Further fruit baskets, blossoms and birds are dotted across the rest of the curtain. These motifs are symbols of abundance and the composition contains elements harking back to themes of fertility associated with the god Dionysus, a popular motif on earlier textiles.

This cloth is also firmly rooted in Christian beliefs, with a female figure holding one half of a medallion featuring a jewelled cross. In addition, the vine and grapes may represent the biblical epithet of 'Christ as the true vine' (**63**) and the grapes may also be a reference to the Eucharist. Thus, both the pictorial programme and the expensive dyes and craftsmanship would have made for a very apt shroud.

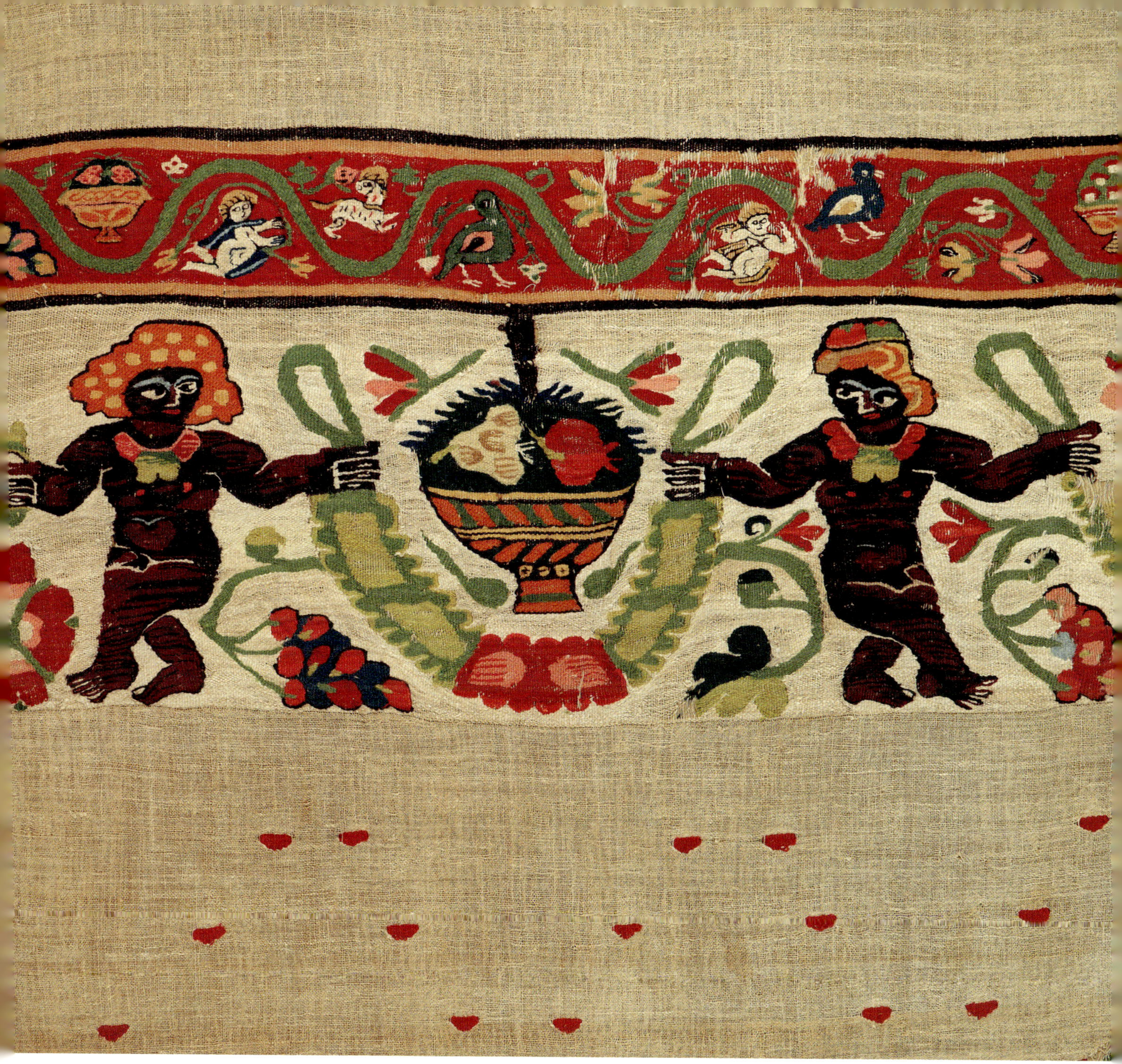

33 TUNIC DECORATION

This *clavus* or decorated textile band from a knee-length tunic was made in a fine, regular tapestry weave. The naturalism of earlier textiles from Coptic Egypt (**24**) has been superseded by a highly stylized, densely packed form of decoration. Clearly delineated fields of different colours, often separated by contour lines, present a more graphic than painterly impression.

Late textiles from the old production centres at Akhmim, Antinoë and in the Fayum are still of superb technical quality. This confirms that the strongly abstracted and formulaic figures and patterns are not likely to be the consequence of a lack of skill, but rather a preference for expressionist ways of representation. Perhaps this was also coupled with an intentional move away from late antique and Byzantine artistic traditions.

Using a palette of colours ranging from a strong royal blue for the horse's eye to a salmon pink for the facial contours, the weaver presents a mounted saint, characterized by his halo and the prominent cross on his chest, perhaps a pendant (**53**, **57**). Religious scenes may have been an expression of faith, but they were probably also thought to have additional evil-averting or apotropaic properties. The belief in demonic forces was widespread in the ancient world. Christian images, as well as the inscriptions or ciphers imitating them, were meant to provide a spiritual shield for their wearer.

But not everyone approved. In the fifth century Bishop Asterios of Amasea complained bitterly about 'some idle and extravagant style of weaving, which... produces... clothing beflowered and wrought with ten thousand objects.... But... rich men and women [who] are more pious, have gathered up the gospel history and turned it over to the weavers.... In doing this they consider that they are acting piously and are clad in garments pleasing to God. But if they take my advice let them sell those clothes and honour the living image of God.'

This passage also confirms that patrons could commission particular motifs. A drawing was made on papyrus and this was then fitted under the loom as a guide for the weaver.

Coptic
Said to be from Akhmim-Panopolis, Egypt
6th to 8th century AD
Length of whole *clavus* 66.5 cm
1887,0402.108 (EA18233), Dept of Ancient Egypt and Sudan

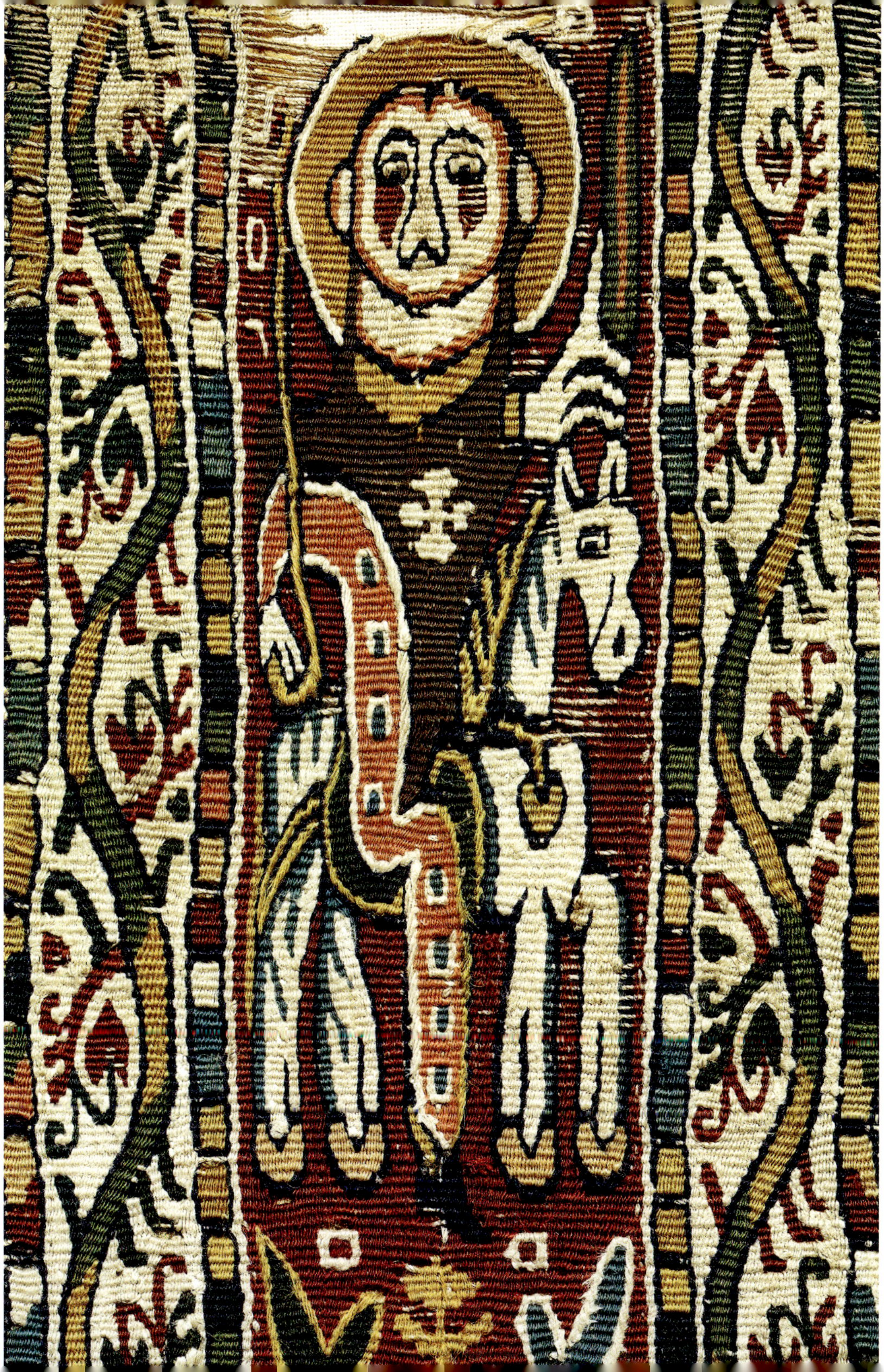

34 BRACELET WITH A MEDALLION OF THE MOTHER OF GOD

One of the most technologically accomplished pieces of Byzantine jewellery in the British Museum is an *opus interrasile* (**5**) bracelet with a hinged medallion at the front. It features an image of the Mother of God which is not unusual as by the sixth century religious themes were common on jewellery.

Mary is shown with a nimbus or halo, and her hands are raised in the *orans* position of a person praying. Tool marks are still visible where the plain background has been smoothed around her head and hands. Over time her wide-eyed stare was to become characteristic of many depictions of the Mother of God, yet the iconography of this piece is unparalleled in early Byzantine jewellery. Most depictions either place Mary in a narrative scene (**29**) or show her in stylized form, especially on small objects such as finger-rings or pendant crosses.

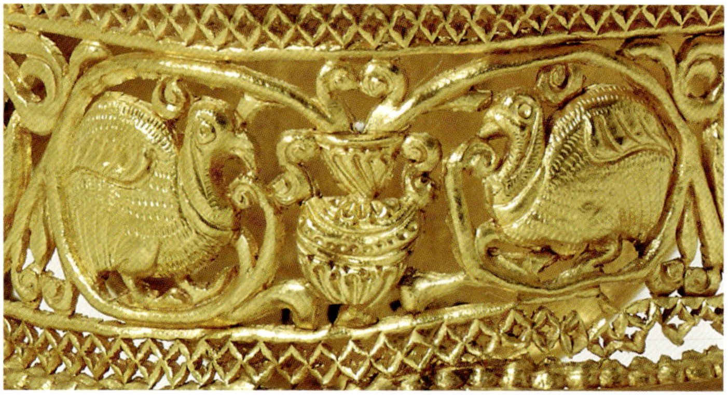

The bracelet's hoop is in the form of a band of paired birds perched inside plant scrolls. At the back, a *kantharos* is flanked by what appears to be a pair of peacocks, as seen here on the left. Already during the late Roman period the peacock had become a Christian symbol for the renewal of life after death, while the *kantharos* with plant tendrils growing from it represented the Tree of Life (**95**).

The three-dimensional relief effect of the procession of birds around the hoop was achieved in a number of steps. The gold sheet was first hammered into a mould in which the design had been engraved. This method would allow for multiple copies of a design to be made. The gold sheet was then turned over and placed on a soft backing which would mould to and support the relief. Mastic is one substance known to have been used by craftsmen in antiquity. Details of the design were then chased and punched from the front, and the openwork decoration pierced through.

Byzantine
Said to be from Syria
c. AD 600
Diameter of medallion 4.4 cm
Bequeathed by A.W. Franks
AF.351

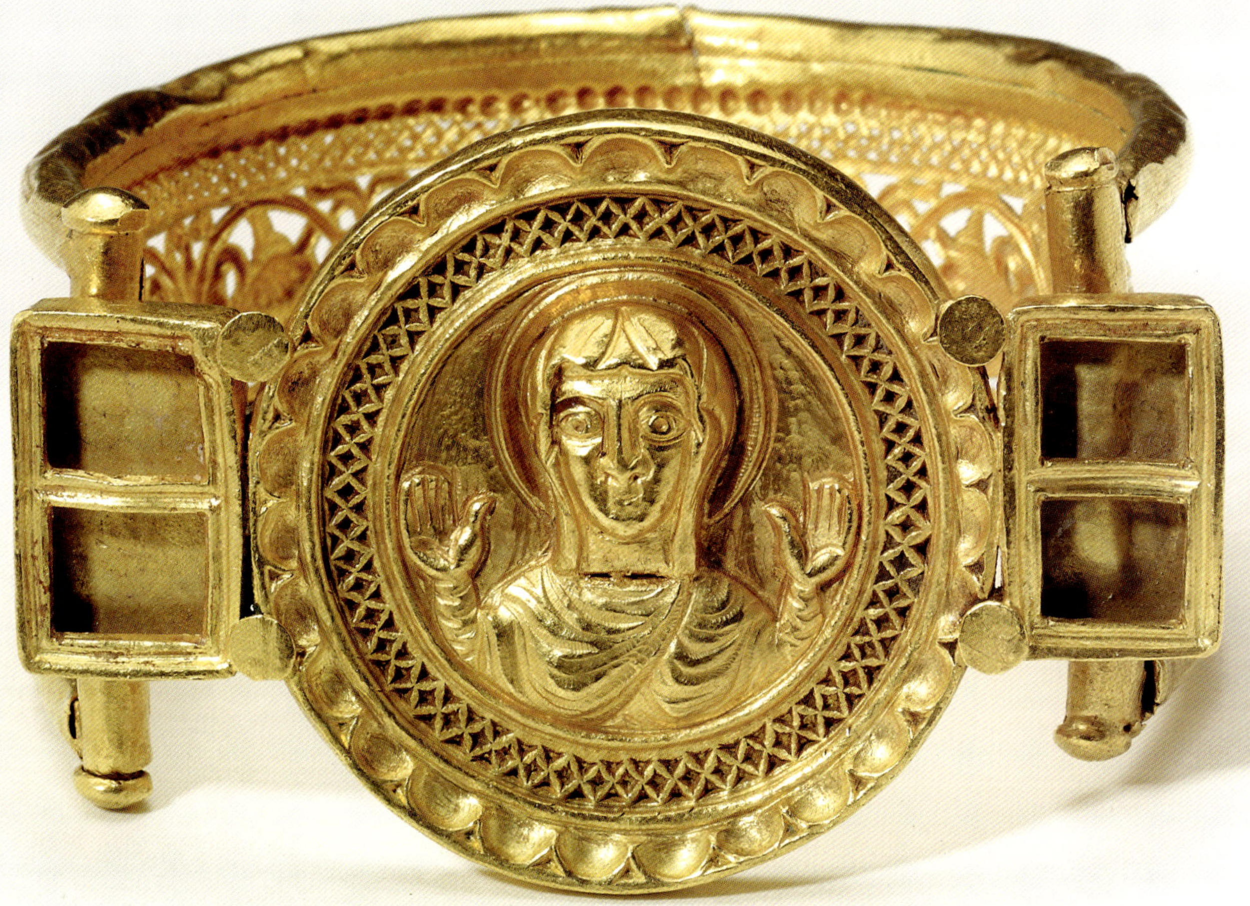

35 BYZANTINE BELT BUCKLE

This small gold buckle forms part of the British Museum's collection of Byzantine jewellery, which with some seven hundred and fifty pieces is one of the largest known.

The oval loop is joined to a long tongue with a decorative shield at the base. Interestingly, the tip of the tongue is also decorated underneath, even though this would not have been visible. It has been suggested that the small arches, triangles and dots could perhaps be a mark of the maker or workshop, as comparable designs have also been found on other buckle tongues.

A tiny red inlay is preserved in the openwork ornament on the back of a similar buckle tongue in the Ferrell Collection in the United States. Perhaps the tongue and plate of the present buckle were once inlaid as well.

The buckle plate is lyre-shaped and ends in a roundel with a monogram. The letters, which are laid out in the shape of a cross, can be translated as 'of Agapios', perhaps referring to the owner who commissioned this piece. Similar buckles, although cast in copper alloy, display cross monograms of the emperor Heraclius (AD 610–41) on their roundels.

Buckles with a lyre-shaped plate, especially in simpler copper alloy versions, were widespread both inside and beyond the Byzantine Empire. Gold coins as well as jewellery were awarded to various friendly and sometimes less than friendly nomadic peoples to the north of the empire, either as gifts or in an attempt to pay them off to leave without harm. Thus belt fittings of the late sixth and early seventh century as well as other precious metalwork were imitated and further developed in these regions. The comma-shaped openwork on the buckle tongue and plate, for instance, was adopted by the Avars (**92**), who developed their own styles out of it. Likewise, a variety of buckles with lyre-shaped plate developed in the western Mediterranean, especially in Visigothic Spain (**93**), where Byzantine influences stayed strong even after the Germanic conquests.

Byzantine
Unknown findspot
Early 7th century AD
Length 4.4 cm
1974,0910.1

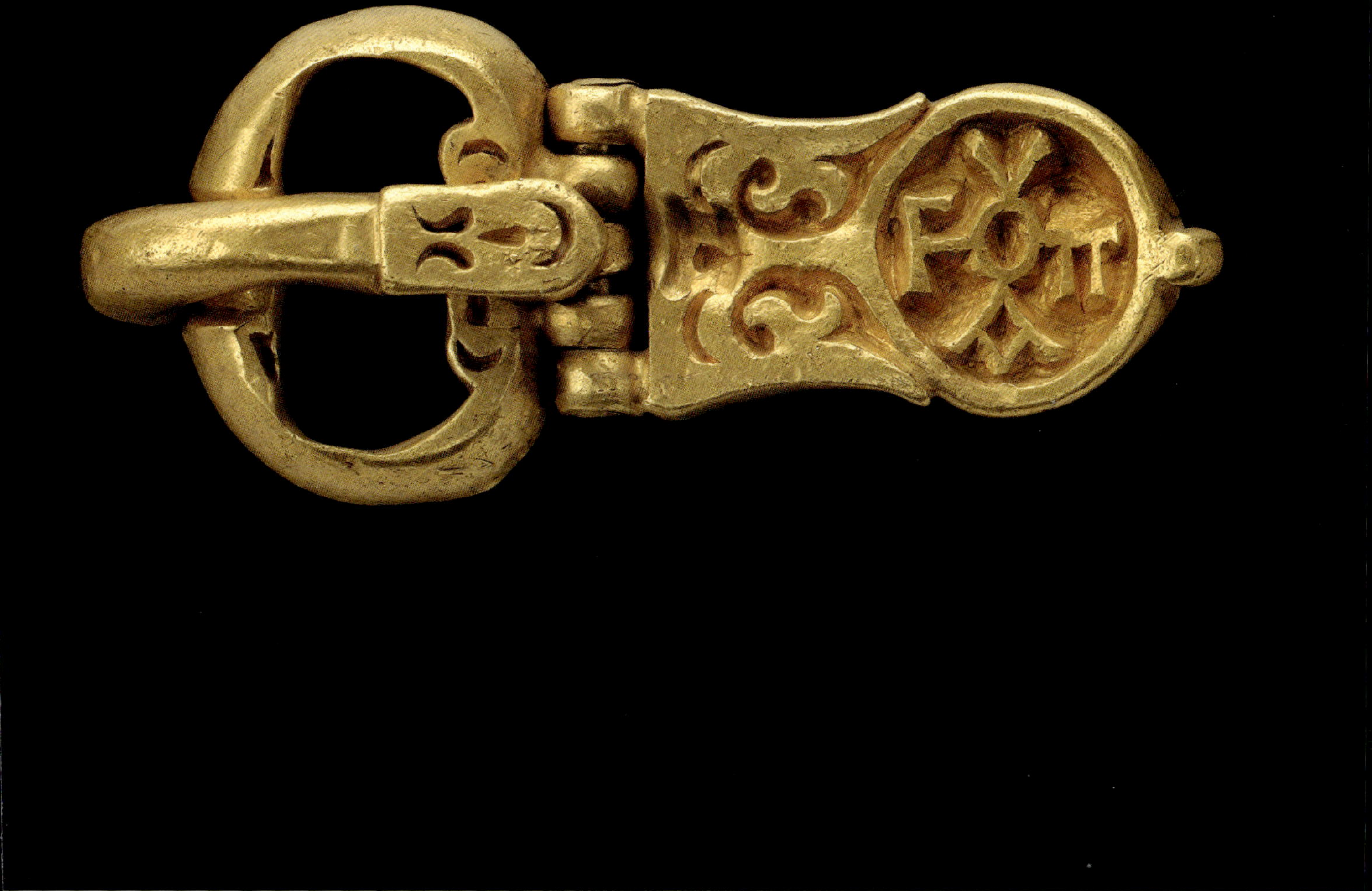
ΓΟΤ

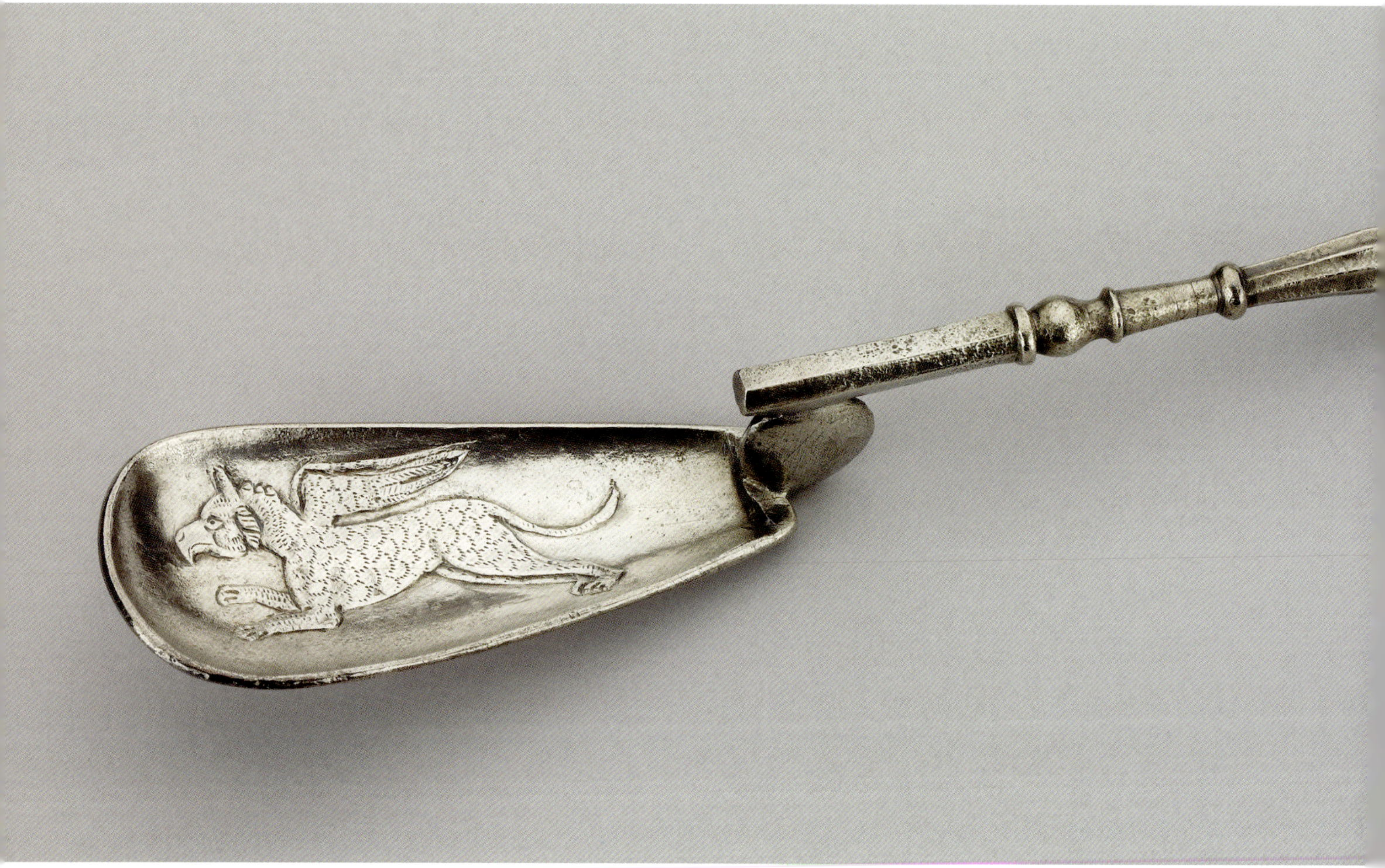

Byzantine
Found near Karavas, Cyprus
c. AD 650
Length 25.9 cm
1899,0425.27

36 GRIFFIN SPOON

In the sixth and seventh century heavy silver spoons such as this one were part of the dinner service for those who could afford them. This spoon has an ovoid bowl with broad tip, which is joined to the massive handle by a vertical disc. This type of spoon was known as a *kochliarion* and was used for eating, as opposed to similar shaped spoons which were employed during the Eucharist.

The back of the spoon's bowl is engraved with a symmetrical leaf design. But even more eye-catching is the inside of the bowl, which is decorated with the relief image of a griffin in mid-pounce. This mythological creature had been a popular motif since antiquity (**27**) and was depicted with the body of a lion, the head of an eagle and wings. While this example does not have the snake's tail that some griffins sport, its body has been covered with scales made up of finely punched lines. This spoon is part of a set of eleven, many of which show animals in full chase: a ram, bull, boar, hare, stag, bear, tiger, lion, leopard and horse. The common theme of this set is the hunt, a popular pastime among late antique elites (**5**, **79**). The horse belongs to the hunter and all the other animals are either his prey or hunters themselves, as was often seen on mosaics or silverware. The griffin was believed to live in India and would have been considered an exotic form of game.

Originally there were probably twelve spoons in this set, as this was the usual complement for a full dinner service. They came from a cache of Byzantine silver known as the 'First Cyprus Treasure', named after the island where a number of important hoards were found. In this case, two plates, a censer for burning incense and a total of twenty-five spoons came to light apparently near the Acheripoetos Monastery on the north coast of Cyprus, in as far as the complicated find history of the nineteenth century can be reconstructed.

37 BYZANTINE EARRINGS

Although the enamel is now largely discoloured, the sumptuous multicoloured effect created by the combination of the enamel with gold and pearls is still evident in this pair of tenth-century earrings.

The upper part of each earring is formed from a plain wire, which springs from a hollow gold bead on each side. The lower segment consists of an enamel field with a border in which pins with pearls alternate with gold pellet pyramids. A medallion disc is fixed to the inner edge of this segment. Originally the disc and outer edge of the lower segment would have been surrounded by pearls, but only the loops onto which they were threaded remain.

The front of each earring shows three birds in delicate cloisonné enamel, a very expensive technique. The birds and the twigs they carry in their beaks are outlined in gold wire, which was then filled with enamel. The enamel has turned iridescent with time, but it seems that the backgrounds were once a translucent green, while the birds had translucent blue bodies, opaque white heads and blue wings. The birds on the medallions were probably only a single colour, with opaque white wings. All the birds are depicted with a lively sense of movement, their heads facing in different directions.

The backs of the earrings are also decorated, which makes it likely that the earrings could be worn with either side facing outwards. Here, a central bird like the one on the front is flanked by a scrolling vine motif. The medallion is not enamelled on this side, but is plain gold with a double rosette. It is possible that the birds and vine had Christian connotations (**34**, **63**).

There has been some debate over the date of these earrings, but the enamel work can be paralleled with examples from two securely dated hoards, the Slav Preslav Treasure from Bulgaria and the Cretan Hoard from Greece, both of which were buried in the second half of the tenth century. Moreover, birds and rosettes belong to the canon of Middle Byzantine motifs, also frequently found on carved ivory caskets or painted pottery.

Byzantine
Unknown findspot
First half of the 10th century AD
Height 4.5 and 4.7 cm
Bequeathed by A.W. Franks
AF.338

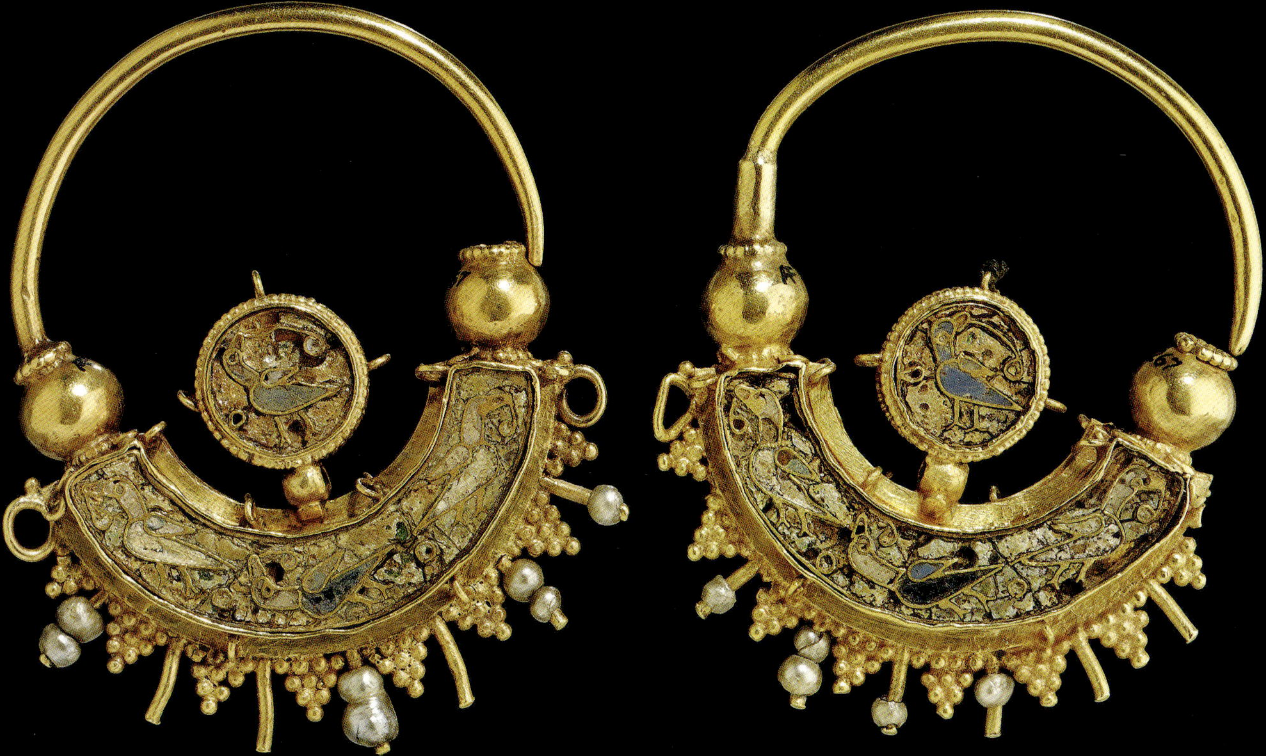

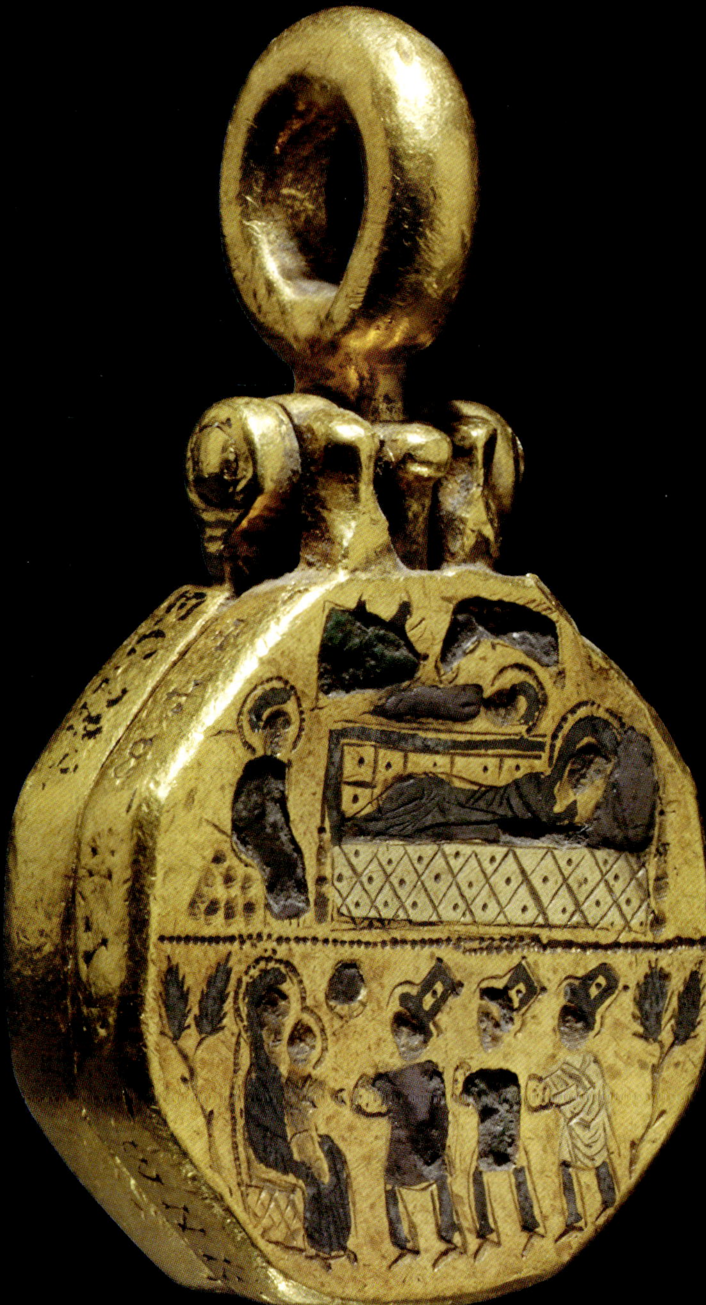

38 RELIQUARY LOCKET

This intricate reliquary presents a microcosm of Byzantine hopes and fears, all of which are encapsulated in the decoration and inscriptions on the pendant or *encolpion* (**29**).

The octagonal locket is made from gold and has a single hinge which allows for a suspension loop and access to the interior. The front is decorated with two scenes, the upper one depicting the Holy Family in the stable at Bethlehem, and the lower one showing the Magi as they advance towards the Virgin and Child bearing gifts. The engraved scenes are inlaid in black niello and silver, giving the impression of a miniature painting.

When a pin which is protruding above these scenes is pulled upwards, the locket opens and reveals a small chamber. Once this would have contained earth from a holy place (**48**), wax from candles at a pilgrims' church or a relic, whether a corporeal part of a saint or a piece of cloth which had become holy itself after coming into contact with a relic.

The potency of the relic would have been heightened by the cross monogram engraved on the back of the reliquary. An inscription placed around the monogram pleads for 'secure deliverance and aversion [from] all evil', while on the rim of the pendant the saints Cosmas and Damian are named. These twin saints had cured the sick for no cost in third-century northern Syria. Their cult spread quickly and by the late fifth century the Pope had a chapel in Rome dedicated to them. It has been proposed that Cosmas and Damian are linked to the Virgin on this reliquary as their shrines were situated near each other in the Blachernae area in the north-west of Constantinople.

With its imagery relating to the birth of the Saviour, an inscription evoking a pair of holy healers and its potential for carrying a relic, this *encolpion* illustrates the very real fear of illness and the attempted ways to evade it during the Middle Byzantine period.

Byzantine
From Constantinople
10th to 11th century AD
Height including loop 3.7 cm
Bequeathed by A.W. Franks
AF.354

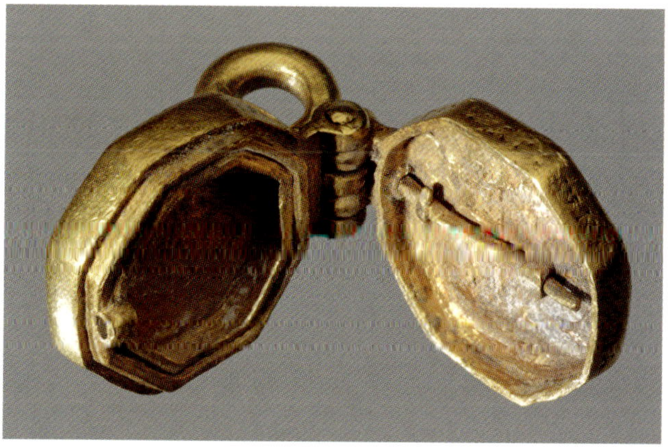

3 THE ANGLO-SAXONS

(FIFTH TO ELEVENTH CENTURY)

Writing in Northumbria in the early 700s, the Venerable Bede described the Anglo-Saxons as descendants of settlers who had arrived from the Continental lands of the Saxons, Angles and Jutes. Archaeological similarities in material culture, funerary customs and house forms do indeed show that people from northern Germany and Denmark moved to an area roughly corresponding to modern-day England from about AD 450 onwards (**Map 2**). The types of jewellery, weapons, costume fittings and daily goods that these people used and buried with their dead also suggest that some of the settlers came from the areas of present-day France, Belgium, the Netherlands and western Norway. Neither historical sources nor archaeology can resolve the question of what happened to the original, Romano-British population in the Saxon-dominated areas, but most likely they continued their lives, albeit in a way that as of yet archaeologists can scarcely distinguish from the newcomers.

Detail of an Anglo-Saxon walrus ivory, late 10th century AD (**71**)

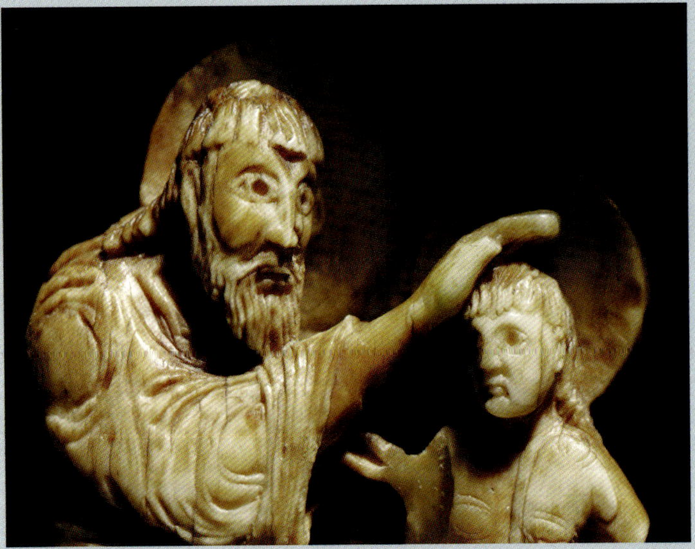

The art of this early Anglo-Saxon period evolved from common Germanic traits and developed its own distinctive forms of dress accessories, jewellery and weapons, as well as a characteristic animal style of decoration (**42, 43**). Over the course of the later sixth century, a number of kingdoms emerged. Two regions particularly notable for their wealth were East Anglia, where the Sutton Hoo ship burial was found (**46–8**), and Kent, which had close ties to the Franks across the Channel. The quality of Anglo-Saxon garnet-inlaid jewellery (**50, 51**) was rarely surpassed in Europe at this time.

The first missionary sent by Rome, St Augustine (d. 604), was received at the Kentish court in AD 597, and by the late seventh century the Anglo-Saxons had been converted to Christianity (**53, 57**). Monasteries and royal or aristocratic residences were centres of activity where craftsmen could find patrons. The Church in particular played a crucial role in the transmission of learning, and monastic workshops produced fine manuscripts, metalwork, ivories and sculpture for secular (**58**) as well as ecclesiastical use (see facing page). Major influences for the development of a distinctly Insular art form came directly from Irish monastic foundations, for example at Iona in Scotland and Lindisfarne in Northumberland (**137**).

From the seventh century a number of kingdoms competed for supremacy in Anglo-Saxon England, with both Northumbria and Mercia dominating at times. In the ninth century the kingdom of Wessex established itself as the pre-eminent power. Anglo-Saxon art and literature flourished (**67**) under Alfred the Great (AD 871–99), especially after he conclusively defeated the Vikings in AD 878.

While localized internal and external conflicts with the neighbouring Welsh, Pictish and British kingdoms were nothing unusual, all parts of the British Isles were blighted by Viking attacks from the late eighth century onwards. The arrival and eventual settlement of the Scandinavians, particularly in the Viking-administered Danelaw (see p. 226), did have some positive outcomes: silver, which had been comparatively rare since the Roman period, now became abundant; new trade routes opened to the north; and Viking art inspired new and hybrid styles characteristic of the British Isles (**121**, **122**).

During the late seventh and eighth century trading centres such as London, Ipswich and York had emerged where exchange with the Continent took place and artisans established various crafts. Later Anglo-Saxon England saw the rise of large-scale wool and pottery production (**76**) for the first time since the Romans. The highest echelons of society had access to exquisite gold work (**72**), prestigious weaponry (**69**) and the finest carvings (**75**), which reflected the love of playful ornament already present in early Anglo-Saxon art. Monumental stone sculpture (**63**), on the other hand, addressed wider audiences and was a prominent feature of churches and the landscape in general, demonstrating how far this art form had come since its first steps in the seventh century.

39 THE CASTLE EDEN CLAW BEAKER

This claw beaker preserves many of the features already visible in earlier examples, such as the Mucking beaker (**20**). Yet the form has evolved, with leaner proportions and finer trails of glass decorating the vessel body, which would remain a characteristic of the type for some two hundred years.

This beaker is distinguished by being one of the few multicoloured early medieval vessels (**90**). The fine trails spun around the body are light blue, while the thicker, indented trails decorating the upper row of claws are of a rich blue tone. This may have been achieved by recycling coloured Roman glass (**45**, **88**).

The body colour is a light, bluish green. Apart from various shades of brown, green hues are the most common colour in early medieval vessels. This is not so much due to preference, but because naturally occurring iron and manganese oxides in the glass mass result in such tones. The art of producing clear glass was known to the Romans, but had been lost in the West. Until Islamic glass makers rediscovered the necessary techniques, the colourless clear glass we are used to today was not available.

The claw beaker is complete, which is nothing short of miraculous given that it did not only survive burial, but also that it was discovered as early as around 1775. It was given to the British Museum by The Honourable Mrs Sclater-Booth in memory of her father, Colonel Rowland Burdon, on whose estate it had been found. In 1790 her great-great-grandfather had jotted down some notes on the excavation, according to which the beaker was unearthed when a hedge was dug up north of the bridge leading to the castle.

It was found in the ground next to the head of the body with which it had been buried. The vessel was so close to the surface that its foot stuck out of the trench and was at first mistaken for the bottom of a broken bottle.

Anglo-Saxon

From Castle Eden, Co. Durham, England

Mid-5th century AD

Height 19.2 cm

Donated by the Hon. Mrs Sclater-Booth

1947,1009.1

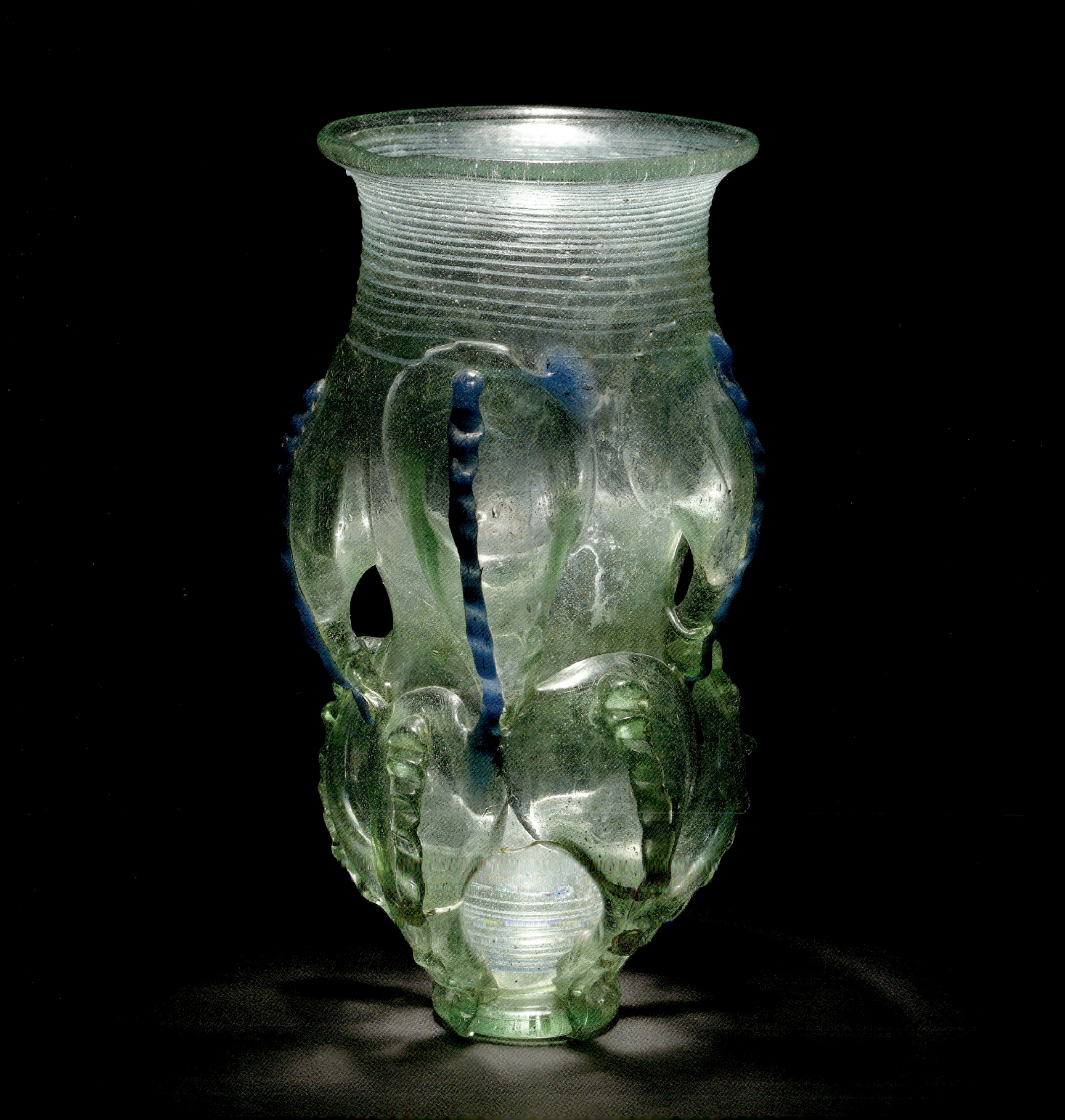

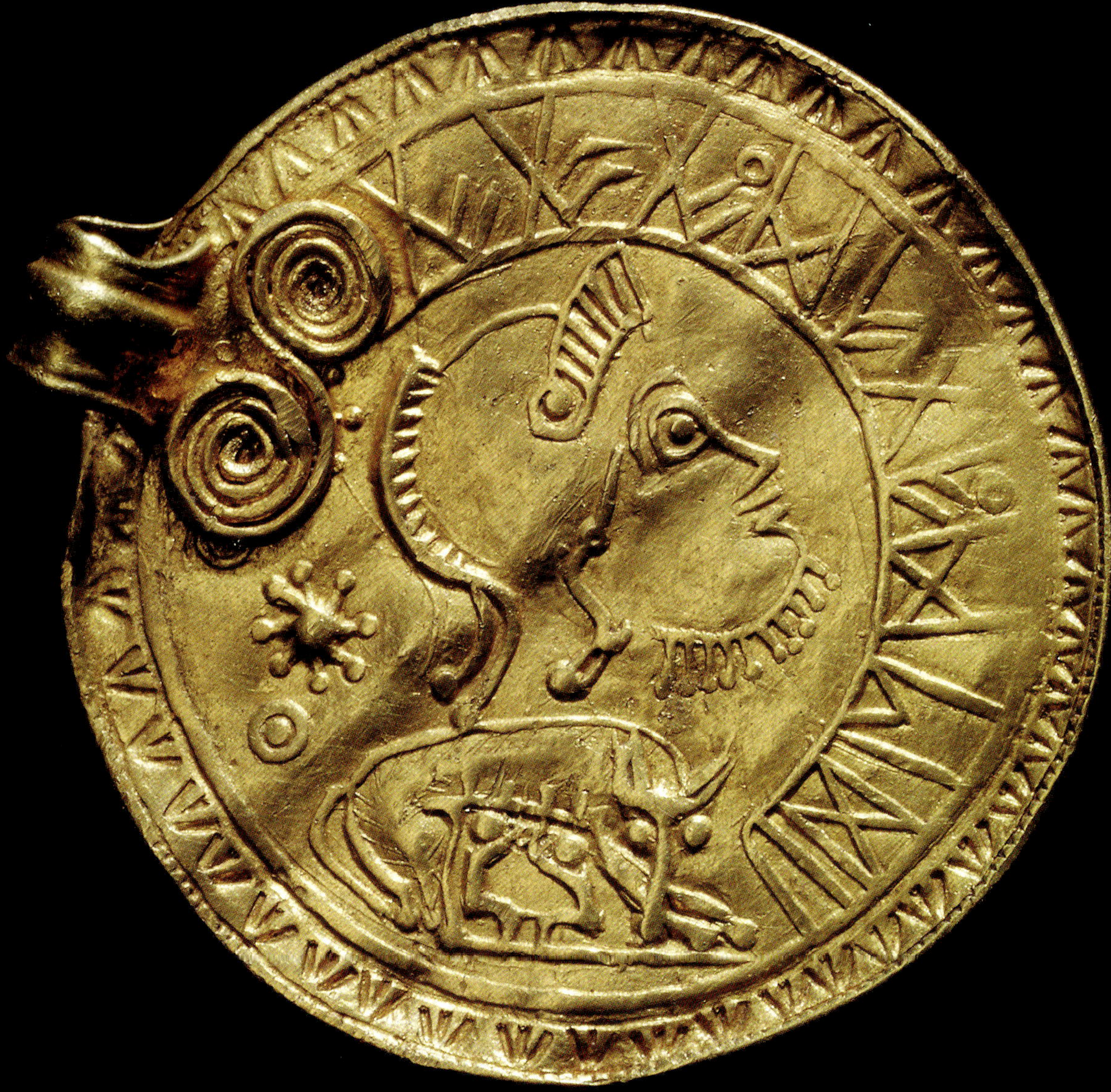

40 THE UNDLEY BRACTEATE

The physical and ideological transformation of Roman imagery is perhaps nowhere better illustrated than in the case of gold bracteates. These Germanic gold pendants have been found in Scandinavia, northern Germany, Frisia as well as Anglo-Saxon England. Smaller numbers are also known from elsewhere in north-western Europe, with a very few finds as far east as Poland. The repoussé motifs on bracteates largely fall into four categories, some consisting of images of human heads which are at times accompanied by animals.

The Undley bracteate presents a helmeted, bearded male head in profile. Beside him a crouching wolf suckles two infants. The prototype for both motifs is Roman, namely imperial portraits with cavalry helmets and the she-wolf suckling Romulus and Remus, the mythical founders of Rome (**58**). The source for the design was a coin type issued by Constantine the Great between AD 330 and 335, but on this bracteate the images on the obverse and reverse have been modified and compressed into one composition. Additionally, what is perhaps the earliest known English runic inscription runs along the edge, the text of which indicates that the bracteate may have been a gift to a female relative.

Where this pendant was made has long been debated. Technologically and stylistically it compares well with Scandinavian pieces, but the depiction on it is – so far – unique. Further evidence suggests that at least some early bracteates were made in England, rather than imported from northern Germany or Scandinavia. This is important as it would mean that the ideas behind the bracteates were developed further by the Anglo-Saxons.

The significance of this type of bracteate seems to have been manifold. They were protective amulets with a transformed image of the Roman emperor, now appearing to represent the chief god Woden. A cluster of these pendants in Norfolk could be related to a centre of cultic activity and ritual depositions. In Kent, a different type of bracteate acted as a badge for elites who wanted to proclaim kinship, whether real or perceived, to Scandinavia, where the earliest examples had come from. This would be echoed later in genealogies of Anglo-Saxon dynasties who traced their origins back to Scandinavia and Woden.

Northern German or possibly Anglo-Saxon

From Undley Common, Suffolk, England

c. AD 450–80

Diameter 2.3 cm

1984,1101.1

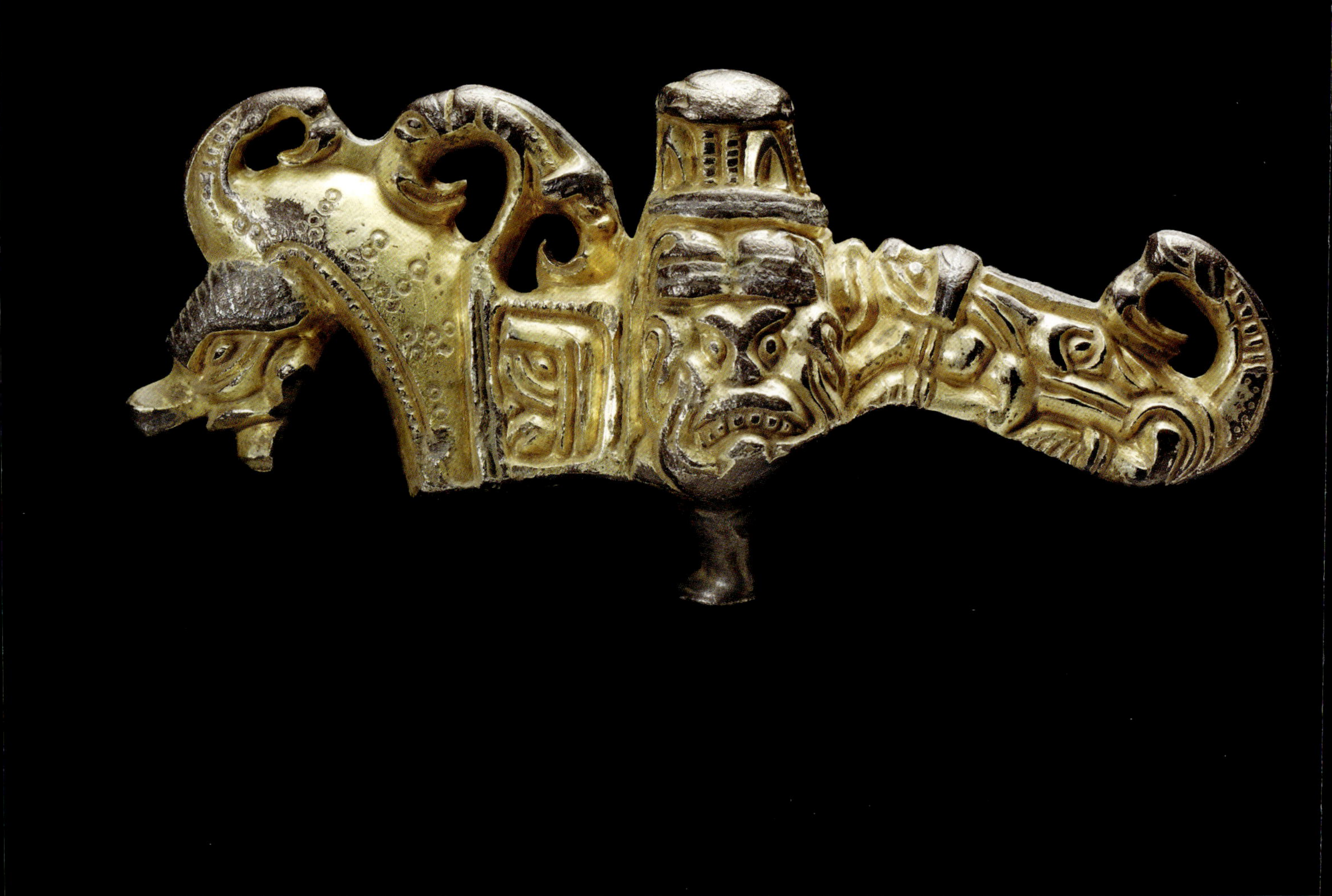

41 BUCKLE TONGUE

The human figure in overt, easily recognizable form is extremely rare in early Anglo-Saxon England and frequently appears in apparently mythical or numinous contexts (**40**, **52**). Where it does otherwise occur it is often in masked form, which requires a trained eye to recognize it (**42**).

This strange, three-dimensional object is an exception. The elongated silver-gilt cast is covered in stylized, but clearly discernible faces. As is characteristic of the Germanic Animal Style I current at the time (**42**), the sculpted design comprises numerous anthropomorphic, animal, bird and monster masks and full heads. Details of the hair on some of the human heads are finely nielloed. The outline of the object is profiled and has a central dowel rod and a carefully shaped hole, which implies that this was a mount that slotted firmly onto something.

The three-dimensional appearance of the cast is almost unparalleled in England at the time, but compares well with a series of large buckle loops and tongues from Scandinavia and the Baltic Sea region. Some of these examples are different in shape to the Thimbleby piece, but close in their execution. They, too, feature distinctive human and anthropomorphic heads, and carefully modelled hair. A buckle from Proosa, Estonia, shows a closely comparable profile while a find from Snartemo, Norway, displays the same grooved underside and circular hole. It is therefore likely that the Thimbleby mount is a buckle tongue, and that the dowel and bore hole facilitated the attachment of the anchorage which allowed the tongue to swivel around the buckle loop.

The Scandinavian buckles largely date to the late fifth to early sixth century. At this time, there was certainly contact between Scandinavia and the east of England, which could explain how the buckle tongue or even the craftsman who made it got to Lincolnshire. It has been suggested that the masks and heads on the Scandinavian finds include representations of Loki, a mischievous Nordic god known from later written sources. Whether this is borne out by the evidence is debatable, but in any case the explicit human imagery on the buckle tongue must have been notable to those who saw it.

Early Scandinavian
From Thimbleby, Lincolnshire, England
Late 5th to early 6th century AD
Length 4.9 cm
2011,8025.1

42 THE CHESSELL DOWN BROOCH

In essence, a brooch is a glorified safety pin, but as far as sixth-century Anglo-Saxon England is concerned, the great square-headed brooch from Chessell Down, Isle of Wight, is the most sumptuous example known. Large and heavy, it would once have been worn horizontally to close a lady's cloak below the neck (**85**).

The front of the brooch dazzles the viewer, both with its substantial gilding, which is contrasted subtly with black niello triangles, and the complex ornament covering the surface. The scrollwork framing the sides of the rectangular headplate is yet another derivation from late Roman ornament (**19**). No fewer than twenty-four beings are visible, including human masks, birds' heads, human–animal hybrids and various beasts. Some are easily recognizable, but others are highly stylized and only apparent to the trained observer. While it may be difficult for the modern eye to decode the imagery, it strictly follows the rules of the Germanic Animal Style I (**41**). The meaning of the composition is hidden to us, but it will likely have had talismanic and apotropaic properties to bring good luck to the wearer and protect them from evil. The central motif on the foot plate – a human face with a beard and a helmet-like cap or hairstyle – below the heads of a conjoined pair of birds of prey could represent Woden with his companions, the ravens Huginn and Munnin (**85**).

A brooch such as this was a statement of the owner's wealth and social status, and perhaps that of her family as well. It is likely that it also had religious and perhaps ethnic connotations. The material would have distinguished this brooch from most others; while the silver content is low at only around 30 per cent, in general great square-headed brooches were made from copper alloy. It appears that silver was a scarce commodity for the early Anglo-Saxons. The Franks on the other side of the Channel did not seem to have had this problem as up to two-thirds of all bow brooches (**85**) in any given cemetery were made of high-grade silver.

Anglo-Saxon

From Chessell Down, Grave 22, Isle of Wight, England

Early 6th century AD

Length 13.8 cm

1867,0729.5

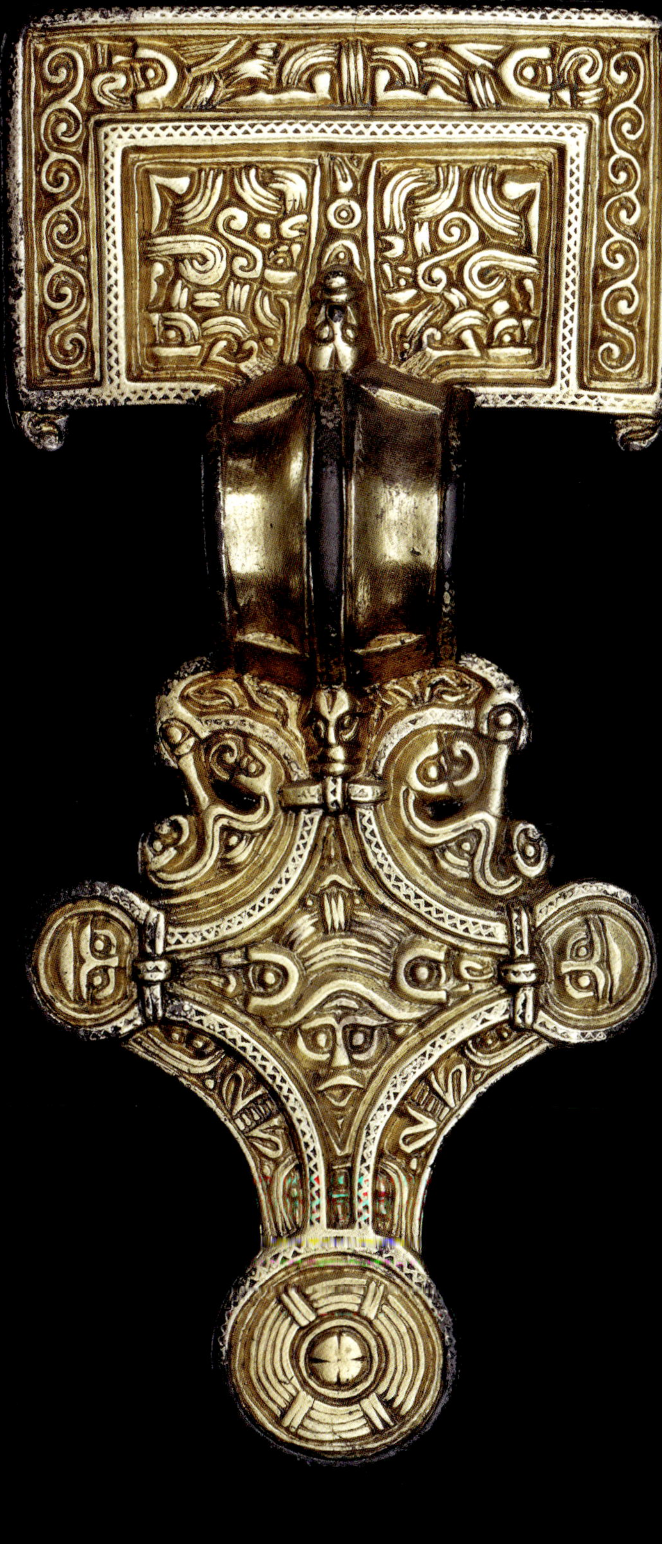

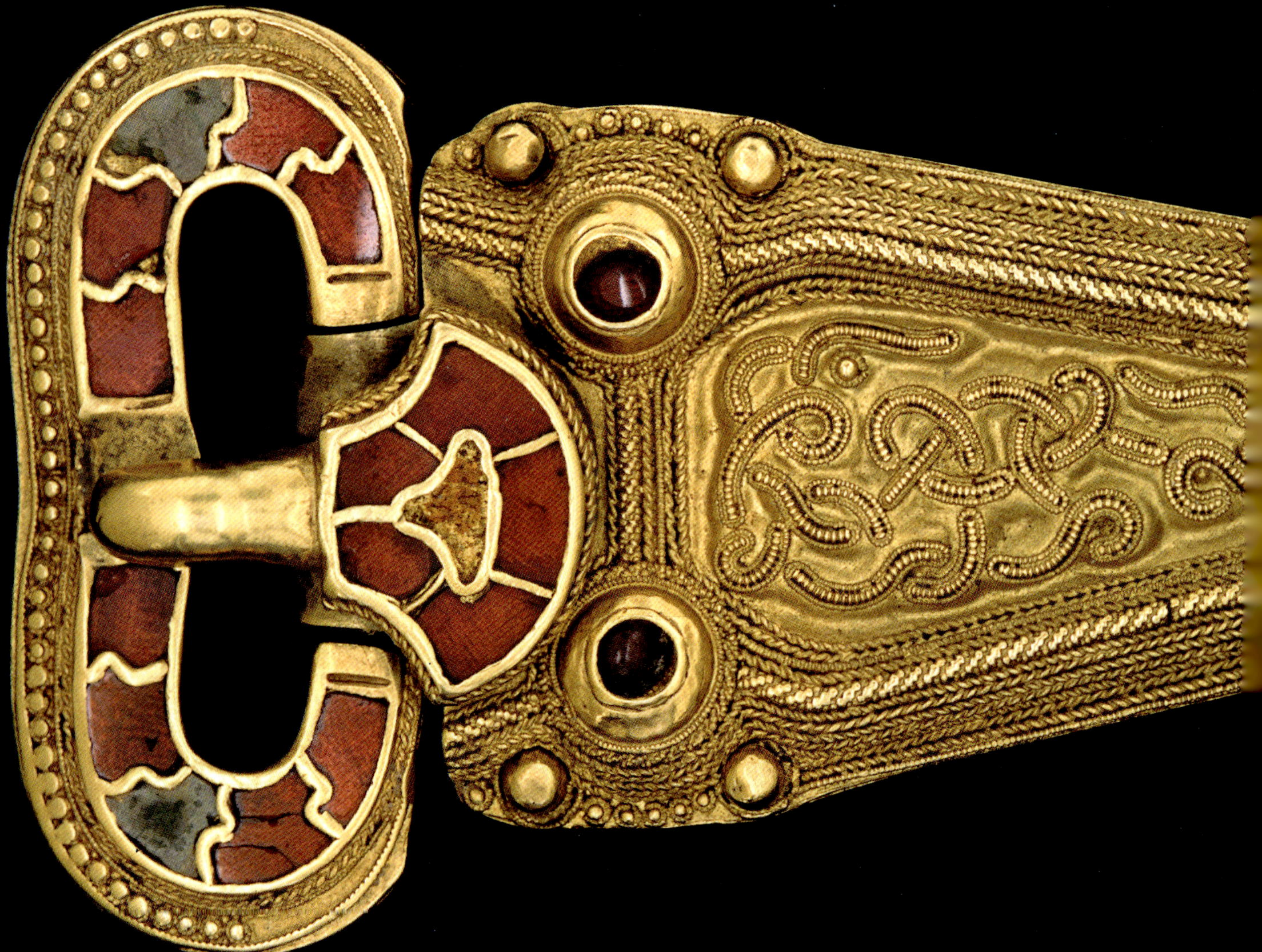

43 THE TAPLOW BUCKLE

The princely burial at Taplow was excavated from a large burial mound in 1883. Unexpected riches came to light, although these would later be surpassed by the discovery of the ship burial at Sutton Hoo (**46–8**).

Among the grave goods at Taplow were a pair of filigree gold clasps and a large belt buckle. This impressive piece has an oval loop inlaid with garnets and slips of green glass. The shield on the base of the buckle tongue is in the shape of a fan or mushroom, a form that first occurs with the Continental Franks around AD 600.

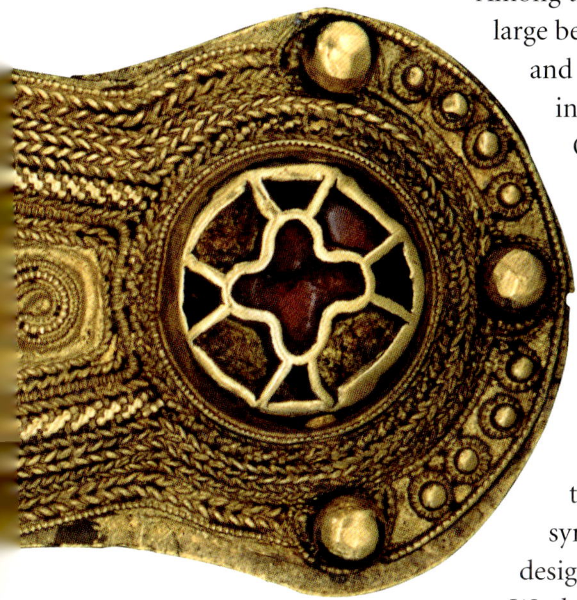

The Franks were also the first to use triangular buckle plates. The Taplow plate is embellished with the finest filigree, in the form of twisted and beaded wires and rivets, as well as tiny gold balls surrounded by wire collars. The main feature is an interlaced animal in the central field. The animal's head is indicated by a simple curved wire near one of the garnet rivets and a gold granule for an eye. The body and limbs are a rather indistinct tangle of filigree wires. It appears that this is a craftsman's early attempt at the new Animal Style II (**50**), as its loose composition is lacking in symmetry and distinct body parts or feet, which contradicts the clear design principles of the style when in full flow.

We do not know who was buried here, nor whether the garnet cross on the boss at the end of the buckle plate had any significance to its owner, who clearly belonged to the top tier of Anglo-Saxon society. Given that large gold buckles were also included in the outstanding burials at Sutton Hoo (**48**) and Prittlewell, Essex, it is possible that they were an integral part of a 'kit' considered appropriate for anyone of a princely rank, along with the prestigious vessels, weapons and lyres also found in these other graves.

The Taplow buckle was probably dear to its owner. It shows clear signs of wear in the asymmetrical edges of the plate and the rubbed appearance of the gold granules on the loop.

Anglo-Saxon
From Taplow, Buckinghamshire, England
Last third of the 6th century AD
Length 9.8 cm
1883,1214.1

44 SHIELD MOUNTS FROM SUTTON HOO

During building works about 500 metres north of the barrow cemetery which comprised the famous Sutton Hoo ship burial (**46–8**), a further group of graves was discovered. It consisted of some thirty-five inhumations and cremations largely dated to the sixth century. This may therefore have been the predecessor of the 'princely' burial ground only a short distance away.

One of the male burials was distinguished by its excellent weaponry. A sword, spearhead and shield with numerous decorative mounts, including the two shown here, were found. The shield fittings were cast from copper alloy and decorated using various punches. After that a thick layer of gilding was added. The final step was the application of thin silver sheets, which were cut to shape and soldered onto the mount. The fittings have a crisp appearance that betrays very little use, or at least little wear, of the shield. Underneath the bird, the remains of the shield board and its leather cover are still visible.

The bird is one of the ubiquitous birds of prey common in early Germanic art (**83, 85**). This one on the right, which may be an eagle, is shown at the moment of the catch, grasping in his talons a snake, shaped like a figure-of-eight, with a silver-covered head. The mount to the left represents an aquatic creature, and while earlier than and entirely different in both appearance and meaning from the fish on the Crundale buckle (**54**), it is also seen from above. Like other shield mounts of its kind it seems to illustrate an underwater raptor, such as a pike.

The combination of an eagle, the king of the sky, and a fierce aquatic predator is likely to have emphasized the martial prowess of the owner, while at the same time spiritually reinforcing the protective qualities of the shield itself. The restriction of such emblems to a small circle of men has been seen as an expression of their status as leaders and protectors of their communities.

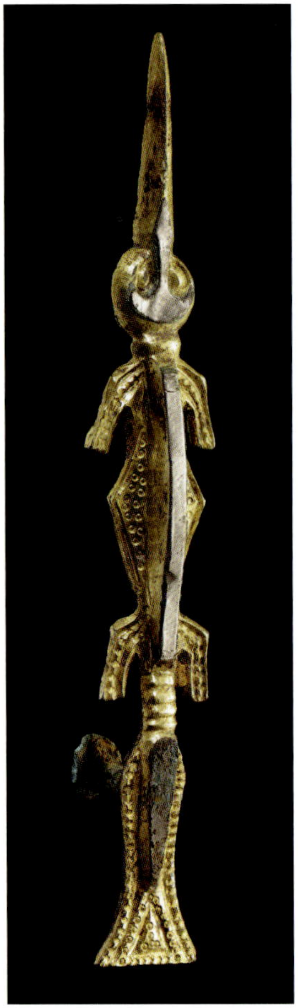

Anglo-Saxon

From Sutton Hoo, Suffolk, England

Late 6th century AD

Width of bird 4.5 cm

Length of fish 9.5 cm

Donated by the National Trust, Sutton Hoo Visitor Centre

2001,0103.3e & f.1

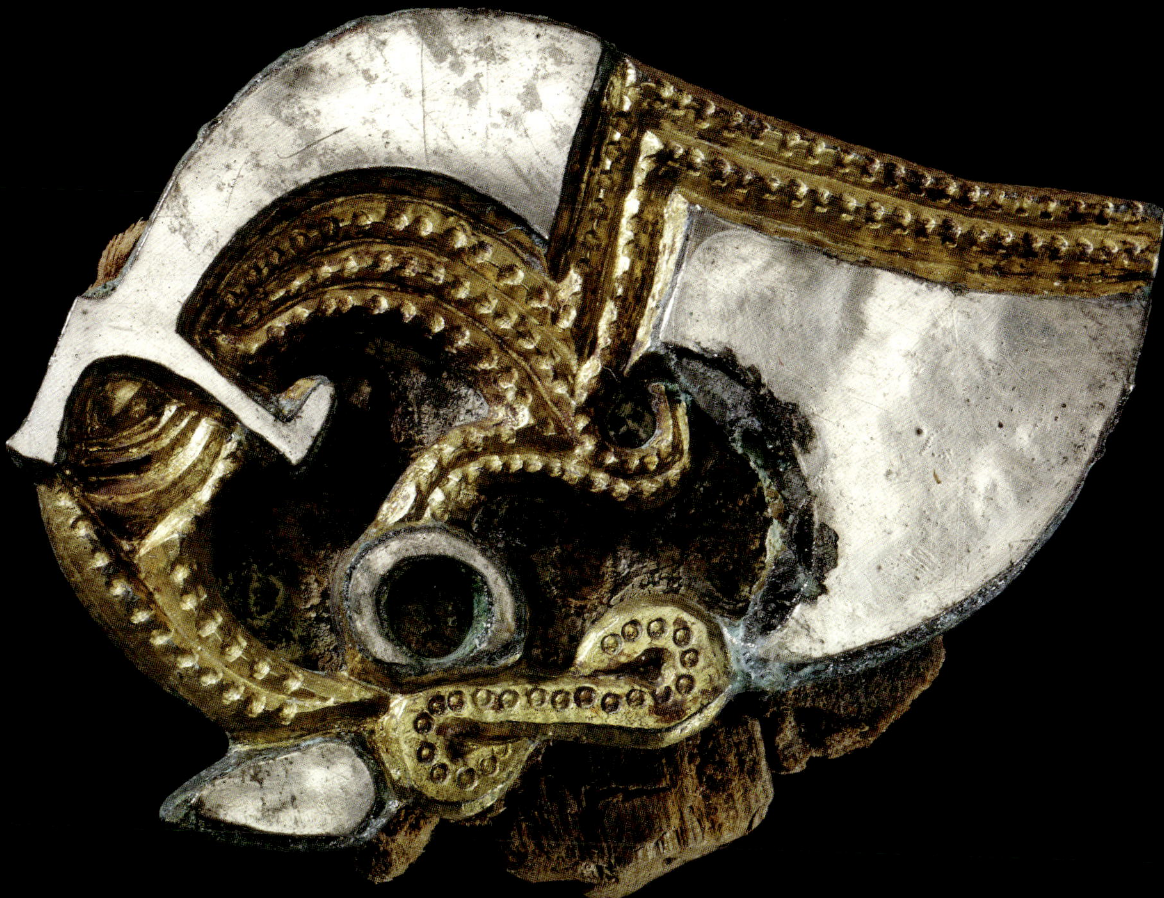

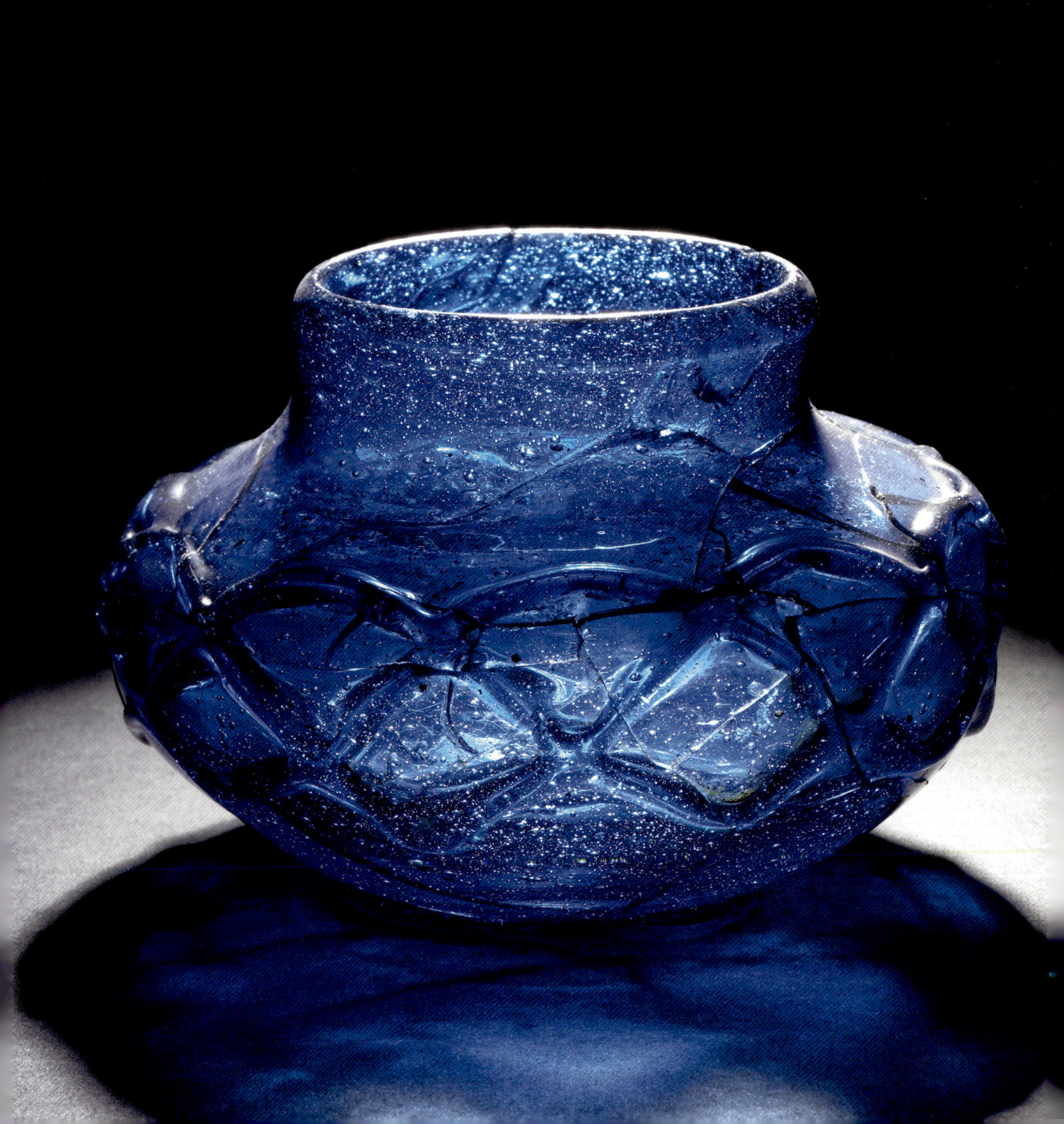

45 A GLOBULAR BEAKER FROM BROOMFIELD

Anglo-Saxon
From Broomfield, Essex, England
Late 6th to 7th century
Height 7.0 cm
Donated by D. Christy
1894,1216.18

Thousands of tiny bubbles are visible in the deep-blue body of this globular beaker which had been trapped in the glass when the beaker was made. A second, almost identical, beaker was found in the same grave, although the present piece is slightly bluer and contains more bubbles. The vessel is thick-walled, with a generous lattice trail around the widest point of its circumference. Another trail on the base forms a four-petal flower pattern. This rare form of globular beaker, sometimes also known as a 'squat jar', is an Anglo-Saxon vessel type and has not been found abroad, with the exception of a pair from Norway.

Scientific analysis of this vessel and its pair has revealed some interesting details. They are very similar in technique, especially in the treatment of the rim, which is straight on the inside, but curved on the outside. On the basis of their appearance they could have been made by the same artisan. While this may be so, the vessels were made from different melts, as far as the chemical composition of the glass mass can reveal.

The deep blue colour is due to the presence of cobalt. In addition, the lead content was found to be high in comparison to other Anglo-Saxon glasses, but in keeping with the concentrations measured in Roman cobalt blue glass. Therefore, recycled Roman glass may have given the beakers their deep hue. It is possible that this came in the form of *tesserae* or glass cullet imported from the Mediterranean. In general, raw glass for vessels in north-western Europe appears to have been produced in the eastern Mediterranean, traded north (**49**) and then processed by local craftsmen. By the time that the Broomfield beakers were made, it seems that the trade was slowing down. Many vessels now contained an amount of locally made glass mass of a composition different to that from the Mediterranean.

The grave at Broomfield, which also included a high-status mound, was a fitting context for this exquisite vessel and its twin. The burial was discovered during gravel digging in 1888 and further excavated in 1894.

46 THE SUTTON HOO SHOULDER CLASPS

Even within the astonishing context of the Sutton Hoo ship burial, the technical mastery of these shoulder clasps is outstanding. The two pairs of hinged clasps were attached to a sturdy backing, previously thought to be leather. However, sets of small loops on the reverse suggest that they were sewn onto a softer material, perhaps a padded linen or wool garment, which could have been worn over the mail shirt also found in the burial.

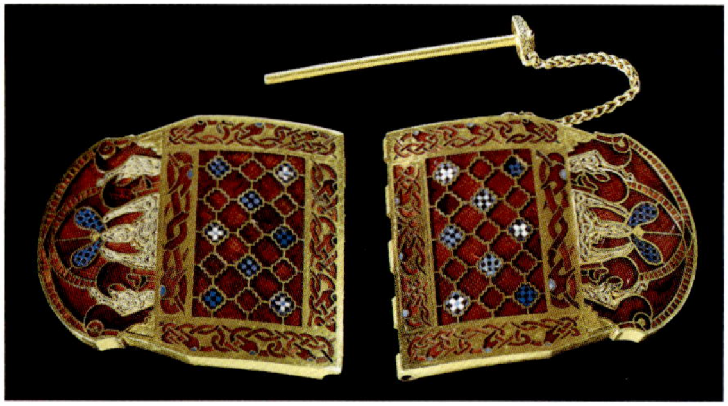

The technical virtuosity of the craftsman or workshop is evident in the absolute precision of the decoration covering the clasps. During the complicated construction process, the garnets, glass inlays and filigree plaques had to be fitted onto a curved object. Even after some 1,300 years of burial no buckling has occurred and the cellwork forms a beautifully smooth surface.

The arrangement of the ornament is complex, with a carpet of large garnet and millefiori glass inlays (**106**) at the centre. The latter are likely to be products of Celtic workshops and therefore not common in Anglo-Saxon contexts (**138**). The frames of the central panels are executed in a rare technique known as lidded cell cloisonné, whereby figural apertures cut into a gold sheet are inlaid with cloisonné and glass. The Staffordshire Hoard also includes a very few pieces which feature this technique. The rounded ends of the clasps contain an intricate depiction of two boars crossing each other. Their down-turned heads, which are framed by fine gold filigree, are the easiest to discern.

Recent stylistic analysis of the cloisonné patterns favours a production date of between the second half of the sixth and the first decade of the seventh century. The models for these shoulder clasps are still debated. Undoubtedly, exemplars from abroad and military connotations will have played a role, be it classical Roman sculptures wearing cuirasses fastened at the shoulders, armour from the empire in the East or the hinged clasps known from the northern peripheries of the Byzantine world.

Anglo-Saxon

From Sutton Hoo, Mound 1, Suffolk, England

Made *c.* AD 560/70–610

Width 5.4 cm

Donated by E. Pretty

1939.1010.4 .4a & .5 .5a

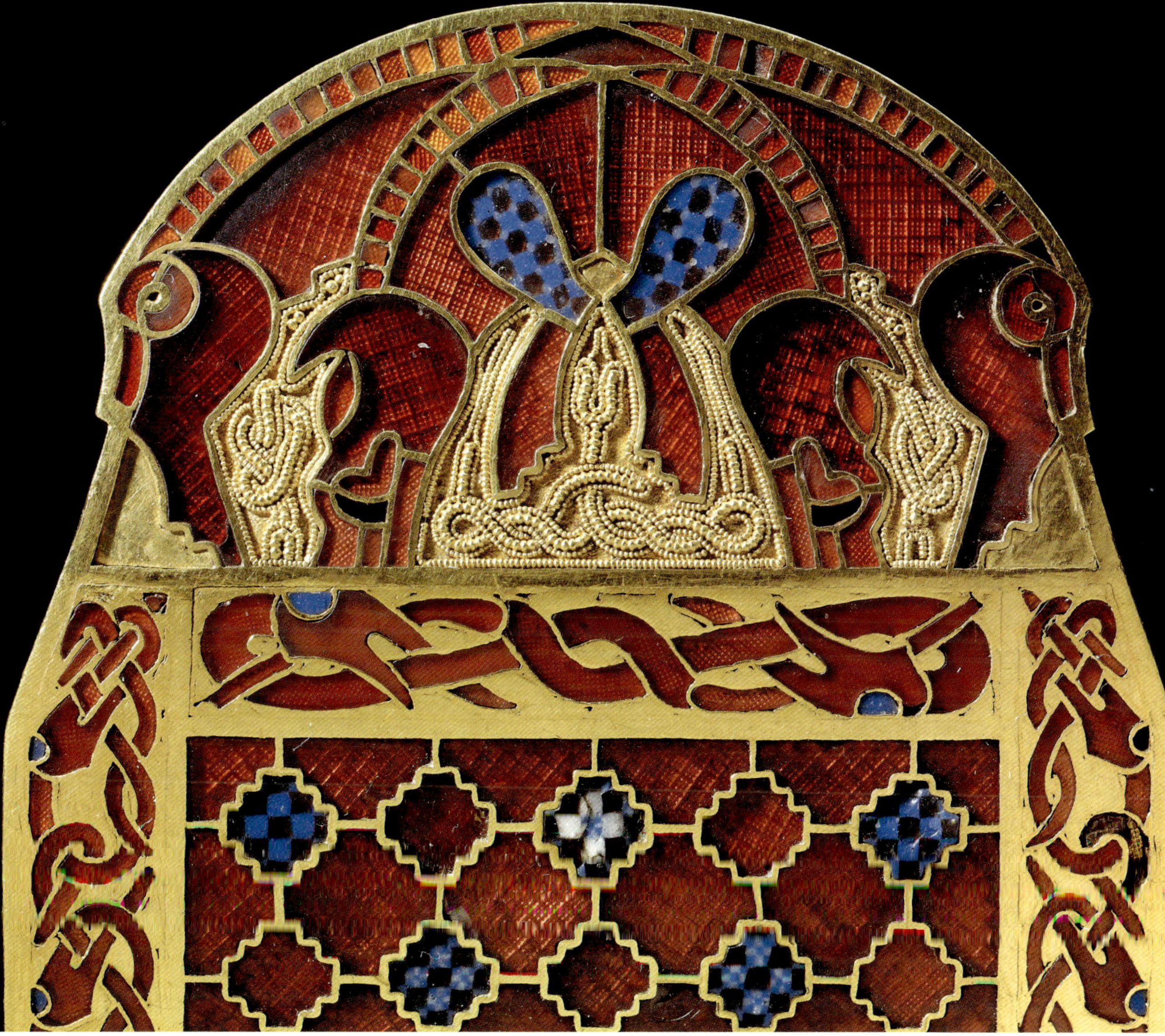

47 THE SUTTON HOO HELMET

When it was made in around AD 600, this helmet would have had a very different appearance from its corroded and largely reconstructed modern-day incarnation. The cap, face mask and neck guard were covered with tinned copper alloy panels in a manner reminiscent of the 'shining helmets' mentioned in the early medieval poem *Beowulf.* The striking appearance was augmented by the image of a flying dragon or bird adorning the face mask. Its tail is formed by the moustache, the nose is equivalent to the bird's body and its wings consist of the two wire- and garnet-inlaid eyebrows. The carefully modelled dragon's head resembles a bird, but with vicious teeth. It is set nose-to-nose with another dragon, which is part of the elaborate helmet crest.

Many of the cover panels were originally embossed with different motifs. There are two kinds of interlace as well as two spectacular figural scenes. One of these features a warrior on horseback brandishing a spear. Behind him, a small figure is kneeling on the rump of the horse. He is also holding on to the spear and his head is thrown back in the exact way that kneeling warriors are portrayed on some of the embossed silver sheet fragments from the Staffordshire Hoard. But the Sutton Hoo rider and his strange companion are not alone. Below the legs of the horse is a fallen, yet by no means helpless enemy: he is plunging his sword into the breast of the steed. Again, the detail of the hand and sword occur in the Staffordshire Hoard, increasing the likelihood that these fragments of silver sheet came from a helmet as well.

The second scene from Sutton Hoo shows dancers with horned helmets, holding up swords and spears. Exact parallels to this imagery are known from Scandinavia. This is also where the nearest relatives of the Sutton Hoo helmet have been found in the form of die stamps for similar scenes, helmets of related constructions and even sets of eyebrows with the characteristic animal-head terminals. The general type of helmet, with a skull cap with hinged cheek-pieces, is derived from cavalry helmets (**40**), ultimately going back to the time of Constantine the Great.

With its late Roman roots and close kinship to Scandinavian pieces and imagery, the Sutton Hoo helmet is an excellent example of the interconnectedness of art and crafts in the early medieval world.

Anglo-Saxon

From Sutton Hoo, Mound 1, Suffolk, England

Late 6th to early 7th century AD

Height 31.8 cm (as restored)

Donated by E. Pretty

1939.1010.93

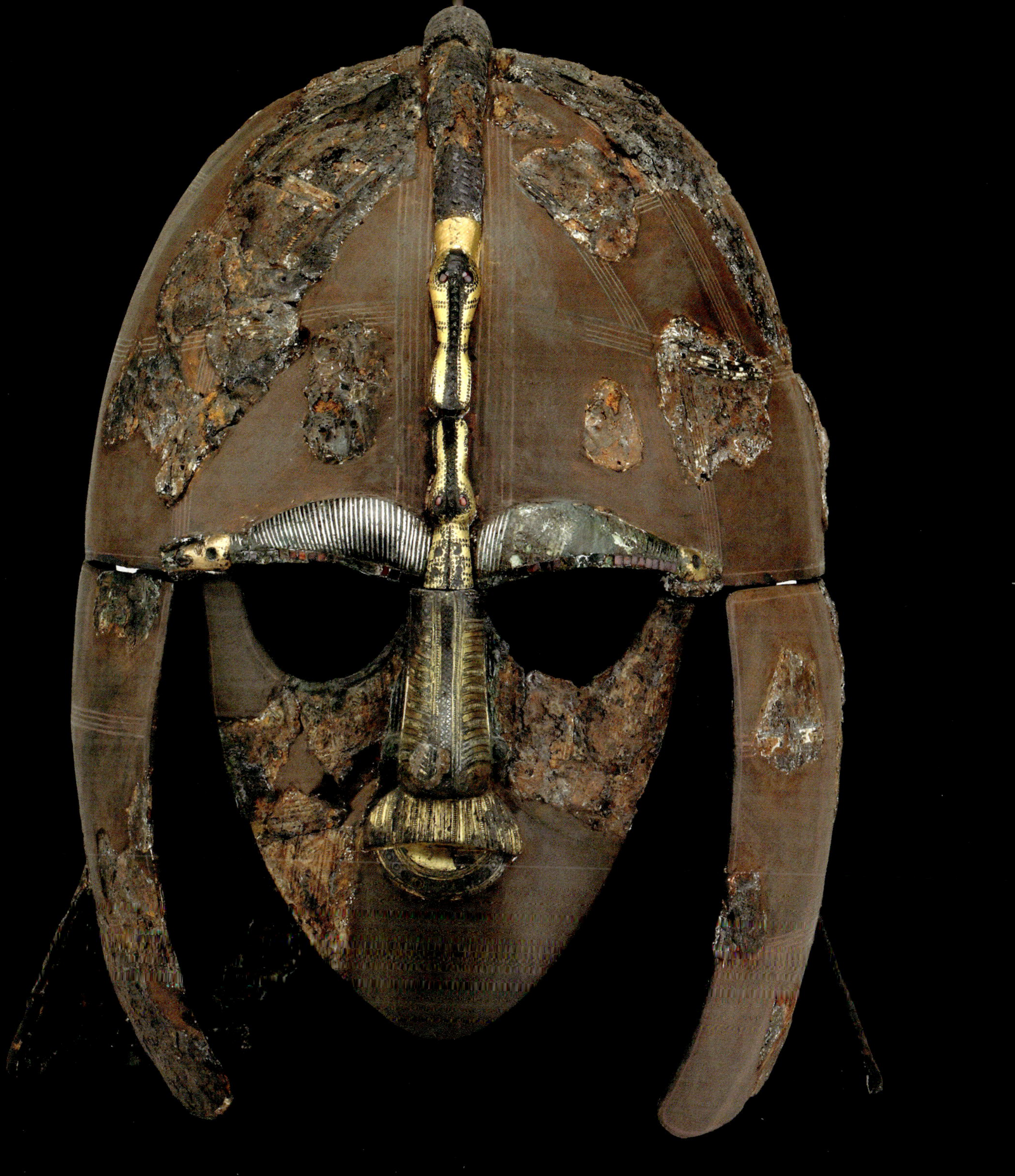

48 THE GREAT GOLD BUCKLE FROM SUTTON HOO

The most superior of the three gold buckles from the Anglo-Saxon 'princely' graves (**43**) is the great gold buckle from Sutton Hoo. Close to a pound of gold was used in its making, or as one scholar suggested, the equivalent of the *wergild* or compensation payable for the life of a Kentish nobleman. An intricate design of interlaced animals writhes on the buckle's loop, round tongue shield and plate. Stylized snakes bite at their own bodies on either side of the tongue rest and a quadruped crouches at the end of the plate. The main body of the plate is covered with a symmetrical, niello-inlaid design featuring intertwined birds of prey, two sets of fantastical long-jawed creatures and snakes. Thirteen animals are depicted in total.

Compositions such as these in Animal Style II (**50**) have been seen as allusions to a passage from the Bible on the creatures of the land, sea and sky (Genesis 1:22–5). The structure of the Sutton Hoo buckle may lend credence to this Christian reading. This interpretation is made more likely by the fact that it is a hollow box, constructed with a hinge and an elaborate locking mechanism of three moveable sliders on the back.

Similarly constructed buckles from the homelands of the Franks and Burgundians – roughly modern-day France and Switzerland – sometimes contained organic residues. Together with their often explicitly Christian imagery, this probably identifies them as reliquaries, which may have enclosed candle wax and even plant remains from pilgrimages. While there is no indication that the Sutton Hoo buckle's owner was Christian, it would have been an outstanding possession, perhaps imbued with special powers through its outward ornament and hidden contents.

We do not know who was buried at Sutton Hoo, but judging by the other grave goods, he certainly had good connections with the Franks. The great gold buckle, or perhaps its maker, is likely to have come from Francia. In addition to the buckle reliquaries found on the other side of the Channel, a similar buckle was discovered in the Merovingian royal cemetery beneath the cathedral of St Denis in Paris, and there are strong parallels for the overall type of buckle in many Frankish cemeteries.

Anglo-Saxon

From Sutton Hoo, Mound 1, Suffolk, England

c. AD 600 to early 7th century AD

Length 13.2 cm

Donated by E. Pretty

1939,1010.1

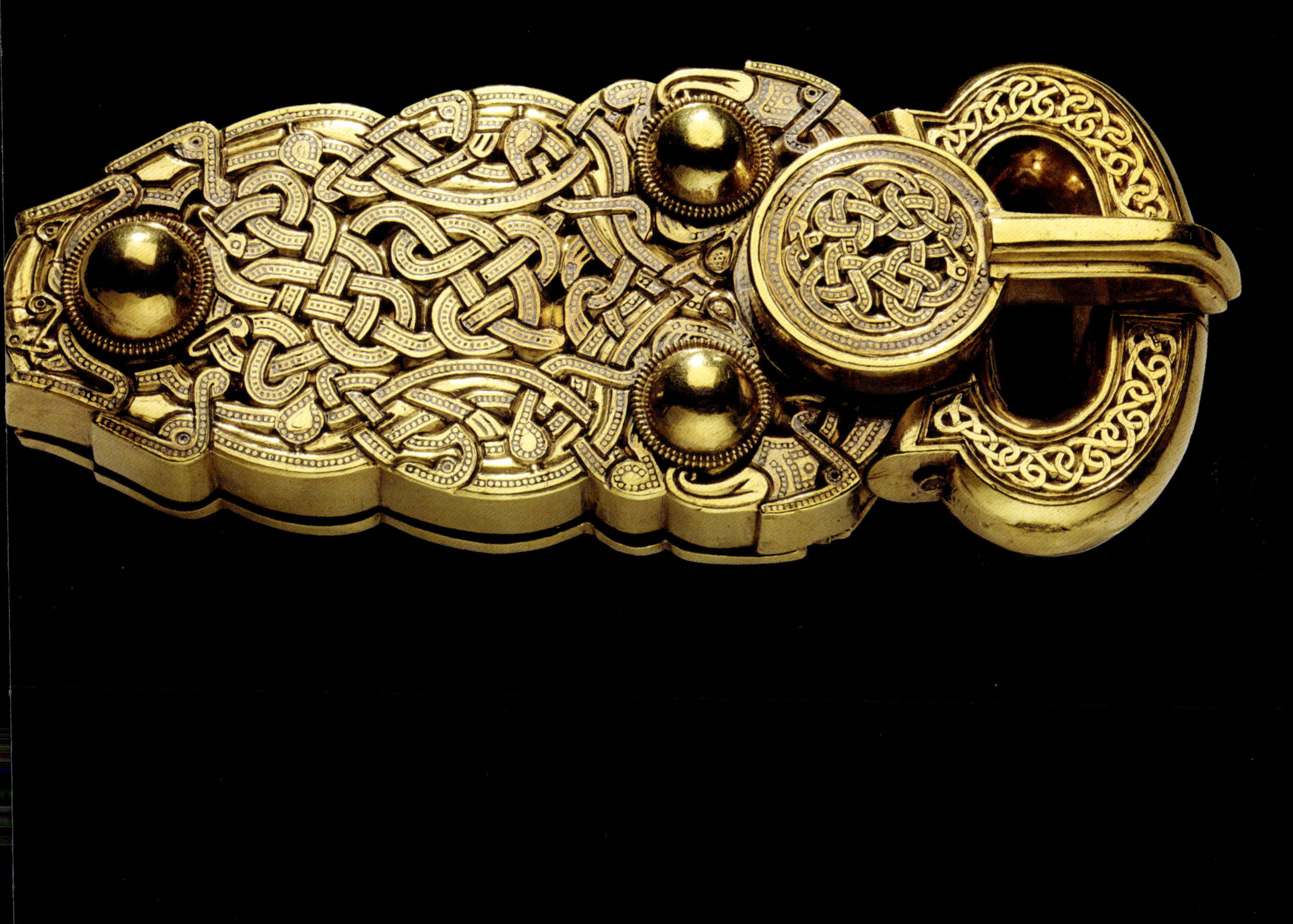

49 EWER

While this attractive copper alloy vessel may look like a teapot, this was certainly not its function. Rather, these ewers were meant for pouring water for handwashing. It is a heavy cast with a practical thumb rest on the handle and three sturdy feet. Concentric lines decorate both body and lid, and underneath there are visible marks from the mandrel, which held the pot while it was turned on a lathe.

Only around a dozen of these 'teapots' are known from all over north-western Europe. Other vessel forms made from cast copper alloy include bowls and basins with footrings and various handle forms, as well as flagons. Notably they have been found in the burials of Anglo-Saxons (including this one from Hertfordshire), Franks in northern Gaul and Alamans in south-western Germany, occurring mostly in well-furnished graves. These vessels follow standardized forms and were particularly popular during the second half of the sixth and the middle of the seventh century.

It is not surprising that they appear in the burials of more affluent and therefore probably well-connected individuals. Such copper alloy vessels are not common and had travelled a long way to northern Europe. It was once thought that they came from Egypt, and hence they are occasionally still described as 'Coptic', but it is now clear that they were produced in manufactories in the Mediterranean, most probably on its eastern shores.

From there they were shipped towards Italy or the south of France, where their journey overland began. The main trade routes to the north were either through the Adriatic Sea, then over the Alps, or via the River Rhône and then along the Rhine Valley. Various luxury goods travelled in this way from the Mediterranean to places as far away as Anglo-Saxon England, including garnets, amethyst beads and probably shell for producing white inlays (**51**).

Mediterranean

From Wheathampstead, Hertfordshire, England

Late 6th to 7th century AD

Height 23.7 cm

1900,0719.4

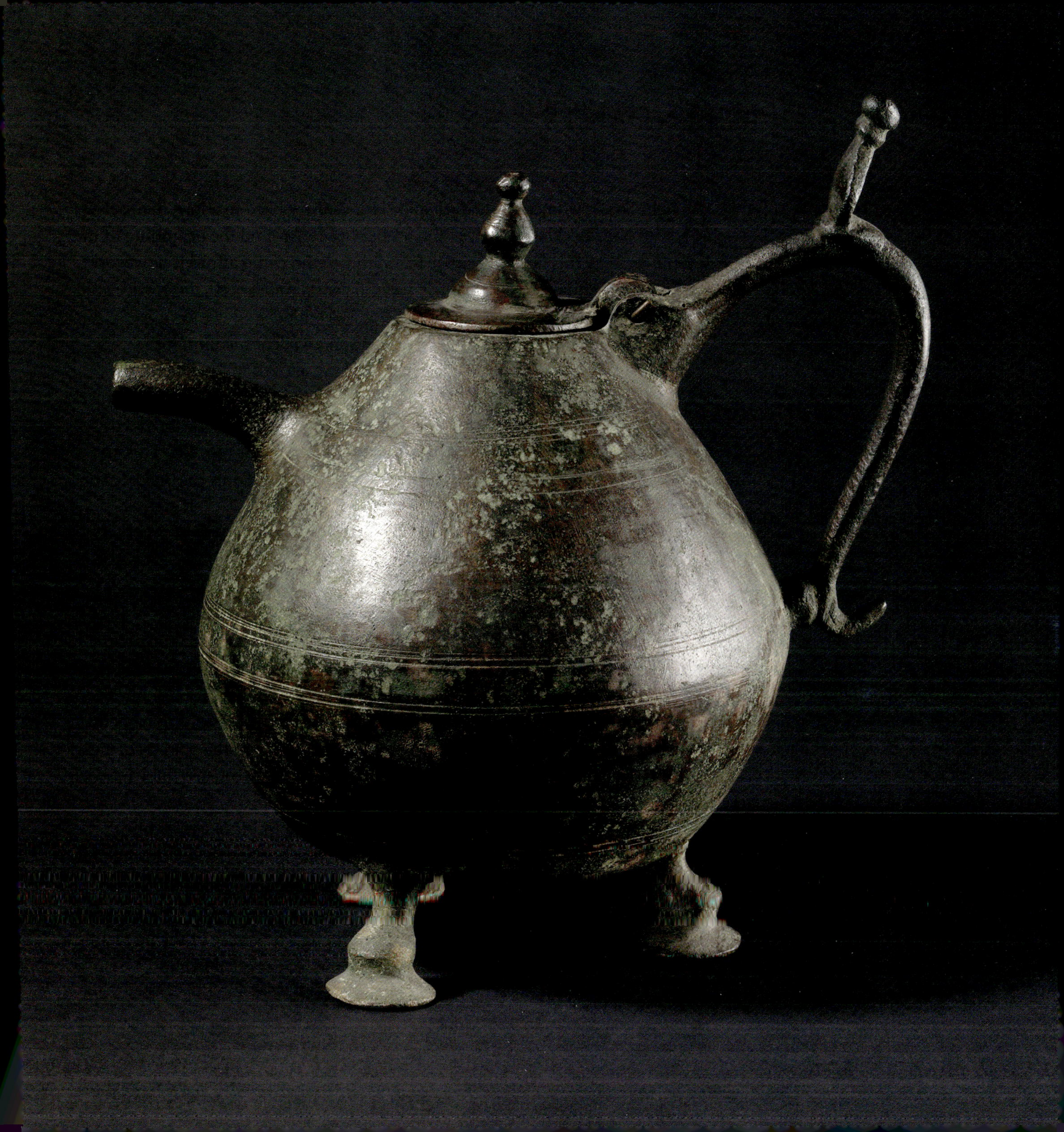

50 GOLD DISC PENDANTS

Anglo-Saxon women of the fifth and sixth century liked to adorn themselves with large necklaces of glass and amber beads. Around the beginning of the seventh century this fashion changed, and those who could afford it now wore eye-catching pendants (**51**) or, as the seventh century advanced, impressive gold necklaces with gem-set jewels (**57**).

These new pendants were at the same time an excellent medium for popularizing Animal Style II, which seems to have arrived in England in the later sixth century. To put it simply, as opposed to Animal Style I which dissolves the depicted creatures into segments (**42**), Animal Style II is characterized by the sinuous interlace of both animal and non-animal forms (**46**, **48**). This art appears to be particularly bound up with elite identity not only in Anglo-Saxon England, but also in Scandinavia and on the Continent.

The gold pendant with a repoussé design of a cross with a central interlace knot and small interlaced triquetras found between the arms of the cross is an example of Style II. This find from Kent echoes the shape of earlier bracteate pendants (**40**), but is also reminiscent of the gold foil crosses which were placed on the faces of the dead in Alamanic south-western Germany and Longobard northern Italy at this time. The cross arms here are formed of four bearded faces inside large frames, which could be misshapen haloes. Similar faces on buckle plates from Francia have been interpreted as depictions of Christ. Arguably this is also their meaning on the pendant displayed here. But given the scarcity of easily recognizable, quasi-realistic human faces in early Anglo-Saxon art, these bearded faces would certainly have had a special potency.

The pendant to the right with a triskele or whirling motif of garnet birds' heads shows filigree patterns of superior workmanship. Filigree was coming into its own with Style II and is found on such high-class metalwork as the Taplow buckle (**43**), the Faversham miniature buckles (**55**) and, albeit in varying quality, on numerous fittings from the Staffordshire Hoard. The centre of the pendant would have held a decorative boss made of garnet (**43**) or shell (**51**).

Anglo-Saxon
Early 7th century AD

Repoussé pendant:
From Ash, Kent, England
Height including loop 3.4 cm
1862,0701.16

Bird pendant:
From Faversham, Kent, England
Height including loop 3.7 cm
Bequeathed by W. Gibbs
1145.'70

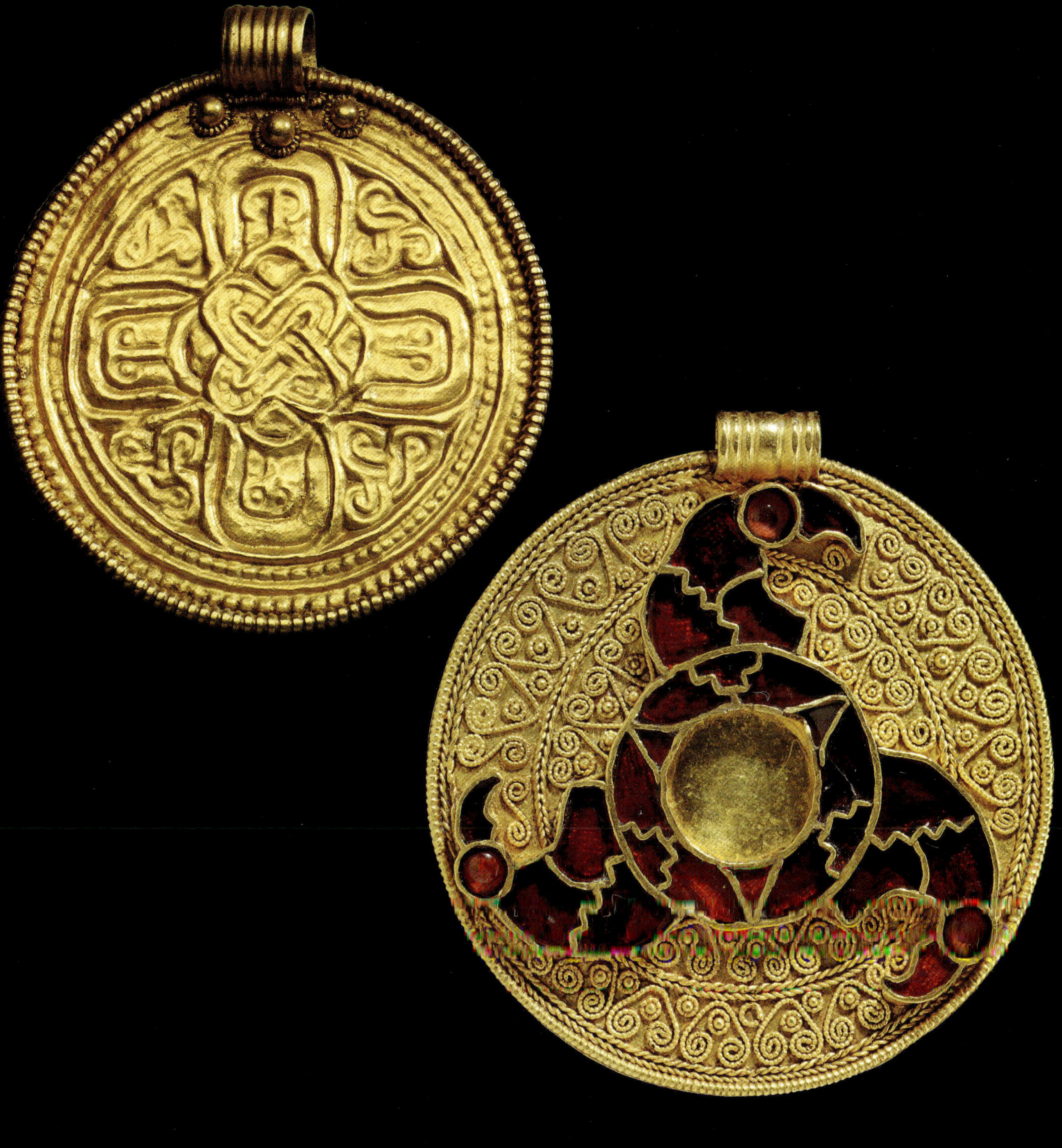

51 DISC BROOCH AND NECKLACE

One of the best preserved Anglo-Saxon composite disc brooches comes from a female grave at Sarre in Kent. The body of the brooch is made up of several layers, the uppermost of which is inlaid with garnets and gold filigree panels, as well as five ornamental bosses in a cruciform arrangement. These are made from a white, crystalline material which has been identified as possibly cuttlefish bone. Bosses on other surviving early Anglo-Saxon brooches and pendants were cut from shell, sometimes from species that would have lived in warm waters such as the Mediterranean, rather than in the North Sea, indicating that some raw material had travelled a long way (**49**).

The short necklace with two amethyst beads at either end, pictured below the brooch, came from the same grave. The beads were imported from the Mediterranean, but the source of the stone may have been Egypt, Afghanistan or Persia. The glass beads are typical late types of the seventh century when barrel shapes in strong, opaque colours were en vogue. They are interspersed with coin pendants, prefiguring a later seventh-century fashion for elaborate gem settings (**57**). At the centre of the necklace is an Anglo-Saxon pendant set with a reused millefiori disc, which may have come from a Roman brooch.

There is one Frankish and one Byzantine coin, but the other two are imitations of Byzantine *solidi* made in southern France around AD 600. This does not imply that Byzantine coinage was being forged. Rather, by modelling their coins on those of the empire, kings and moneyers who minted the coins invested them with an air of authenticity and ensured that they were widely accepted. This principle was common in the early medieval world (**84**, **128**) and still employed some one hundred and fifty years later by the Mercian king Offa (**60**).

The owner of the Sarre brooch and necklace was not only demonstrating that she and her family could afford high-status jewellery, but also that they had access to exotic goods from the other side of the Channel and beyond, as well as to rare, ancient materials.

Anglo-Saxon
From Sarre, Kent, England
First half of the 7th century AD
Diameter of brooch 6.7 cm
1860,1024.1 & 2.a–e

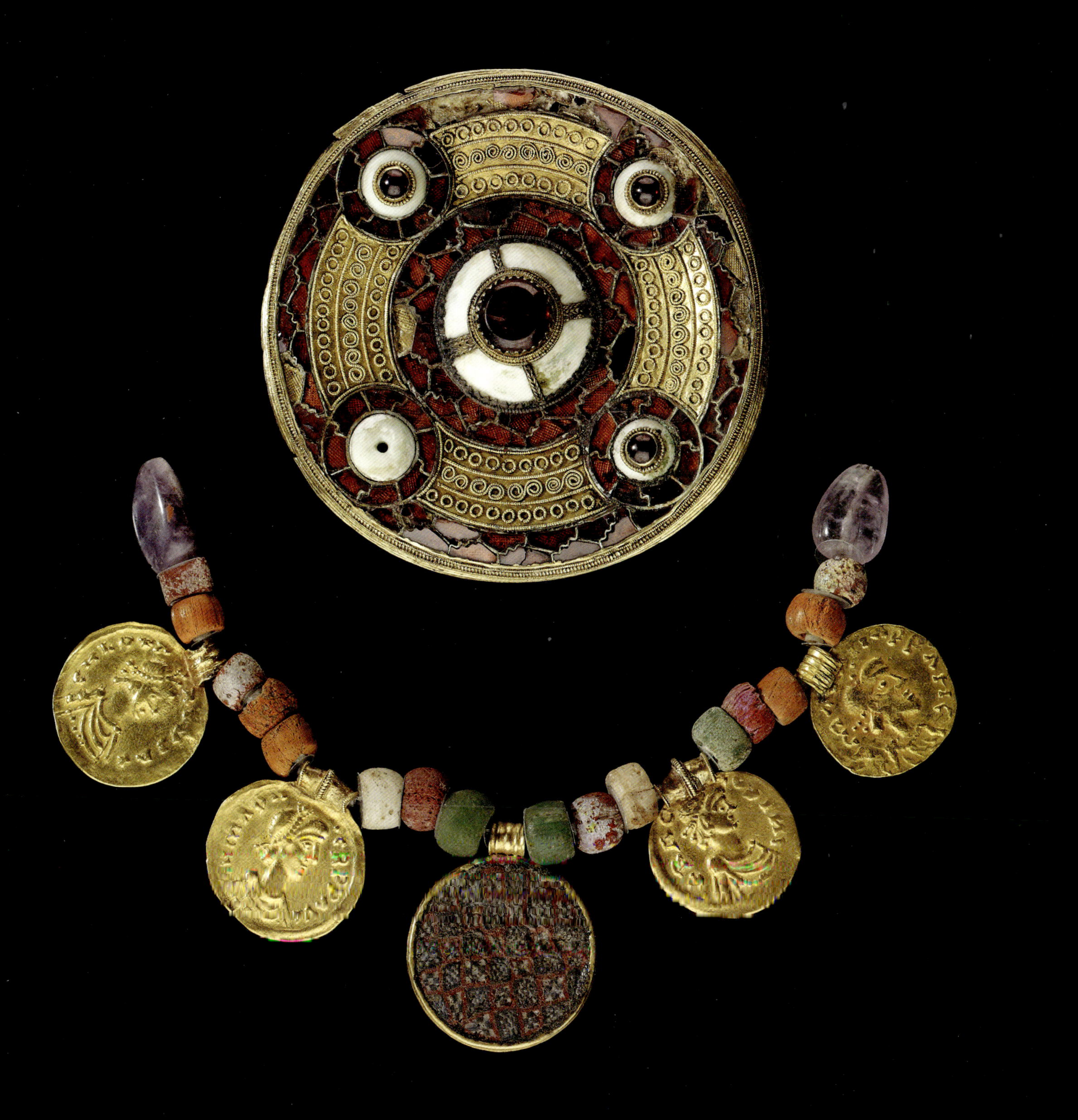

52 SILVER FIGURINE

The human form must have held a powerful meaning for the Anglo-Saxons of the fifth to seventh century. If depicted at all, it is usually in the broken-down configuration of Germanic Animal Style I (**42**) or as stylized masks. Naturalistic representations (**40**) such as this silver figurine of a bearded male are extremely rare.

The man is shown in a formal pose, his left hand touching his beard, his right laid across his torso. His face and hands are gilded, as is part of his lower body. It is unclear whether he is wearing a pair of knee breeches, but if so, they leave little to the imagination.

Five other figures known from Kent and the east of England, both male and female, show similar postures. While the two females from Kent are naked and seem to be pointing towards their genitalia, another male figure wears the same clinging 'trousers' as those of the Carlton Colville man. This apparent emphasis on fertility, expressed through the potent depiction of the human form, suggests that these figurines had an amuletic function and were perhaps associated with cultic practices. The presence of a loop on this and several other figurines suggests that they could have been worn as personal amulets.

Further instances of these tiny men and women with strange fused feet and expressive gestures have been found in Scandinavia. Some, like the figure here, are carefully modelled while others are more basic, like two of the Kentish finds. Gilded heads occur in Scandinavia as well. The English examples are either from graves or stray finds without context, but in Scandinavia, a number have been found deposited in large timber buildings, for example at the major cult site at Uppåkra in southern Sweden.

It may be of significance that the Anglo-Saxon figurines seem to have started to appear in the seventh century, the time when Christianity was taking root in the Anglo-Saxon kingdoms. It is possible that this new religion, with its canon of imagery centred on the figures of Christ, the Virgin Mary and the Apostles, may have catalyzed the development of miniature anthropomorphic sculptures with a pagan significance.

Anglo-Saxon

From Carlton Colville, Suffolk, England

First half of the 7th century AD

Height 4.3 cm

Acquired with contributions by The Art Fund and the British Museum Friends

2001,0902.1

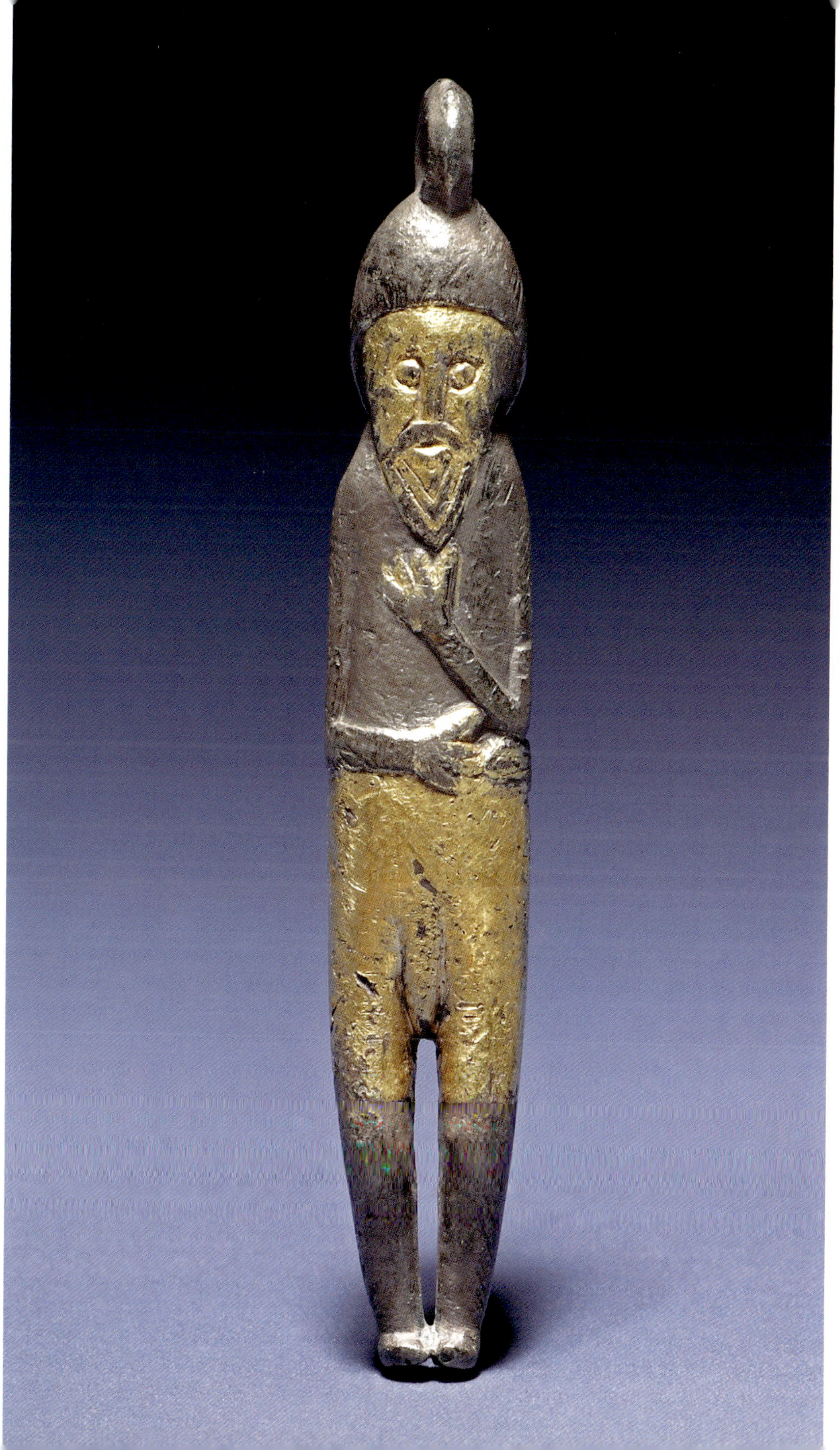

53 THE WILTON CROSS

There are a number of Anglo-Saxon garnet pectoral crosses now known to us. One was found in the coffin of St Cuthbert at Durham, and there are stray finds from Ixworth in Suffolk and Holderness in East Yorkshire, but the most complex of them all is this cross from Wilton. It was at one point in the possession of William Chaffers, an antiquities dealer and ceramics historian, before the British Museum bought it in 1859.

The Wilton cross is distinguished by its outstanding level of craftsmanship, characterized by evenly set garnets in very regular gold cells. The availability of garnet slips does not seem to have been a problem because, as opposed to most of the other crosses, the Wilton artist did not need to make do with reused garnets of varying shapes, which would have led to irregular cloisonné. The cross would originally have been a colourful piece of jewellery, as the one remaining light blue glass inlay suggests. The quality of the inlay as well as the cell patterns link the cross with some of the jewellery from Sutton Hoo (**46**) and elsewhere.

The centre of the pendant is taken up by a lightweight Byzantine *solidus*, minted approximately after AD 616 and before AD 625, which has been set upside down. The depiction of the Cross on top of the stylized hill of Golgotha is thus the right way up for the wearer glancing down at it, while at the same time it becomes an image of a pendant cross for those looking directly at the wearer. In addition, as the obverse of the coin had been struck upside down in relation to the reverse, the imperial double portrait on the back of the coin, shown here on the left, had the correct orientation.

The Byzantine coin would have been a rarity in itself, even though Frankish ones were reasonably common. It shows traces of use and had indeed already been mounted as a pendant before it was integrated into the sumptuous garnet frame. It has been suggested that this transformation reflects the impact of the conversion to Christianity in East Anglia: a gold coin pendant following older traditions, such as bracteates (**40**), was turned into an overt statement of the new faith.

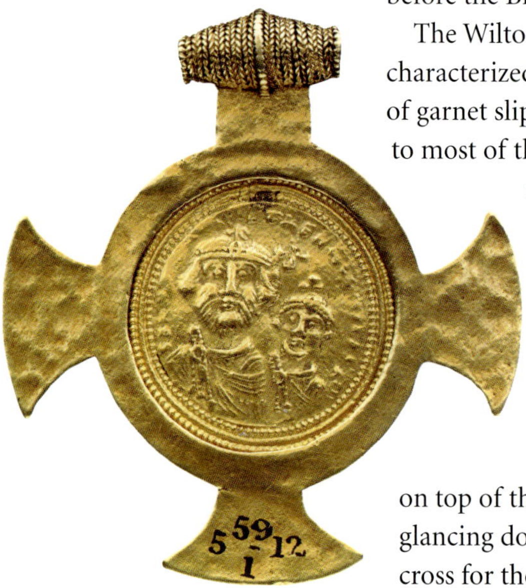

Anglo-Saxon and Byzantine
Thought to be from Wilton, Norfolk, England
7th century, perhaps *c.* AD 635
Height 4.7 cm
1859,0512.1

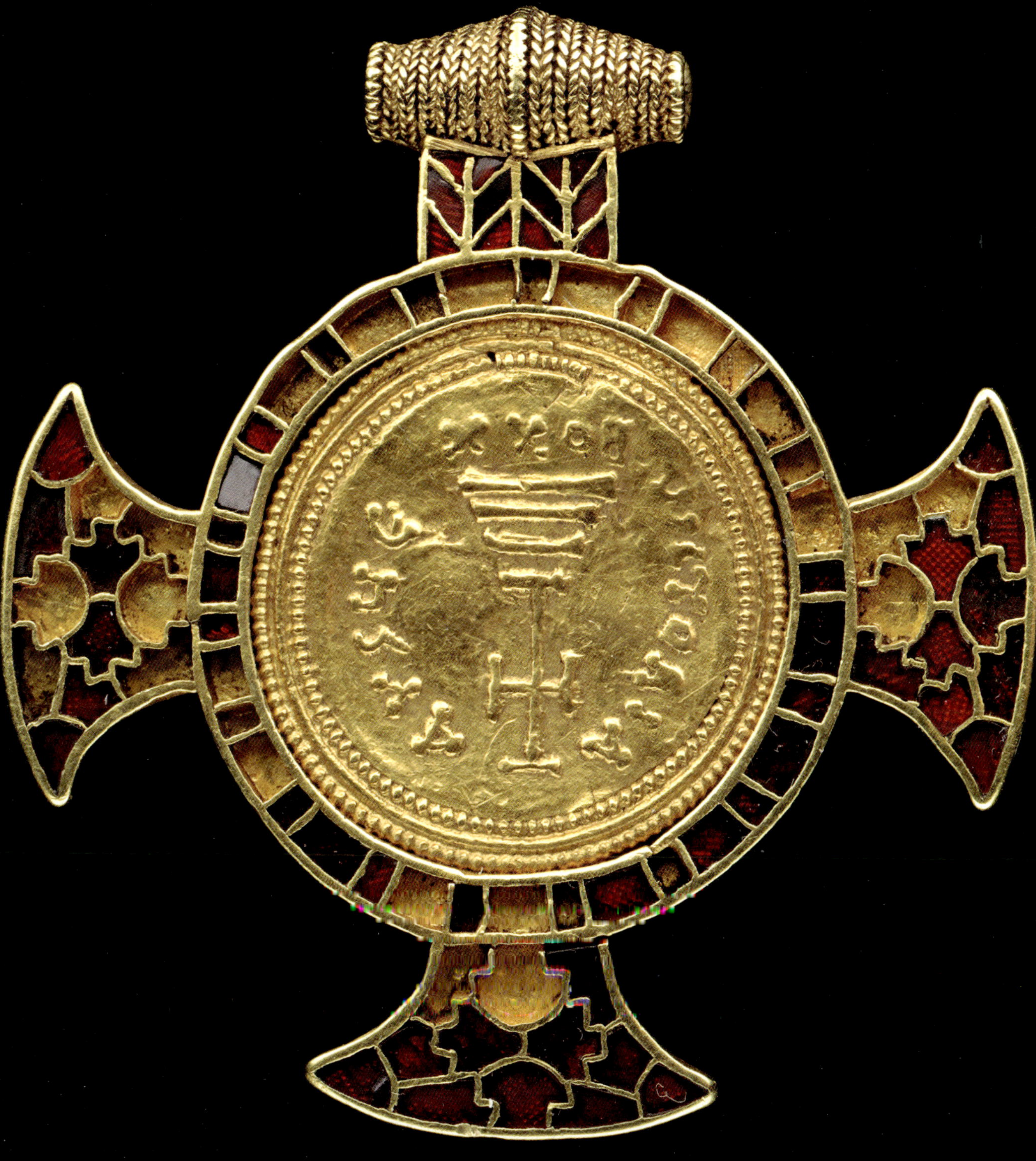

54 THE CRUNDALE BUCKLE

The Crundale buckle is one of the most unusual to survive from Anglo-Saxon England. Its plate is of a triangular shape, which is not particularly common and mostly restricted to more elaborate buckles worn by people of status (**43**). Its outstanding feature, however, is a three-dimensional appliqué in the form of a fish. Fine wires indicating the scales and four small flippers, two of which are now wedged beneath the fish effigy, were originally inlaid with garnets, just like the eyes. Further garnets, parcel-gilding, filigree and gold granulation increase the precious character of this buckle. Notably, the remains of a similar fish appliqué have recently been discovered near Westleton in Suffolk, now also in the British Museum.

The fish first became a Christian symbol in the Mediterranean during the Roman period. The letters of its name in Greek, *ichthus*, could be decoded as an acronym for *Iesous Christos, Theou Uios, Soter* (Jesus Christ, Son of God, Saviour). Anglo-Saxon fish images are also known in more stylized form, especially as shield appliqués (**44**). But the Crundale buckle is younger than such shield ornaments and it can be assumed that by the time it was deposited in the mid-seventh century, Christianity was well established in Kent, which gives this dress accessory a religious dimension. In addition, the buckle plate is hollow and could apparently be opened. This is reminiscent of the Sutton Hoo gold buckle (**48**) and of Continental buckles from Francia and Burgundia, which functioned as reliquaries. Like the Crundale buckle, they are often decorated with Christian imagery, although the fish is not one of the known motifs.

The buckle was discovered in 1861 in a male grave on the Crundale Downs. It additionally contained another buckle and a sword. One buckle may have been for a waist belt, while the other may have come from the weapon harness.

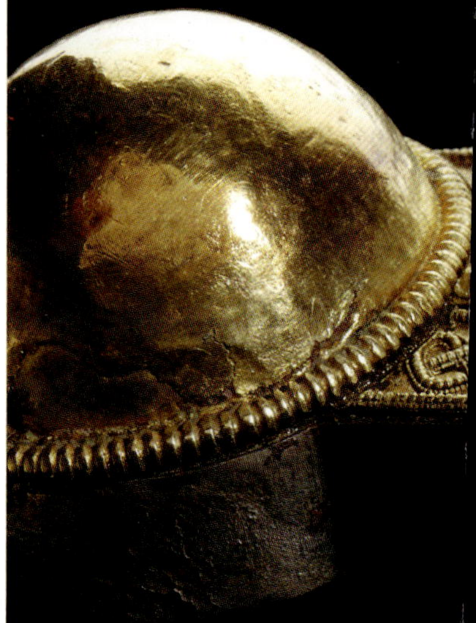

Anglo-Saxon
From Crundale, Kent, England
Early to mid-7th century AD
Length 15.0 cm
1893,0601.204

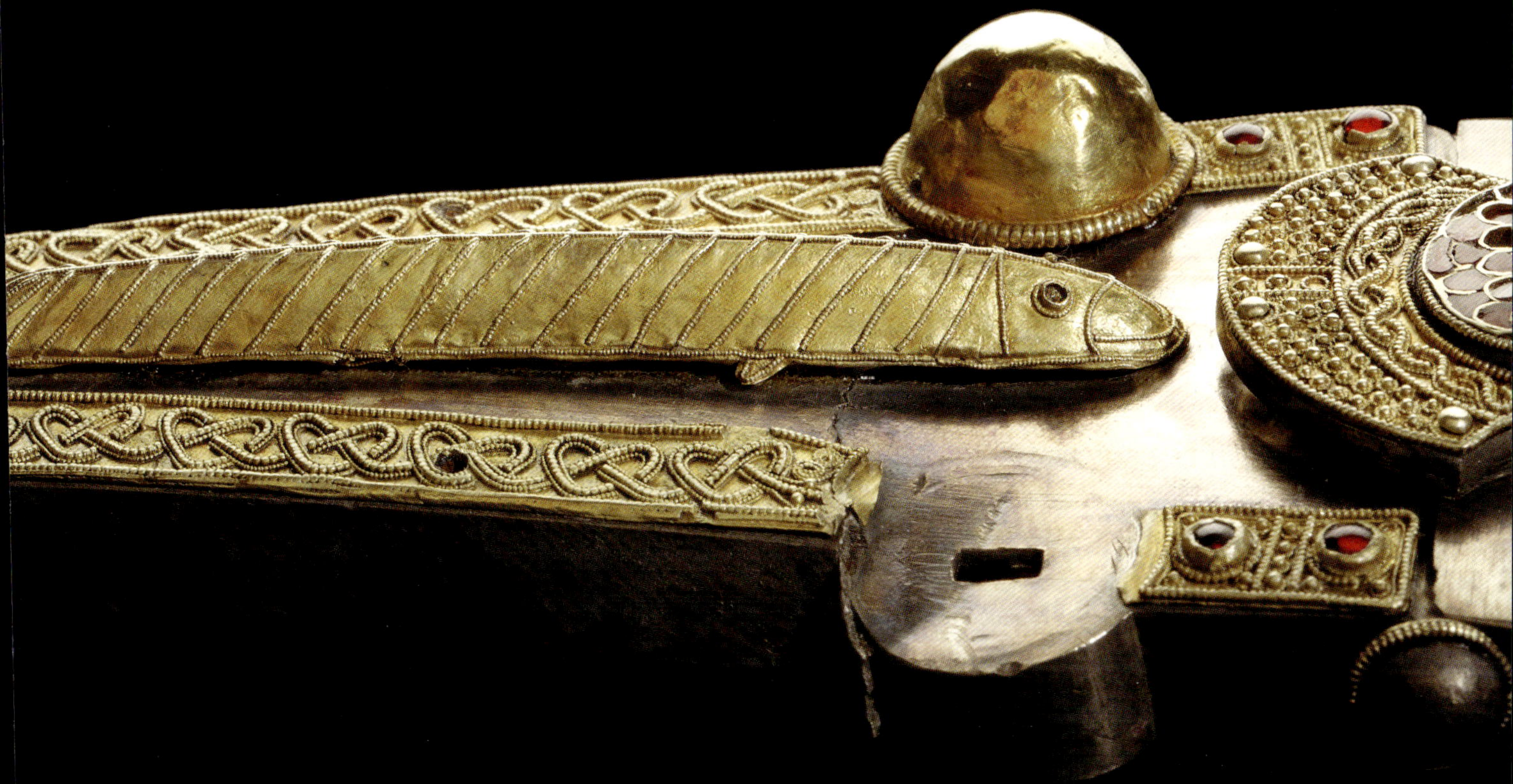

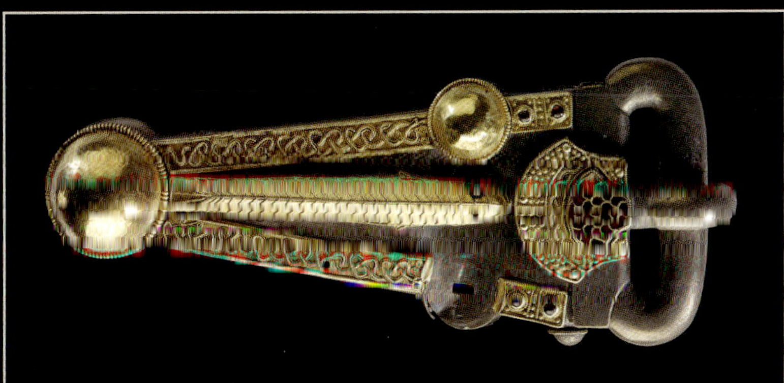

55 FILIGREE BUCKLE FROM FAVERSHAM

A pair of miniature buckles is one of the best examples of filigree known from the early Anglo-Saxon period.

Each buckle is cut from gold sheet which has been shaped and engraved to show two pairs of back-to-back birds' heads. In the characteristic manner of the Germanic Animal Style II (**48**, **50**), the birds have large eyes, in the form of gold granules, and their heads are indicated by angled frames and strongly curved beaks. Birds of prey appear to have been an important part of the mindscape of all Germanic peoples, as they occur in many different guises (**44**, **85**).

The birds enclose a rectangular central panel showing two interlaced snakes. Their heads are only indicated through U-shaped wires, but each one is evidently biting the other's tail. The strict symmetry of the composition is characteristic of the Kentish adaption of Animal Style II.

The construction of the filigree in the central field is technically superb and follows a rarely seen method. The wires are applied to a repoussé gold sheet, rather than just to a flat surface, which lends an extra depth and plasticity to the snake panels. As this requires superior skills from the artisan as well as an additional investment in gold sheet, it appears that only the highest quality pieces such as the buckle (**43**) and clasps from Taplow, or the Market Rasen sword fittings from Lincolnshire – also in the British Museum – were made in this way. Notably, only a small proportion of the large number of filigree fittings in the Staffordshire Hoard features this technique.

The buckles from the King's Field at Faversham come from perhaps the richest Kentish site. It was discovered during railway works in the nineteenth century and further finds from the Anglo-Saxon period were made during the exploitation of brick earth deposits. Often there is little information about the objects and their contexts, but we can make a good guess at how the pair of buckles was used. Due to their delicate nature and the presence of little, right-angled hooks on their backs they were probably meant to close a small bag, and were attached to its lid, most likely made of relatively stiff leather.

Anglo-Saxon
From Faversham, Kent, England
Early 7th century AD
Length 3.2 cm
1094. & 1094a.'70

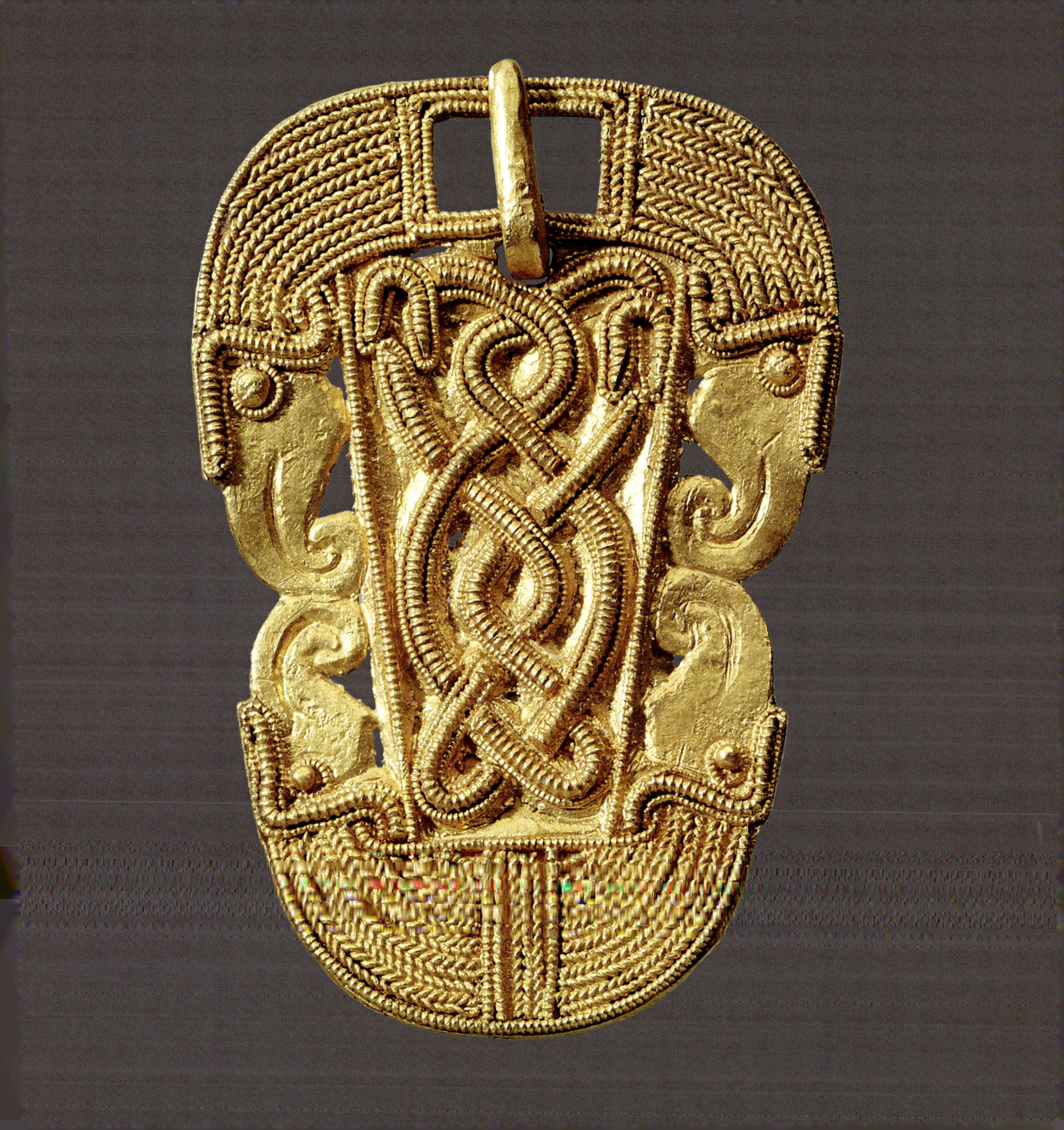

56 THE EWELL PENDANT

The stern face of a man is facing towards the right on this gold pendant. He is bearded and wearing a Phrygian cap, with its distinctive, forward-curled peak (**29**). In the use of a portrait cameo the Ewell pendant is so far unique among seventh-century Anglo-Saxon female jewellery.

The popularity of necklaces with large pendants set in gold frames (**50**, **57**) superseded the older fashion for strings of glass and amber beads during this period. Substantial garnets, either round-topped cabochons or flat slabs, were mounted in gold frames.

By the seventh century, garnet was no longer easy to obtain in northern Europe. The exact reasons for the shortage are unclear, but the expansion of the Muslim dynasties across the Arabian peninsula and into Egypt may have disrupted existing trade routes, which ran over sea and land from the Indian subcontinent and Sri Lanka into the Mediterranean and from there northwards (**49**).

In addition to its obvious expense and luxurious appearance, jewellery rich in garnets (**46**) must have held an additional cachet since only the privileged had access to this dwindling commodity. Garnets of all sizes were reused and the small number of sizeable cabochons without settings in the Staffordshire Hoard, for example, must have been of significant value. But not all the stones were plain, as demonstrated by the Ewell pendant and the discovery of a scallop-shaped garnet set in a gold pendant at Street House in north-east Yorkshire.

The Anglo-Saxons, like other Germanic peoples, obviously appreciated the prestigious connotations of Roman or Byzantine gems (**80**), and not only because they were technological marvels which could not be replicated.

In light of this, it seems of secondary importance whether this gem is an ancient Roman piece or a roughly contemporary Byzantine jewel, and what the exact significance of the so far unidentified Phrygian figure was.

Anglo-Saxon, with a Mediterranean gem

From Ewell, Surrey, England

Late 7th century AD

Width 2.2 cm

1970,0301.1

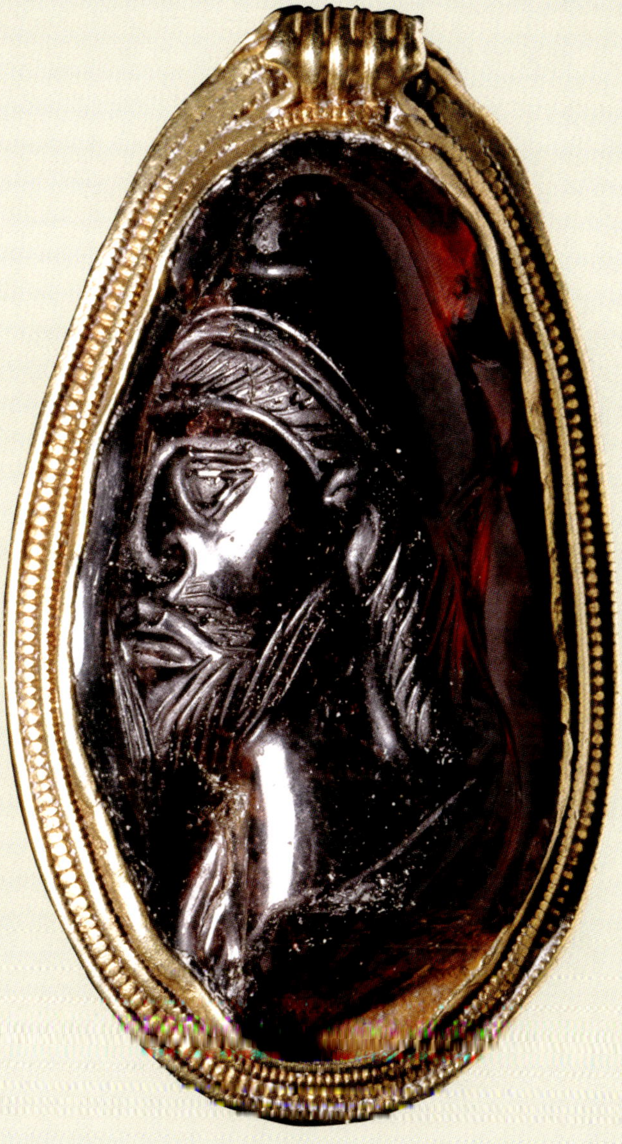

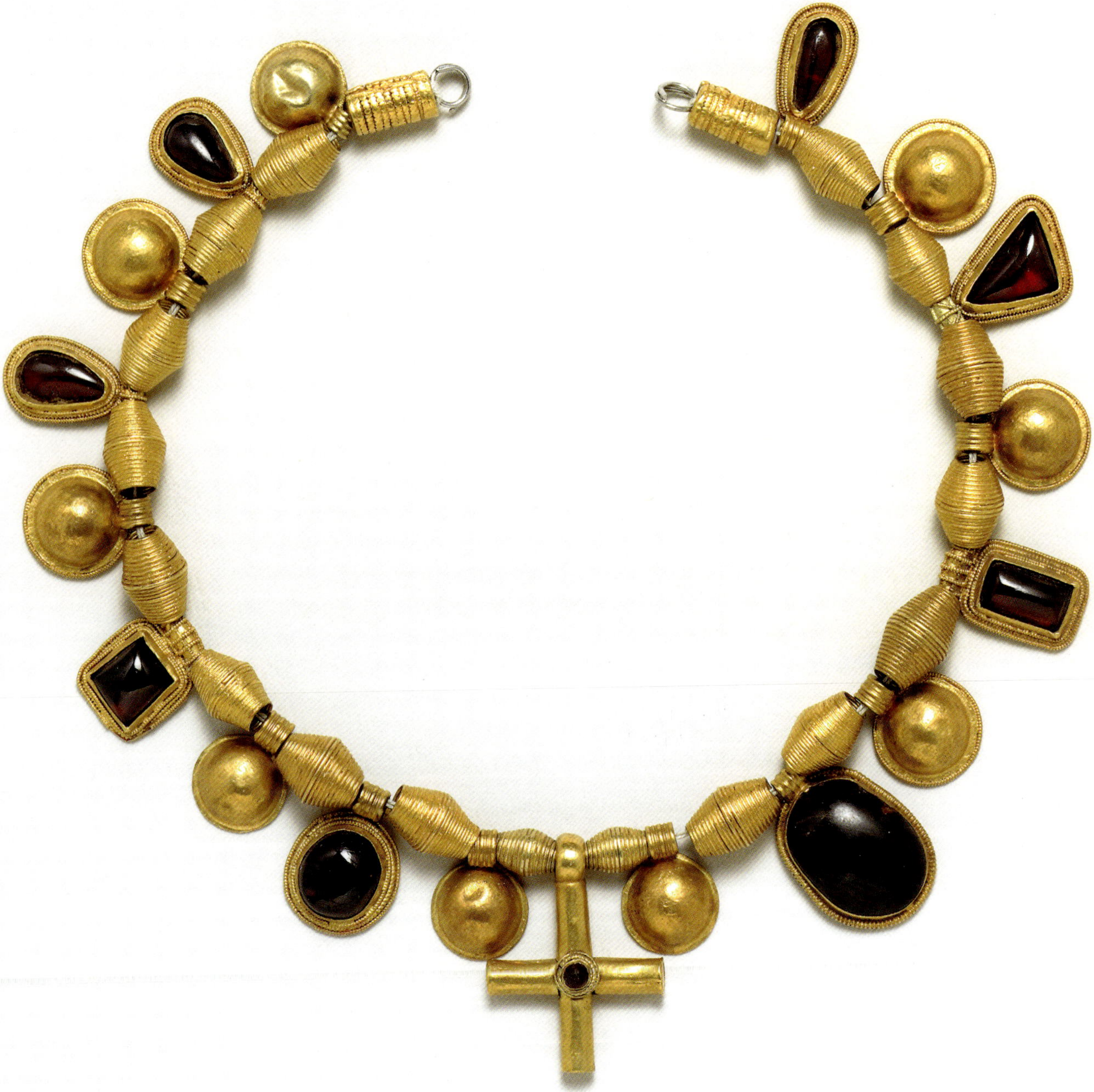

57 THE DESBOROUGH NECKLACE

The Desborough necklace is arguably the finest among the pieces of high-status jewellery dating from the end of the early Anglo-Saxon period. The sumptuous nature of all of these items is characterized by the contrast between their gold mounts and large, colourful settings (**51**, **56**).

On this necklace, biconical gold beads made from coiled wire are interspersed with gold sheet pendants, or *bullae*, and large pendants set with cabochon garnets. These come in various forms, including ovals, rectangles and drop-shapes. A small number of single pendants has been recovered as stray finds in recent years, but the examples from the Desborough necklace are still notable for their size and the quality of the mounting.

The focus of the necklace is a cross, made from two hollow gold tubes. A small cabochon garnet has been set where these intersect. While the construction of the pendant is slightly awkward, it is clearly modelled on Byzantine examples of jewelled crosses. Indeed, the fashion for gold necklaces with various kinds of pendants was inspired by Mediterranean jewellery. Ideas are likely to have been transmitted through the Frankish kingdom, which had close connections to both the Mediterranean and the north. It may be significant that Christianity, which was closely associated with missionaries from Rome, had firmly taken root in Anglo-Saxon England around the time that the owner of this necklace was buried. This may have contributed to an interest in Mediterranean styles, including new dress fashions.

Instead of the old mode of wearing a dress pinned at the shoulder by a pair of brooches, which had once been common all over the Germanic world, tailored tunics now became the principal garment for women. Heavy cloak brooches (**42**) were replaced by more delicate, circular forms, perhaps closing a veil at the neck (**51**). Large strings of glass and amber beads were no longer popular. A much more uniform kind of high status women's attire had replaced the previous regional diversity in Anglo-Saxon England.

Anglo-Saxon
From Desborough, Northamptonshire, England
Late 7th century AD
Length of necklace 25.0 cm
1876,0504.1

58 THE FRANKS CASKET

This whalebone box is perhaps the most famous piece of small sculpture from Anglo-Saxon England. Named after Augustus Wollaston Franks (1826–97), a great benefactor of and Keeper at the British Museum, its complex iconography has mystified viewers since it was first observed in the Auvergne, France. It is probable that it travelled there from the north of England, where it was undoubtedly made.

The casket is covered in narrative carvings depicting the Adoration of the Magi (**29**, **87**), together with an episode from the Germanic tale of Weyland the Smith on the front; Romulus and Remus being suckled by the she-wolf (**40**) on the left side panel; the capture of Jerusalem by the Roman emperor Titus in AD 70 on the back; and another siege scene portraying the Germanic hero Egil on the partly damaged lid. Today the right side panel, depicting an unknown scene from Germanic mythology, is in the Bargello Museum, Florence. Labels and longer inscription strips in both Old English (in runes) and Latin name some of the settings and protagonists. The long text running around the front is a riddle referring to the material from which the casket is made.

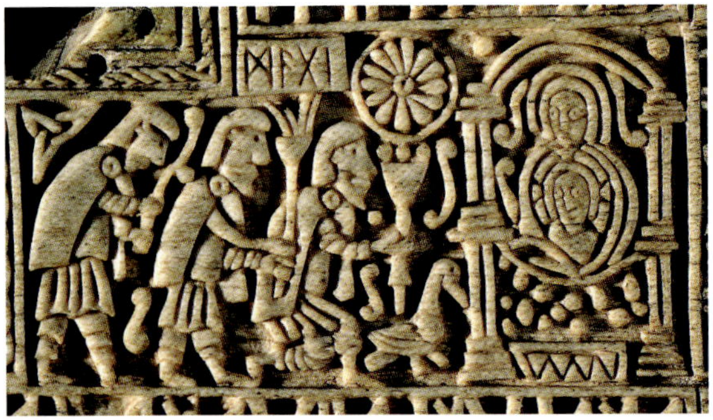

Detailed analysis has unravelled the seemingly random selection of religious, historical and mythical topics, including both Christian and pagan themes. They can be read as an illustration of the early medieval Church's notion of universal history. This saw the incarnation of Christ as the point to which all of history had been leading, while the end of history would follow the Second Coming of Christ.

Such a complex iconographic programme could only be devised in a learned environment. Stylistic and linguistic evidence suggests a Northumbrian monastery as a likely place of manufacture. The high-quality workmanship, expensive whalebone and the long-gone, possibly jewelled, metal fittings imply a high-status, perhaps even royal patron. A casket with an extensive religious and moral commentary such as this would have been eminently suitable for holding a precious text, such as a psalter.

Anglo-Saxon
Probably made in Northumbria, found at Auzon, France
First half of the 8th century AD
Width 22.9 cm
Donated by A.W. Franks
1867,0120.1

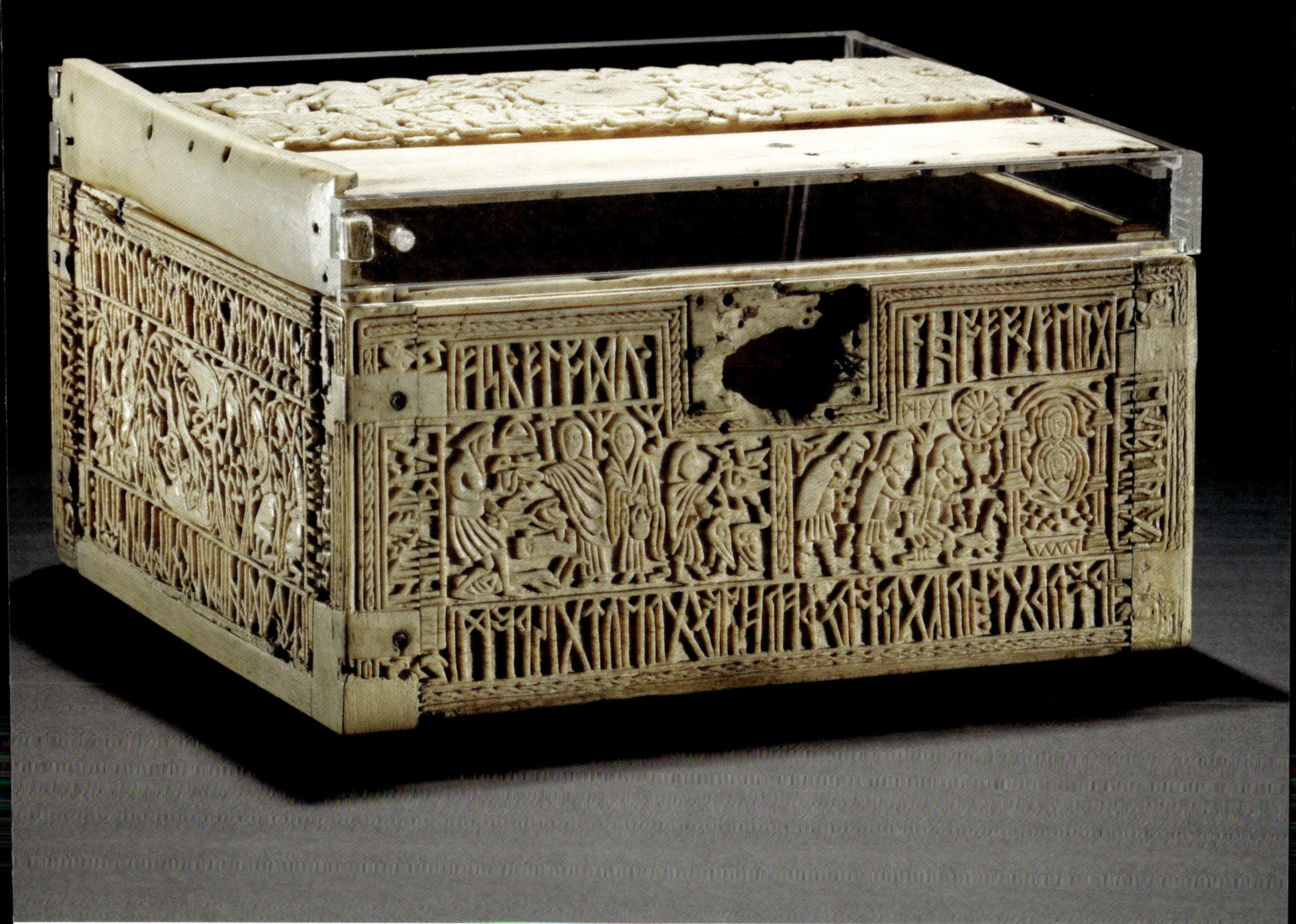

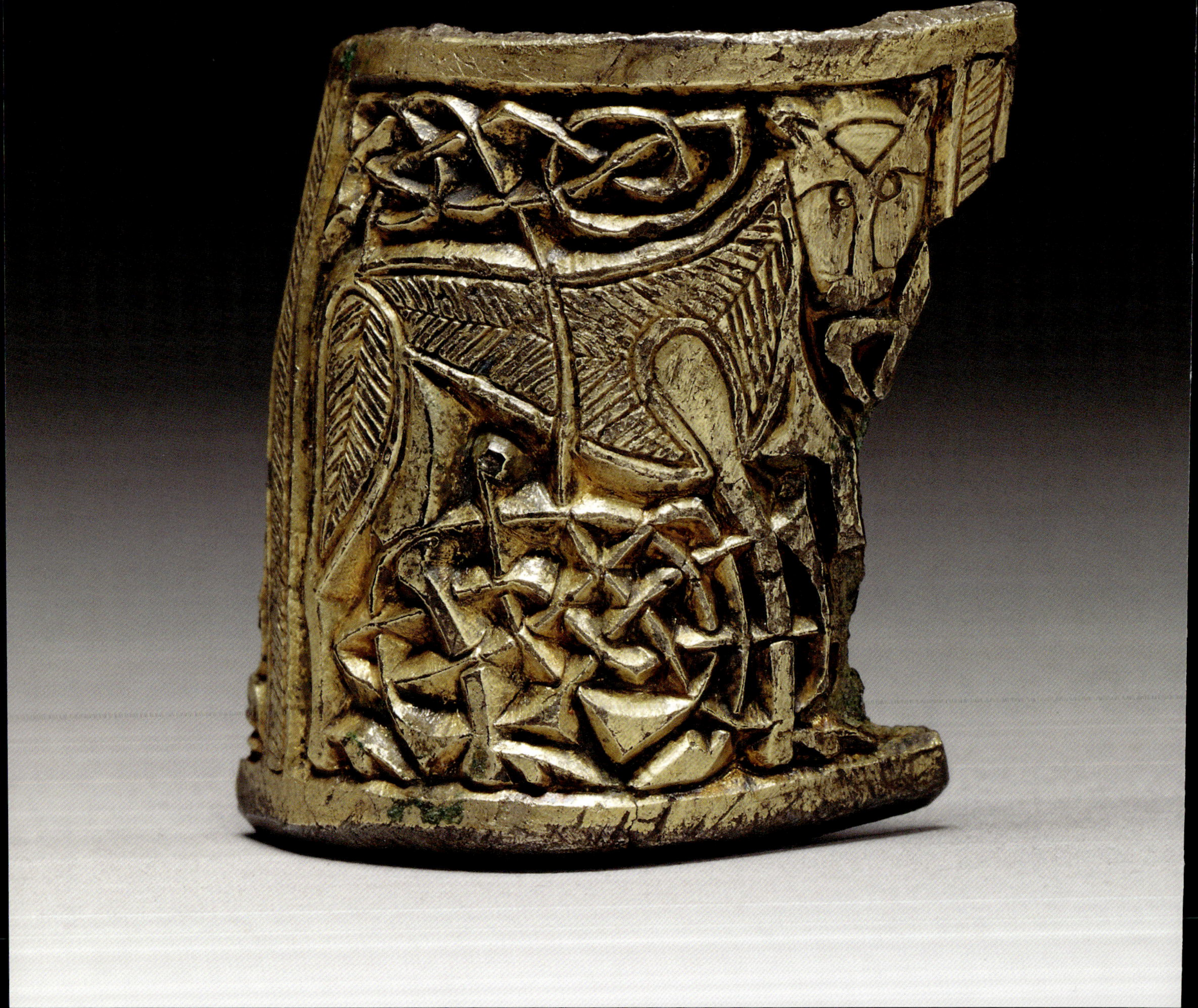

59 INTERLACE FRAGMENT

Like much other high-quality Anglo-Saxon metalwork of the eighth century, this silver fragment is characterized by a fine interlace network into which an animal has been integrated. Other prime examples of this style include a set of three linked pins with large disc heads from the River Witham, also in the British Museum, and a sword pommel from Oxfordshire (**62**). This ornament is also used to great effect in other media, for example in book illumination, on stone sculpture, textiles and carved ivories, such as the well-known Gandersheim Casket, which was possibly made in East Anglia, where the present fragment was found.

Many of these artworks of the later eighth and early ninth century are associated with the kingdom of Mercia and the areas over which it exerted influence at the height of its power (**66**). Conversely, small, perfectly portable objects with this form of decoration, such as jewellery and weapon fittings, are notably scarce outside the Mercian sphere. One distinctive element of the style, the so-called Mercian beast with its imposing posture and lolling tongue, reappears in later, ninth-century metalwork (**65**).

The high quality of the fitting is reflected in its superb execution. After the fitting was cast with the basic decoration in place, it was sharpened up, resulting in deep-cut interlace with precise, narrow ridges, which was then gilt. A cat-like creature is facing the viewer. Its fur is indicated by narrow, engraved ridges and its tail is intertwined with both its body and the interlace background. While this must remain speculative, the striding feline could be a representation of the lion of St Mark. If so, the missing panels on either side of this one may have contained the other Evangelists' symbols (**102**). After all, another precious metal plaque from East Anglia features the symbol of St John (**64**).

Whatever this fragment depicts and however it was used or attached – the back is plain and gives no clues – it certainly came from a high-status and perhaps ecclesiastical object.

Anglo-Saxon
From Surlingham, Norfolk, England
8th century AD
Maximum height 2.5 cm
2003,0904.1

60 THE OFFA DINAR

One way of describing the Offa dinar is as a masterpiece of marketing through the appropriation of an established brand. Although it was minted in England for Offa, the famous king of Mercia (AD 757–96), the dinar copies the design of a proverbial gold standard of its time, the coinage of the caliph al-Mansur (AD 754–75), a ruler from the Muslim 'Abbasid dynasty (AD 750–1258).

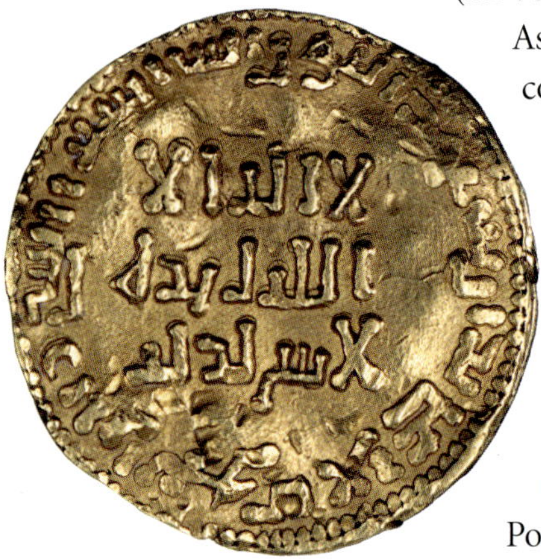

As the most important gold sources during the Middle Ages were either controlled by or only accessible through the territories of Islamic sovereigns, their high-quality coinage was sought after all over the Mediterranean. In northern Europe, eighth-century Muslim gold currency has also been found along the passes of the Alps and major rivers. In fact, the Arabic term for a dinar carrying an inscription, *al-dīnār al-manquš*, was transformed into a more generic term for a European gold coin, a *mancus*, and is still used today.

The Offa dinar is unique and its purpose is uncertain. It first appeared in Rome and it has been suggested that it was minted as a gift for the Pope. However, it is doubtful that a Muslim coin featuring the *Shahada*, the Islamic profession of faith, would have been copied for such an occasion. Instead, its similarity to the widespread and well-regarded 'Abbasid denomination may identify it as a trade coin. Similar considerations most probably lay behind the imitation of Byzantine gold coinage by Germanic rulers (**51**, **84**) or the Viking Age copies of Muslim silver coins (**128**).

Whoever produced the design must have had access to genuine coins from the Near East, as the inscription was copied well enough for us to ascertain that it was based on a coin minted in the Islamic year AH 157 (AD 773–4). But, as with the Ballycottin brooch (**109**), the craftsman who cut the die clearly could not read Arabic, as the Latin name and title of the Anglo-Saxon king, OFFA REX, are upside down in relation to the Arabic inscription.

Anglo-Saxon
Found in Rome, Italy
Minted in the kingdom of Mercia, England
AD 773–96
Diameter 2.0 cm
1913,1213.1

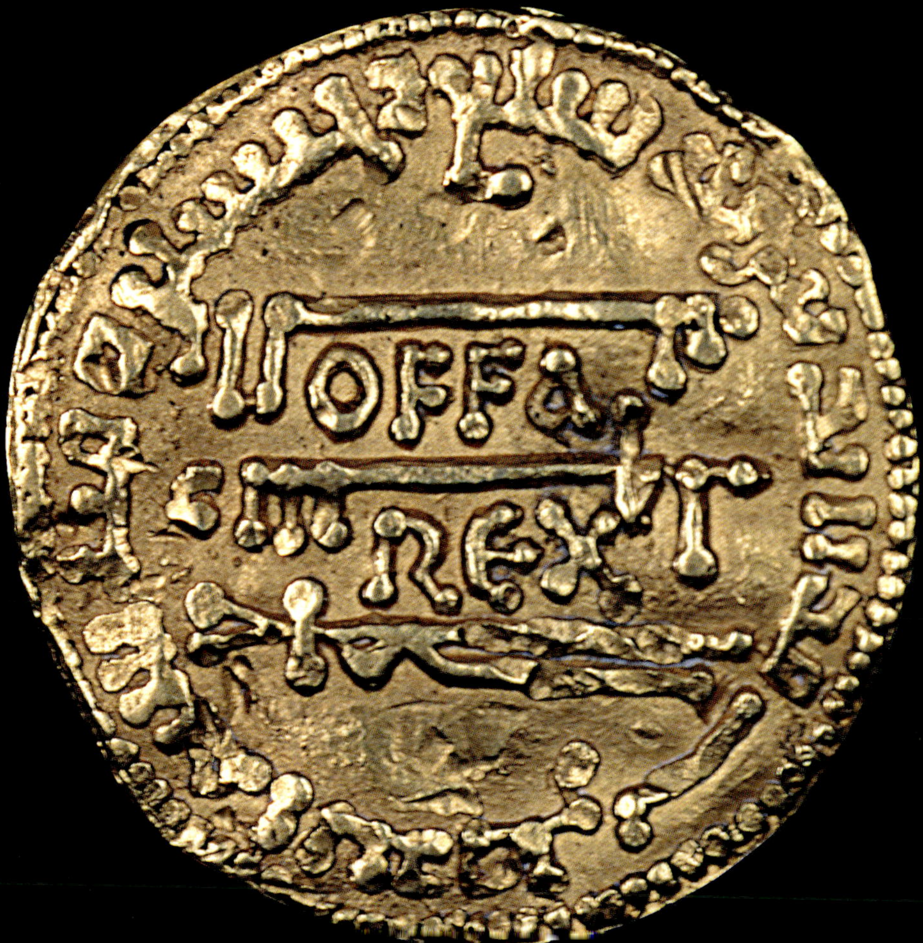
OFFA
REX

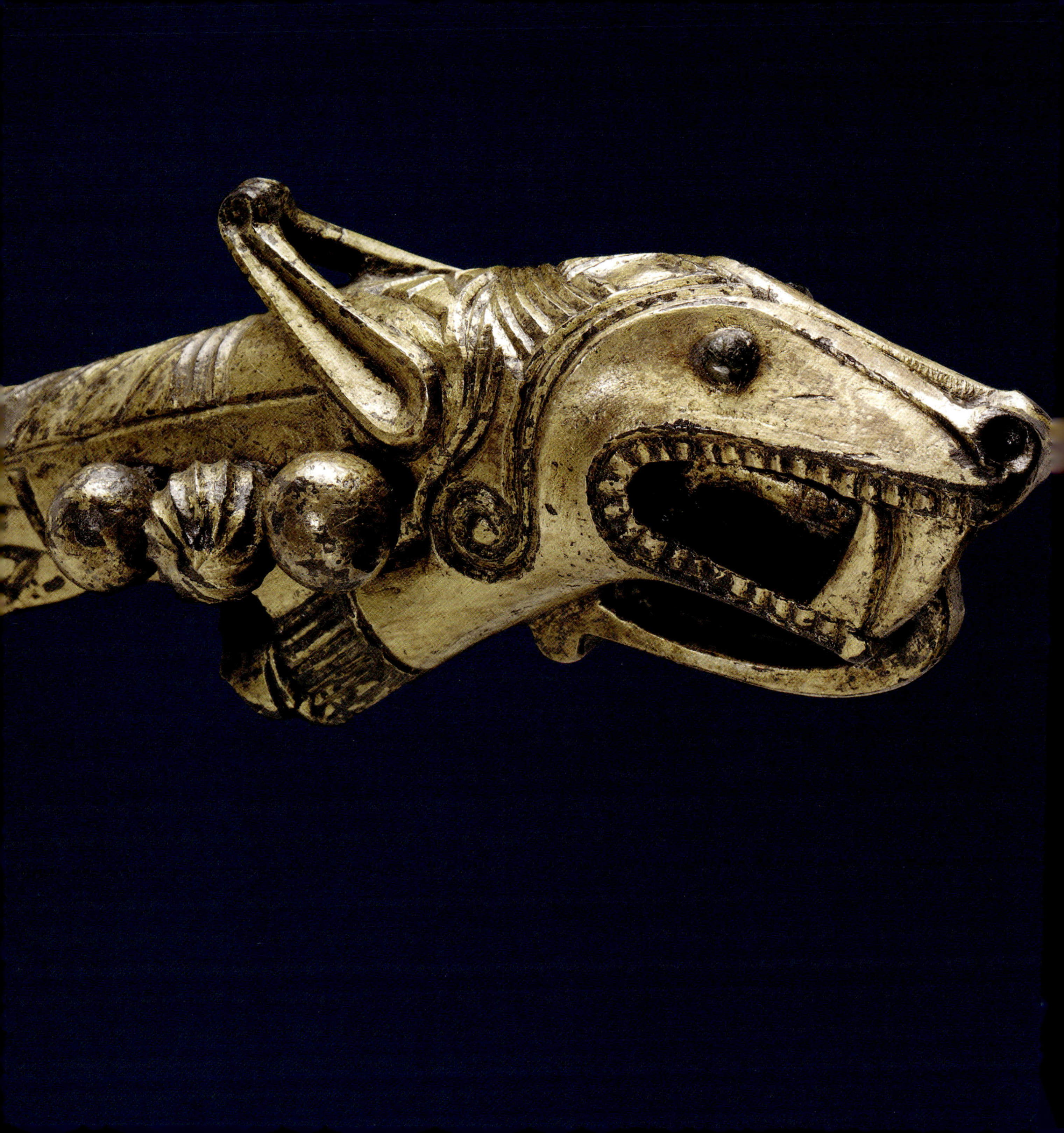

61 SCABBARD MOUNT

An act of generosity brought this silver-gilt fitting into the collection of the British Museum. A letter dated May 1869 reads, 'Should the Metal object bearing Runic Inscription be considered worthy of a place in the National Collection be pleased to add the same in the name of Yours Obliged Thomas D.E. Gunstone.' The note goes on to say that the mount came from the River Thames.

The original function of the fitting is unclear. It is made from two U-shaped metal strips which terminate in a carefully modelled animal head. The lower strip has now broken off, but it met with the upper one at a sharp angle. Decoration is restricted to the front of the mount, on which there are also groups of large ornamental rivets. This suggests that the fitting was fixed to a curved and pointed object, perhaps made of leather or wood, which was only seen from one side. Most likely this was a scabbard for a knife or a seax (**69**). Other asymmetrical scabbard fittings with decoration on only one side have been found in Wiltshire, and the treasure from St Ninian's Isle, Shetland, included two contemporary scabbard mounts with animal-head terminals.

The vicious teeth, curled-back tongue and indication of a mane seem to suggest that this is meant to be a wolf. Its eyes are formed from inlaid blue glass roundels, which are also used as animal eyes on jewellery and strap-ends at this time. A ferocious creature such as this would certainly have been an appropriate ornament for a weapon. In addition, the front of the fitting carries a series of twenty-one incised runes, which are spread out between the rivets in the same way that a Christian prayer is laid out on the terminals of the St Ninian's Isle mounts. The runes do not seem to have any specific meaning, but may have had an amuletic function meant to enhance the power of the weapon in order to protect its owner

Anglo-Saxon
From the River Thames, London, England
Late 8th century AD
Length 18.8 cm
Donated by T.D.E. Gunstone
1869,0610.1

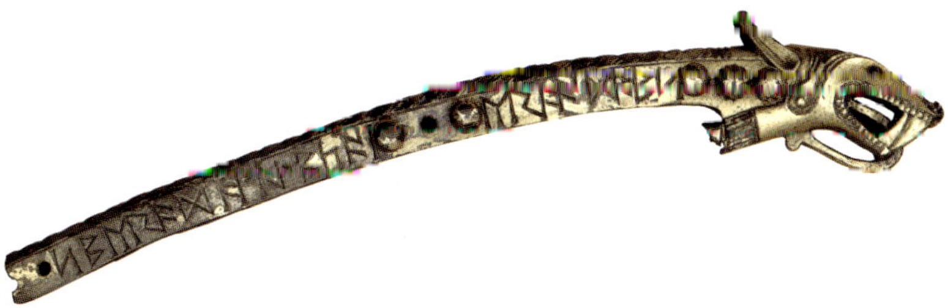

62 THE BECKLEY POMMEL

The dead were laid to rest with dress accessories, weapons, jewellery, vessels and other trappings of daily life from the fifth to about the mid-seventh century. The material culture of middle Anglo-Saxon England is much less familiar to us than that of the early Anglo-Saxons as by then the custom of being buried with goods had come to an end. While the Church did not regulate this practice, adherence to Christian ideas about the afterlife will have played a role. At the same time written sources became more common, and we now occasionally hear of weapons, including swords, decorated scabbards and precious pommels, being bequeathed in wills. Therefore this chance find from an Oxfordshire field fills a significant gap in the archaeological record.

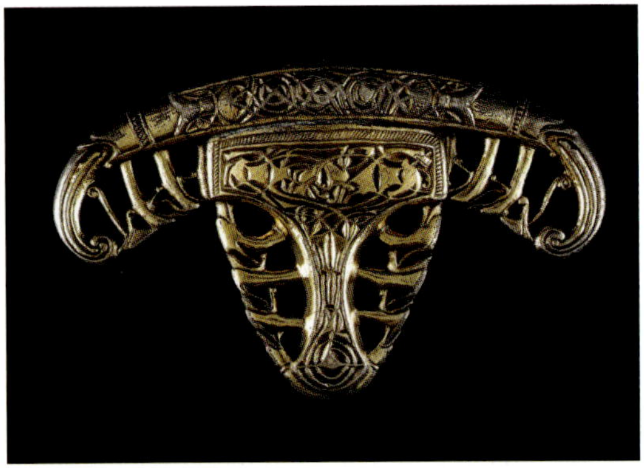

Unlike the majority of sword pommels known from this period, the Beckley pommel was cast from silver, which is consistent with its superior craftsmanship. The unparalleled openwork design has been gilt and shows clear signs of wear, as the gilding has rubbed off on the pommel bar in particular. This bar was cast separately from the upper part of the pommel, to which it was then riveted and soldered.

A microcosm of strange animals is encapsulated in the pommel's design. The easiest to discern are the two large birds' heads at the ends of the pommel bar, which can be identified by their scrolled beaks. A procession of odd creatures with gaping maws moves inwards away from the birds, with the inner ones flanking the interlaced spine of the pommel. These elements, as well as the scrollwork at the bottom of the pommel, reflect the influence of Pictish style elements.

When the blade is raised, the whole pommel transforms into an image of a bovine head, as one scholar has pointed out. Strength and aggression were qualities associated with bulls (**143**) and worthy of a high-status weapon such as this. Moreover, the visual puzzle fits well with the Anglo-Saxon predilection for riddles, a popular pastime, which were also recorded in written sources and even carved onto objects such as the Franks Casket (**58**).

Anglo-Saxon

From Beckley, Oxfordshire, England

Late 8th century AD

Length 9.9 cm

Acquired with a contribution from The Art Fund

1994,0407.1

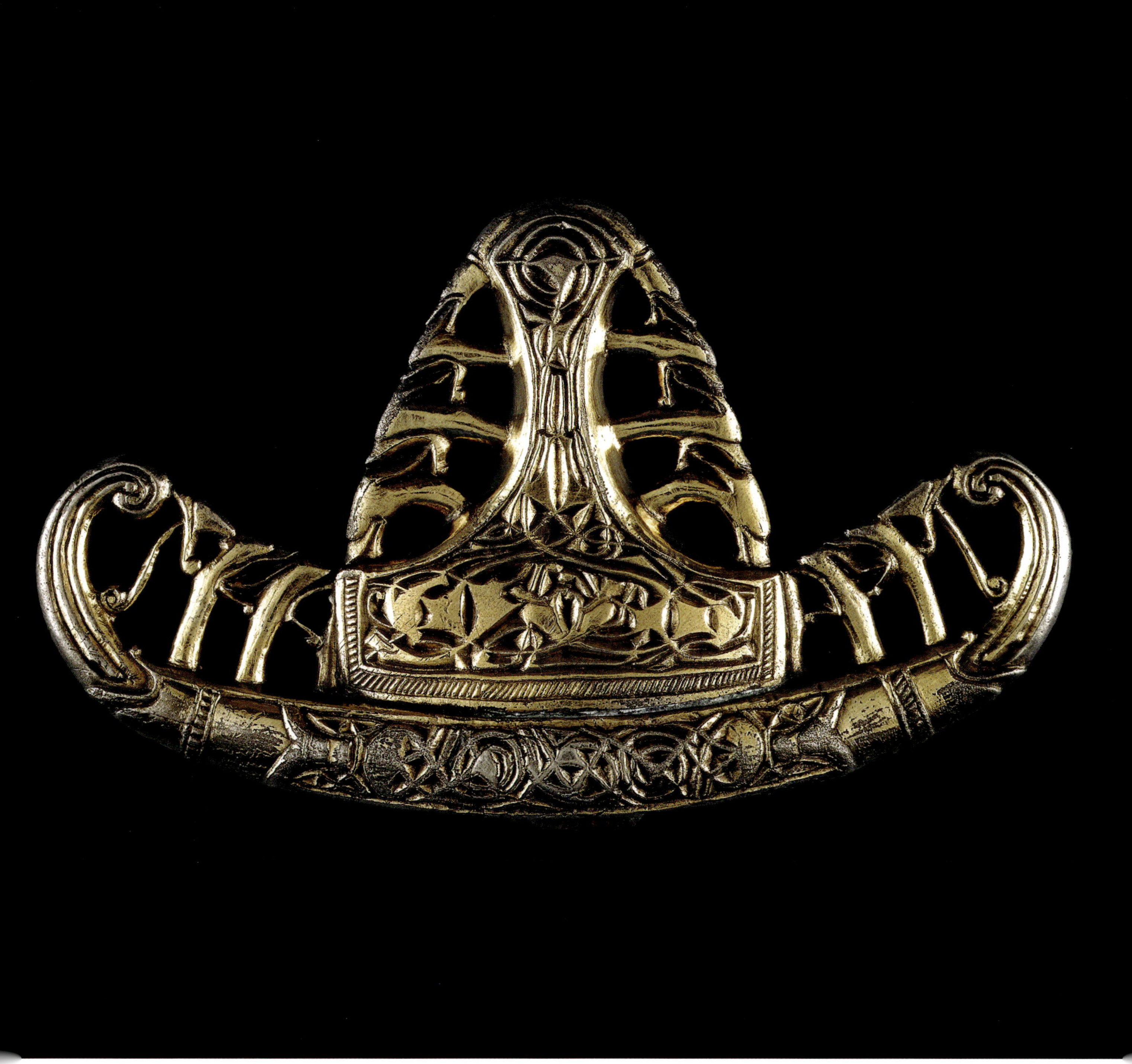

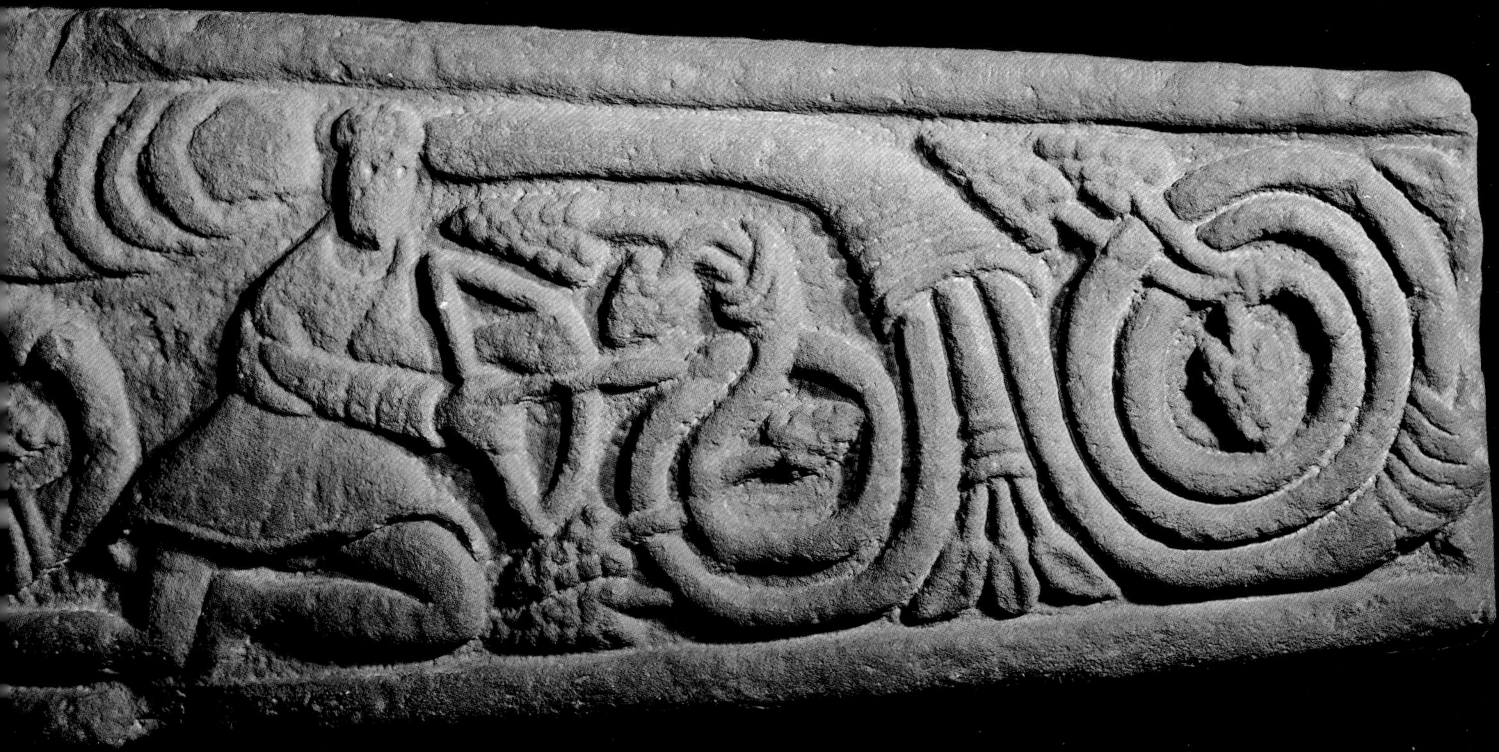

63 THE SHEFFIELD CROSS SHAFT

All that remains of a large sandstone cross that once stood by St Mary's, a parish church which was later to become Sheffield Cathedral, is the lower part. Freestanding crosses were an important part of the Anglo-Saxon landscape. Some were memorials, while the biblical events depicted on others were designed to instruct the faithful.

The narrow sides of the Sheffield cross shaft are decorated with vine scrolls, a motif which had been widespread since antiquity. Originally a Mediterranean symbol associated with Dionysus (**32**), the god of wine and fertility, to Christians it was a manifestation of the biblical description of Christ as the 'true vine' in which the faithful live (John 15:1–7). Moreover, it was a reminder of the Eucharist, in which wine represented the blood of Christ and his sacrifice for the redemption of mankind. The large front of the cross shaft shows another vine scroll, at the base of which an archer is perched. He is shown in a typical tunic from the mid-Saxon period and seems to be wearing a pair of hose. Although he is aiming his bow, we cannot see where exactly. The image of the archer is found elsewhere in Anglo-Saxon art as a metaphor for the Word of God seeking out its target.

It may be significant that the cross was carved from stone rather than wood. The early Anglo-Saxons built with wood and the first stone buildings to be erected after the departure of the Romans were associated with churches and monasteries, constructed with the help of craftsmen from the Continent.

The stone cross was removed from the church in the sixteenth century, presumably in connection with the religious turmoil following the dissolution of the monasteries under Henry VIII (1509–47). It was broken up and the part preserved today was hollowed out and used as a trough for watering horses before it came to the British Museum.

Anglo Saxon

From Sheffield, South Yorkshire, England

Early 9th century AD, modified in the 16th century (?)

Height 153.0 cm

1924,1015.1

64 THE BRANDON PLAQUE

This gold plaque with unusual imagery was found on the banks of the Little Ouse river. A human figure with a haloed eagle head is dressed in a long-sleeved garment with a decorative neckline, worn beneath loosely falling drapery. In his hands, the beast-man is holding a book and a quill pen. The nielloed outline of the image is precise and naturalistic, and for those who might not recognize the iconography as the symbol of St John the Evangelist, the artist has added the inscription 'SC̄S IOHANNIS EVANGELISTA'. The depiction of the beast-man is a rare departure from the usual representation of St John by an eagle (**102**).

Several extensive excavation campaigns at Brandon identified a high-status settlement of the middle Saxon period from around AD 600 to AD 900. It included some thirty-five buildings, a church and a cemetery. An area where large-scale cloth-processing took place was also discovered. Suffolk has no sources of metal ores, and yet there was evidence for metal working. The numerous high-quality finds confirm the impression of an important site which is given by the gold plaque. Ecclesiastical material, inscribed objects and writing implements (*styli*), as well as the layout of the settlement, which placed special emphasis on the church and a number of high-status buildings clustered around it, may suggest that there was a monastery on this site.

Holes in the four corners of the plaque show that it was attached to a hard surface, for example a book cover (**145**) or crucifix (**151**). The lack of a niello border at the top of the plaque, as well as the upturned gaze of the beast-man, make the latter possibility less likely, although the symbol of St John the Evangelist is commonly found at the top of crucifixes.

The confident execution easily rivals contemporary book illumination, such as the Mercian Book of Cerne, and it has been suggested that the metalworker was closely familiar with manuscript art as the figure looks as if it has been drawn with ink. The outstanding quality of the object and the precious metal from which it was made indicate that the Brandon plaque was a commission for a pre-eminent patron or community. It is feasible that it was made either for or at the possible monastery at Brandon.

Anglo-Saxon
From Brandon, Suffolk, England
Early 9th century AD
Length 3.4 cm
1978,1101.1

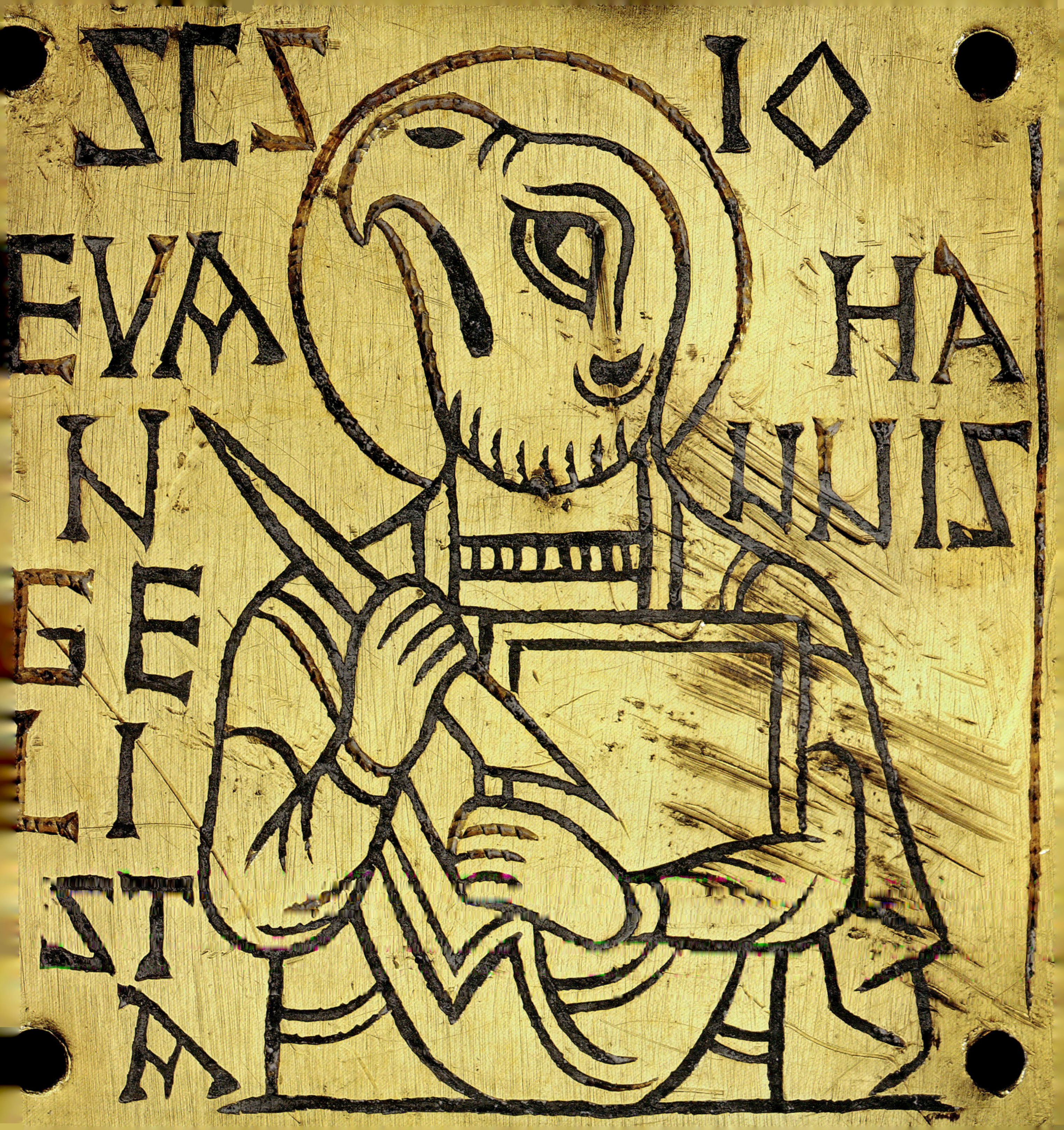
SCS IOHANNIS
EVANGELISTA

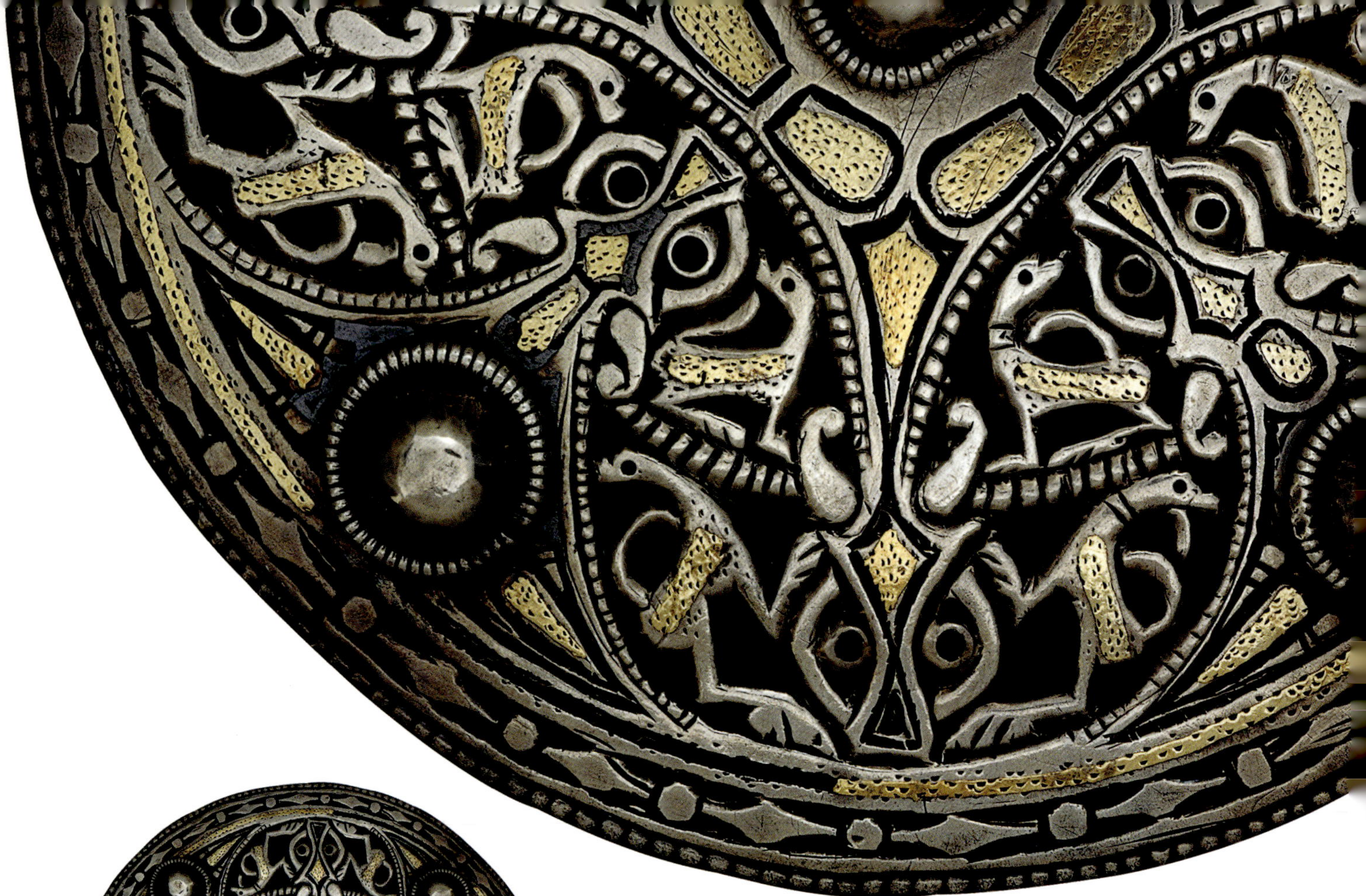

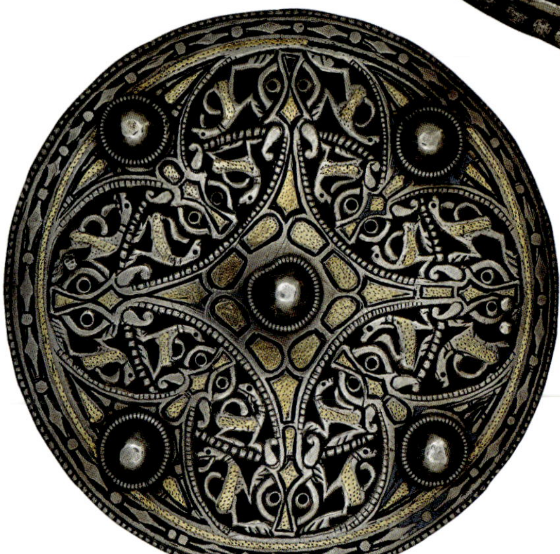

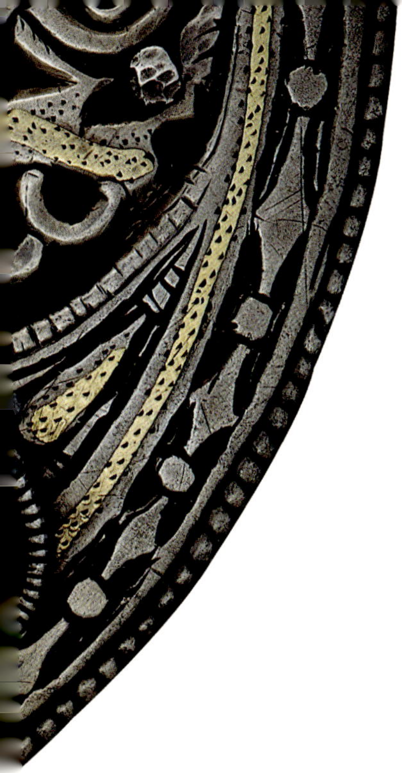

65 THE STRICKLAND BROOCH

One of the most opulent silver disc brooches from Anglo-Saxon England is the Strickland Brooch, named after the family to whom it once belonged. Its surface is brought to life by the contrast of cast and openwork sections as much as by the polychrome or multicoloured effect of the contrasting silver, niello and gold. The presence of the latter is unusual as the brooch was made at a time when gold was scarce in England, save for the occasional finger-ring (**66**). If used at all, gold was restricted to inlays, as here, or to small areas of gilding, as on the King's School, Canterbury, brooch, also in the British Museum. The openwork construction of the brooch was not only attractive and in keeping with the style of the time, but also reduced the amount of precious metal needed.

At first glance the layout of the brooch may seem confusing, but on closer inspection a more orderly menagerie emerges. Four large animals spring from the central boss of the brooch and divide the round surface into sections. Inscribed into these are four additional animals with large heads and goggly eyes, seen from above. These, however, point inwards from the frame of the brooch. In between the large heads are sixteen small cavorting quadrupeds. Some resemble dogs with lolling tongues, while others are fantastic creatures with lappets or flaps growing from their heads.

The repertoire is an example of the Trewhiddle Style, named after a hoard from Cornwall, which contained very distinctive metalwork with beaded frames and speckled surfaces (**68**), animals wearing collars and animal heads with curled ears. The lolling tongues are reminiscent of the style element known as the Mercian Beast (**59**), which is found on late eighth and early ninth-century metalwork associated with the kingdom of Mercia.

Like many other objects in this book, the brooch had a chequered history in its afterlife. The previous owner found it 'in the bottom drawer of a "Queen Anne" bureau', which he had inherited. He took a liking to it and then used it as a paperweight on his desk for two or three years before offering it to the British Museum for purchase.

Anglo-Saxon
Previously kept in Yorkshire, England
Mid-9th century AD
Maximum diameter 11.2 cm
1949,0702.1

66 THE ÆTHELSWITH RING

By coincidence, the British Museum's collection contains two rings associated with the royal house of Wessex. One mentions Æthelwulf, father of Alfred the Great, while the ring here names Æthelswith, Alfred's sister, on its back. Æthelswith married Burgred of Mercia in AD 853 or 854 and probably followed him into exile when he was expelled by Danish Vikings in AD 874. She remained in Italy after his death and died in AD 888 at Pavia, while on a pilgrimage to Rome.

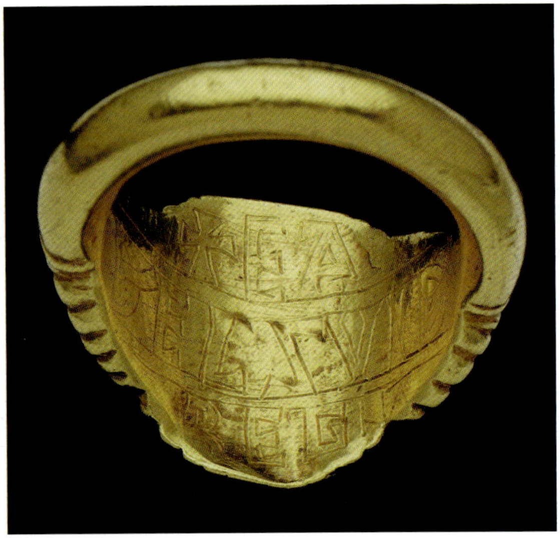

The ring is heavily cast in gold and the plain hoop expands into curved shoulders. Each shoulder panel is inhabited by a quadruped on a nielloed background. On the round bezel a small animal in the Trewhiddle Style (**65**) is shown in profile between the letters A and Đ, which provide a clue to its interpretation as the Agnus Dei or Lamb of God (**93**). The lamb as a symbol of the risen Christ appeared in contemporary Frankish manuscript illumination, but its presence on a piece of Anglo-Saxon metalwork is rather unusual, as are the find circumstances of the ring. It was discovered in a ploughed field in West Yorkshire in 1870 and the finder is said to have attached it to the collar of his dog, before it attracted the attention of a jeweller who bought it. Today, it is one of the most iconic pieces of the Trewhiddle Style with its stylized animals which could have stepped out from the pages of a comic book, interspersed leafy sprigs and the attractive colour contrast between the precious metal and the black niello.

The inscription '+ EAÐELSVIÐ' is engraved on the back of the bezel in capital letters. This may not have happened at the time when the ring was made, but it seems to confirm its significance as a token of office, a means of identification for a messenger or a gift from Æthelswith to a loyal follower, rather than indicating that it was her personal possession.

Anglo-Saxon
From Aberford, West Yorkshire, England
Probably AD 853/4–74
Height of bezel 2.0 cm
Bequeathed by A.W. Franks
AF.458

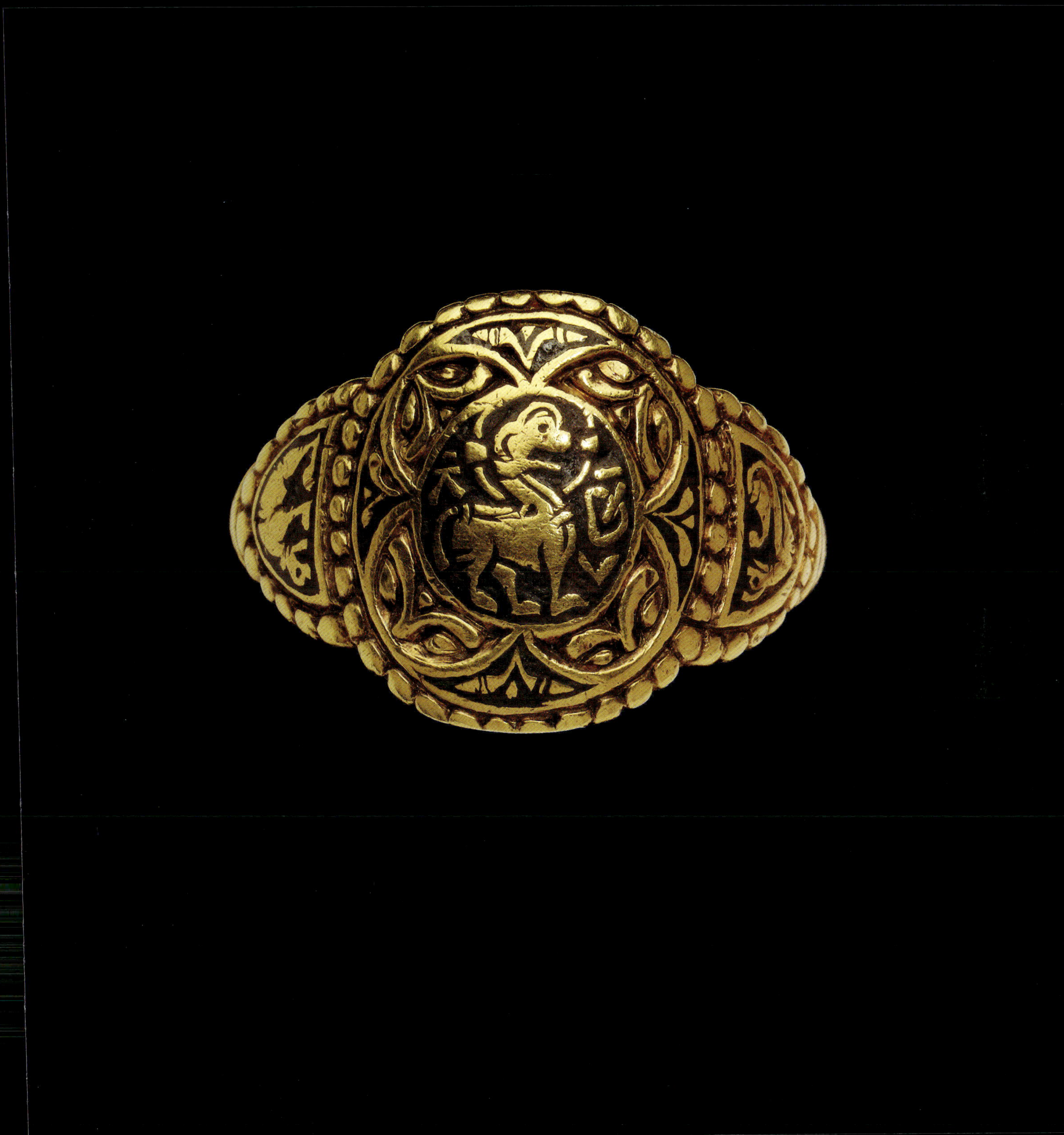

67 THE FULLER BROOCH

This large silver disc brooch, described by one scholar as being 'severely beautiful', is indeed so splendid that it was at one point considered to be a fake and removed from the Ashmolean Museum in Oxford, where it was on loan. It was subsequently forgotten, but the emergence of the Strickland Brooch (**65**) prompted renewed interest. After detailed scientific examination and academic study, its authenticity was reinstated and the brooch was acquired by the British Museum.

The brooch follows the traditional form of the disc type where niello is used to delineate the design, but it is distinguished by its novel iconography. Four segments are inscribed in the central disc, each of which contains a naturalistic human figure. On the top right, a man stands with his arms folded behind his back smelling a stylized plant. The bottom right segment is filled by another man seeming to touch his right hand with his left. Next to him, a third man holds his hand behind his ear, while the fourth one, at the top left, has his whole hand inserted into his mouth. They clearly represent the senses of smell, touch, hearing and taste. At the centre of the brooch is a figure holding two stylized plant leaves and staring at the beholder with large eyes. This is a depiction of sight, which was considered to be the most superior of the senses as it was the one with which God's creation was beheld. Creation is reflected in the roundels framing the central medallion, which is decorated with humans, birds, quadrupeds and geometric ornament reminiscent of a starry sky.

The brooch's style and its programme of complex imagery places it firmly within the intellectual climate prevalent at the court of Alfred the Great (AD 871–99). The significance of the sense of sight has been linked with Alfred's references to 'the Mind's Eye', through which wisdom could be sought and ultimately achieved. The brooch may illustrate his quest for wisdom through learning. In his writings, Alfred explicitly encouraged others to follow this path and perhaps the brooch was a visual admonition to seek wisdom through study using all the senses God had bestowed.

Anglo-Saxon
Unknown findspot
Late 9th century AD
Diameter 11.4 cm
Partly donated by A.W.F. Fuller
1952,0404.1

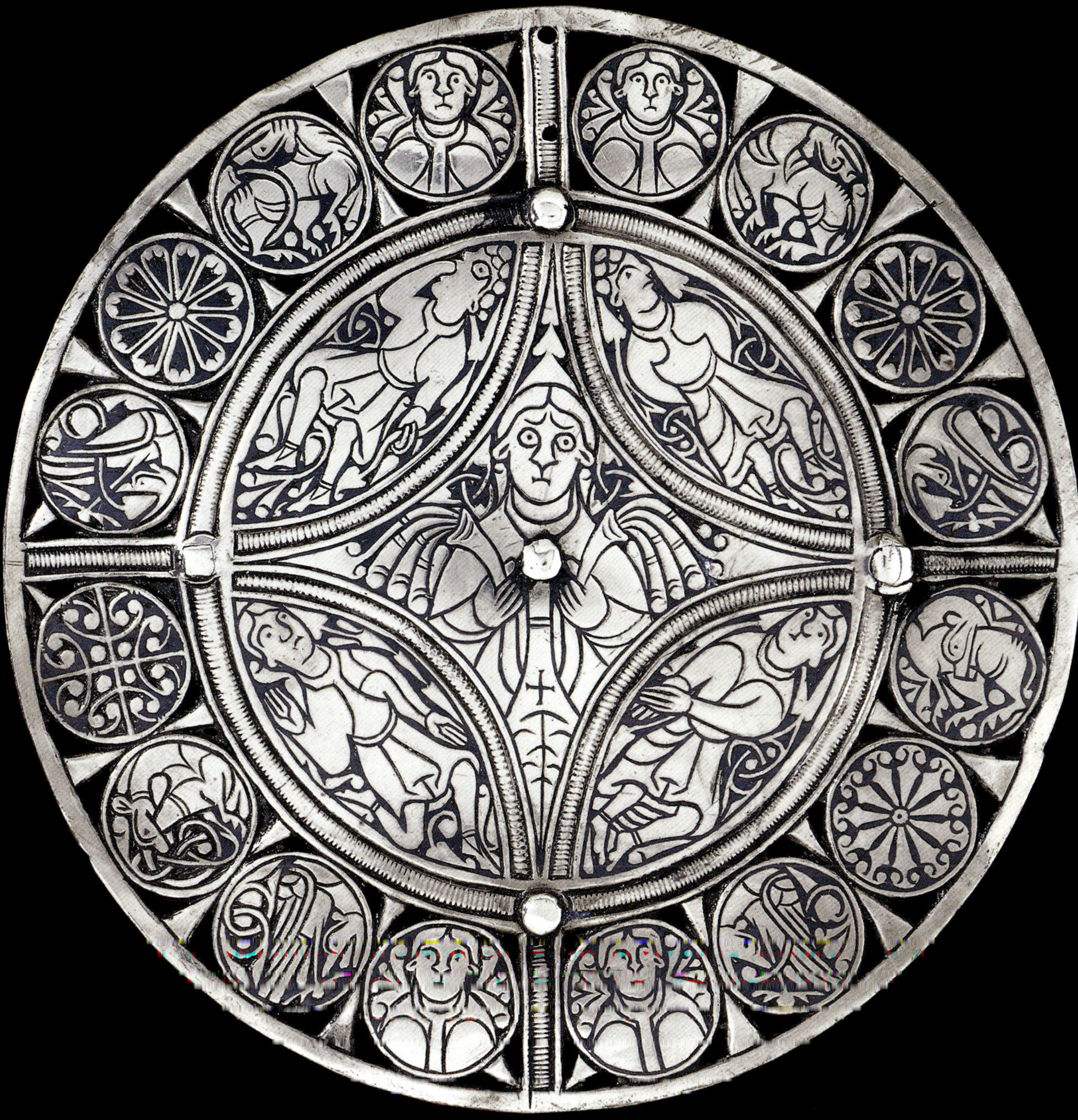

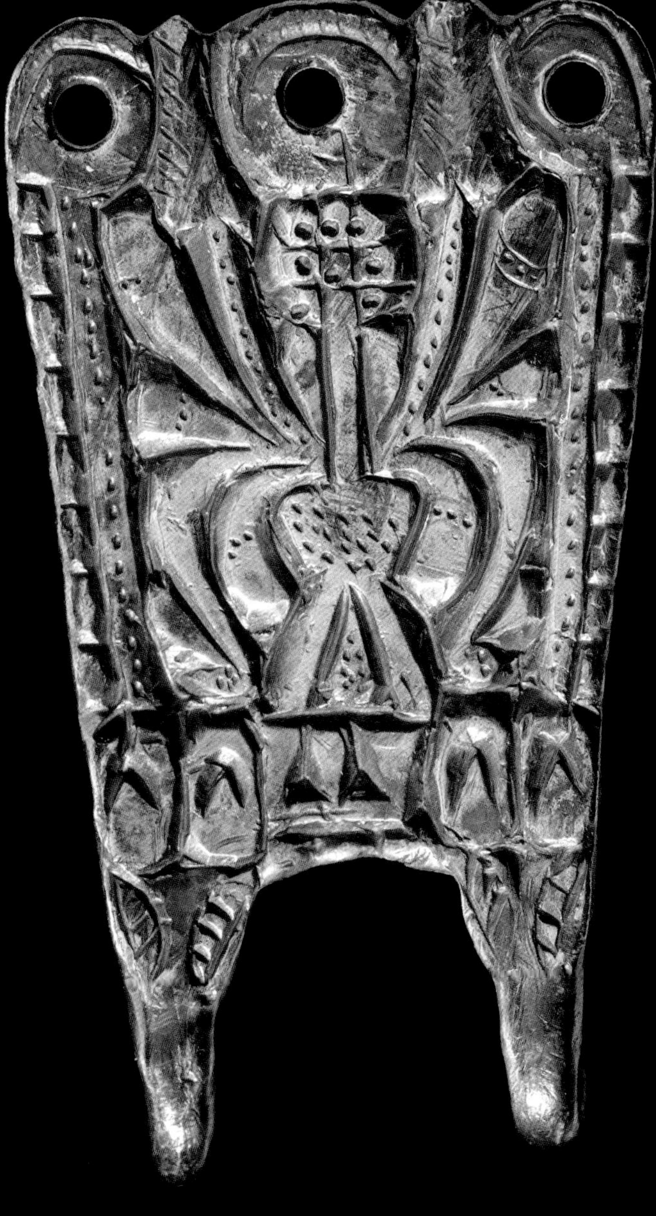

68 HOOKED TAG

Hooked tags were the zip fasteners of their day. They were used for fastening clothing, but also for closing bags and pouches. A huge variety was produced in both copper alloy and silver, and even the smallest and simplest were often decorated. The wide distribution of silver hooked tags and the niello inlay on many examples indicate that even for those living in the country, there was moderate wealth to allow for the purchase of the odd nice dress accessory. Hooked tags were an enduring fashion and in use from the late eighth century onwards, but they did not outlast the Norman Conquest.

The large size of the Charminster find, its intricate ornament and the presence of two hooks distinguish it from the majority of other tags. It is very solidly made as a generous amount of silver was used. The plate is decorated with an ornate flower, and some of the curving leaves and flower stems are textured with fine dots and incisions. A dotted and beaded bar frame the composition on either side. Below, two stylized animal heads extend into the hooks. When seen from above, as they are here, only their long ears are visible. Between the animal heads there is a cipher resembling the letter 'E' lying on its back.

The animal heads are paralleled by those on a hooked tag from Hampshire, which is dated to the tenth century on the basis of its Winchester Style ornament (**71**). The beaded border and finely stippled ornament of the Charminster piece are characteristic of the Trewhiddle Style (**65**, **66**), which is commonly dated to the ninth century, although the date range has recently been extended into the tenth century.

From a construction point of view, hooked tags were a slight failure. Many examples have torn eyelets, testifying to the way in which they were lost. Likewise, the tip of many hooks is missing, as it is from one of the hooks here. The tag is otherwise unblemished, but faint green traces of corrosion on its back may mean that it went missing while attached to another object which had a copper alloy component.

Anglo-Saxon

From Charminster, Dorset, England

Late 9th to early 10th century AD

Length 3.5 cm

2009,8029.1

69 THE SITTINGBOURNE SEAX

The seax is a single-edged knife or short sword. It was never as popular with the Anglo-Saxons as with their Continental neighbours, but some of the most elaborate examples have been found in England.

The iron blade has a characteristic angled back and tapers to a sharp point. Both sides of the blade are embellished with complex inlay and appliqués of silver, copper, brass and niello. The attractive contrast of silver and red copper is also used on a slightly earlier spearhead from the River Thames (**114**). Even the spine of the seax was inlaid with polychrome or multicoloured wires and panels up to the angle of the blade. As on the sides of the blade, much of this is now missing.

A number of panels are arranged on the left face of the seax. The one nearest the tip contains a winged animal. Its wing ends in an acanthus leaf and lush acanthus foliage is found in several other panels. Another animal, this time S-shaped, inhabits the plaque nearest the handle. The two central panels contain Old English letters reserved against a metal background. These are still legible and read '+ S[I]GEBEREHT ME AH', or 'S[i]gebereht owns me'. This inscription is matched by lettering on the other face of the blade, proclaiming that someone called Biorhtelm made the seax. While not particularly common, inscriptions naming individuals are known from objects dating to the middle and later Saxon period. This includes those where a name was integral to the purpose of the object, such as seals (**74**), as well as those where it was not (**66**, **121**).

Another seax which was found in the River Thames in London, now in the collection of the British Museum, names in runes a certain Beagnoth, along with a full runic alphabet, and there are a small number of other seaxes inlaid with male names. This may well be a reflection of the prestige a skilled weapon smith enjoyed in late Saxon society.

The Sittingbourne seax was discovered when foundations were dug near the *Daily Chronicle* paper mills, and was later donated to the British Museum.

Anglo Saxon
From Sittingbourne, Kent, England
Early 10th century AD
Length 32.1 cm
Donated by E. Lloyd
1881,0623.1

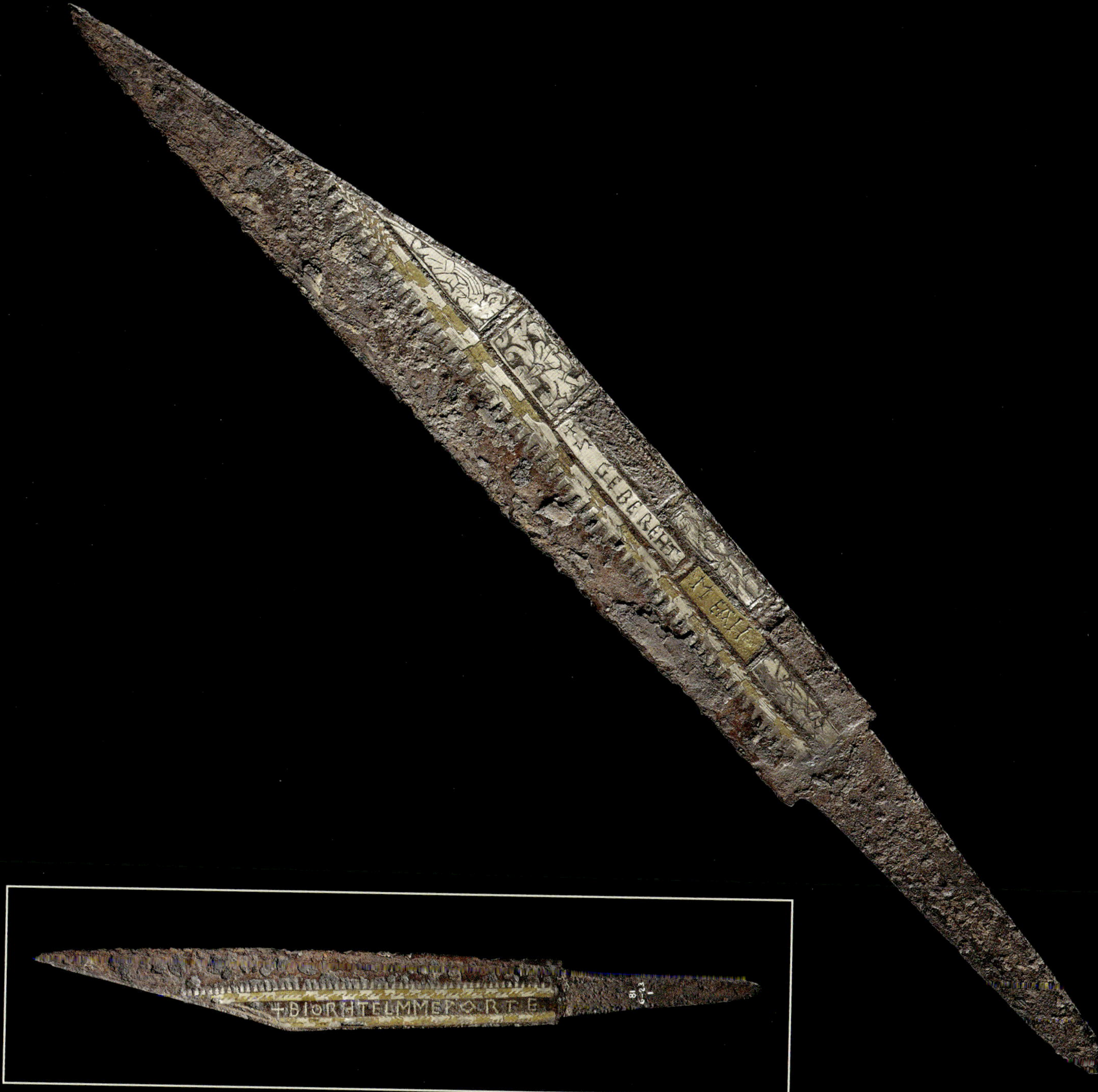

70 CRUET

Ottonian (?)
Unknown findspot
10th century AD
Height 7.2 cm
Bequeathed by A.W. Franks
AF.3175

This miniature cruet would probably have been used during Mass to pour water or wine into the chalice. If so, it is an outstanding surviving example of pre-Reformation church plate, of which little is known. Its precious appearance would certainly have been fitting for an Anglo-Saxon church or monastery. For instance, a chronicle for Abingdon near Oxford describes a lavish tenth-century donation of gold and silver altar plate, including cruets and gem-encrusted gospel books. According to the author of the chronicle, these precious trappings were not only considered appropriate for the Mass, but were also meant to enhance the beauty of the church.

A veritable menagerie covers the surface of the cruet. Pairs of back-to-back birds are shown feeding on the acanthus leaves under which they perch (**95**). Animal masks are interspersed between the birds, and the spout is formed of a fantastical beast with large eyes, a mane and a wide-open mouth. The handle is in the shape of an animal devouring a serpent and above it the remains of a hinged lid are preserved. The body of the vessel, with its complex relief decoration, spout and foot ring were cast in one piece in the lost-wax technique (**144**).

For a long time the cruet was considered to be Anglo-Saxon due to its affinities with southern English manuscript illumination and metalwork in the Winchester Style (**71**). Yet a recent reassessment has highlighted the differences to other copper-gilt Anglo-Saxon work on the one hand and the similarities with Ottonian German metalwork on the other. There are a number of parallels to various features of the cruet in book mounts, liturgical candlesticks and a range of different fittings. There is a close comparison of the detail of the snake being swallowed by another animal in Ottonian book illumination and elements of the plant ornament on the cruet foot also appear in Ottonian manuscripts. Therefore it seems more likely that the cruet was cast on the Continent, rather than in Anglo-Saxon England.

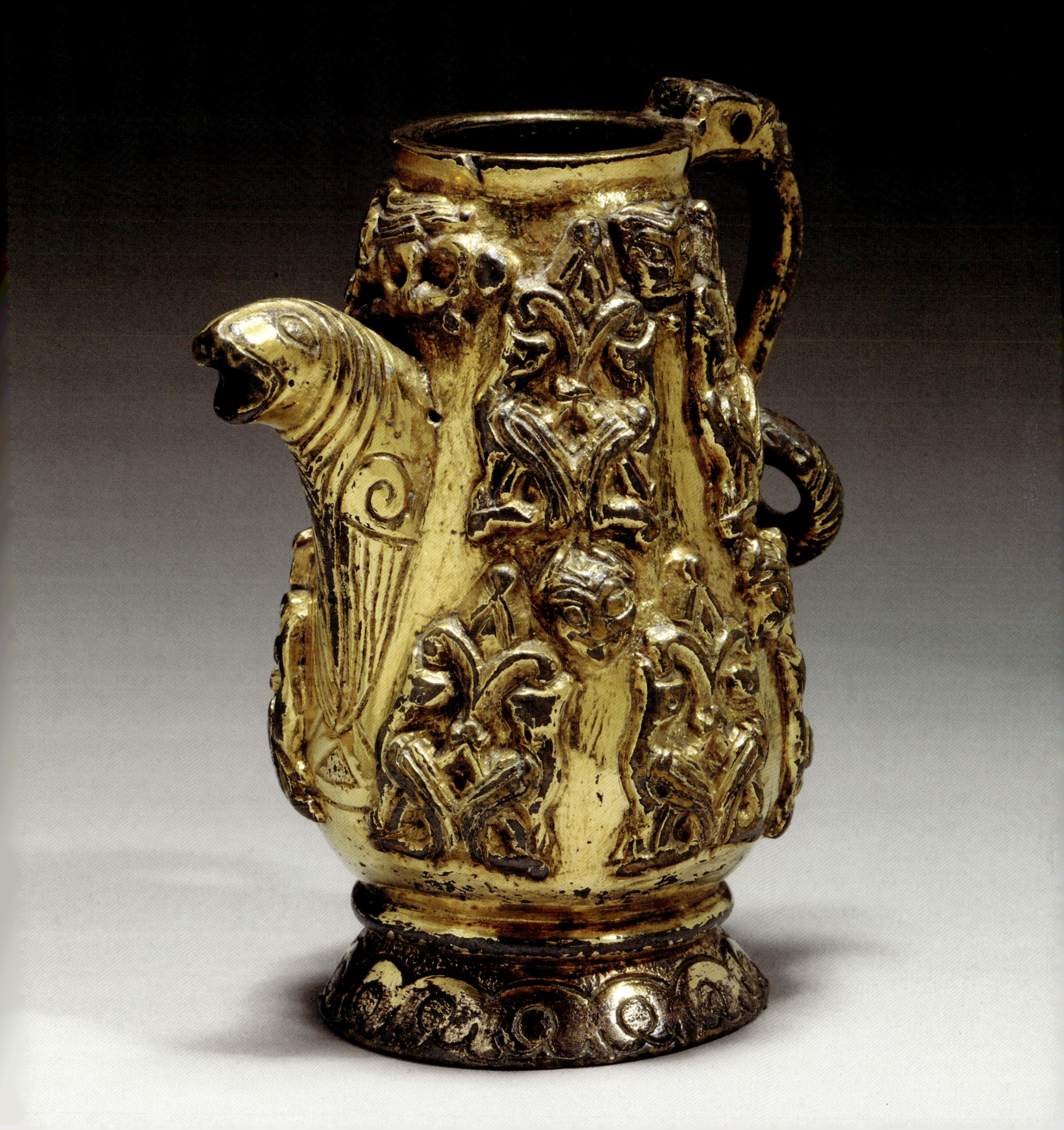

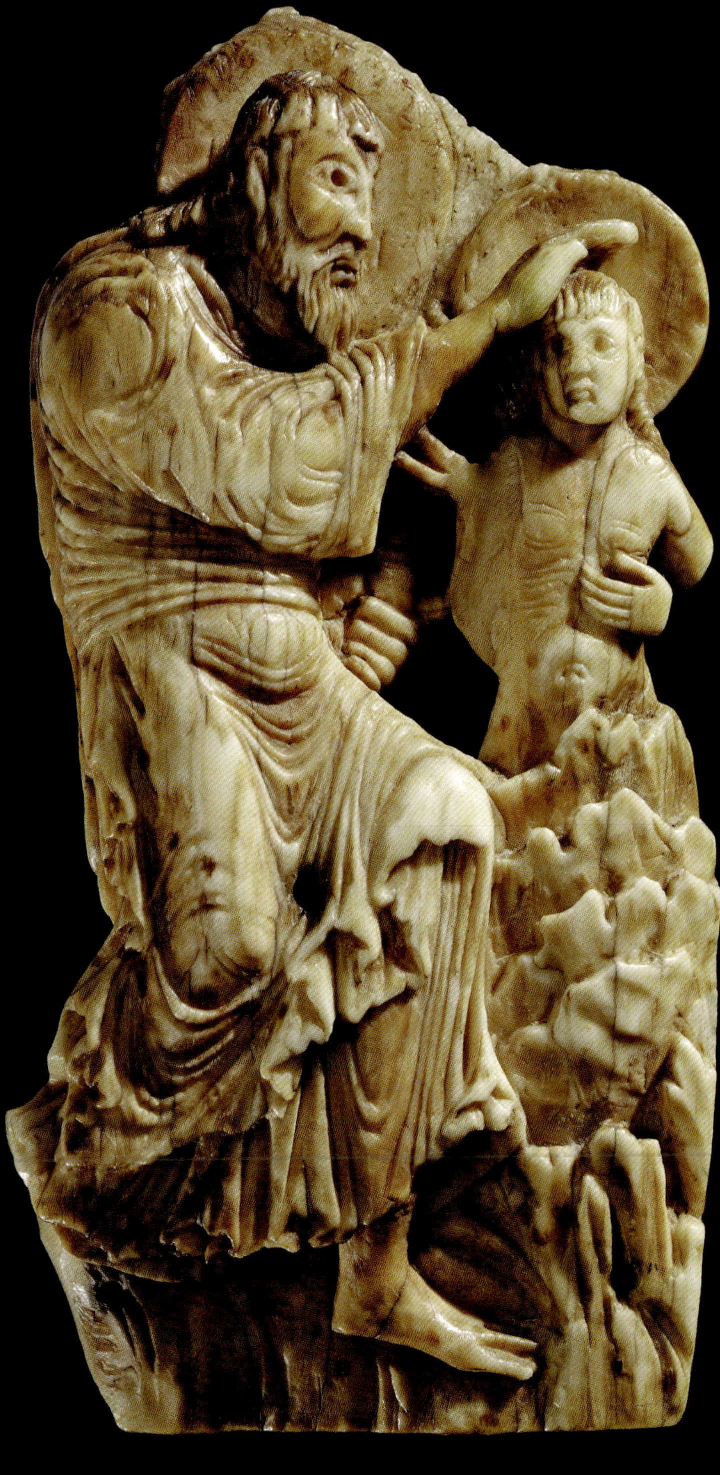

71 THE BAPTISM OF CHRIST

This Anglo-Saxon walrus ivory could not be more different in appearance from the late antique carving (**25**) depicting the same subject matter. This present scene appears to be all about movement: St John the Baptist is in the process of kneeling down or rising up, his torso turned towards Christ, and his lower body facing the viewer. The folds and hems of his two-layered attire are likewise in motion, echoed in the frothing waters of the River Jordan. Perhaps the biggest difference between the two ivories is, however, in the figure of Christ. Although his face is ageless and could be that of a young man, he is small, almost child-like. He is naked, although strategically placed waves shield his lower body. The rounded form of his abdomen and the grooves indicating his ribs resemble geometric ornament rather than anatomical detail.

The panel was carved around the same time as a Byzantine ivory in the Treasury of the Church of St Servatius, Quedlinburg, Germany, which was later mounted on a Gospel book named after the emperor Otto III and his sister Adelheid, an important abbess. Again, St John the Baptist is placed on the left, holding his hand over Christ. The latter is shown as a full-length, bearded portrait and although naked, he is also sexless. The scene appears static through the strictly vertical arrangement of all the figures and shows none of the vigour that characterizes Anglo-Saxon ivories of this period. Despite all the differences in style, it is remarkable how similar these panels are, faithfully following an iconography ultimately based on late Roman and early Byzantine models (**25**).

This late Saxon panel was originally larger before it was trimmed back to these two figures and has a number of links to manuscript art. The figure of St John the Baptist closely resembles an image of Christ in the Benedictional of St Æthelwold (fol. 9b) from approximately AD 971–84, perhaps hinting at a common model for both. Moreover the dynamic pose of St John the Baptist, the fluid lines of drapery with jagged hems and the choppy appearance of the waves are elements of the Winchester Style (**68**), which are also seen in book illumination.

Anglo-Saxon
Unknown findspot
Late 10th century AD
Height 9.3 cm
Acquired with contributions by The Art Fund and the Pilgrim Trust
1974,1002.1

72 THE DOWGATE HILL BROOCH

Dowgate Hill in the City of London was the findspot for this brooch which was uncovered during sewer excavations in the nineteenth century.

A bust fills the central roundel of the brooch, executed in cloisonné enamel (**37**), with extremely fine gold wires separating the differently coloured fields. Three roundels on golden stalks on the head of the male figure may represent a diadem or crown, whereas the two golden volutes curling either side of it could represent the kind of decorative hanging ornaments known as *pendilia* which adorn depictions of Byzantine emperors on coins, ivories, mosaics and in manuscripts. A composition of the finest goldwork surrounds the enamel. The ornament is formed of winding tendrils made from filigree wires, surrounded by a plethora of gold granules and curled leaves. It is possible that this imagery had Christian overtones (**63**). The intricacy of this foliage is heightened by the lack of a backplate, which means that the gold frame had to be constructed as an openwork mesh. Four pearls set in dog-tooth gold collars complete the design.

This brooch may have been made in England, but it is more likely to have come from abroad. Some technical details, such as the combination of cloisonné enamel with gold and pearls, and a pin apparatus set towards one side rather than across the middle of the reverse, are also present on other high-status jewellery, such as the Townley brooch (**104**) and several marvellous brooches possibly associated with the German Ottonian and Salian imperial houses. The production of the latter has been debated recently and it seems likely that they were made in Italy rather than Germany.

On the other hand, there are a few comparable objects from England, such as a gold, filigree and pearl disc from Worcestershire, and a cloisonné roundel showing the Hand of God, both of which are in the British Museum, which could be either late Saxon or Ottonian. Charles Roach Smith (1807–90), a previous owner of this brooch, certainly had an opinion. He thought that 'the arrangement of the dress and the simplicity of the crown, have altogether a purer and chaster stamp than the Byzantine works exhibit'.

Ottonian, Italian or late Saxon
From London, England
Late 10th to 11th century AD
Diameter 3.6 cm
1856,0701.1461

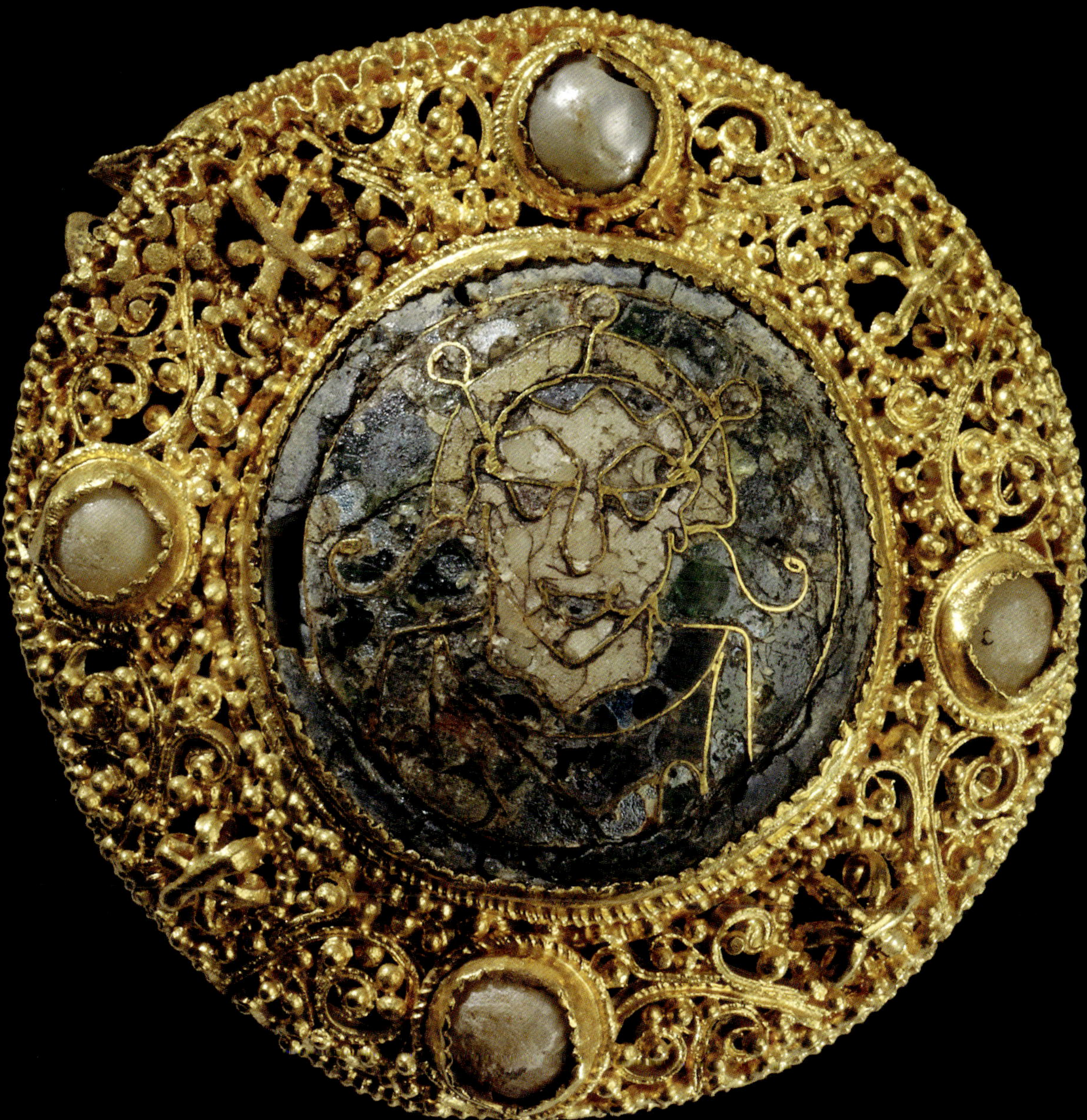

73 THE ALCESTER TAU CROSIER

Church staffs of office came in two basic forms: some with crooked heads (**149**) and others less commonly with a T-shaped head. The Alcester crosier falls into the latter category and it is called a Tau crosier after the Greek name for the letter T. Judging from manuscript illumination, this form of crosier was particularly popular with abbots in England and France during the eleventh and twelfth century. This preference may stem from a late tenth-century order recorded in a French manuscript which advises abbots to use Tau crosiers rather than the crooked variety. In late antiquity the Tau shape had been commonly used to depict the Cross on which Christ was crucified (**15**), before the Latin cross became the standard form.

The walrus ivory relief of the Alcester crosier is exceptional in the depth of its carving and the degree to which the freestanding parts were undercut. Small flecks of gilding are still visible in a few protected places. Originally, it formed a shining backdrop to the carved relief. The imagery on both sides of the crosier is centred around the figure of Christ. On the side shown here he is seen purposefully striding from the grave, vindicating Sin and Death who are represented by a lion and a dragon on whose necks he steps. The other side features the Crucifixion. From this central point two volutes curl outwards, covered in stylized foliage and large flowers. The plantwork is inhabited by small fantastical animals with big bellies and ends with two griffin heads, one of which is now missing. The upper corners of the Tau are formed from the profiles of the sharp-toothed monsters.

There are excellent parallels for the griffin heads in an illuminated psalter from Canterbury. Both the abundant acanthus foliage inhabited by small beasts and the trumpet-shaped flowers have close affinities with an illuminated manuscript probably from the same school. These examples, as well as the overall appearance of the carving, suggest a date in the early eleventh century.

Anglo-Saxon

From Alcester, Warwickshire, England

Early 11th century

Width 14.0 cm

Donated by the Friends of the British Museum with a contribution from The Art Fund

1903,0323.1

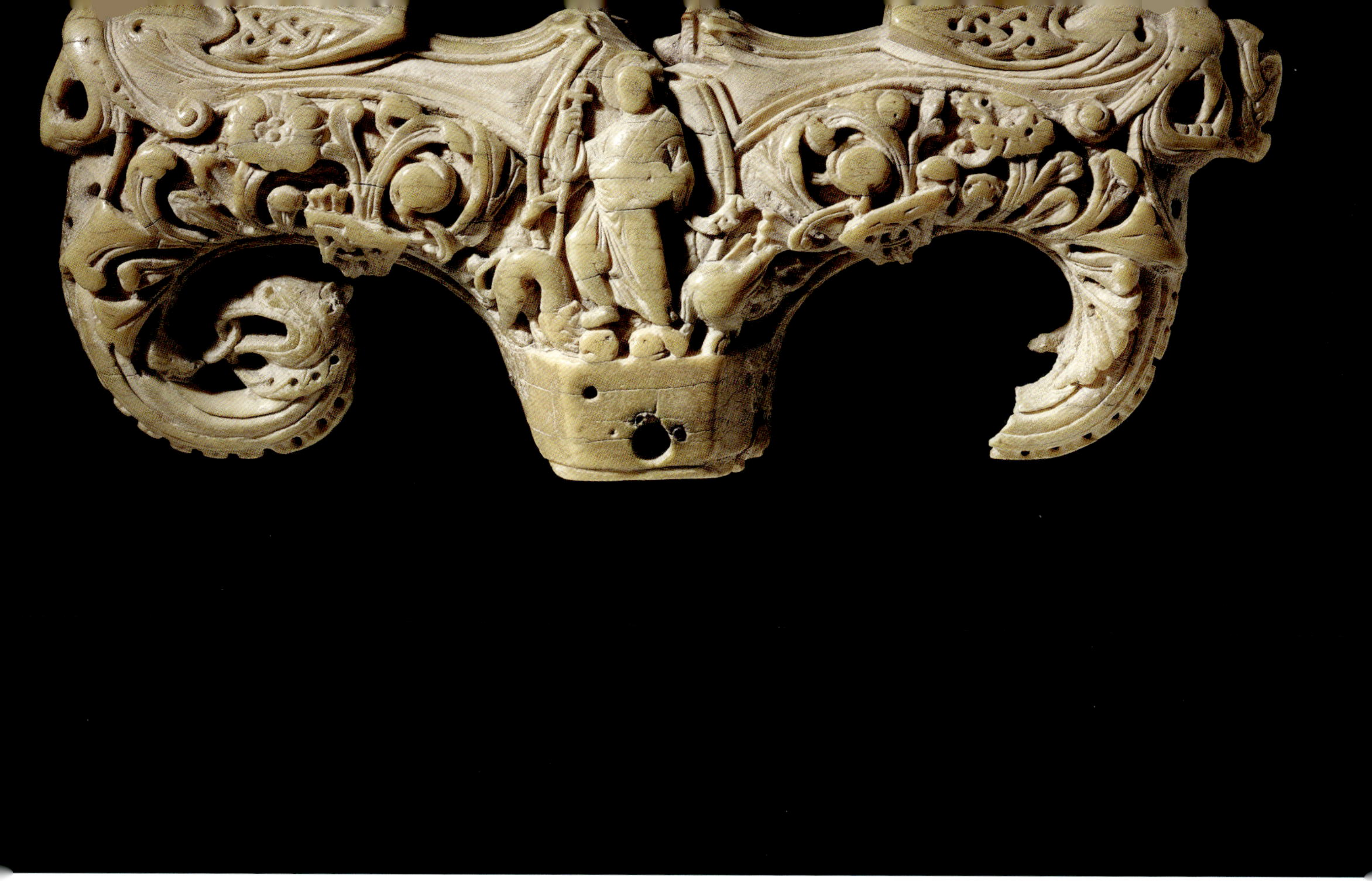

74 SEAL DIE

Anglo-Saxon
From Wallingford, Berkshire, England
Mid-11th century, before 1066
Length 8.6 cm
1881,0404.1

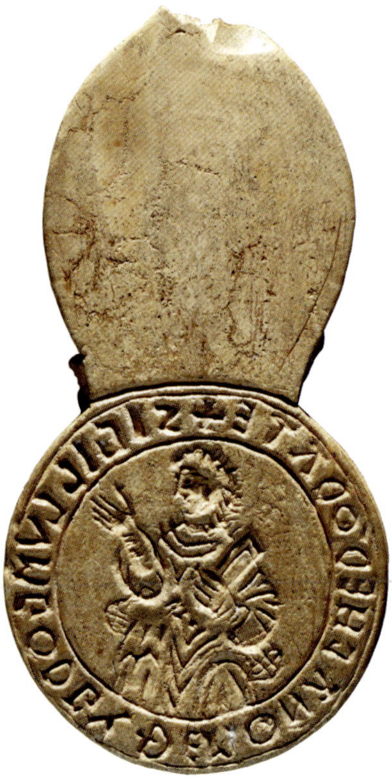

A small cache of objects comprising a double-sided comb, a whetstone and this seal die was discovered in a garden at Wallingford in August 1879. The latter had been carved from walrus ivory, as elephant ivory was no longer available in northern Europe at this time (**75**).

On the front of the seal die the image of a man holding a sword is surrounded by a Latin inscription identifying him as 'Godwyn the thegn'. In other words, he was a nobleman in service to a higher lord. The image is close to that on a coin type issued by King Harthacnut, the Danish ruler of England between 1040 and 1042. Royal seals were modelled on coinage and so presumably the Godwin example follows the design of the coin in order to lend the seal, and by implication the missive that it sealed, more authority. This point is reinforced by the fact that swords were regularly shown on seal dies.

On the oval handle above Godwin two seated male figures are turned towards each other, while their feet rest on a human figure lying face down. This is an illustration of Psalm 109 which begins: 'The Lord said unto my Lord: Sit thou at my right hand, until I make thine enemies thy footstool.' This is another clear reference to authority and obedience.

The back of the handle is plain, but the roundel bears another engraving, cut by a less accomplished carver than the one who decorated the front. A woman seated on a cushion is surrounded by an inscription naming the seal as that of 'Godgytha, a nun given to God'. The seal die is one of the few objects from England before the Norman Conquest which specifically names a woman (**66**, **121**). As Godgytha's seal is on the back of the die, it is likely that it was added later on. It is possible that she was Godwin's wife or daughter, who used the seal after his death. Godgytha's placement on a cushioned seat is an ancient symbol of a person's importance (**22**), a point which was further emphasized through the document scroll she appears to hold in her left hand.

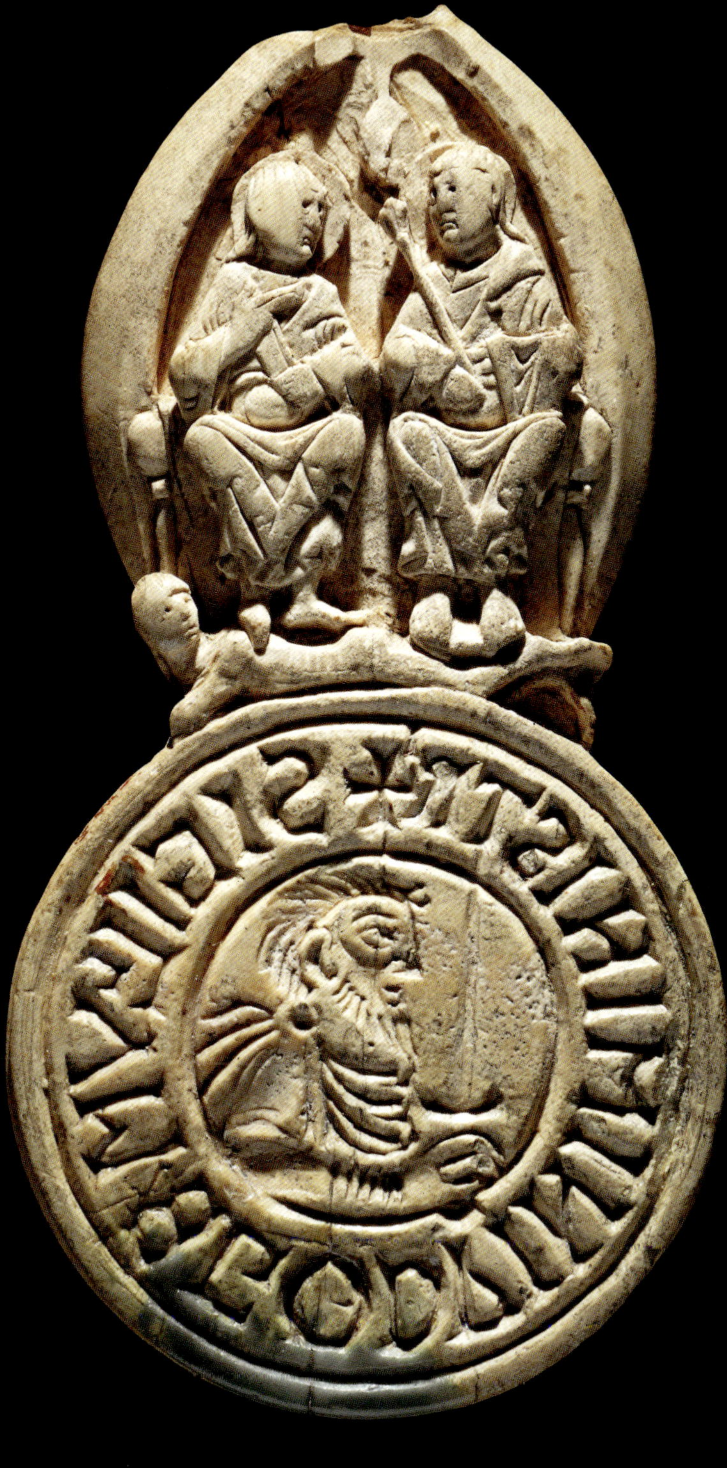

75 WALRUS IVORY CASE

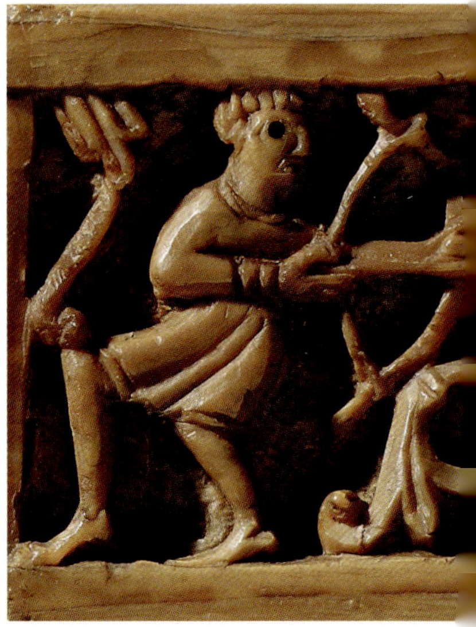

While elephant ivory was a precious, but available, commodity in the Roman and Byzantine Empires, it was very scarce during the early Middle Ages. The Carolingians (p. 167) still seemed to have some access to it, although during that period antique diptychs were on occasion already planed and then recarved. In late Saxon England walrus ivory was used as a substitute and during the Viking period this was imported from northern Norway as well as Greenland. While it is hard and glossy, it does not exhibit the same sheen as elephant ivory as it cannot be so highly polished. Nonetheless, it was a luxurious material, suited to the production of high-status secular (**127**) and religious (**73**) objects.

Lively reliefs cover the top and sides of this box. They are carved and undercut so deeply that they almost give the impression of openwork decoration set over a plain background. A mounted warrior fighting dragons, lions attacking a man, animals crouching in lush foliage and archers aiming at birds, as shown here, all follow a hunting theme.

Parallels for the vivacious scenery can be found in manuscripts spanning the eleventh century. The carvings are firmly rooted in Anglo-Saxon traditions, but the rise of the Romanesque Style (**76**, **127**) is already discernible in the loosely asymmetrical composition of some of the panels, and the physicality and mannered postures of the figures. Depending on how late the case is dated, this may represent Norman influences.

The function of the object has proven to be elusive. One scholar, who acknowledged that there is no evidence to support his theory, suggested that it may have been a case for quill pens. The hunting imagery and prominent depictions of birds in particular led another scholar to propose recently that it may have been a case for a bone whistle. Whistles could be made from bird bones and moreover certain types of bone pipes were used to lure birds.

The quality of the carving as well as the material from which it was made indicate that the original setting for this box would have been one in which both scholarly activities and hunting as a pastime were at home.

Late Saxon
From London, England
Mid- to late 11th century
Length of case 22.7 cm
1870,0811.1

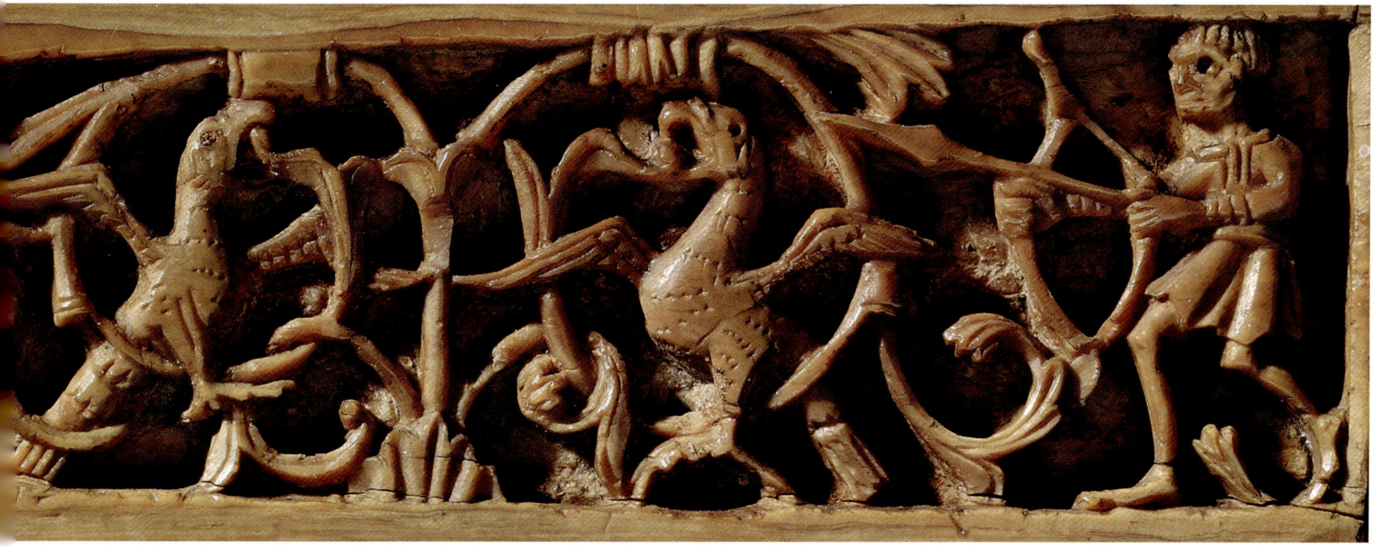

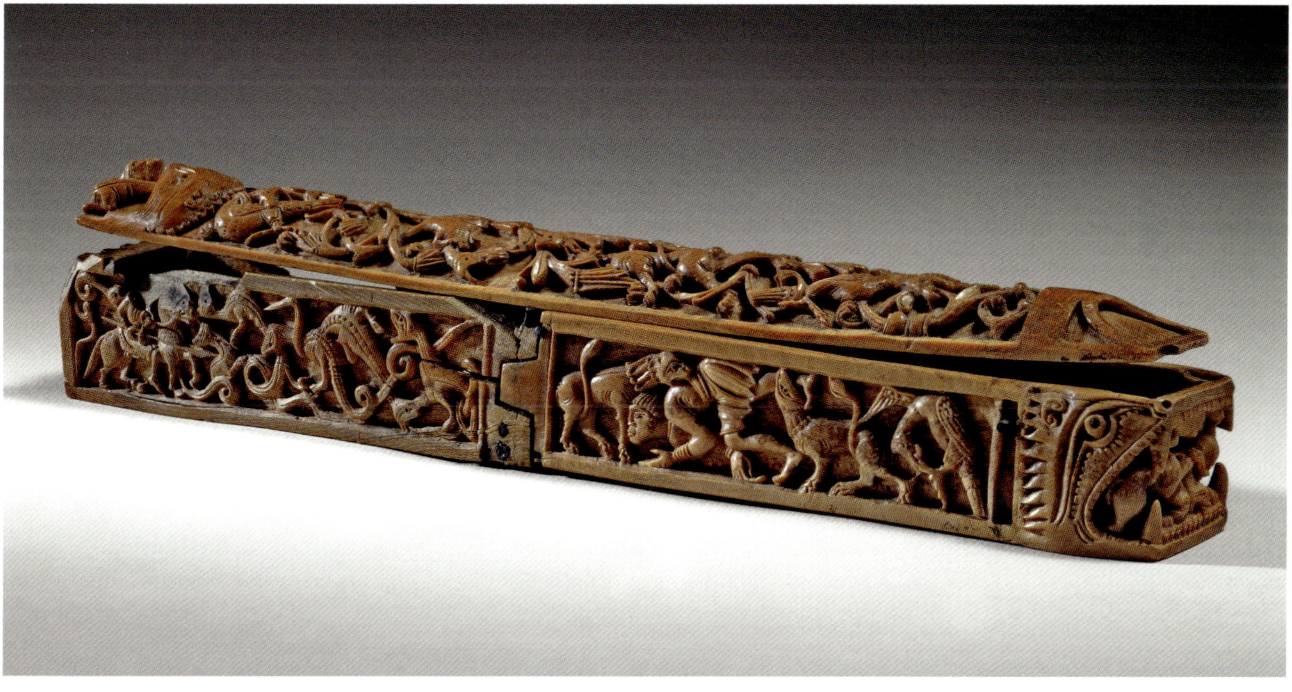

76 PITCHER FRAGMENT

A small bird is perched on the shoulder of this vessel fragment, its beak seeming to hold on to the neck of the vessel. It was formed from a single piece of clay, with the wings made separately and attached to the back. While the clay was still soft, it was incised with a simple but effective pattern of lines to emphasize the shoulders, back and wings.

The sherd once belonged to a tubular pitcher, the spout of which is still intact. To increase stability, a clay band connected the spout to the neck of the vessel. It was decorated with figure-of-eight loops, which seem rather casual when compared to the carefully modelled bird. This pitcher would once have been a piece of high-quality tableware, serving spiced wine, for instance. It is likely that it originally had a lid as well.

The pitcher is an outstanding example of Stamford-type ware. This is named after ceramics from the town in southern Lincolnshire where a major pottery industry sprang up in the ninth century. Stamford produced wheel-thrown ceramics in large quantities, some of which have been found as far away as Scotland and Norway. The link may well have been a Viking one, as Stamford was an important town of the Danelaw, the area controlled by Danish Vikings. Despite the political turmoil of the time, the conditions were apparently right for the first large-scale pottery production to emerge in England since the Romans, and Stamford ware was an integral part of it.

Our green-glazed pitcher followed this potting tradition, but zoomorphic decoration is extraordinarily rare on such ceramics. Nevertheless, Stamford ware and associated types such as this piece can be distinguished from other Romanesque pottery of the eleventh and twelfth century through their high quality and technological mastery. As it appears that only three such pitchers with bird appliqués are known, all of which compare well with one another, it seems possible that they all came from the same workshop, one which was already experimenting with elaborate decorations that would become popular in the course of the thirteenth century.

English
From London, England
Second half of the 12th century
Height 14.4 cm
Donated by the Trustees of H. Christy
1866,0627.147

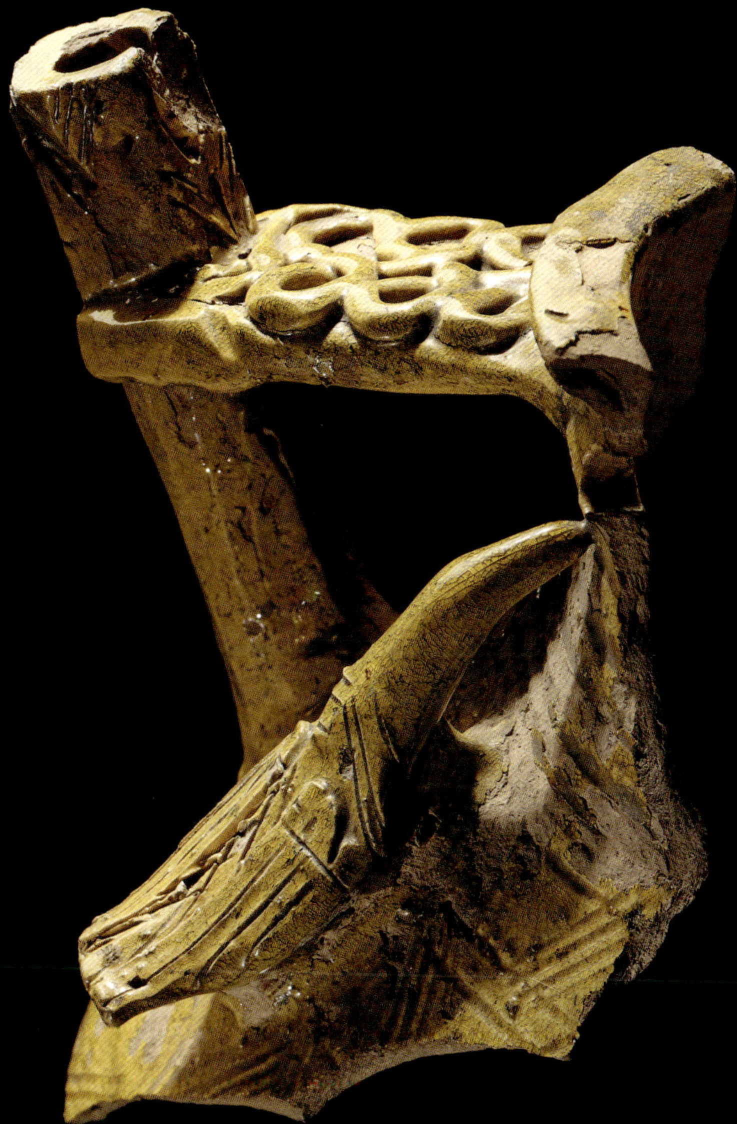

4 GREAT MIGRATIONS

(FIFTH TO TWELFTH CENTURY)

Late Roman authors wrote of the movement of 'barbaric' peoples, in other words those who did not speak Latin or Greek. They presented a picture of people gradually migrating, for example, from central and eastern Europe to North Africa or from Scandinavia to Italy, which is partly compatible with archaeological evidence. For this reason the era is commonly referred to as the 'Migration Period'. What is clear is that these movements were not planned, military invasions. Moreover, the 'peoples' of the ancient authors were not homogeneous blocks, but made up of the descendants of many traditions who affiliated themselves to larger groups with a dominant culture. By outsiders, they were seen collectively as Goths, Vandals, Longobards, Saxons, or any one of the multitude of non-Romans who made an appearance in written records from the fourth century onwards (**Map 2**).

Grave group from Sutri, Italy (see **88**; 1887,0108.2 to 9)

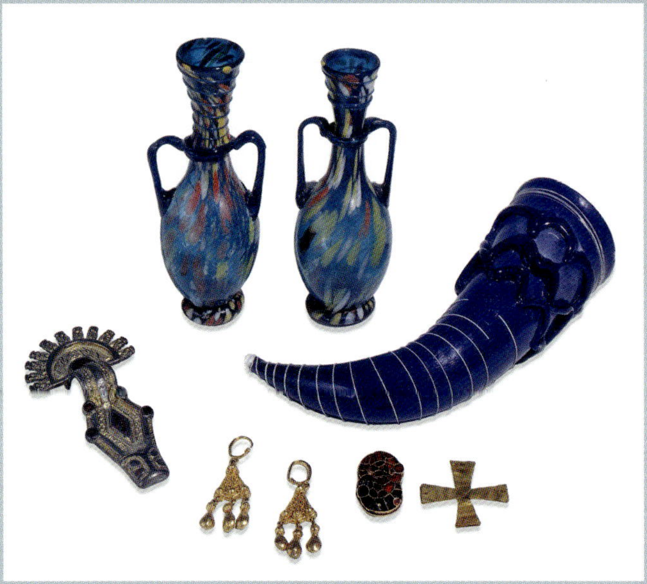

What motivated the onset of these migrations has been much debated, but many factors will have played a role. The advent of the Huns, a horse-riding, nomadic people who swept in from the Eurasian steppes, may have started a domino effect of displaced peoples. On occasion the Romans employed tribal groups, including the Huns, for military service, in return for which they could be granted land inside the empire. In addition, warfare, a deterioration in environmental conditions and the long drawn-out decline of Roman civil and military authority may all have encouraged people to leave their homelands and seek security, opportunities and wealth elsewhere.

Roman objects were prized, integrated into jewellery (**80**) and imitated. Furthermore, some Roman styles and techniques inspired Germanic craftsmanship and evolved into new techniques or forms of ornament. In graves of newcomers around the Mediterranean, for example, we see a rapid fusion of traditional and Roman elements (facing page, **79**).

While the Roman Empire in the West came to an official end in AD 476, some of its social, economic and political structures continued, even if in truncated and altered forms. The Germanic and, later, Slavic elites still looked to the Mediterranean and Byzantium for luxury goods and political recognition. They were the 'Heirs of Rome' and the most successful of them, the Franks, had risen to pre-eminence by the eighth century. Under the Frankish king Charlemagne (AD 768–814), in particular, an interest in the classical heritage was promoted, not least as it positioned the Carolingian dynasty firmly in the Roman imperial tradition (**95**). Their court art inspired new heights in ivory and gem carving (**96–8**), book illumination and architecture, while the Church still played an integral role in preserving literacy and the transmission of iconographies and artistic conventions that had first developed in late antiquity (**15**).

The Frankish Empire split into several kingdoms and out of its eastern part rose the polity which would later be known as the Holy Roman Empire. At its greatest extent it reached from the North Sea to Sicily and its diplomatic links culminated in a marriage between the Ottonian and Byzantine imperial houses (**103**). The Holy Roman Empire was therefore a major conduit for Mediterranean styles and fashions (**72**).

In the eastern Mediterranean, the rise of Islam from AD 622 and the Muslim conquests in the Near East, North Africa and Spain did bring disruption, but also the conservation and further growth of late antique and Byzantine arts (**99**), architecture and scholarship. Numerous classical texts, for instance, are only known today as they were preserved in Arabic transcriptions which were later, for example under Frederick II (1194–1250; **105**), retranslated into Western languages.

By about AD 1000, large power blocks had emerged (**Map 5**), which to a degree are still visible in the political geography of modern-day Europe and the Middle East.

77 SWORD SCABBARD SLIDE

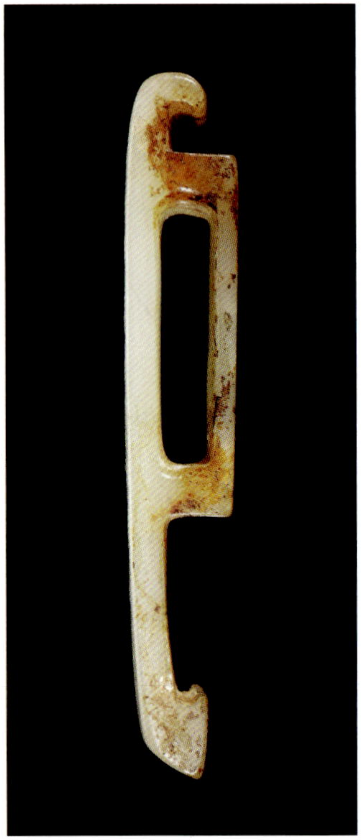

Chinese, with Sarmatian(?) reuse

From the Kuban area, Russia

Made late 2nd century BC to 2nd century AD

Reused 3rd to 4th century AD

Length 9.5 cm

1923,0716.88

This beautifully carved mount from a sword scabbard, shown here from two different angles, is a prime example of how objects can transcend time and space by travelling huge distances and being prized in cultures far away from those which made them.

The mount was originally cut from jade and engraved with a scrollwork pattern in China. This would have been an arduous task as jade is very hard, but it is this quality that explains why the mount and ornament are relatively unworn. Numerous slides of this type are known from the Han Dynasty (206 BC–AD 220).

However, this slide is said to have been found in the Kuban area, north-east of the Black Sea, and would then most likely have been in the possession of a Sarmatian. If the scabbard slide still had its original function, it would have come from a male burial. Given that several sumptuously equipped burials in Bulgaria and the delta of the River Don in southern Russia contained sword scabbards with Chinese jade slides, this is not an unreasonable assumption.

The shape of the slide is governed by its function. Some Roman examples of the late second to the beginning of the fourth century are very similar in form, which appears to be ideally suited to holding and adjusting the straps of a sword harness. These would have run under the curved 'tails' at the top and bottom of the back of the mount, which was fastened to the scabbard through the opening in its middle. It is unclear whether, and if so how, the Roman and Chinese types are related. If they are linked, both may follow prototypes that had developed in the regions north of the Black Sea and which were then adopted and adapted both in the East and West.

This jade slide may have been a chance find or a valued gift that travelled through the eastern steppes or along the Silk Route. Perhaps it was handed down within one family for generations. After all, heroic poems from northern Europe such as *Beowulf* describe old and honoured swords that heroes inherited from their ancestors.

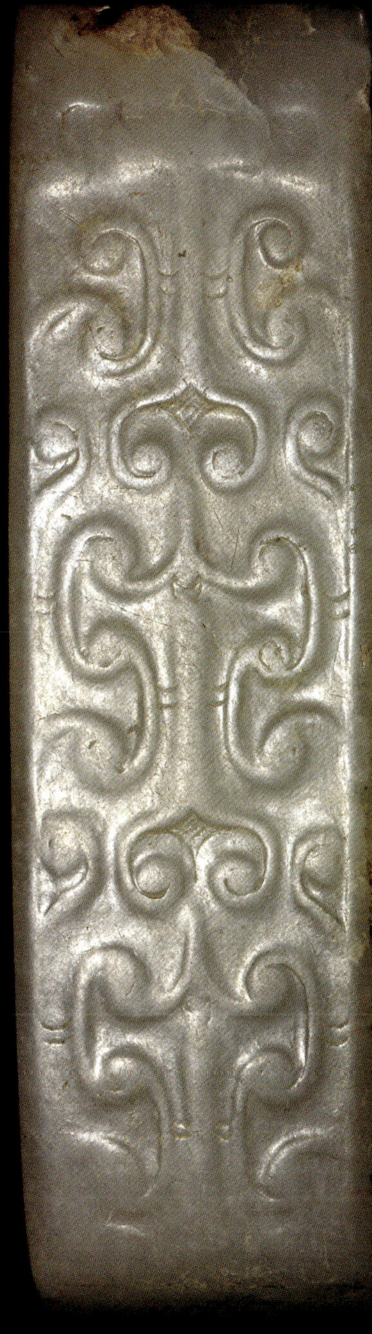

78 BROOCH

Some of the most distinctive gold and garnet work in the collection of the British Museum comes from the areas north of the Black Sea. During the fourth and fifth century artisans here produced exquisitely crafted jewellery, probably influenced by Byzantine fashions. The high standards of the goldsmiths may also have benefited from the traditions of late Scythian metal craft, while some of the techniques in evidence on this brooch belong to a common, late Roman repertoire.

Round late Roman brooches with colourful enamel and millefiori inlay may have been the model for this unique brooch, especially as some of these are also constructed like a wheel with four spokes. The British Museum brooch was cast from silver in one piece before a silver gilt grid with metal cells was applied, which were then inlaid with garnet slips. The border was not simply made from beaded wire, but from single silver granules which were each painstakingly soldered to the edge of the brooch before the seven decorative wedges were added. All in all, a dozen metal parts, ninety-five granules and forty-six garnets were assembled perfectly.

As opposed to later jewellery (**46**), the garnets were not set over gold foil impressed with a waffle pattern, which would have reflected the light falling through the stones and made them glow. Without the reflective foil, the red garnets on this brooch would have appeared almost black unless in direct sunlight.

A diverse and changing population inhabited the areas north of the Black Sea and the Crimean peninsula. The region was originally part of the Roman Empire, and Greeks as well as Scythians and Sarmatians lived there. Later, in the third century, it came under Germanic control by groups such as the Goths and Alans. At least in the Crimea, there is evidence for Jewish people and in AD 325 the first Christian communities emerged. The Huns occupied part of the Crimea during the fifth century and after the demise of the Western Roman Empire, part of the Crimean peninsula remained a Byzantine dominion. This brooch would have been compatible with the aesthetics of many of these groups.

Sarmatian, east Germanic or Hunnic (?)

From Olbia, modern-day Mykolaiv, Ukraine

End of 4th to first half of the 5th century (?)

Diameter 5.5 cm

1923,0716.73

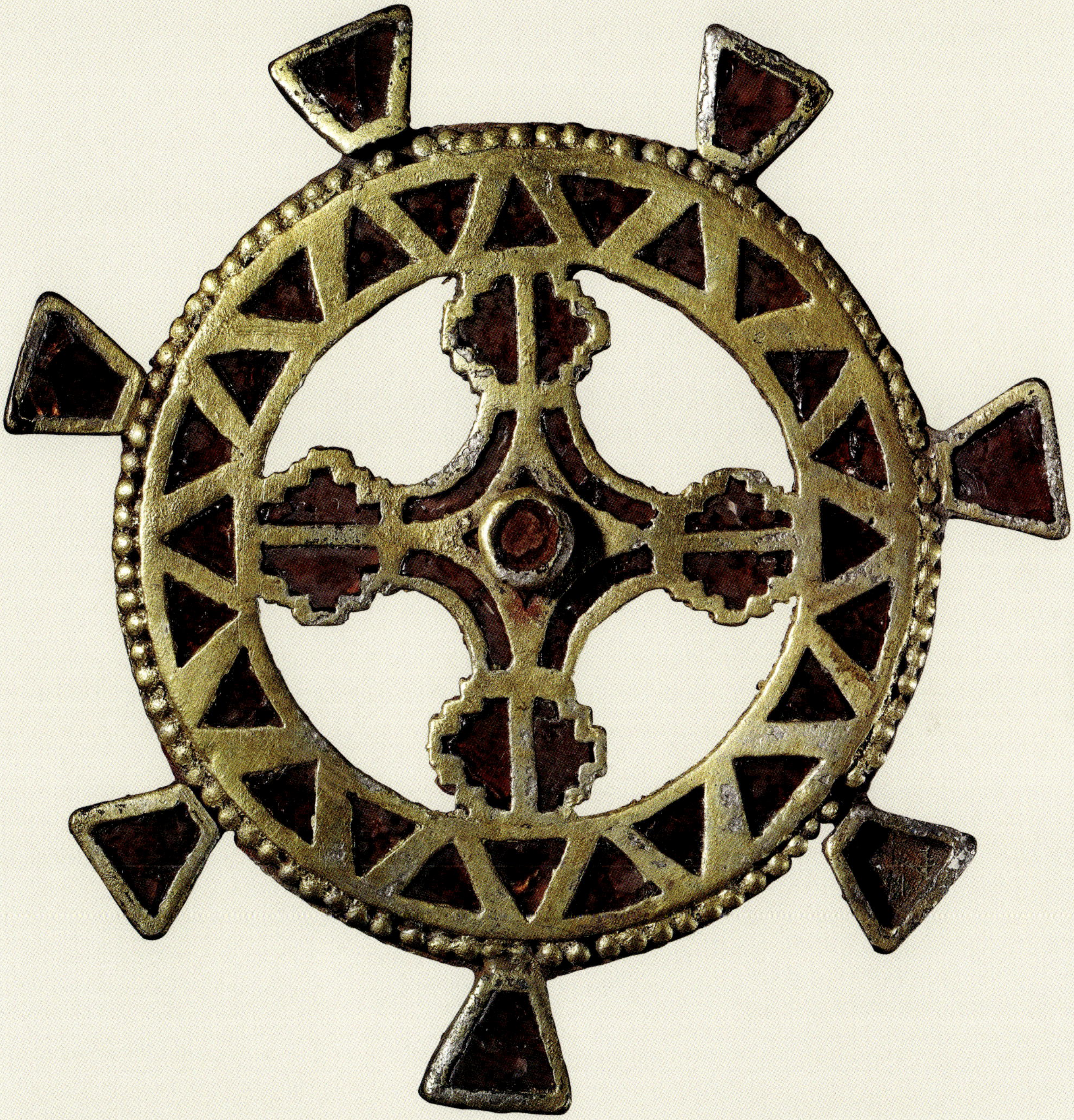

79 BELT BUCKLE FROM NORTH AFRICA

Another example of the hunting scenes so popular in late antiquity (**5**, **12**) unfolds on the oval plate of this belt buckle. The hunter, his feet planted firmly on the ground, is spearing a lion. The animal is roaring and rises up on its hind legs.

Yet despite the gruesome subject matter, the scene has a certain lightness to it, unlike the stern nature of the leopard hunt shown on a Byzantine weight (**23**). The design was punched into the copper alloy plate and then gilt. Various tools with rounded and pointed ends were used, skilfully highlighting the texture of the lion's mane and coat. The hunter is sketched and yet every detail is clearly recognizable, from his short tunic or cuirass worn over a longer undergarment to the effort it takes him to hold back the lion.

Similar buckles have been found as far away as Hungary, but they are most common in the eastern Mediterranean. The buckle plates depict a variety of human and animal images, and many also feature Greek inscriptions, suggesting that they were made in Byzantine workshops.

The present buckle was one of the many sumptuous objects discovered in the grave of a woman near 'Annaba, known in antiquity as Hippo Regius, which was famous because St Augustine was its bishop (AD 395–430). The burial also contained a large pair of disc brooches with colourful glass inlays. It is likely that the woman in this grave was of Vandal descent.

The Vandals were a Germanic people who crossed the Straits of Gibraltar from Spain in AD 429 and by AD 439 had conquered Carthage (**10**, **11**). After this initial turmoil they founded a prosperous kingdom on North African soil, which at times was even recognized by the Byzantine emperor.

The association with the Vandals for this burial cannot be deduced from the buckle alone as it is of Byzantine manufacture and there are parallels of similar brooches from elsewhere in North Africa and the eastern Mediterranean. As opposed to the local Romano-Byzantine population, the Vandals sometimes buried their dead with dress accessories and grave goods, and so the small number of burials like this one stand out in North Africa as they follow a different funerary rite.

Byzantine, from a Vandal grave
From 'Annaba, Algeria
Mid-5th century AD
Length 5.0 cm
1865,0518.3

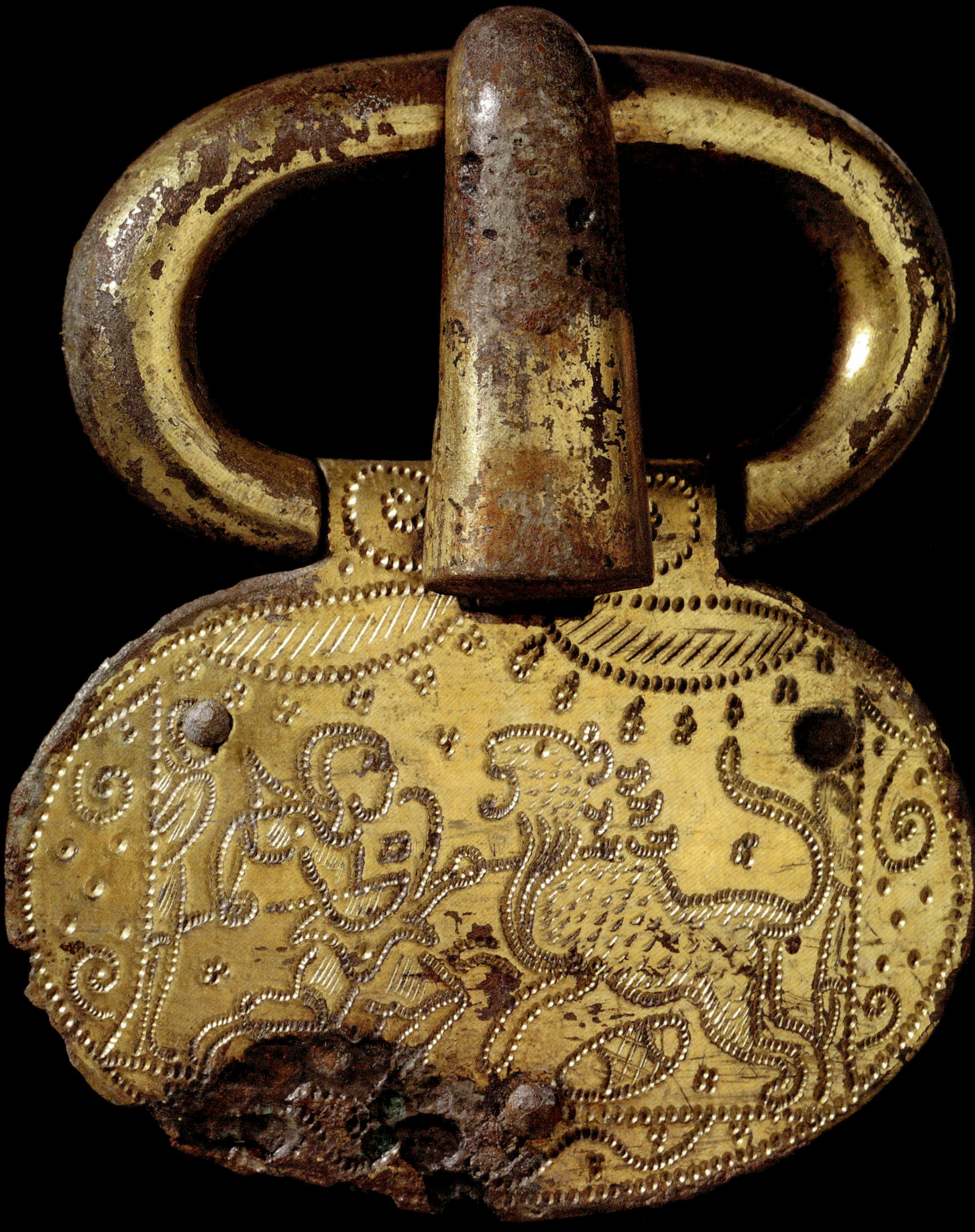

80 GOLD BUCKLE

At first glance, this heavily cast gold belt buckle set with a large chalcedony gem fits well into this general buckle type. Such buckles feature a massive round or oval loop, a long tongue with a strongly curved tip, and a round or sometimes oval plate with garnet cloisonné, occasionally also with coloured glass inlays.

Yet this buckle from Hungary differs from most of its companions through the use of a very special inlay. The gold plate has a kidney-shaped opening, into which an antique gem has been mounted. The stone is set flush with its frame, and the original low-relief design is clearly visible. A naked male figure is reclining on a rock, propping himself up with his left arm. The upper part of the torso, the head and the right arm are all missing, but the small wings on the figure's sandals identify him as Mercury, the Roman god of commerce and messenger of the gods. A fine line above his right knee may represent the lower end of his characteristic staff, the *caduceus*.

The first- or second-century gem would originally have been used as a seal. As the buckle dates to the mid to late fifth century, the gem must have been a treasured possession by then. Whether it broke or was cut in two for reuse is unclear, but the goldsmith who made the buckle deliberately chose to show off the design, as he could have set the gem with the other, rounded side upwards (**82**). The classical, ancient look of the gem must have given a special air of importance to the buckle and its wearer (**56**).

Buckles of this type are particularly common in the area north of the Black Sea and the Carpathian Basin, but they occasionally occur all around the Mediterranean. It is likely that Byzantine goldwork, which reached the areas to the north of the empire in the form of gifts and sometimes tributes, contributed to the development of the type. Buckles with inlaid plates were enthusiastically adopted by Germanic peoples, such as the Goths or the Vandals (**79**), as well as the nomadic Huns.

East Germanic or Hunnic
Said to be from Tolna, Hungary
Gem 1st or 2nd century AD
Buckle mid–second half of the 5th century AD
Length 4.8 cm
1900,0714.1

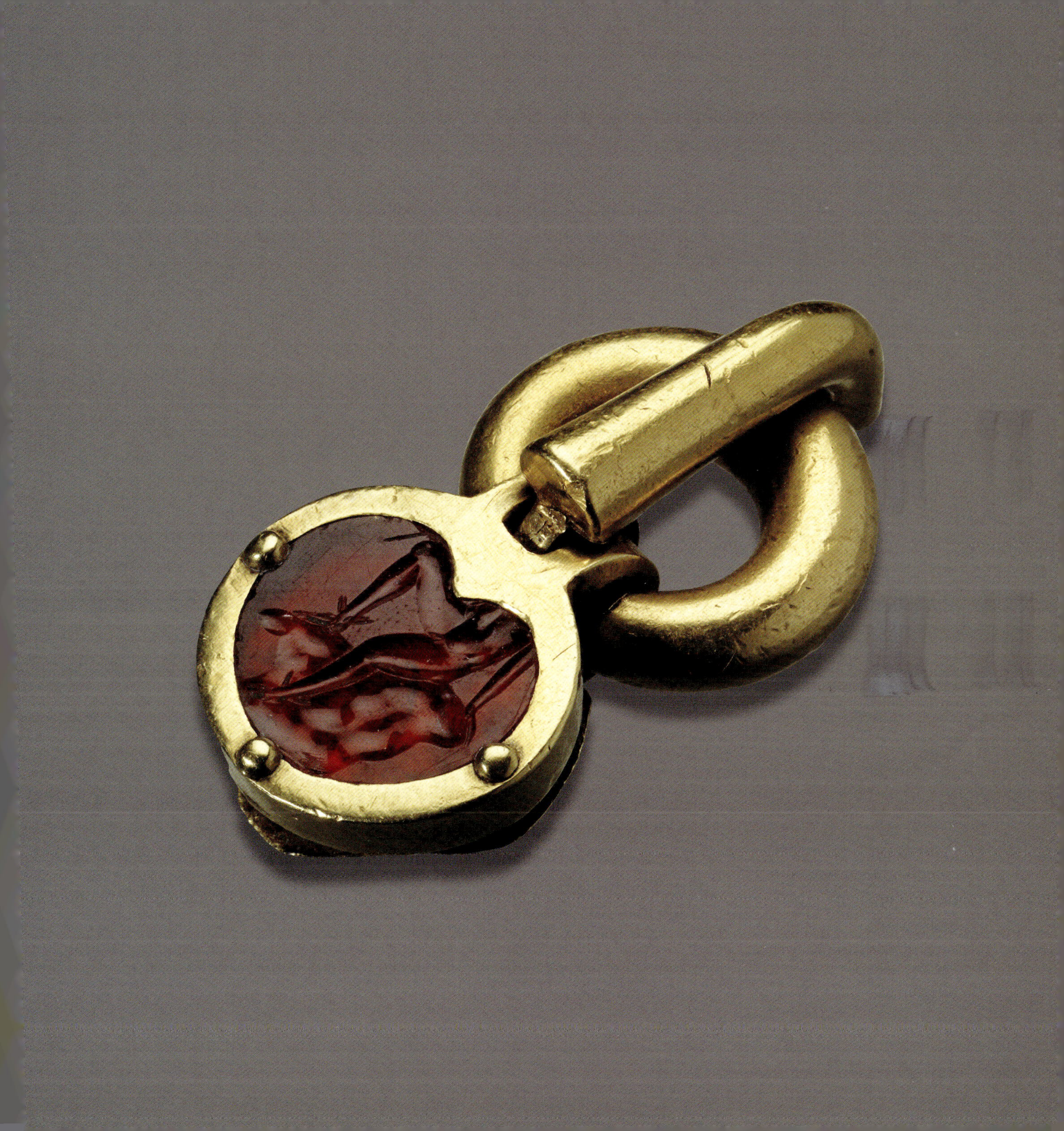

81 GLASS BEAKER

During the Migration Period in Sweden (*c.* AD 400 to AD 550–60) glass vessels were a rare, imported commodity. They were not only prestigious items for high-status individuals, but it is possible that they also played a specific role in ceremonial drinking practices. There were only two main types, the most frequent being Snartemo beakers, named after a Norwegian findspot. Over fifteen examples are now known from Sweden, with sherds of probable further examples from important sites such as the cultic centre at Uppåkra, near the modern town of Lund, and the major trading hub of Helgö. As this British Museum beaker is complete, it probably came from a grave rather than a settlement site.

The distribution of such early beakers in Sweden is related to the Baltic Sea. Indeed, the origin of the Snartemo type has been traced back to central or south-eastern Europe on the other side of the sea. This is an important difference to other forms of glass vessels, which came to Scandinavia from Francia or Anglo-Saxon England in the second half of the sixth and seventh century, while eastern imports in general seem to cease soon after about AD 550.

It is difficult to interpret this shift, but it may be linked to changes in the power structures of central and eastern Europe. The Avars (**92**) pushed westwards in the mid-sixth century, which precipitated the Longobard move into Italy in AD 568 (**94**), as well as an expansion of Slavic peoples towards the west and north. It is possible that these changes disrupted established routes for goods from the Black Sea region. Scandinavians focused more strongly on connections with the west until the Vikings re-established the trade routes through the river valleys of eastern Europe towards the Black Sea (**Map 4**).

Like most of the Gotlandic antiquities in the British Museum this beaker came from the collection of James Curle (1860–1944; **107**, **120**), a Scottish antiquarian who became interested in Gotlandic archaeology on a visit to the island in 1888 and quickly built up a large collection. Curle acquired this beaker in 1891 on a journey which also took him to Lund and Stockholm on the Swedish mainland.

Central or south-east European
Found on Gotland, Sweden
5th century AD
Height 20.5 cm
Acquired with a contribution from The Art Fund
1921,1101.381

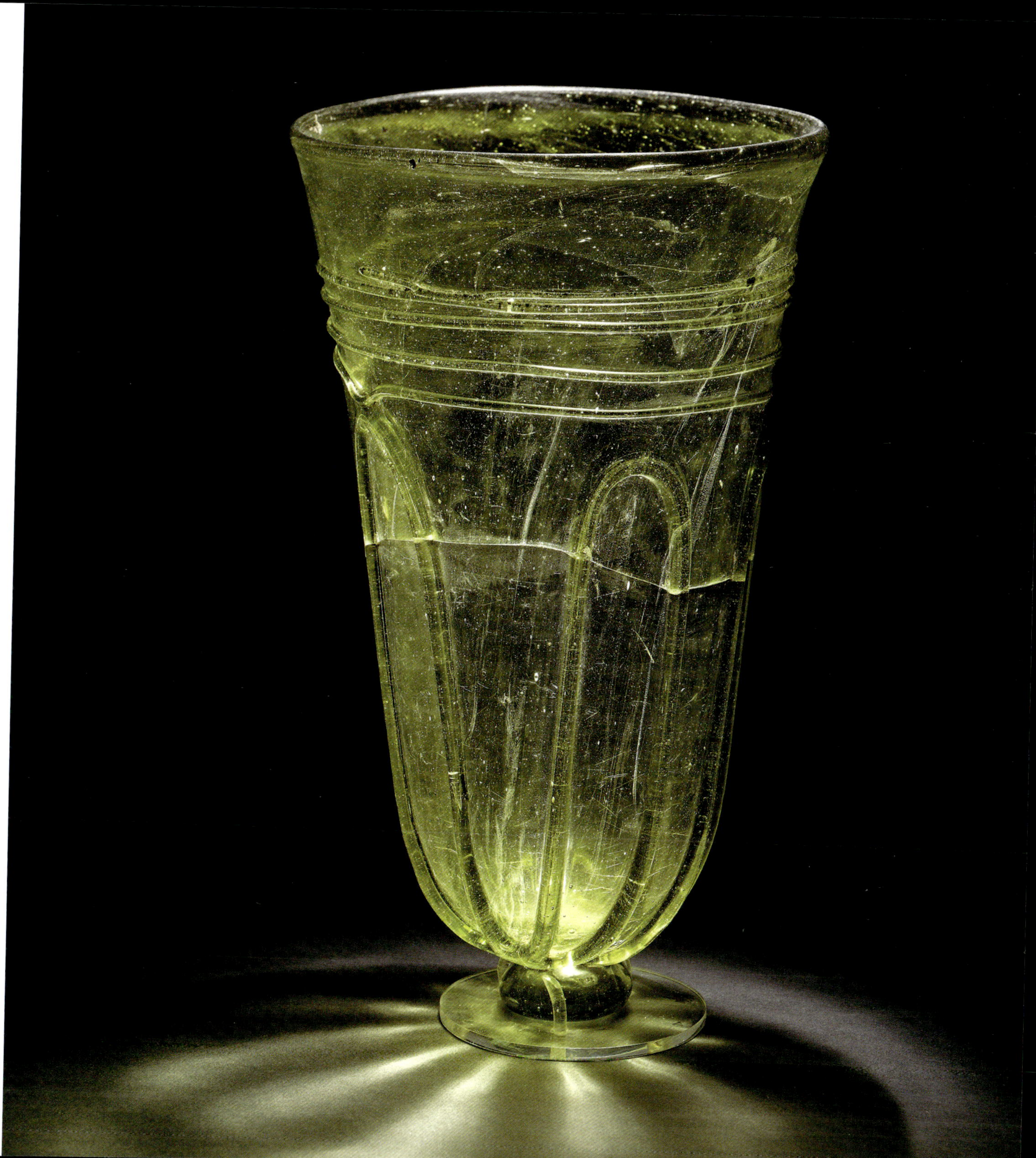

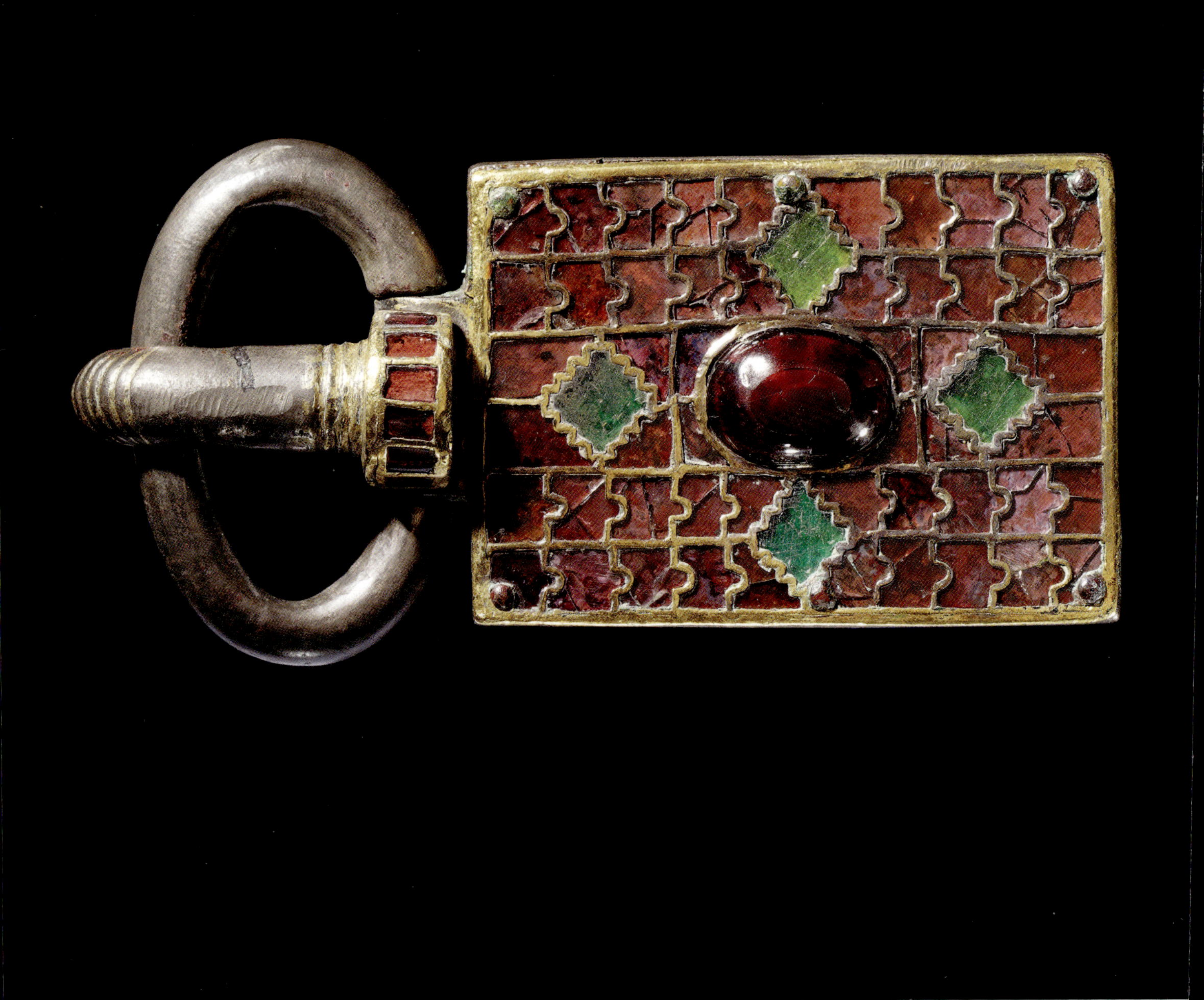

82 GOTHIC BELT BUCKLE

A taste for large and elaborate buckles is seen as a characteristic of Gothic belt fashions. This applies to both the early finds from the Crimea, where the Goths settled from the fifth century onwards, and to finds from those areas of the Mediterranean where the Visigoths (**93**) and Ostrogoths arrived later.

This substantial belt buckle is said to have been found together with a pair of earrings and two finger-rings, all of which are possibly identical to other objects in the British Museum which were acquired in the late nineteenth century. One account of the find also mentions a round brooch, which is now lost. Such an ensemble would be consistent with a female grave from Ostrogothic Italy, an interpretation which is backed up by an assessment of the shape and decoration of the buckle. Although there are only a few Ostrogothic women's graves from Italy, they are among the most sumptuous known; the Domagnano purse mount (**83**), for example, is from arguably the richest of them. It should be noted, however, that buckles with large cloisonné plates also occur in Visigothic burials in northern France and the nineteenth-century collector who owned the finds before they were dispersed just noted that they were 'found on the Continent'.

This buckle is made from gilt copper alloy and the massive tongue was originally silvered. Garnets are set in a row at the base of the tongue and also cover most of the plate, the centre of which is taken up by a cabochon garnet. Its size and careful polish, as well as the slightly awkward choice of a stone that is not fully rounded but has a flat top, indicate that this is a reused Roman gem (**56**, **80**).

Cells of green glass with a stepped outline are arranged around it. Such lozenge-shaped cells are not particularly common, but the form was popular enough to still be present on much later material, such as the shoulder clasps from Sutton Hoo (**46**). In accordance with their superior quality, the millefiori glass and garnets from the ship burial are, however, much more precisely set.

Gothic
From Italy or France (?)
5th century AD
Length 9.7 cm
1865,0318.1

83 THE DOMAGNANO PURSE MOUNT

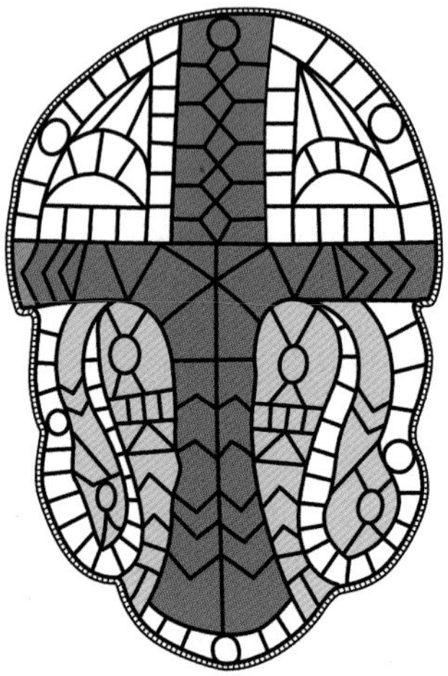

Ostrogothic

Found near Domagnano, Italy

Late 5th to beginning of the 6th century AD

Length 5.3 cm

Acquired with a contribution by The Art Fund

1933,0405.1

The famous, female grave from Domagnano, near San Marino in Italy, contained an outstanding array of gem-inlaid jewellery, some of which is in the British Museum today. This gold and garnet mount came from the lid of a purse which would have been worn on a belt. The mount is roughly oval in outline and is covered in a complicated network of gold cells which were once filled with garnet slips and perhaps white inlays as well.

Numerous interpretations of the inlay patterns have been put forward, and some have caused heated debate. One way of reading the mount, for example, is as the representation of a helmeted warrior. In this case, the top half of the fitting is the helmet, from which a long nasal reaches down the middle of the mount, while two lateral flaps protect the ears (**47**). Two round cells next to the nasal are the warrior's eyes. Another reading sees these cells as the eyes of a pair of fish with rounded heads, looking upwards. The 'earflaps' could be either another two fish looking downwards, or a pair of birds' heads with curved beaks pointing upwards.

A prominent cross is also visible, which could otherwise be the crest, brow band and nasal of the helmet. Parallels have been introduced in support of each idea, and indeed good comparisons can be made with both late antique helmets and engraved seals featuring Christian symbols such as doves, fish, crosses and anchors.

But perhaps the design was intentionally ambivalent and all these interpretations are correct? Visual ambiguity is a feature of early Germanic art, be it in the form of chip-carved animal ornament (**42**), wire-inlaid patterns (**91**) or garnet inlay, as is the case here. Riddles were, after all, a popular early medieval pastime (**58**). Therefore there may not have been a single accurate reading of this mount, but several possible versions. We may even go as far as to speculate whether this potential fusion of martial and Christian imagery could have been an especially powerful apotropaic or evil-averting design.

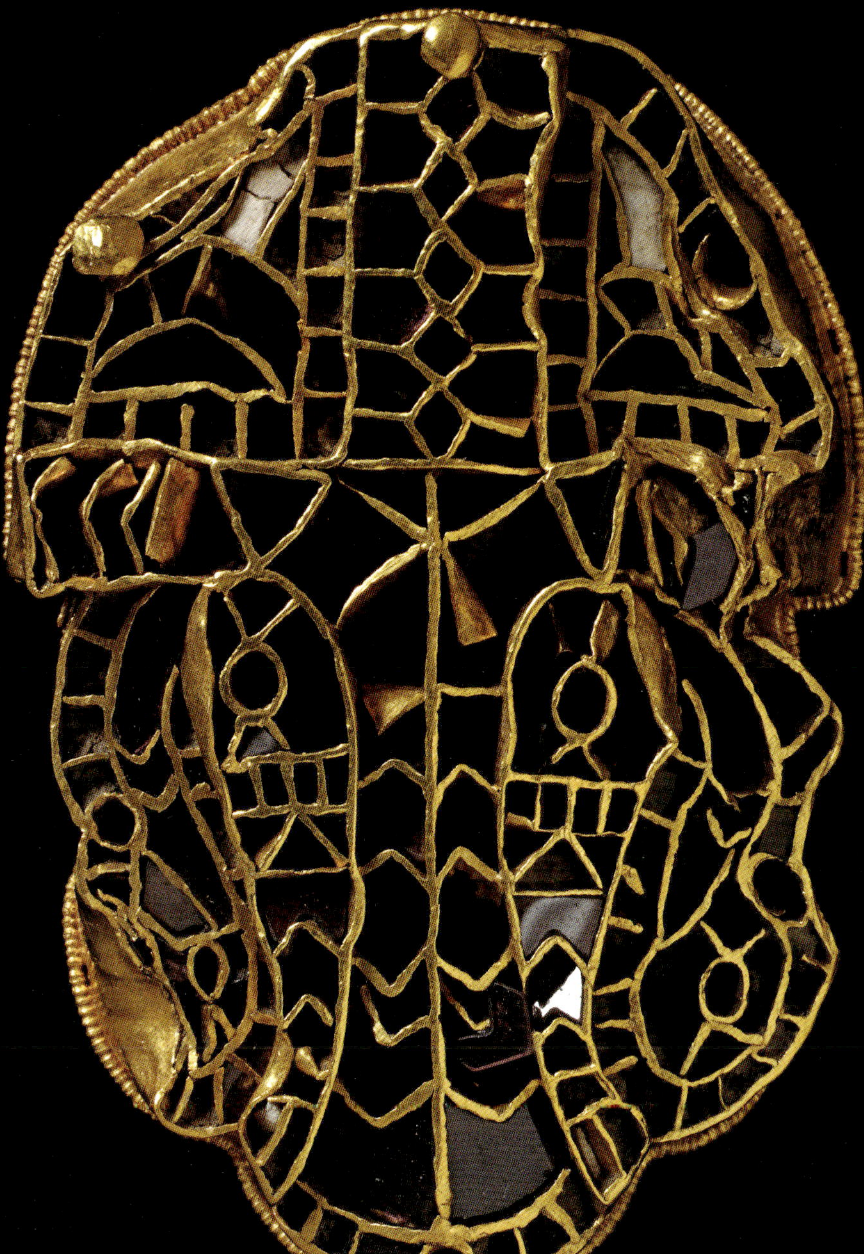

84 *SOLIDUS* OF THEODEBERT I

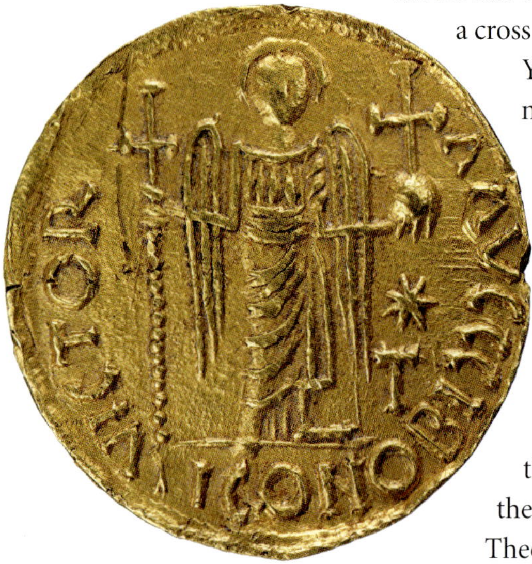

To the untrained eye, this gold coin appears to have all the trimmings of a Byzantine *solidus*, for instance one of Justinian I (AD 527–65; see p. 52). On the obverse, there is a portrait showing the ruler in a frontal pose, with a spear in his right hand which is laid across his shoulder, a diadem in his hair and a nimbus. On the reverse of the coin, a personification of Victory holds in one hand a globe with a cross on top, which symbolizes the world, and in the other a cross staff.

Yet this coin was not minted in Constantinople or any other imperial mint, but in the eastern Frankish kingdom of Austrasia, centred around Metz in modern-day France. After the demise of the Western Roman Empire in AD 476, the various Germanic successor states, initially with the exception of the Anglo-Saxons, started minting their own coinage. All gold coins still carried the portrait and name of the Byzantine emperor. These pseudo-imperial coins were based on imperial prototypes, but could differ in their style, which was not necessarily inferior, but simply and consistently different. In general, mostly gold coins were struck and there was little use for smaller denominations up until approximately the seventh century.

Theodebert I came to power in Austrasia in AD 534 and he issued gold coins such as this one. He was very ambitious and broke with one important convention: his own name is clearly legible around the portrait of the ruler on the obverse of the coin. Although the names of Germanic rulers had cropped up on silver and bronze coins, where they were still in use, this was a novelty on gold coinage. The Byzantine court was not happy about this impertinence, as the naming of emperors, even on Germanic coinage, was considered to be a sign of respect and acknowledgement of the superior authority of Constantinople. But it is possible that this custom had only been kept up in the West because gold coinage needed to be accepted widely and therefore initially drew on the prestige of imperial coins. Such a strategy of imitating well-known coins was widespread in the early Middle Ages (**60**, **128**).

Frankish
Unknown findspot
Minted AD 534–48
Diameter 1.9 cm
Donated by J.F.W. de Salis
B.10331, Dept of Coins and Medals

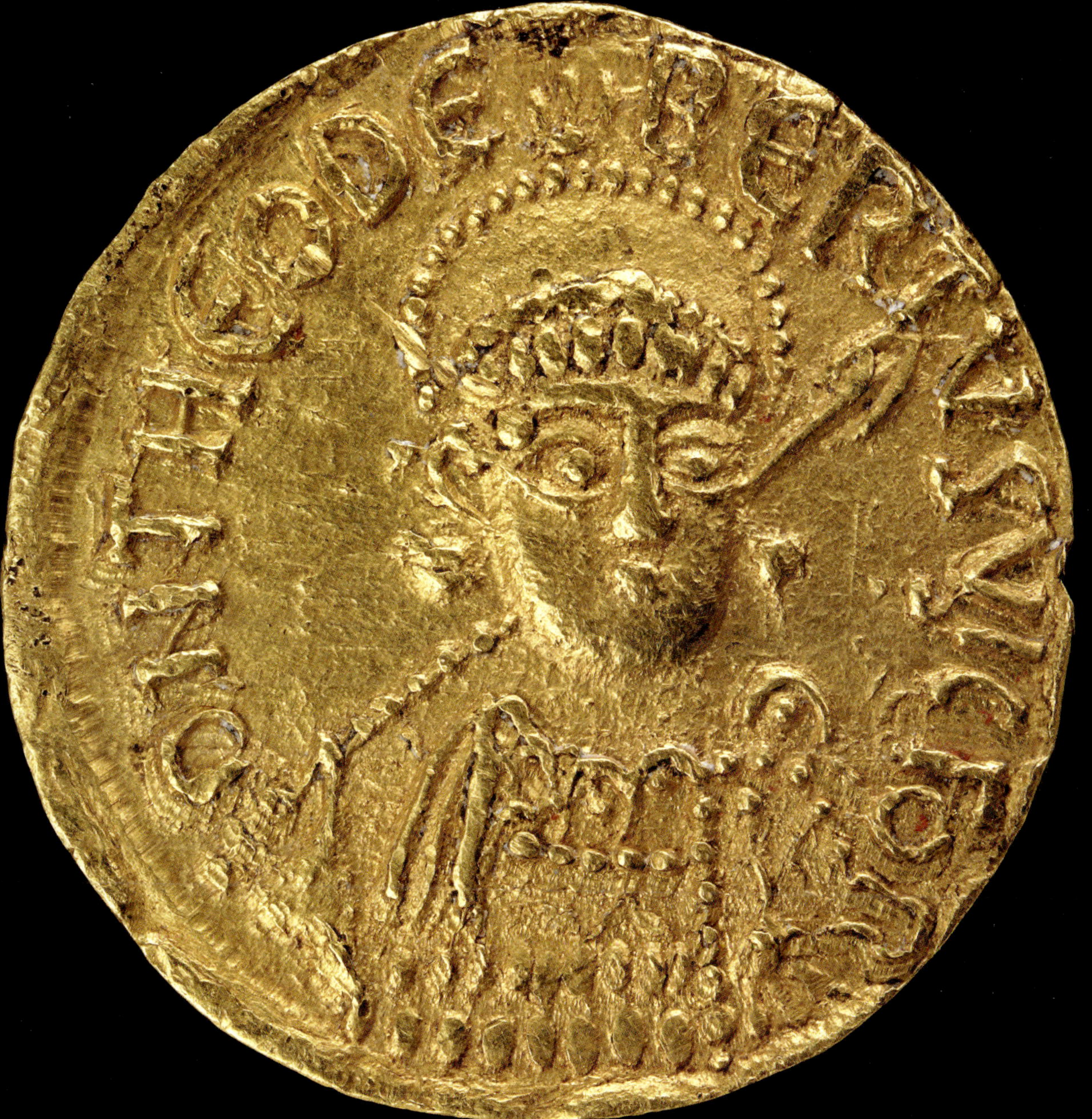

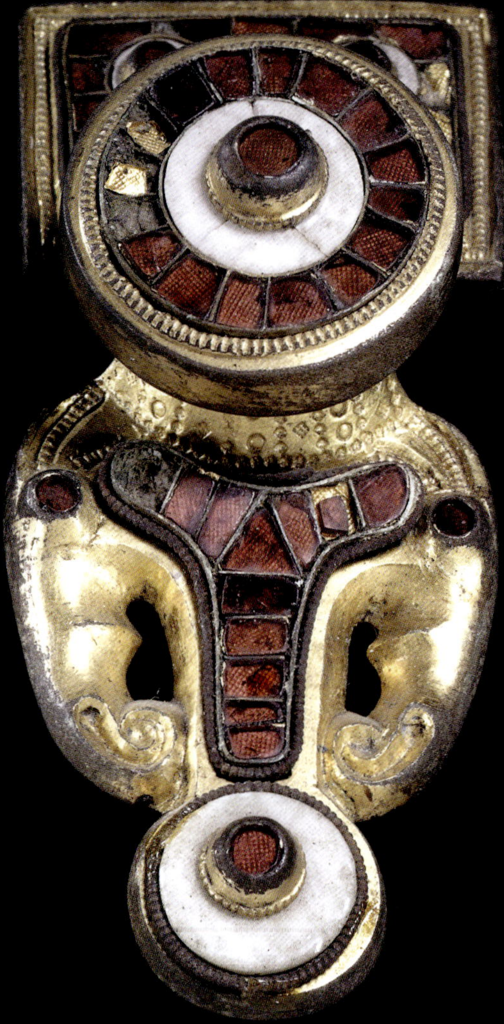

85 DISC-ON-BOW BROOCH

Scandinavian brooches of this type are named rather blandly after the way in which they were constructed. They are part of the large family of brooches which have an arched middle into which the fabric to be pinned was gathered (**42**), and are among the most ornate bow brooches known. Fortunately, there are several depictions on small gold votive plaques of women wearing such brooches. According to these images, the brooches fastened cloaks vertically just below the neck. The brooches are found in small numbers throughout Scandinavia. The largest group comes from Gotland, as does this example, perhaps due to the island's affluence (**116**, **120**).

No expense was spared in the making of this brooch. The thick gilding is still largely intact, as are most of the garnet inlays. Opaque white glass paste rings provide a pleasing contrast and are notable for the accuracy with which they were set. The brooch was cast from copper alloy rather than precious silver, but so were most brooch types current in Scandinavia at the time.

While the decoration is restrained and relies largely on the effects of colour and texture, this brooch does feature some of the ubiquitous animal ornament of the early Middle Ages. Two birds' heads reach outwards from the bow of the brooch and their strongly curved beaks join the foot just above the terminal roundel. They appear to be birds of prey, an omnipresent motif in all Germanic societies (**44**, **50**). Their meaning is unknown, but the eagle certainly symbolized strength and courage, while the raven-like birds may represent Huginn and Munnin who were the companions of Woden, the chief of the gods.

In the second half of the sixth century such brooches were imitated in Kent. The originally Scandinavian gold bracteates (**40**) are also more common here than anywhere else in Anglo-Saxon England and disc-on-bow brooches may have been another way of displaying links with Scandinavia. Perhaps they were even a visual manifestation of the mythical kinship with Scandinavia that some of the elite appear to have claimed (**40**).

Scandinavian
From Gotland, Sweden
6th century AD
Length 8.5 cm
1921,1101.221

86 ROCK-CRYSTAL BUCKLE

Rock crystal must have been greatly valued by the early Germanic peoples. In appearance it is much like ice, but it is hard and durable. Many people would never have seen anything remotely similar, as glass, when it was available, was not clear but for technological reasons always had a green or brown hue (**39**).

This buckle loop was found in a grave at Châlons-sur-Marne in north-eastern France in the nineteenth century. The rock-crystal loop was faceted and has a roughly heart-shaped outline. The buckle tongue has a decorative shield with drawn-in sides. These so-called shield-tongues frequently occurred in Germanic contexts both on the Continent and in Anglo-Saxon England during the sixth century. The buckle loop, however, is a rarity.

A number of heart-shaped crystal loops have been found in northern France, the Rhineland, south-western Germany and as far away as the Crimean peninsula. Similar loop forms in other materials are primarily known from the lower Danube, Turkey and the Levant, with two pieces from Egypt. The non-Germanic examples therefore show a clear affinity with the Byzantine Empire. In the north they are only found in burials, usually those of men.

It is likely that these buckle loops were cut and polished in the workshops of the Byzantine Empire dealing with precious and semi-precious stones. They could have made their journey northwards in many ways, for example with Germanic mercenaries who had served in the army. Local forms of buckle tongue could be added once travellers returned home with these unusual objects which spoke of exotic contacts and perhaps long voyages abroad. It is significant that the Châlons buckle has a silver tongue, in itself a statement of prestige and affluence.

Rock crystal remained an exclusive material into the Early Modern era and its clarity was later equated with spiritual purity. It was therefore eminently suitable for use in Christian art (**97**, **98**).

Byzantine

Found near Châlons-sur-Marne, France

6th century AD

Width 4.5 cm

ML.3527

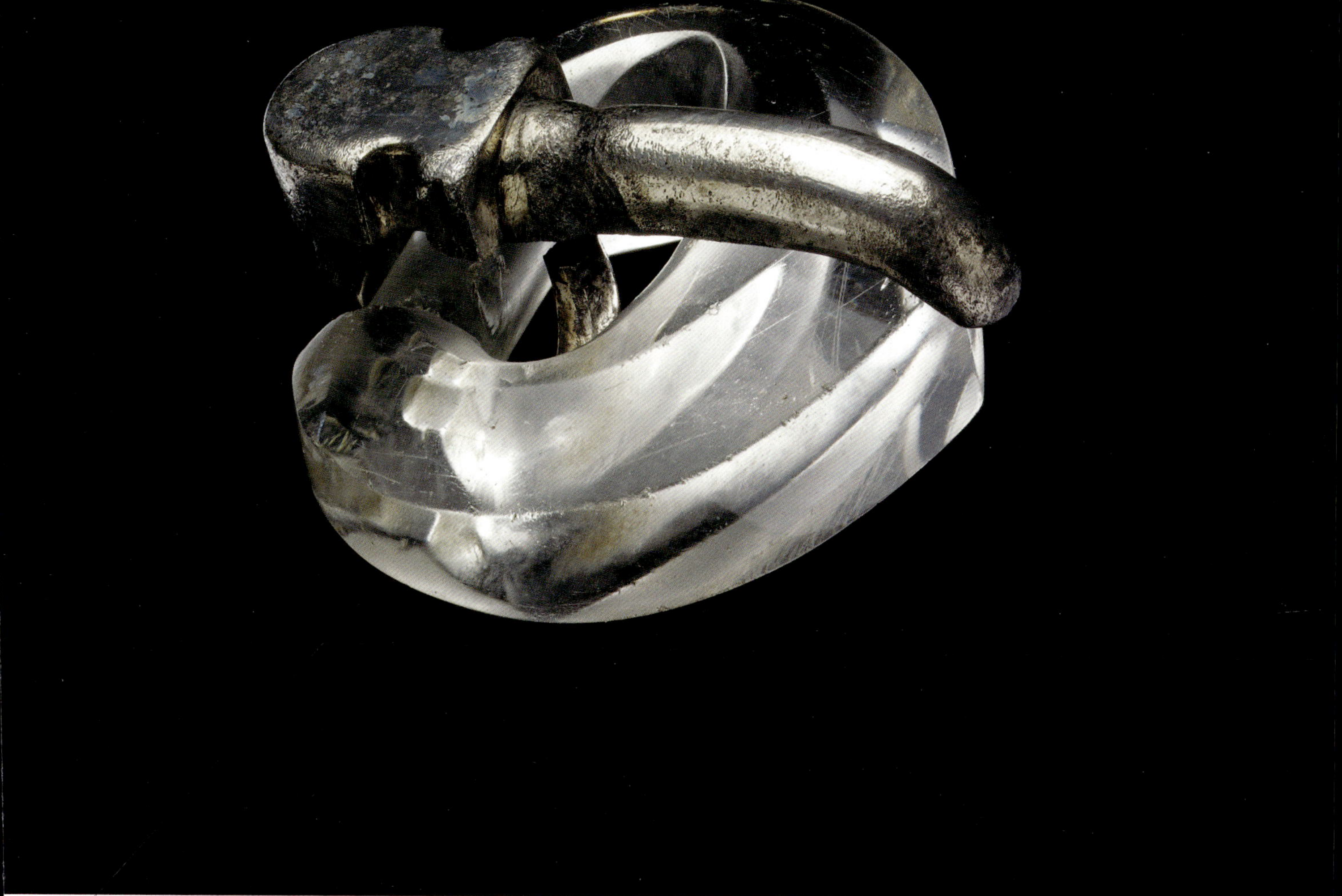

87 BOX BROOCH SHOWING THE ADORATION

A silver gilt repoussé panel has been mounted on a box-shaped body made from bronze or perhaps a very impure silver alloy. On the sunken central field three bearded men approach a seated figure with a child on her lap. A large hole mars the composition, and the head of the seated adult as well as that of the angel floating above her is missing. Nonetheless, it is clear that this is a depiction of the Adoration of the Magi, who have come to pay their respects to the new-born Christ child in the stable at Bethlehem. The setting is completed by the donkey splayed out below the feet of the figures.

Essentially this is the same scene as that which appears on a Byzantine medallion (**29**). This brooch is a faithful copy of an original such as that medallion, down to the star above the head of the child. The Magi on the brooch wear a simplified version of the usual Byzantine draped dress. The Phrygian hats they are often shown wearing have morphed into topknots.

Remains of mineral-preserved textiles on the brooch pin imply that it came from a burial and had been worn by the person laid to rest. Although no findspot is recorded for the brooch, it most likely came from Pannonia, a part of modern-day Hungary which had once been part of the Roman Empire. Even after the empire's demise in the West, Romanized populations seem to have continued living around former Roman towns, notably that of Keszthely.

The people of the Keszthely Group were distinct from their early medieval, steppe nomadic overlords, the Avars (**92**). The Keszthely population seem to have remained Christian and maintained contact with northern Italy as well as the south-east Alpine region, probably by continued use of the Roman roads. During the sixth to seventh century settlers from the Balkans joined them, affirming existing links with the Byzantine Empire. The people of the Keszthely Group were thus part of a Mediterranean cultural milieu, which was expressed in their practice of Christianity as well as in their jewellery.

Keszthely Group
From Hungary (?)
6th to middle of the 7th century AD
Diameter 6.4 cm
1987,0101.1

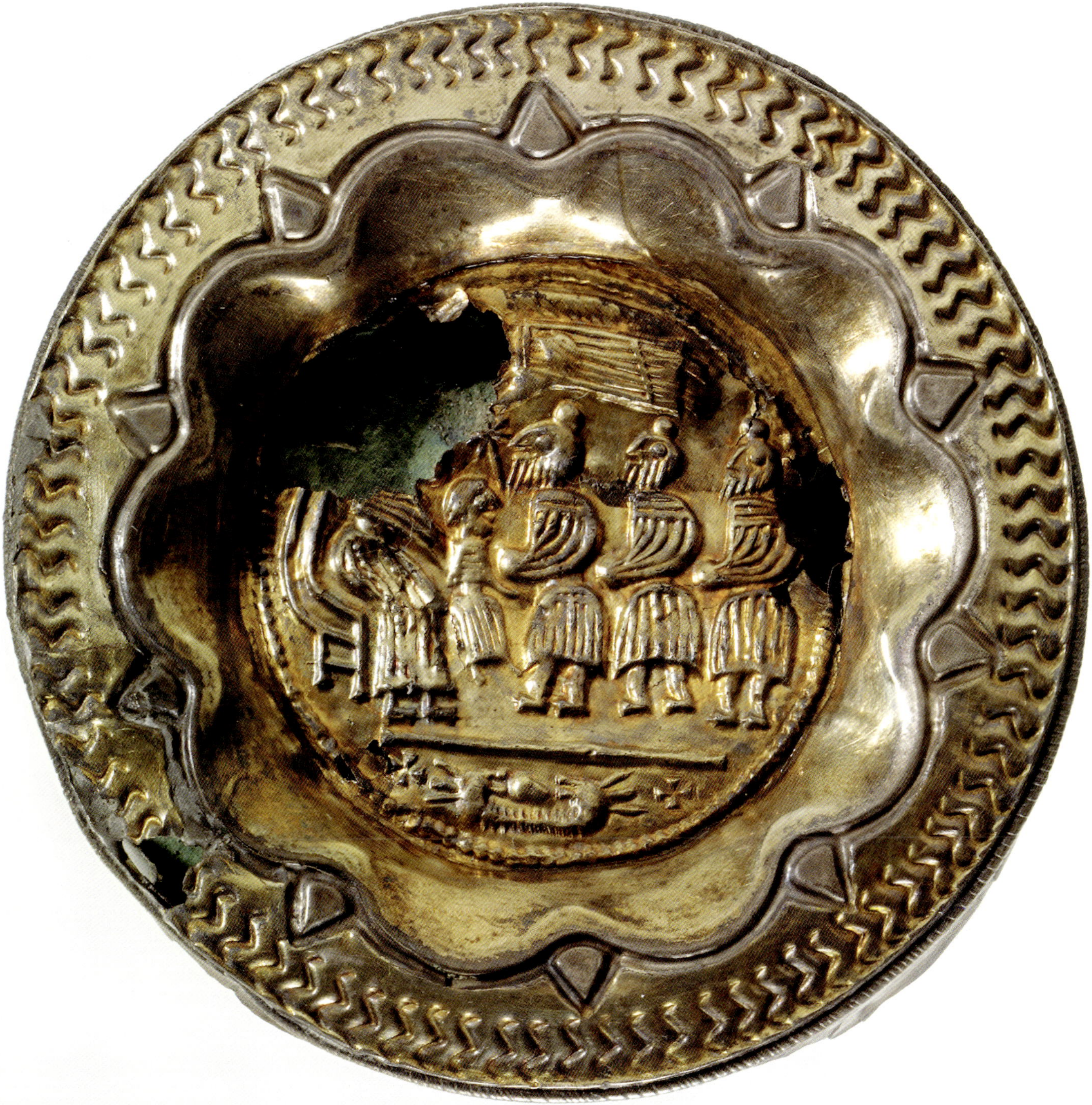

88 THE SUTRI HORN

Drinking horns were a northern European form and popular with all Germanic peoples. A number of examples from Anglo-Saxon England use actual aurochs horns with elaborate silver-gilt mounts. The most famous are the pairs from the Sutton Hoo and Taplow princely burials, and it is clear that due to their size some skill was needed to use them elegantly. Drinking horns were occasionally used in the Celtic areas of the British Isles as well, as is demonstrated by the metal fitting from Lismore, Ireland (**146**), and the stone carving from Angus, Scotland, of a Pictish warrior enjoying a drink while on horseback.

Glass horns were rarer, but no less elaborate, as shown by the two olive green examples from Rainham, Essex, also in the British Museum. Green and brown tones appear to be typical of north European horns and predominate in most glass vessels from north of the Alps (**39**, **90**).

The vibrant, dark blue colour of this horn may be due to the presence of cobalt in the glass mass (**45**). This colourant may have been available through the recycling of glass cullet or the melting down of mosaic *tesserae*. Sutri is some fifty kilometres from Rome and therefore access to either material would probably have been easy. That this atypical vessel form was nonetheless made in the Mediterranean is also suggested by the presence of the opaque, white glass trail decoration, which is rare in the north.

The female burial from which this horn came illustrates excellently the history of the Longobards as conveyed by the written sources. The Longobards lived in Pannonia (**87**) but in AD 568 migrated to Italy, where they formed a number of dukedoms and quickly assimilated local customs. The grave goods from Sutri (see p. 166) are a mixture of traditionally Longobardic material, such as the large bow brooch and the garnet-inlaid S-shaped brooch, and Mediterranean fashions, including Byzantine-style gold earrings and a pair of Roman vases. The glass horn appears to represent an amalgamation of both of these backgrounds.

Longobard
From Sutri, Italy
Late 6th to 7th century AD
Length 23.0 cm
1887,0108.2

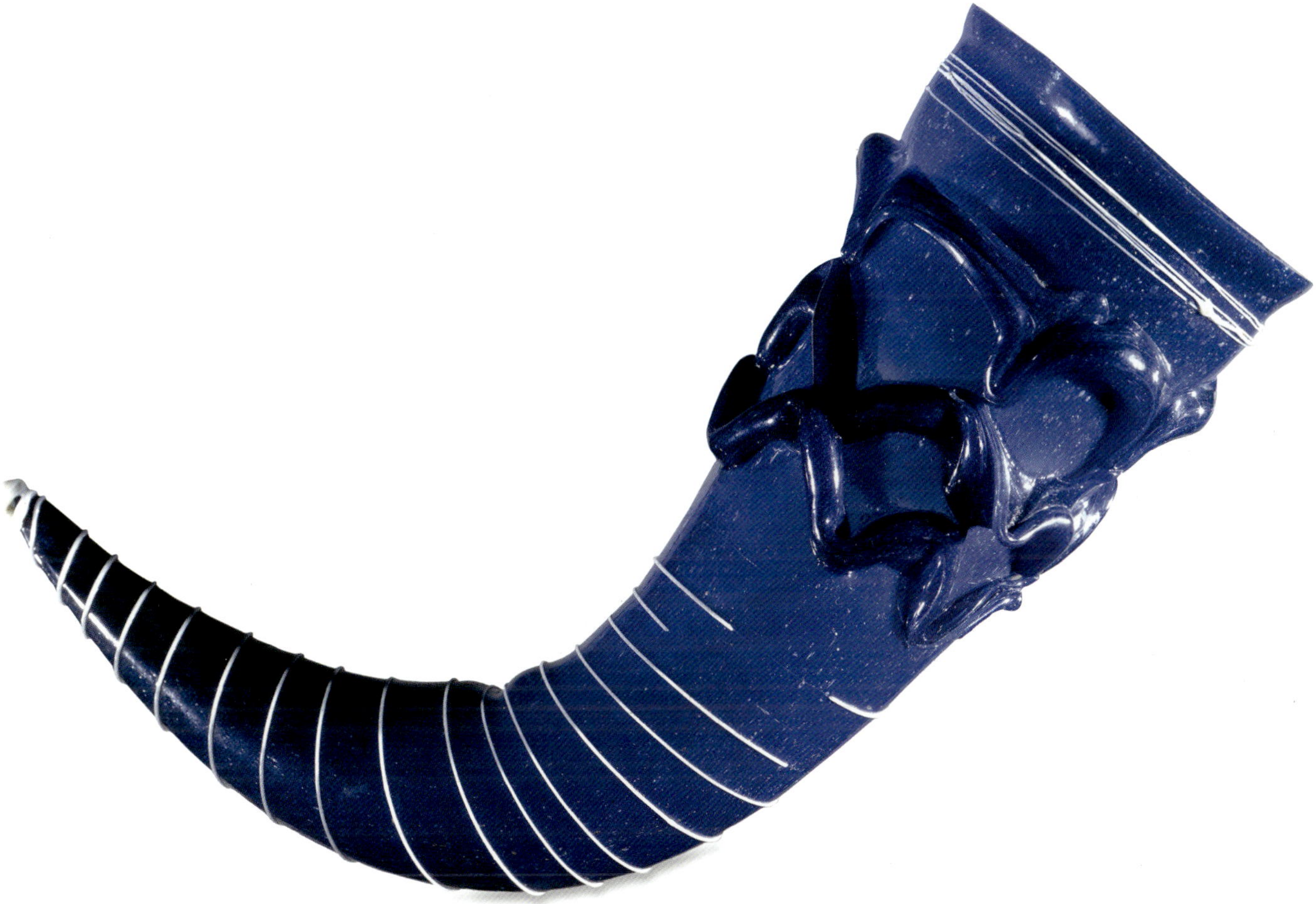

89 THE MARTYNIVKA HOARD

After the discovery of the Martynivka hoard in around 1907, it was concealed and then quickly dispersed by the finders. The British Museum acquired twenty-seven fittings, buckles, arm-rings, animal plaques, brooches and assorted silver fragments in 1912. Today, a total of 115 silver objects are preserved in various museums amounting to a weight of 3.3 kilograms, though it is most likely that this does not represent all of the pieces which originally existed.

The quality of the silver varies widely between different objects from the hoard. The female jewellery, for example, is mostly made from low-grade alloy. On the other hand, the parts of a Byzantine dinner service and fittings from a sword are of very pure silver. Since all the objects have been used, but none have been chopped up, they most likely represent the possessions of a local grandee, rather than of a silversmith who collected material for recycling.

The contents of the hoard come from diverse cultural backgrounds. It has been suggested that this represents the far-reaching contacts of those living in the forested steppes of Ukraine during the sixth and seventh century, and the goods available to them as a result.

This is illustrated well by the horse-shaped fitting and the bow brooch shown here. The former may have come from a saddle or a shield, although in a reconstruction it has been affixed to a leather cuirass used to protect the torso. The exuberant design, enhanced by the partially preserved gilding, and the general importance of the horse in these cultures, suggest a steppe nomadic background (**92**, **132**). The woman's brooch and its pair, on the other hand, follow Germanic models in their construction (**42**, **85**). The human masks seen at the top are a feature found on what are thought to be Slavic brooches. The lateral peacocks with upturned beaks recall Byzantine tastes and the silver plate from the find and many of the belt fittings are Byzantine. Thus, the Martynivka hoard reflects the location of the findspot between all these existing and emergent power blocks.

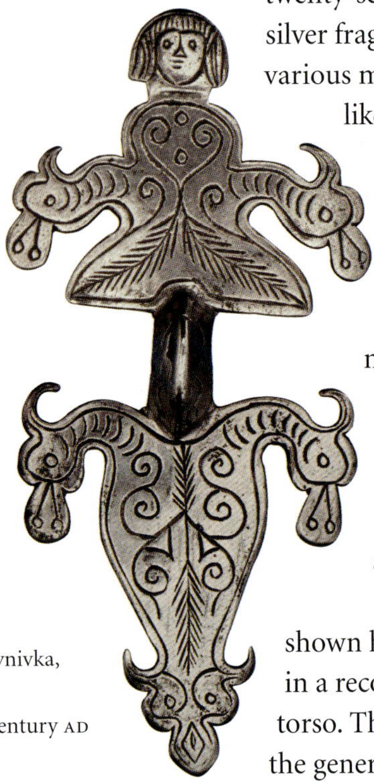

From Martynivka, Ukraine

6th to 7th century AD

Brooch:

Slav

Length 13.1 cm

1912.0610.1

Mount:

Steppe nomadic (?)

Length 8.1 cm

1912,0610.4

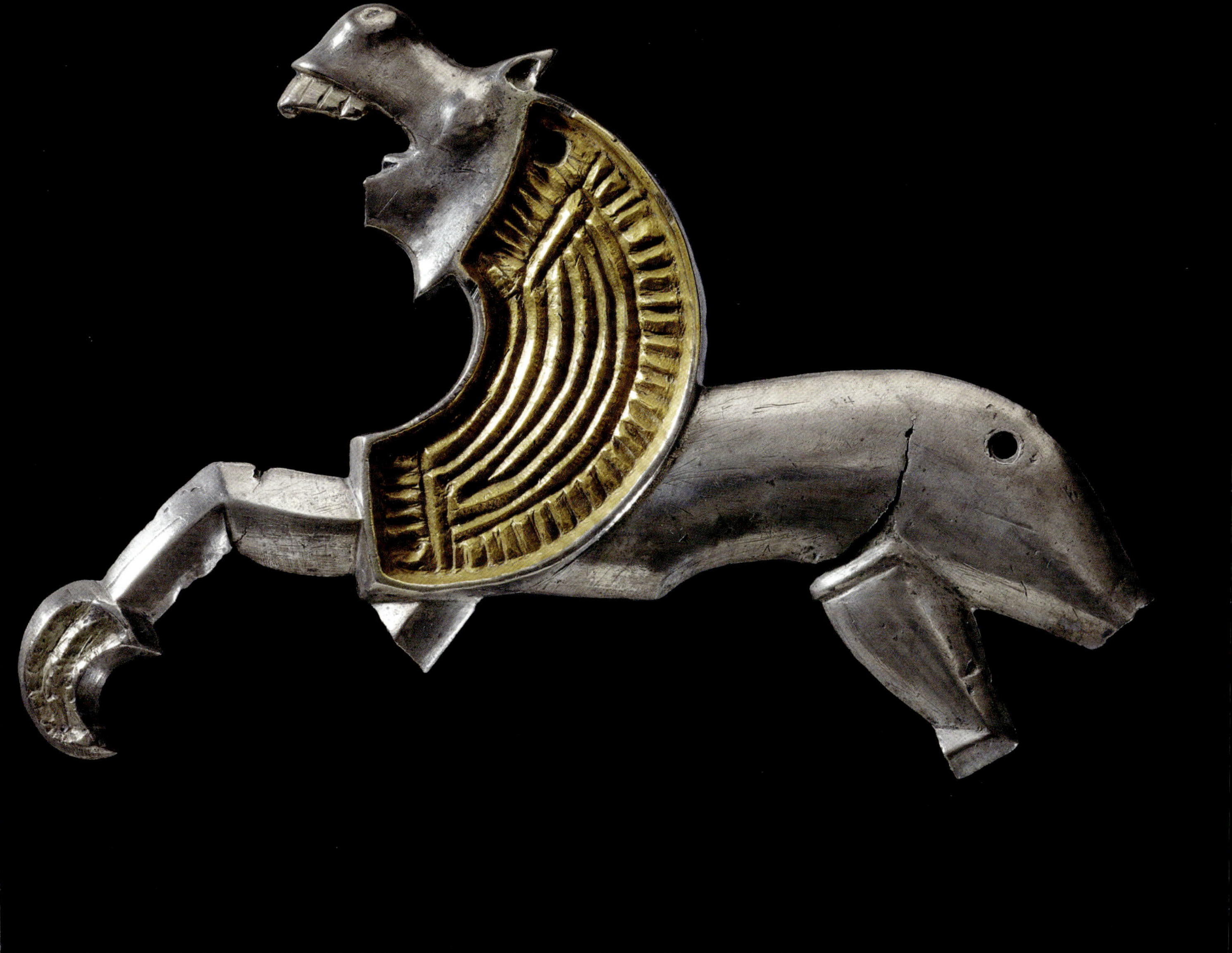

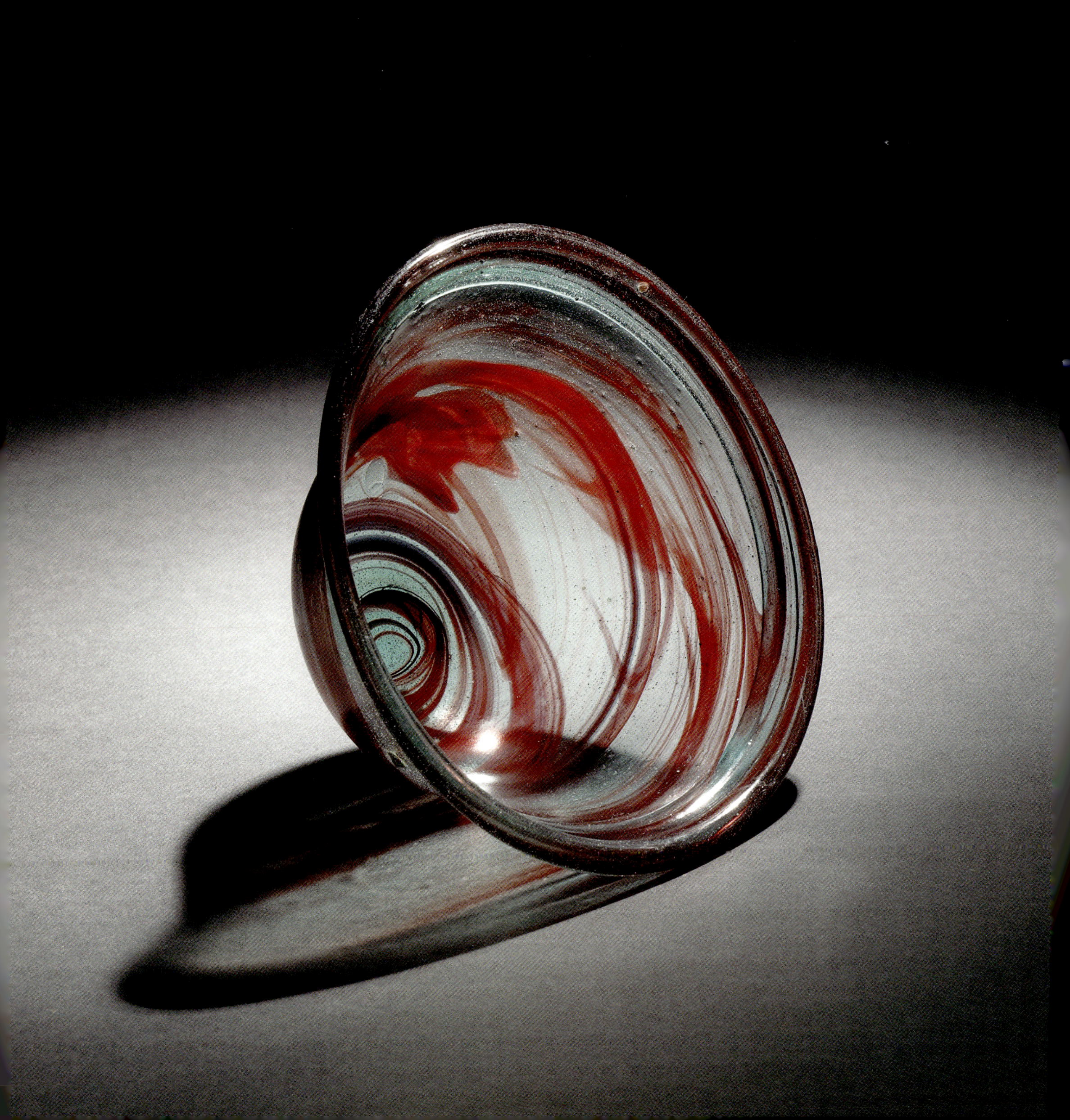

90 PALM CUP

One of the most attractive and unusual examples of this type of cup is this piece from Reims in northern France. It was blown from translucent, pale blue-green glass embellished with ethereal spiralling trails of red glass. Early scholars envisaged Germanic elites cradling such vessels in their hands and therefore bestowed the name 'palm cup' on the type. Due to their hemispherical form and wide flaring mouth, the cups could not stand up and had to be emptied before they could loll on the table.

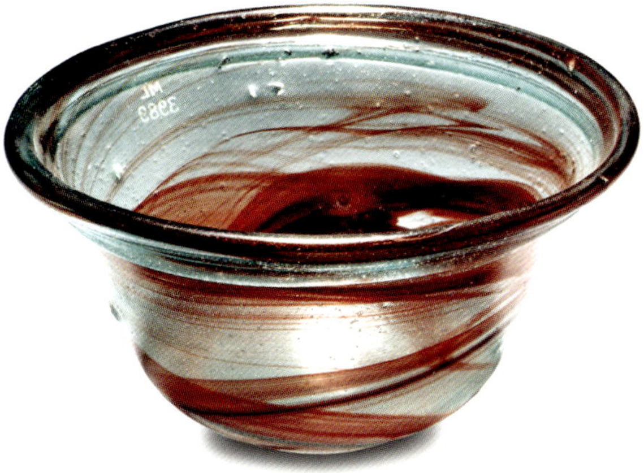

Palm cups were popular in the late sixth and seventh century and a considerable number have been found in early medieval cemeteries in the Rhineland, Belgium and northern France. Over fifty are known from England alone, and as they are made in a similar way it is difficult to say where exactly they were produced. In burials they often occur in pairs, which evokes the notion of communal drinking, as does the large size of the present example.

Green and brown tones are prevalent among palm cups, as with many early medieval vessels (**39**). The spiral streaks in this cup are highly unusual. Only a few examples, among them one from Desborough, Northamptonshire, which is also in the British Museum, show more than one colour and the vibrant red of the Reims cup stands out among early medieval vessels in general.

However it is by no means certain that this colour effect was intentional and as yet it has not been determined which metal oxide or oxides caused the red marbling. During this period, red glass was rare and precious, and only glass makers in the Byzantine Empire knew how to produce it. Whether accidental or not, the harmonious form and the very neatly folded, hollow rim are a testimony to the high proficiency of the glass blower who made this particular vessel.

Frankish
From Reims, France
7th century AD
Diameter 13.0 cm
ML.3989

91 WIRE-INLAID AXE AND BROOCH

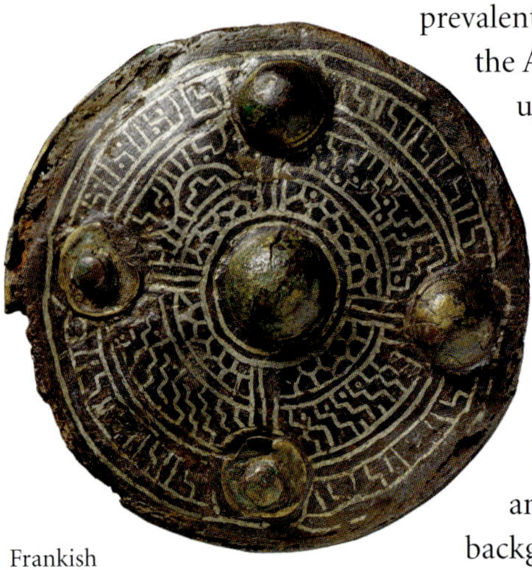

Frankish

7th century AD

Brooch:

Said to be from the Rhine or Moselle regions, Germany

Diameter 6.6 cm

Donated by the Friends of the British Museum

1902,1108.139

Axe:

Thought to be from Kärlich, Germany

Length 17.5 cm

Acquired with a contribution from the Christy Trust

1961,0505.1

Wire-inlaid dress accessories such as brooches and buckles were hugely popular on the Continent during the seventh century. They were most prevalent in the regions settled by the Franks and Burgundians as well as those of the Alamans and Baiuvars in southern Germany. The fashion never picked up in Anglo-Saxon England, except for a few buckles and belt fittings which are likely to have been imported into Kent and elsewhere in southern England.

Like the *opus interrasile* technique (**5**, **8**, **34**), wire-inlay is an excellent way of achieving a spectacular impression while being economical with the precious metal required. During the seventh century, this would have been silver wire, which was sometimes combined with brass inlays of a golden tone. The designs were cut into the surface of an object, the wires were rubbed into the grooves and the finished design was then hammered over and polished. The iron background was probably heat-treated to give it a dark appearance, which provided an attractive contrast to the inlay patterns.

Geometric patterns dominate the ornament, although zoomorphic elements, such as snakes or the heads of birds of prey, were also common. The designs may seem familiar, as many are modelled on the decoration of earlier objects with garnet cloisonné. This female brooch, for example, features a ring of honeycomb inlay around the central boss, and T-shaped cells in the adjacent band of ornament. Both designs have parallels in Anglo-Saxon cloisonné, for instance, the latter in the somewhat uneven inlay on the buckle loop from Taplow (**43**). As on the Sarre cloisonné brooch (**51**), the brass bosses on this Frankish piece are arranged in the shape of a cross, although it is difficult to say whether this had any Christian meaning or was simply a good way of dividing a circular object.

But it was not only female accoutrements which were inlaid. Large belt suites for both men and women, sword harnesses and the occasional piece of weaponry, such as this axe, were either inlaid with wires, or had larger areas plated with silver designs (**132**).

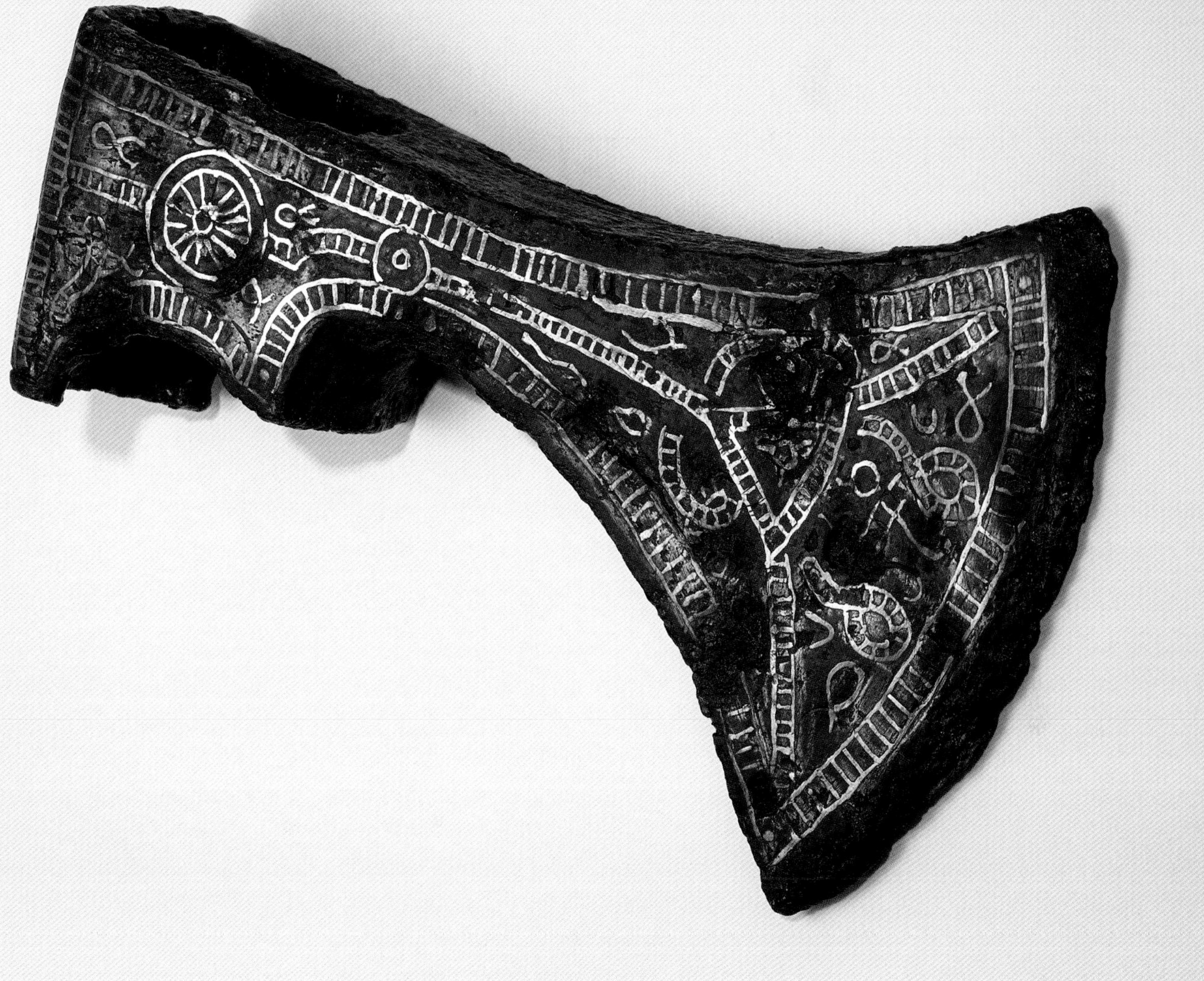

92 AVAR STRAP-END

While a strap-end had the very simple function of protecting the end of a belt from fraying, it has also always lent itself to elaboration. Through the late Roman, Byzantine and early medieval periods, strap-ends were a form of male adornment. In the later Roman army, belt fittings were a primary way of displaying rank (**18**). The expression 'cingulum dare', translated literally as 'to give someone a military belt', was synonymous with appointment to office. During the Byzantine era, precious metal belt fittings were a means of displaying status (**35**). Through its close association with the body, the belt could also have apotropaic properties, in particular if the buckle or fittings bore religious or evil-averting imagery (**93**).

The remains of gilding on this strap-end provide an attractive contrast with the dark patina which is the result of corrosion, but it once would have been entirely gilded. The embellishment on both sides was influenced by Germanic animal ornament. As in Animal Style II (**48**), sinuous body parts and feet with many toes are discernible on the front, but no coherent animal emerges from the pattern. Characteristic blocks of transverse lines have been added in groups of threes and the most notable aspect of the curvilinear interlace pattern on the back is the heart-shaped volutes at the upper and lower ends of the strap-end.

Both features are key to understanding the cultural background of this object. Similar motifs were popular on Avar belt equipment, although they were usually executed in a deeply moulded technique. The Avars were originally a steppe nomadic people, who migrated westwards into the Carpathian Basin during the course of the sixth century. Men wore belts with one large main strap-end that was passed through the belt buckle, with many small decorative ones on short straps positioned all along the length of the belt.

While the use of casting, animal ornament and shallow relief reflect the style of the Germanic peoples further west, the shape of the strap-end is Avar and its decoration contains overtones of steppe nomadic traditions, some of which were ultimately derived from Byzantine models (**35**).

Avar
Probably from Hungary
7th century AD
Length 8.5 cm
2008,8013.1

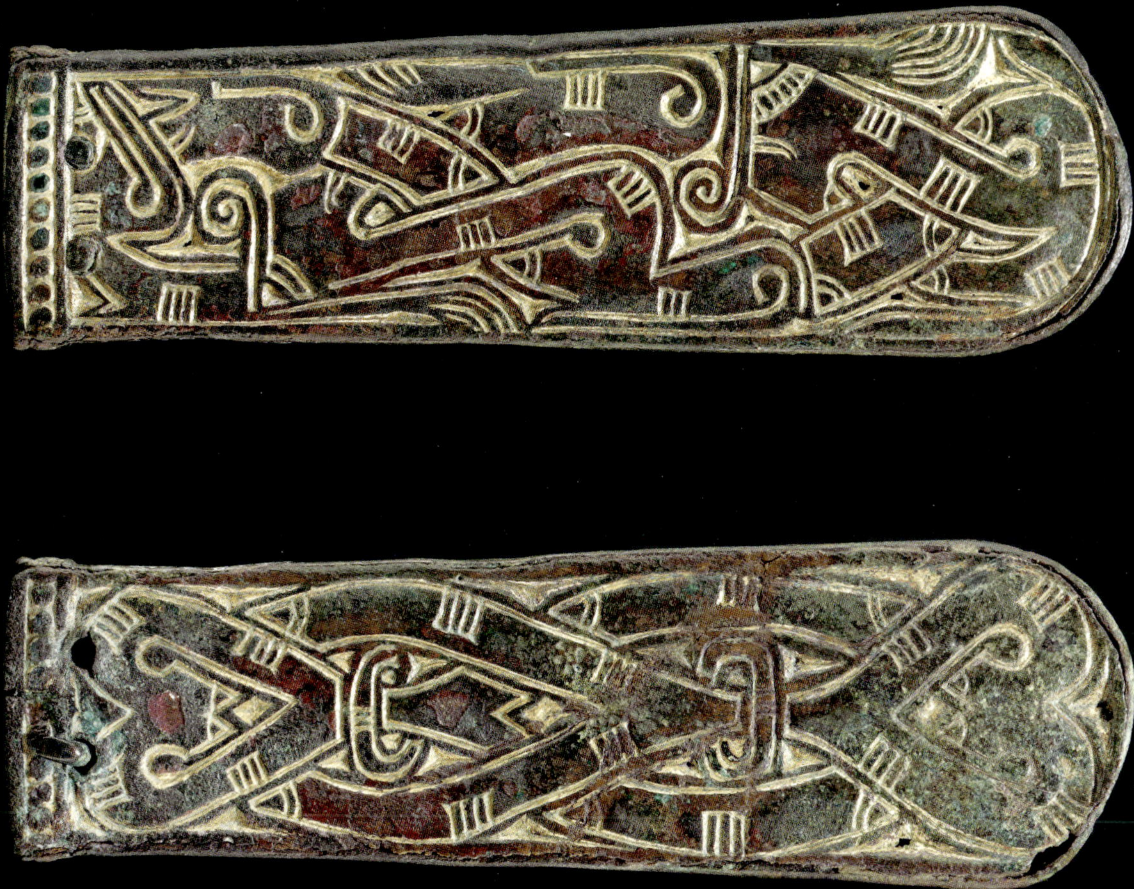

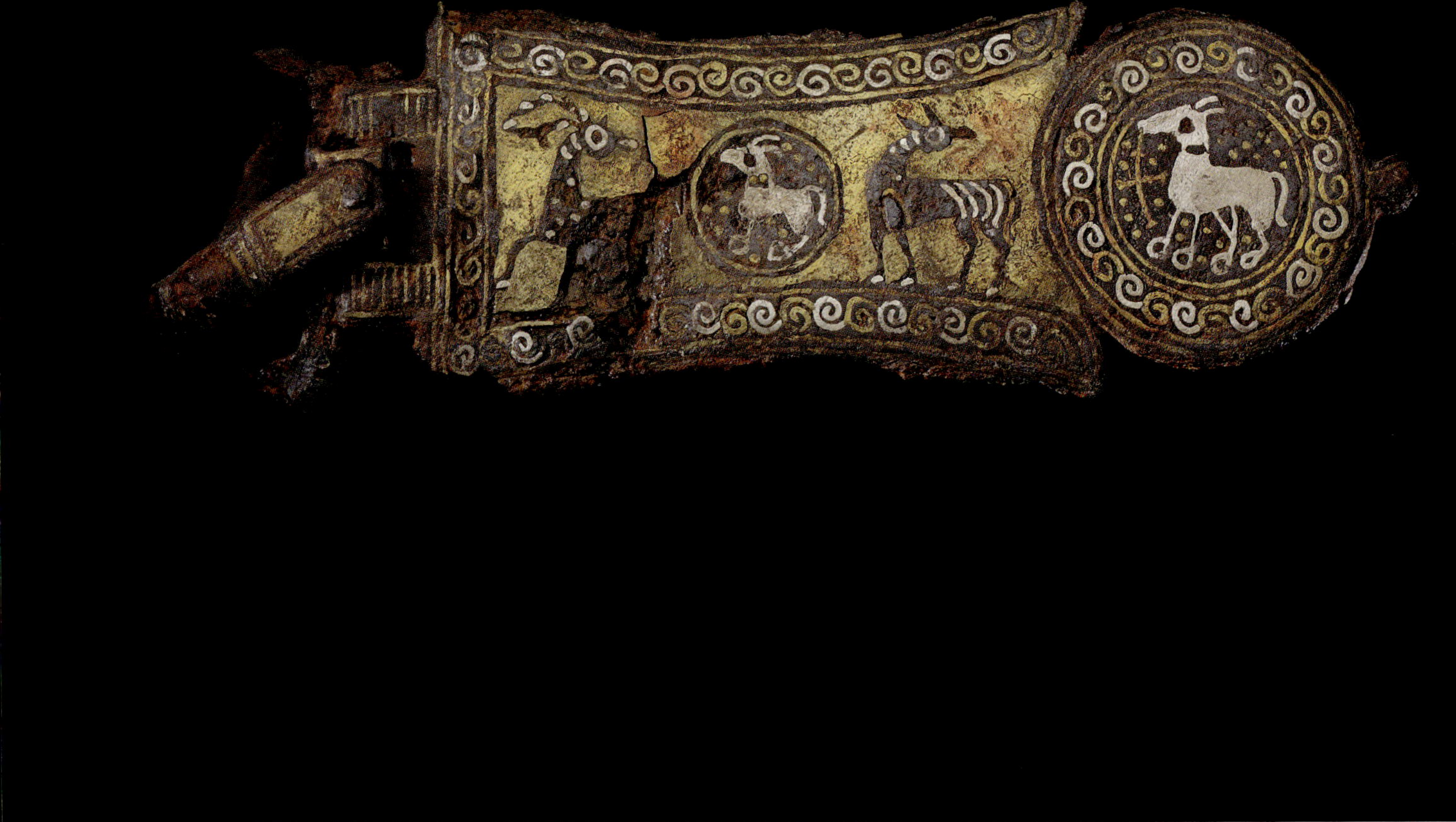

93 VISIGOTHIC BELT BUCKLE

Despite its corrosion, this belt buckle is still the 'striking and important piece' that it was described as in the British Museum's purchase report. The buckle loop to the left is badly damaged, but the elongated plate is in good condition. On it, a multicoloured design shows a parade of animals, including a stag and a doe, on either side of a central medallion depicting a lamb. The terminal roundel contains another lamb with a prominent cross. This has been interpreted as the Agnus Dei, the Lamb of God (**66**).

In the Old Testament the lamb is a sacrificial animal, while in the New Testament there are numerous explicit references to Christ as the sacrificial lamb, giving up his life for the redemption of humankind. The iconography of a lamb with the Cross became the symbol representing this idea and appeared from the fifth century onwards, for example in church apse mosaics in Rome.

It is not unusual to find religious imagery on belt buckles. For example, there are some fine carved bone examples with biblical scenes, especially from the life of Jonah (**7**). Buckle reliquaries are known (**48**, **54**), while northern French buckles with portraits of a bearded man are thought to show the image of Christ (**50**). Like jewellery and clothes with religious imagery (**29**, **33**, **38**), these depictions were meant to award the wearer spiritual protection against all evil.

The shape of this buckle fits well into the canon of Visigothic belt buckles, in particular those from Spain. Late Roman and Byzantine influences stayed strong there, even after the Gothic conquests from AD 414 onwards. The influences also found expression in elite jewellery and belt fashions, and this buckle's concave sides and terminal roundel follow Byzantine models closely (**35**).

Scientific analysis at the British Museum confirmed the golden-coloured metal to be brass. Polychrome compositions of silver and brass set against a dark, iron background were also popular elsewhere, for instance on high-status metalwork among the Burgundians and Alamans in Switzerland and southern Germany, as well as the Baiuvars and the Franks (**91**).

Visigothic
From Spain (?)
7th century AD
Length 13.7 cm
1987,0509.1

94 THE CASTELLANI BROOCH

This brooch has polarized opinion like few other objects in this book, as its date of manufacture, who it was made for and its cultural background have all been debated. While some scholars advocate an origin in the seventh or eighth century, dates as late as the ninth have also been suggested. Moreover, there are arguments for it having been made in either a workshop in Constantinople or a southern Italian, Longobardic one. Whatever the truth may be, the brooch certainly reflects the refined tastes of a Mediterranean environment. The cloisonné enamel (**37**) set into a gold and pearl frame is handled exquisitely, highlighting the quality of the workshop.

The lady depicted on the brooch is portrayed wearing a brooch just like this one. It sits centrally on her chest and the three drop-shaped pendants echo the three loops on the bottom of the Castellani brooch. It has been suggested that the loops were for strings of pearls, but they could equally have been for suspended *pendilia* of pierced or mounted gemstones and pearls. Brooches with three *pendilia* have been interpreted as an imperial privilege from the fourth to tenth century, though some scholars have argued that the Longobard dukes of southern Italy saw themselves as successors of the Byzantine emperors and therefore adopted this sign of rank.

As for how they were worn, Isidore of Seville noted in the seventh century that men fastened their cloaks with brooches on the shoulder, while women wore them on the chest (*Etymologies* XIX.xxxi.17). This is indeed borne out further by pictorial evidence. Whether on portraits of emperors and their wives in stone, ivory and mosaic, on coins, or in illustrations of biblical scenes in the ninth-century Stuttgart Psalter, Isidore's observation largely holds.

The brooch was acquired from the collection of Alessandro Castellani (1823–83) in 1865, together with a number of other outstanding objects. Alessandro was the son of the founder of the jewellery firm famous for its designs inspired by archaeological finds. He also collected and sold antiquities and set up an art and antiquities gallery in Rome in his later years.

Byzantine or Longobard
Said to be from Canosa di Puglia, Italy
Late 7th to early 9th century AD (?)
Diameter excluding loops 5.9 cm
1865,0712.1

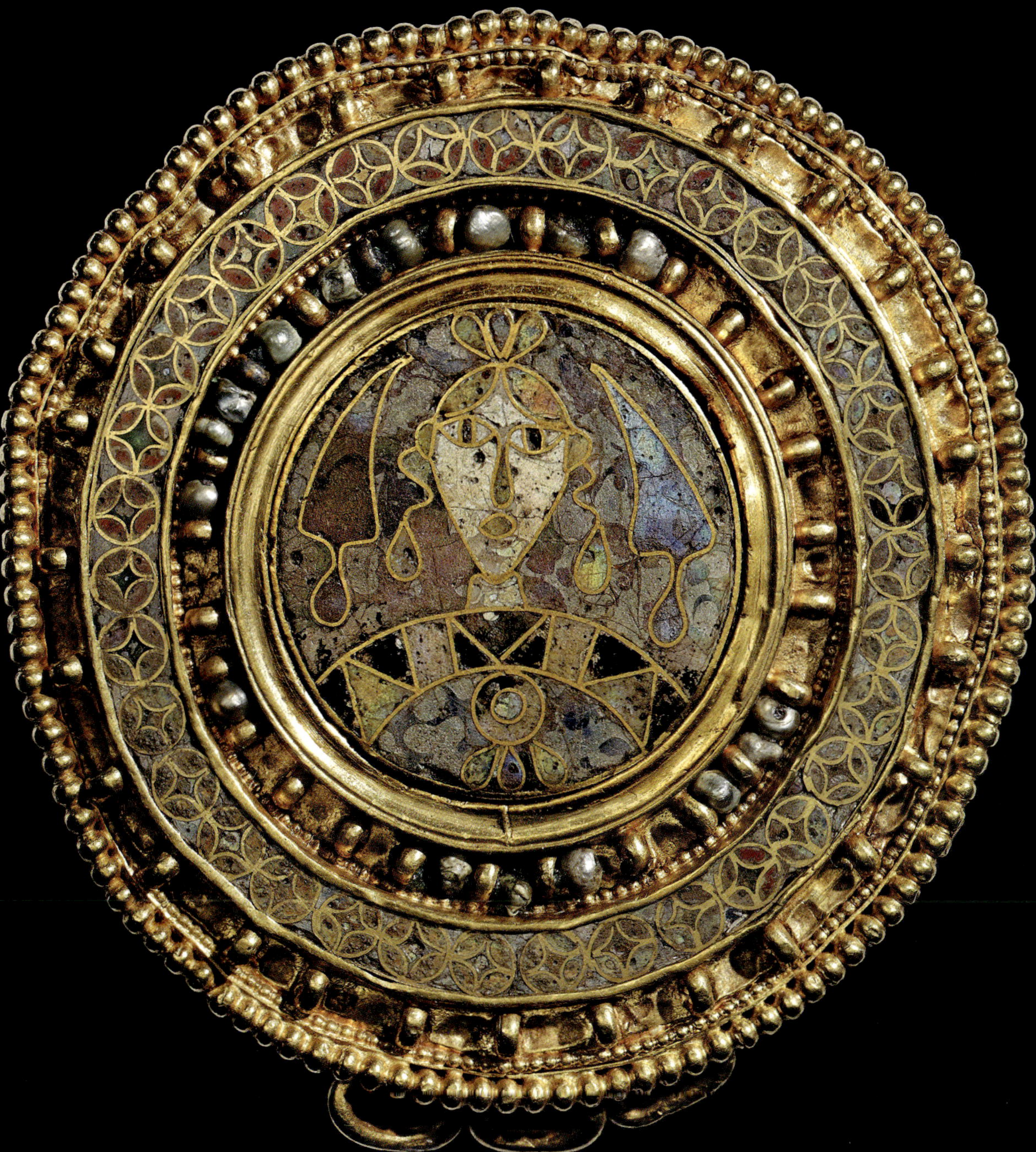

95 PYX

A number of squat silver vessels with a bulbous body and inward drawn lip are known from Carolingian and Viking Europe. Like this example here, another two finds from Anglo-Saxon England, namely the Vale of York (**111**) and Halton Moor cups, are in the British Museum. This Carolingian pyx is one of the most elaborate known and, unusually, retains its original lid.

A delicately modelled web of acanthus foliage covers both body and lid, the former inhabited by birds turning their heads backwards to pick at bunches of grapes. The gilded background contrasts with the silver fruit and birds, which are heightened in niello. The Christian symbolism is evident, and harks back to the biblical metaphor of Christ as the vine (**63**). The birds and grapes are also Christian motifs that had likewise long been in use and would continue to be depicted (**34**, **37**). The religious character is further emphasized by the cross-shaped rosettes which are inscribed into the acanthus, their centres formed by parcel-gilt floral crosses.

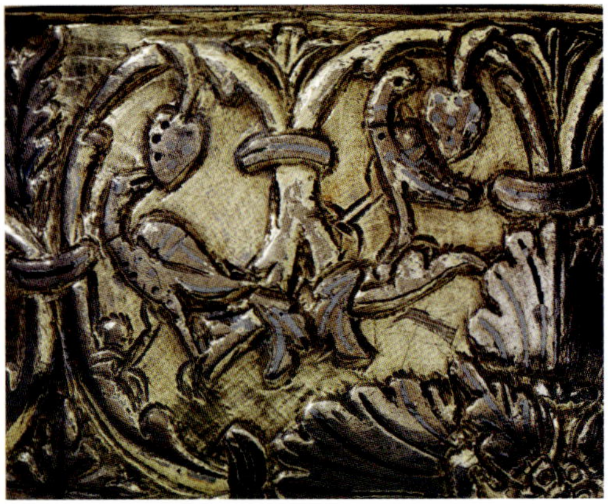

The precious nature of this vessel hints at its function as a container for the Host during Mass. The imagery refers to Christ, who nourishes the community of the faithful in the same way as the grapes sustain the birds, while the evergreen acanthus plant was a symbol of the Tree of Life. The latter alludes to a passage from the Book of Genesis (1:29–30) in which the lush vegetation inhabited by man and all the animals of Creation stands figuratively for Paradise and eternal life. At the centre of the lid, and crowning it in the form of another four-leaf rosette, is the Cross.

While the shape of this pyx is still similar to that of plainer pieces from the early Carolingian period, such as the Fejø and Pettstadt cups, its flamboyant surface decoration is an example of the conscious reuse of antique motifs such as acanthus foliage under Charlemagne around AD 800. Stylistic comparisons suggest production in Lotharingia, perhaps at Metz or Reims (**97**).

Carolingian
Said to be from Spain
Mid-9th century AD
Height including cover 12.6 cm
Bequeathed by A.W. Franks
AF.3041

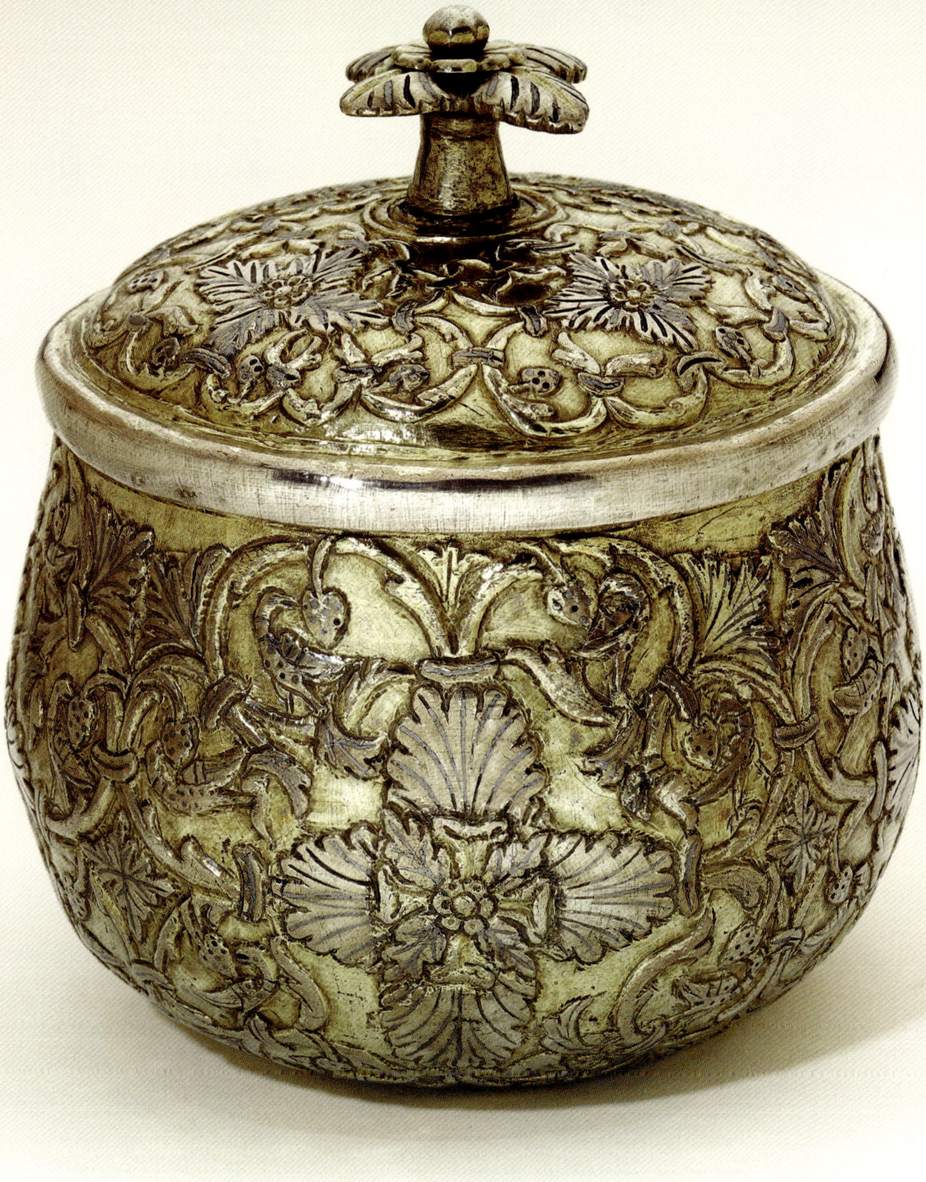

96 IVORY OF THE WEDDING AT CANA

One of the miracle stories from the New Testament concerns a wedding party in Cana. Christ, his mother Mary and the Apostles are invited, but when they arrive, they discover that the wine has run out.

This is the moment at which we join the narrative. The upper half of the ivory shows the arrival of Christ as well as the festivities which are already under way. The scene in the lower half shown here focuses on the distress of the steward, who opens his hands in a helpless pose. Christ, distinguished by his halo, stretches out his right hand in a placating gesture. This may be the crucial moment when he transforms the water, which servants are pouring into pots, into wine. The setting is depicted in loving detail, such as the neat roof tiling and the fine curling acanthus foliage. However, the perspective and proportions of the scenic elements are clearly secondary to the events portrayed.

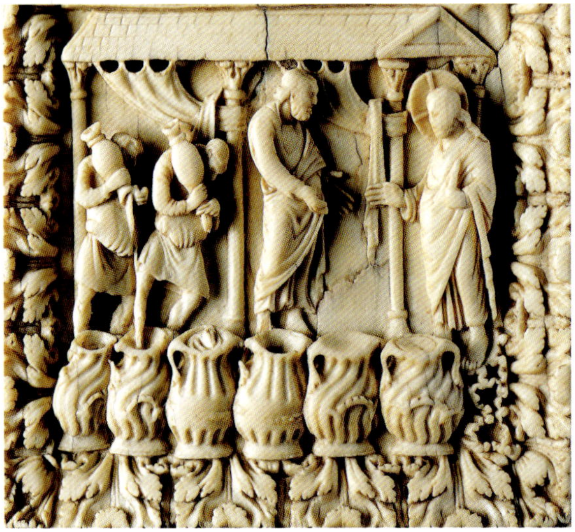

The scene is full of classical components, as one might expect from a Carolingian ivory (p. 167). Buildings are rendered in the *aedicula* style familiar from mosaics, wall paintings and ivories (**13**) since antiquity. Curtains have been pulled back and slung around columns, again in a traditional manner (**32**). Yet the expressiveness of the stances and gestures is a new element and allows the viewer to relate easily to the pitiful resignation of the steward.

The carving takes its inspiration from the Utrecht Psalter, an illustrated manuscript dated to around AD 825–35. Its dynamic ink drawings were hugely influential not only on other manuscripts, but also on ivories, such as this one, which copies some of the illustrations extremely faithfully.

This panel was once mounted on the cover of an illuminated book. It was produced in the palace school of the Carolingian king, Charles the Bald (AD 843–77) (**98**), and is an excellent example of the exquisite art that court schools had been producing since the time of Charlemagne (AD 768–814).

Carolingian
Probably from Germany
Middle to second half of the 9th century AD
Height 14.2 cm
1856,0623.20

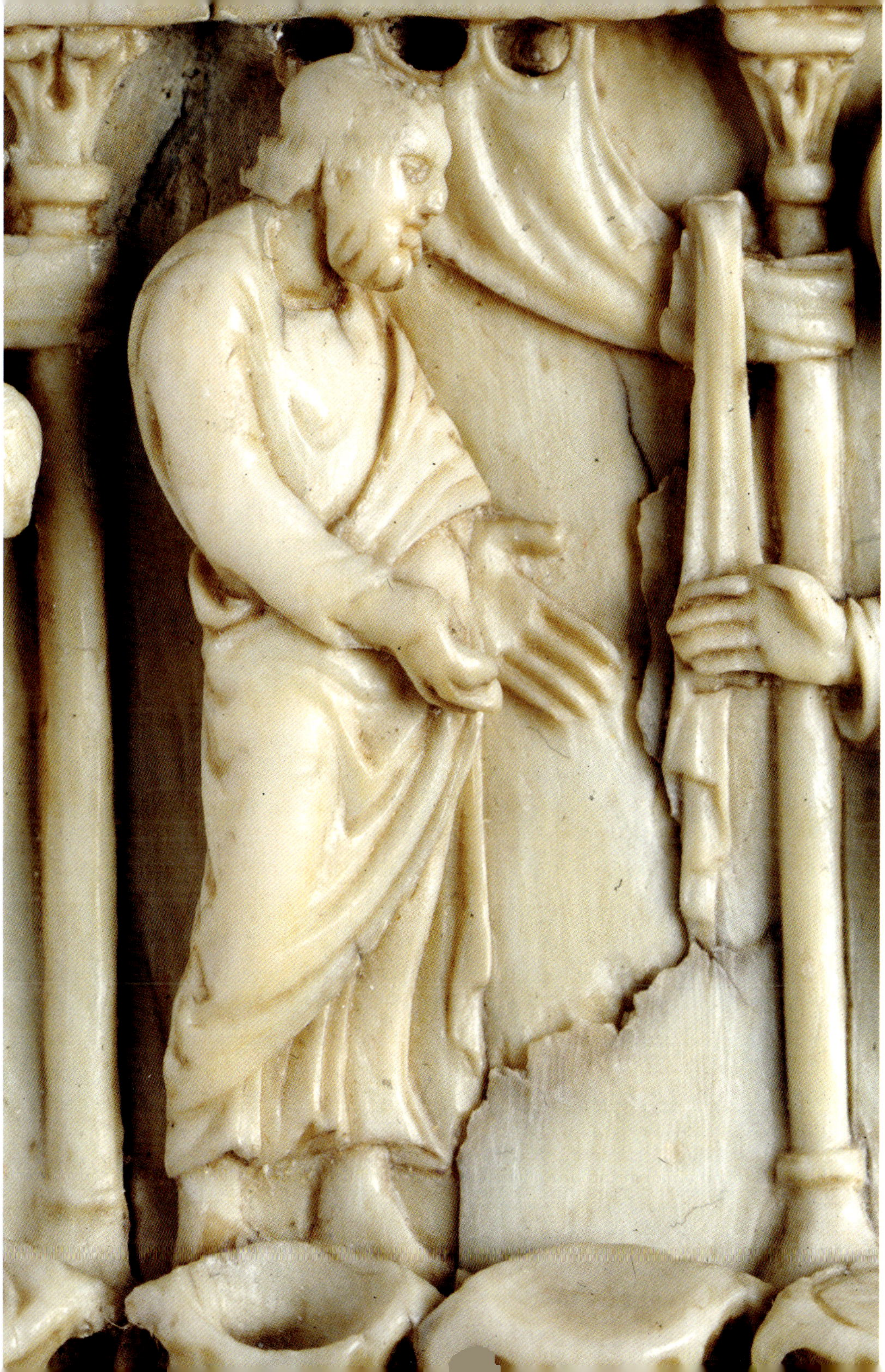

97 THE LOTHAIR CRYSTAL

This large rock-crystal disc is one of the very few objects in this book which can be associated with a historical person with some certainty. The central engraved medallion is surmounted by a Latin inscription stating 'Lothar, King of the Franks, had me made'. Given the subject matter of the narrative pictured on the crystal – namely the biblical story of Susanna, who was accused of adultery but proven innocent – the king in question is likely to have been Lothar II.

Lothar II (AD 855–69) was the ruler of Lotharingia, a territory wedged between the eastern and western Frankish kingdoms in the ninth century. As Theutberga, his wife, had not borne him any sons, Lothar tried to have the marriage annulled on a fabricated charge of adultery. But Theutberga successfully appealed to the Pope and they remained married. Lothar had to acknowledge publicly that the charges were false and it is tempting to see the crystal as a moralistic artwork connected to these events. But beyond this moral dimension, the central depiction carries a message about good governance: Susanna is standing in front of the king who exonerated her and Lothar is named above. The just ruler, a recurring theme in eighth- and ninth-century art, is overtly referenced here.

A large disc of rock crystal would have been rare and precious. The engraved decoration is of the highest quality, and the hardness of the crystal would have required a very experienced artist to work on it. The Carolingian court schools (**96**, **98**) provided the environment where outstanding craftsmen could collaborate with learned scholars who had the capacity to design sophisticated picture programmes such as this. This milieu also encouraged links with manuscript and ivory art. These are reflected here in the expansive gestures of the figures, with particular emphasis placed on their hands to convey fear and astonishment (**96**).

When Lothar II died without legitimate heirs in AD 869, his fears became reality and Lotharingia was divided up between the east and west Frankish kings. The crystal stayed at a nunnery, probably until the French Revolution, and may at one point have been converted into a morse, a brooch for fastening a liturgical garment.

Carolingian

Said to be from the River Meuse at Waulsort, Belgium

Crystal probably carved between AD 855–69

Copper-gilt frame 15th century

Diameter including frame 18.3 cm

1855,1201.5

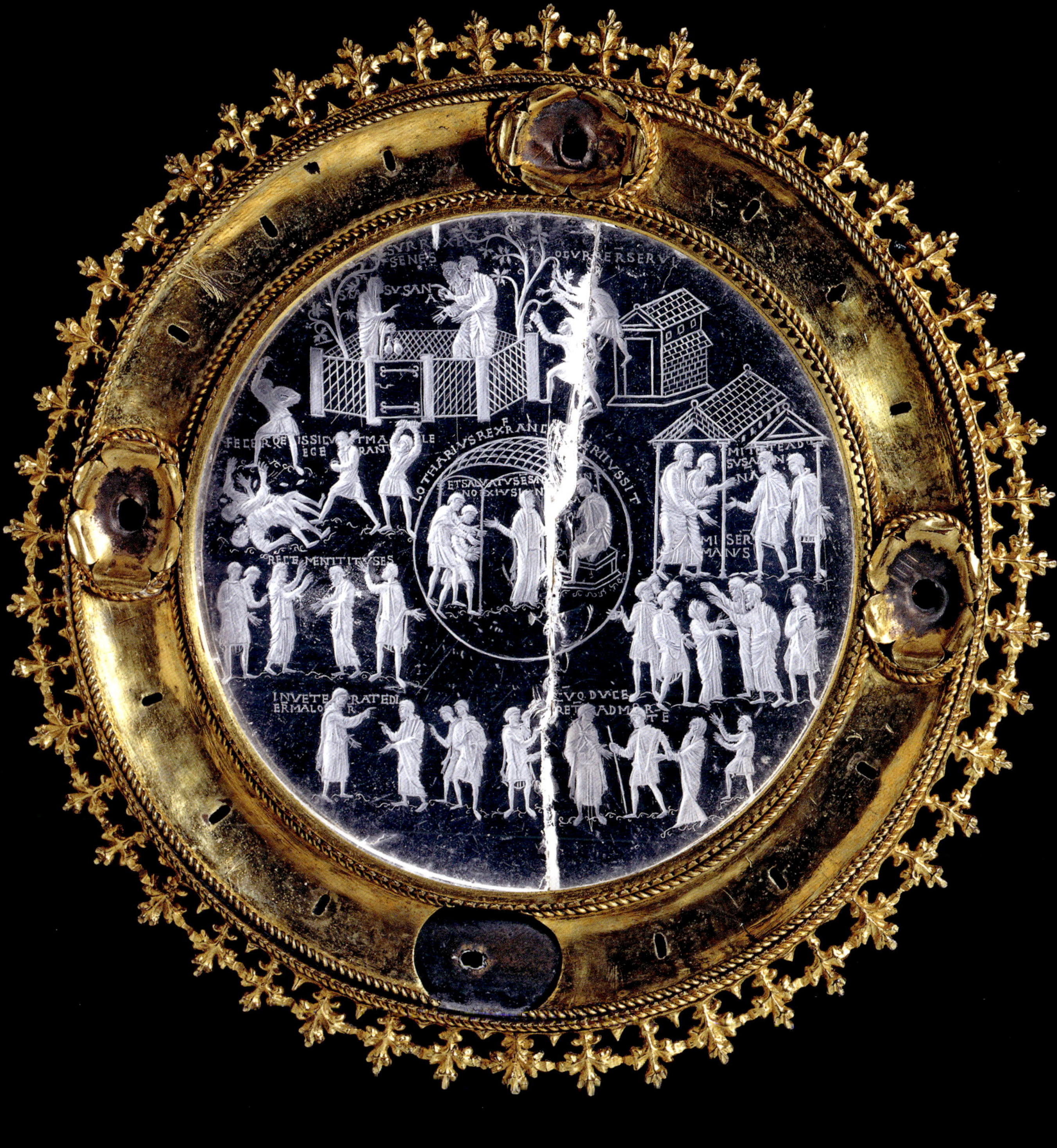

98 THE SAINT DENIS CRYSTAL

The Saint Denis Crystal has had an eventful history. A note describes it as being mounted on a shrine in the cathedral of St Denis, near Paris, by 1534. It is mentioned again in an inventory a hundred years later, after the tabernacle had been demolished and the crystal taken to the cathedral treasury. At this point it had an ornate frame set with smaller gemstones and pearls, which was illustrated in an engraving in 1706. At that time, it was considered to be a reliquary containing fragments from the clothing of St Louis. When the French Revolution reached St Denis in 1793, the crystal was removed from its frame and sent to a museum, but it was then auctioned in 1798. It was shown at the Society of Antiquaries in London in 1839 and finally sold to the British Museum in 1855.

Engraved on the back of the crystal is the Crucifixion with the Virgin Mary mourning on the left and John the disciple on the right. Christ's eyes may be closed, but the image is ambiguous, perhaps intentionally so. His head is tilted to the left and he seems to be either dying or already dead, in striking contrast with the pose of defiance shown on the late Roman ivory (**15**). Personifications of the sun and the moon are looking on from above, the former as a man with his cloak clasped on the right shoulder with a halo of rays. This is essentially the same iconography as that on the late Roman Symmachi diptych (**13**). Below the Cross a bearded serpent with feathered ears is curled up.

The crystal is a large cabochon. This gives it a magnifying effect, of which the engraver was clearly aware. In laying out the design, he left a margin of about seven millimetres around the edge. However, when seen from the front, the scene is enlarged by the optical properties of the crystal and fits perfectly.

Like the Lothair crystal (**97**), this piece may have been commissioned by a Carolingian ruler and it is possible that the crystal was his gift to the important abbey at St Denis. In this case it would have been Charles the Bald, who is also thought to have been associated with the previously illustrated fine ivory book cover (**96**).

Carolingian
From St Denis, France
c. AD 865–75
Height 15.5 cm
1855,0305.1

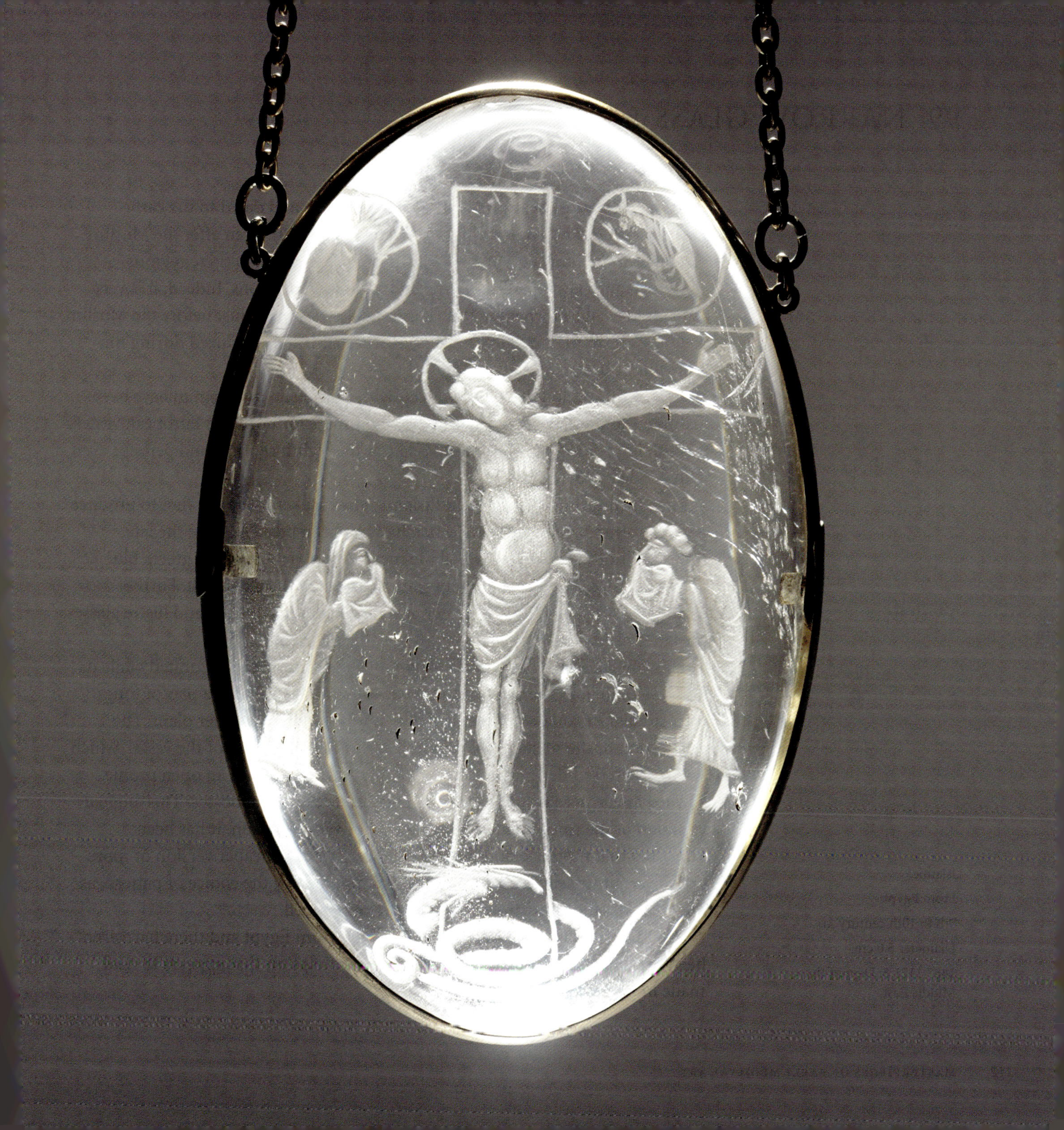

99 NARROW GLASS BOWL

Some of the most beautiful glass preserved today and dated to the early medieval period comes from the Middle East (**100**). Even after the Muslim conquest of the Near East and North Africa, glass makers in these regions continued and developed Byzantine and Sasanian traditions. Indeed, it is very difficult to establish whether Near Eastern glass was made just before the Muslim conquests from the AD 630s onwards, or whether it was produced during the following 150 years.

During this period the trade contacts with Europe do not seem to have been disrupted, and in fact it appears that the glass mass for northern European vessels was still imported from the Levant as late as the eighth century, and perhaps even a little longer (**45**).

The art continued to evolve and Islamic glass makers were the first to produce perfectly clear, colourless glass, which had not been possible since the late Roman period. They rediscovered the methods for removing the green, blue or brown tinge that was caused by natural oxides in the glass melt. Further accomplishments included the later development of enamelled and lustre glasses, the latter of which were covered with metallic pigments.

This small bowl or beaker was blown into shape and then decorated while its body was still hot. The walls of the vessel were impressed with a pair of tongs with circular or square ends, one of which was shaped, the other plain. The application of the metal tongs required access to the interior of the vessel, which is why impressed decoration is mostly found on vessels with an open profile.

The pattern here is composed of rectangles with central bosses. This angular variation of the round *omphalos* design is not very common. It has been suggested that moulded and impressed glasses were a cheaper version of more exclusive, cut vessels. This theory may be supported by the choice of pattern, as the *omphalos* motif exists in cut-glass versions as well.

The majority of such small, open vessels are from Egypt and there have even been two finds which were stamped with an inscription that appears to read 'made in Egypt'.

Islamic
From Egypt
9th to 10th century AD
Diameter 5.0 cm
1887,1121.5, Dept of the Middle East

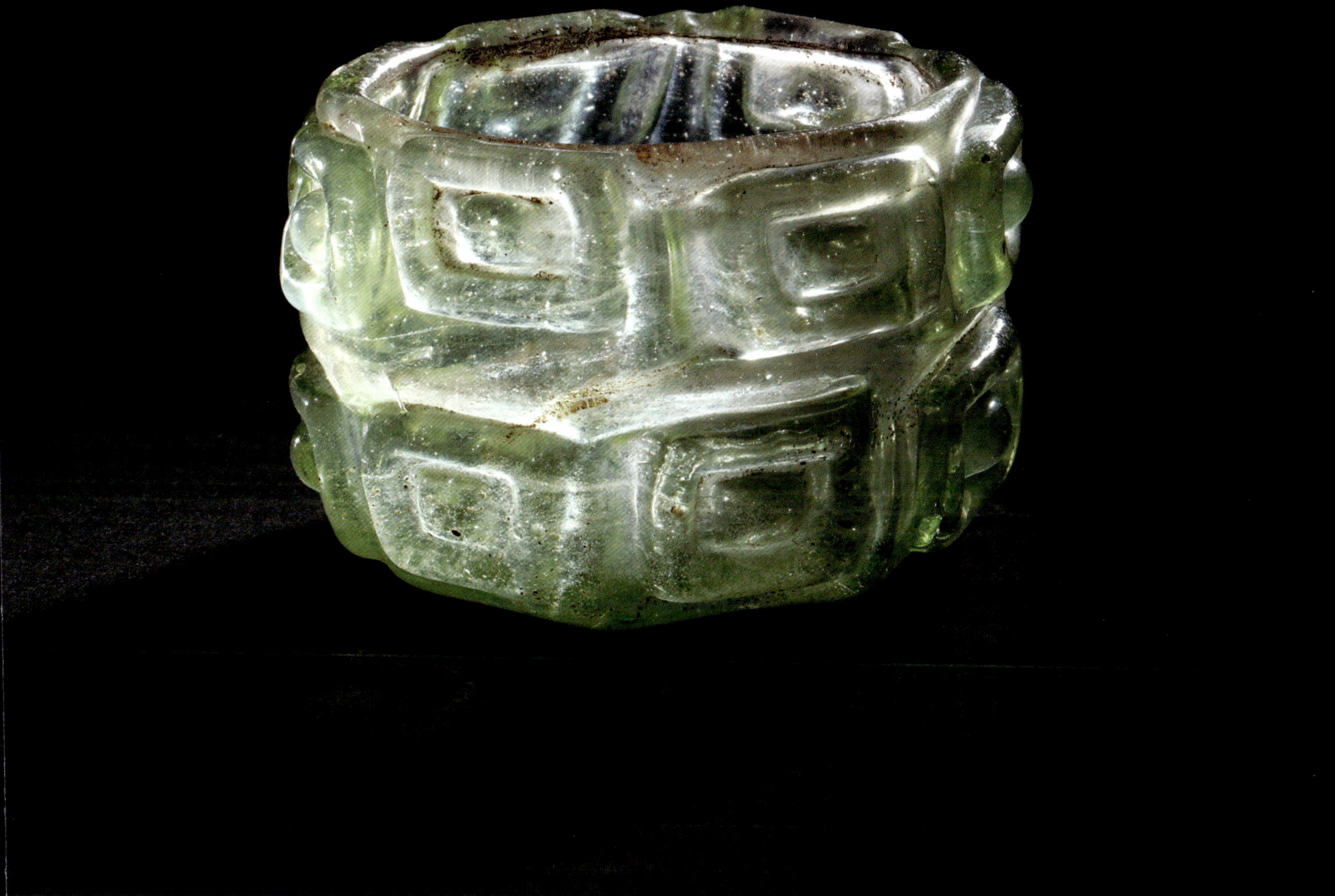

100 SHALLOW GLASS BOWL

This shallow bowl was produced in the same way as the previous more closed example (**99**), but instead used an animal motif for the tong impressions. After the medallions were moulded, the hot vessel was further worked by blowing and shaping the rim with a special, pincer-like tool to achieve the perfectly round shape. The continued blowing elongated the originally round medallions.

Only two zoomorphic motifs – birds or four-legged animals – were used for these impressions. This type of quadruped occurs on a number of vessels of varying shape, but is almost identical on all of them. Its appearance, with a long tail and elongated ears, could represent a feline, a design which is also found elsewhere in Islamic art. The Egyptian provenance of the bowl is in keeping with the form of this animal, which has mostly come to light on finds from Egypt or Syria.

Plain containers and vessels, as well as pottery, would have been available to a large number of customers, but the finer and more complex glass vessels were fit for wealthy households. In contrast to other arts such as rock-crystal cutting or book illumination, glass making enjoyed only brief periods of courtly patronage, even though high-quality glassware was certainly appreciated. This may have contributed to the continuity in the development of vessel forms and glass technologies from the pre-Islamic period into the Muslim era.

This bowl came to the British Museum as a gift from a nineteenth-century Egyptologist, who also donated several other pieces. One of them is a bowl of the same colour as the present vessel and is also decorated with quadrupeds, but of a narrower shape similar to the previously illustrated example (**99**).

Islamic
From Egypt
9th to 10th century AD
Diameter 9.1 cm
Donated by Count Riamo d'Hulst
1902,0517.4, Dept of the Middle East

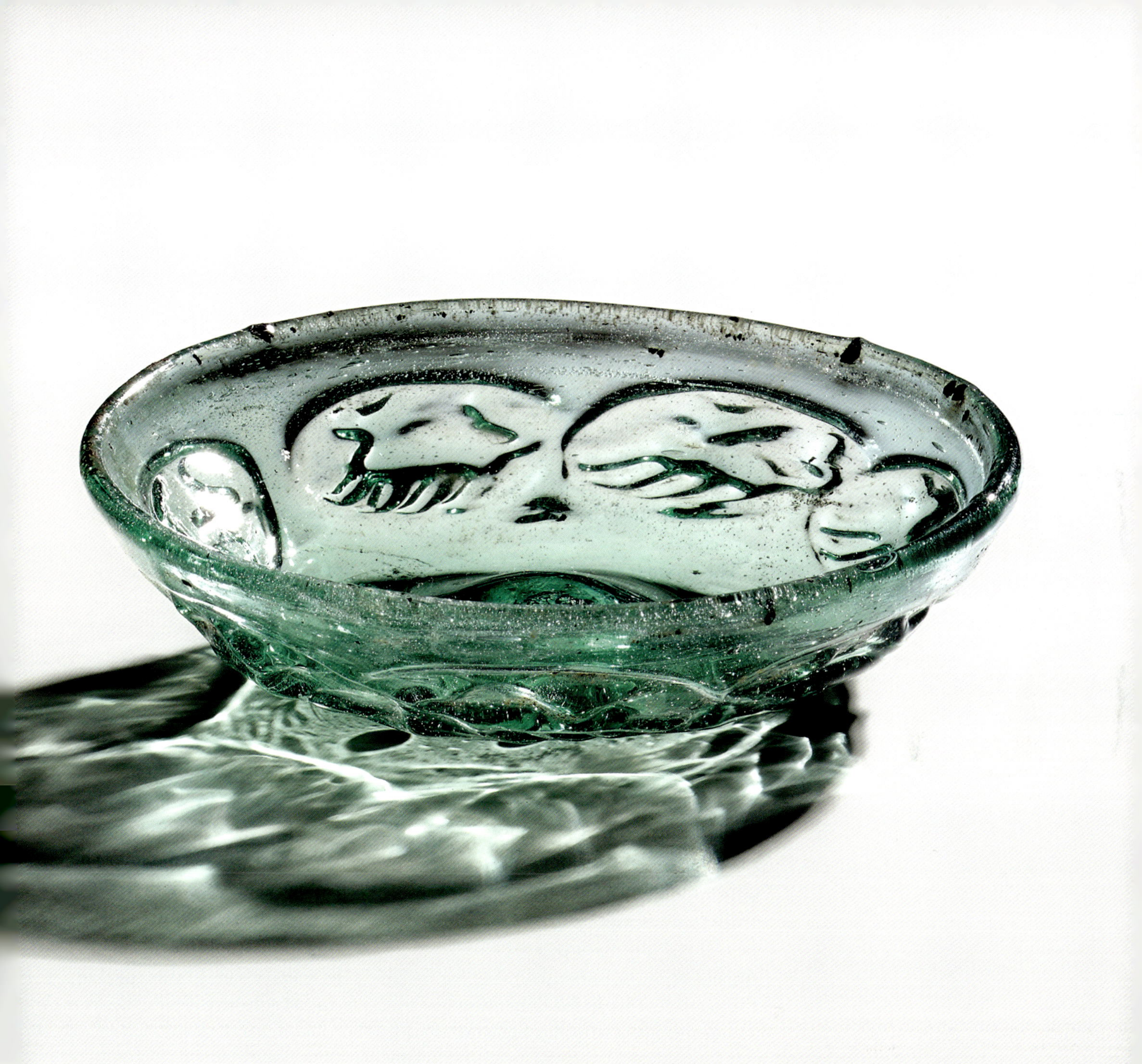

101 CHRIST RAISING THE SON OF THE WIDOW OF NAIM

Christ, accompanied by his disciples, encounters a procession leaving the city of Naim through a gate. A dead man is being carried on a bier. His mother is shown below it, her eyes fixed on the large figure of Christ. With an imposing gesture, he bids the deceased to return to life and, indeed, the young man is shown at the point of raising his head.

This is one of sixteen surviving elephant ivory plaques from the cathedral at Magdeburg in Germany. Otto the Great had them carved some time between becoming emperor of the Holy Roman Empire in AD 962 and his death in 973. It is likely that the commission took place during the time he spent in northern Italy, where the foremost ivory workshops in the Ottonian Empire were situated. Stylistic variations between the panels suggest that three different artists worked on them.

The carvings are probably linked to the elevation of Magdeburg to an archbishopric in AD 968. The plaques would have covered the surface of a piece of church furniture, perhaps a pulpit or a bishop's throne. The effect must have been very striking, as the pierced ivory plates were mounted on a gilt copper background which would have shimmered through the openwork. The broad frames of each panel would have been covered with metal bands, possibly encrusted with precious stones. During the first half of the eleventh century the cathedral was remodelled and the plaques were probably dismantled then.

The theme of this series of carvings is the life of Christ, from his childhood to his Resurrection. Originally there must have been a much larger number of plaques, as all the major events described in the New Testament are missing. The panels do not just tell a narrative, but interpret theological ideas current in the tenth century. The figure of Christ is always shown larger than any other and he is repeatedly presented as enthroned, symbolizing for example his role as a teacher or judge, rather than simply portraying the actual events as described in the Gospels. This added dimension distinguishes the Magdeburg ivory cycle from earlier traditions of biblical illustration (**96**).

Ottonian
From Magdeburg, Germany
Probably carved in Milan, Italy, *c*. AD 968
Width 11.8 cm
1856,0623.25

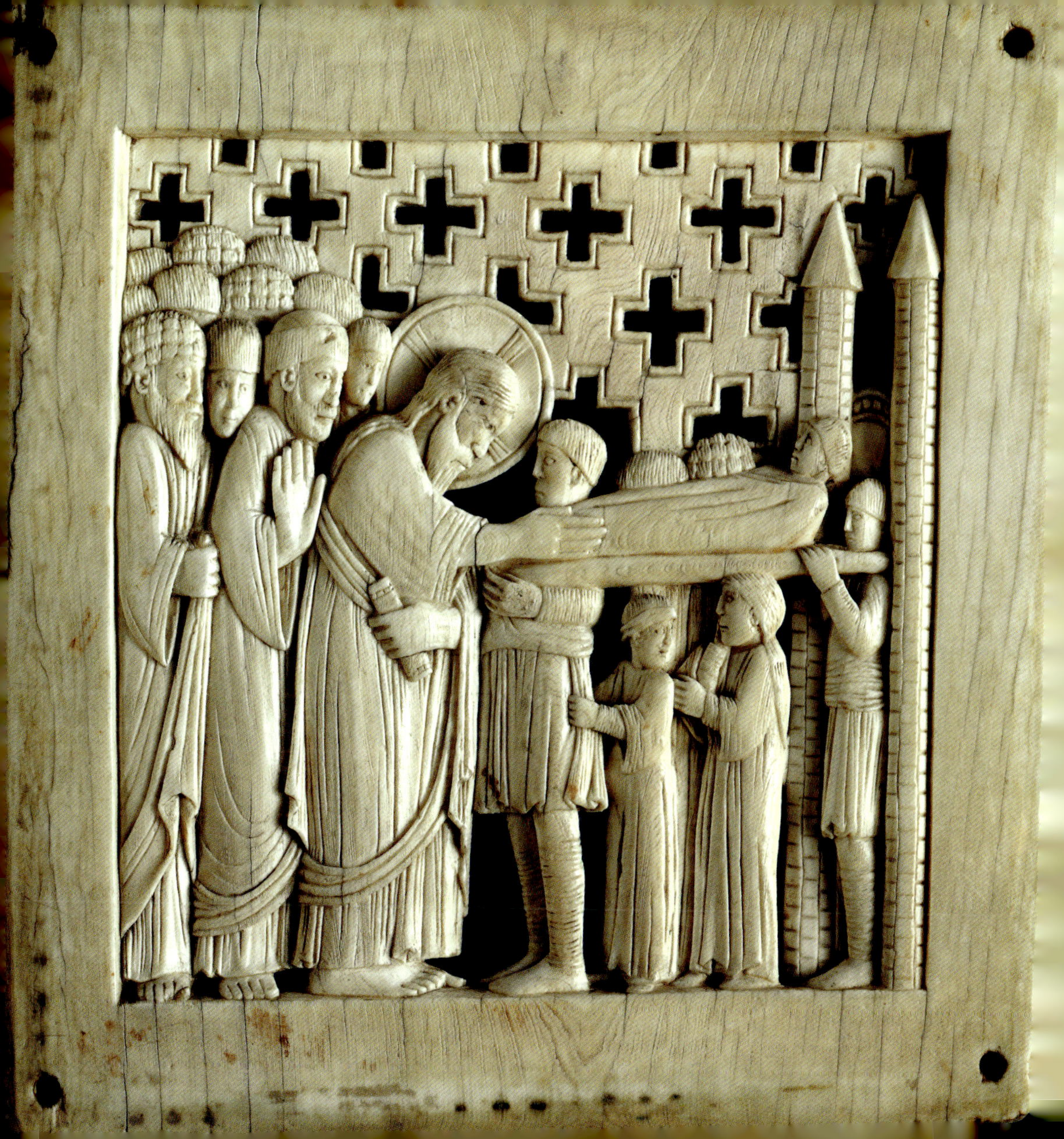

102 IVORY RELIQUARY

Complex religious ideas are encapsulated in this hollow ivory carving. Its base is sculpted with key scenes from the Christian faith, including Christ's Crucifixion, the empty tomb and his Ascension to Heaven. In the next register, the symbols of the four Evangelists are used to represent the New Testament, through which the events depicted on the base were communicated to the faithful. The composition is crowned by a now-damaged figure of the enthroned Christ sitting in front of a socket disguised as a tiled roof. The socket is hollow and would probably have secured the lower part of a cross. The body of the object is hollow as well and most likely acted as a reliquary, which originally could have been closed by a lid.

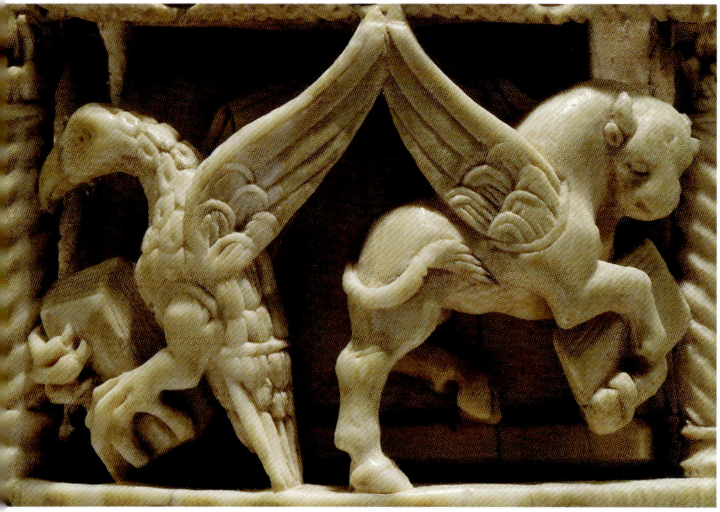

The Evangelists' symbols are rendered in beautiful detail. They have been carved in deep relief out of a thick section of elephant tusk and are therefore more or less three-dimensional. The special nature of these symbols is signified by the presence of wings not only on the eagle of St John and the angel of St Matthew, but also on the bull of St Luke and the lion of St Mark. The eagle and the bull each clutch a book in their talons and between their hooves respectively, reinforcing their status as emblems of the four Gospel authors. This is a very different and much more conventional way of illustrating the Evangelists' symbols than the man-eagle hybrid on the gold plaque from Brandon (**64**).

The large holes once held precious gems and it is possible that the reliquary was actually painted. The material in itself was hugely valuable. As ivory is very durable, it was an appropriate metaphor for the eternal nature of God. It also reflected the belief that the remains of the saints, fragments of which may once have been enclosed inside the reliquary, were incorruptible as well. The clearly architectural construction of the reliquary may be an allusion to the Heavenly Jerusalem, which was also echoed in later tower reliquaries.

Ottonian
Unknown findspot
c. AD 1000
Height 17.4 cm
Donated by W.D. Conybeare
1855,1031.1

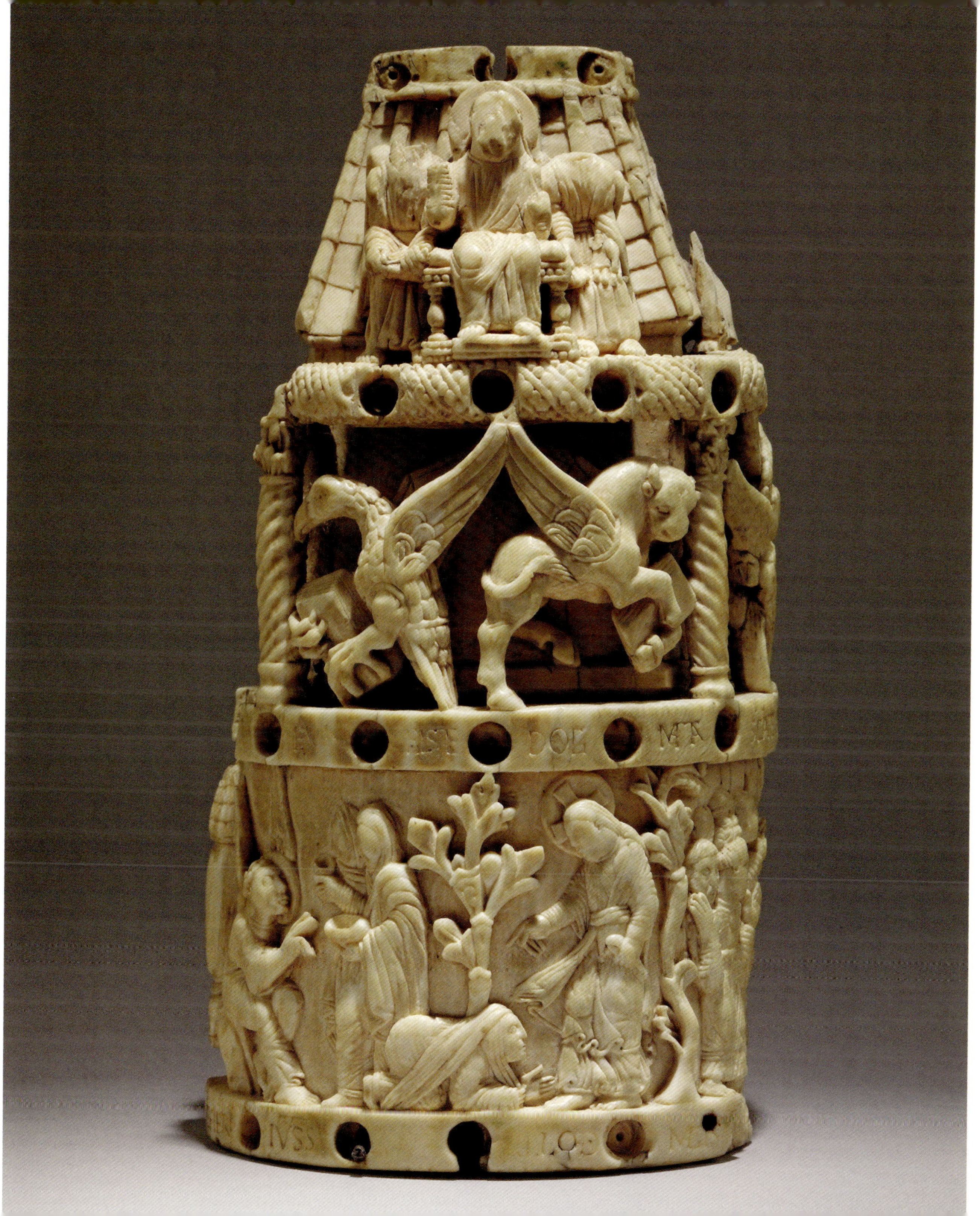

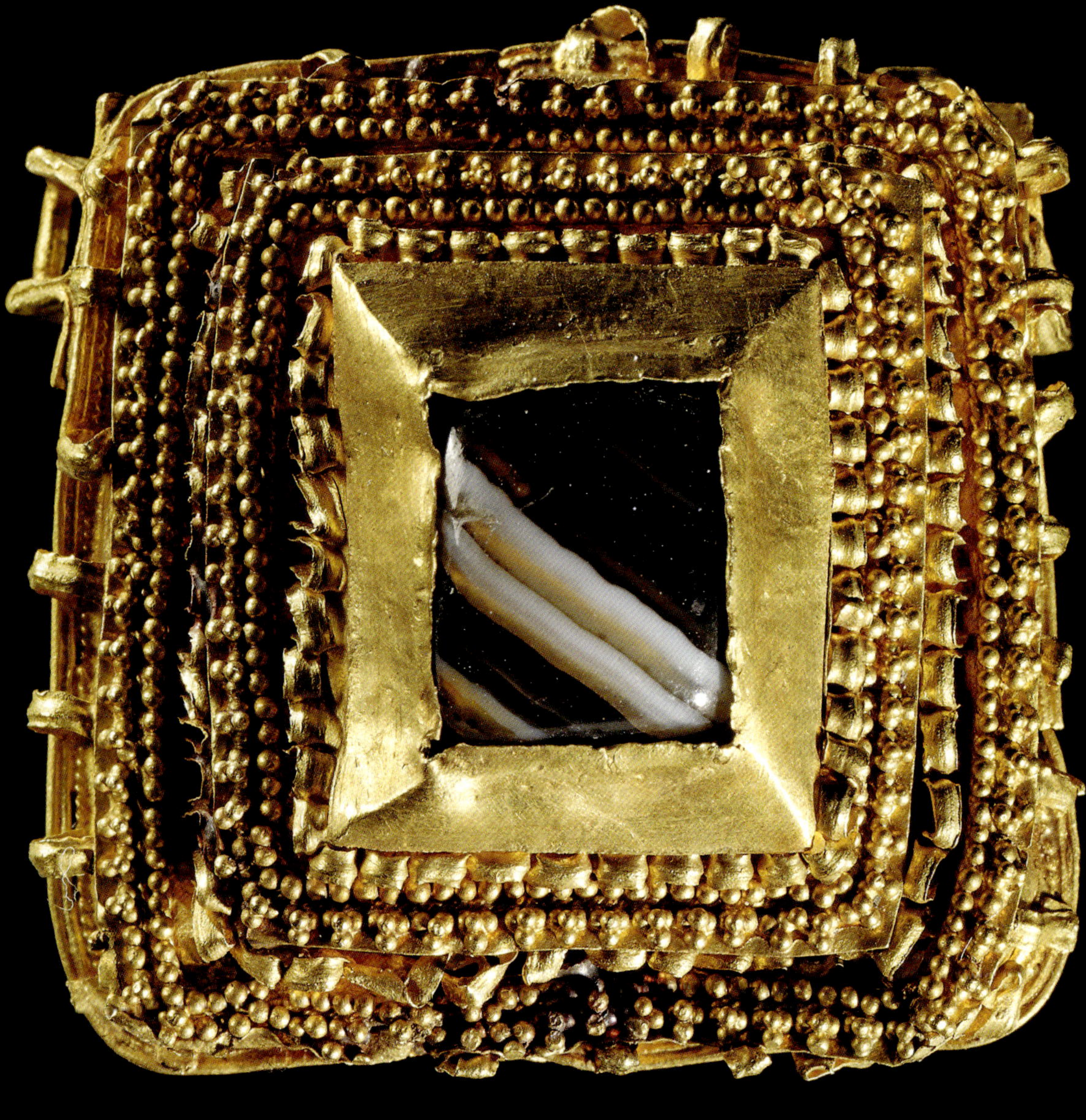

103 PYRAMIDAL BROOCH

A rectangular, banded onyx gem has been used to great advantage as the focus of this gold brooch. Banded gemstones such as onyx, sardonyx or agate had been sought after since antiquity. They were sculpted into vessels, set in imperial brooches or carved into cameos.

The delicate framework of the present brooch is constructed from several tiers of goldwork, embellished with pyramids formed from gold granules and alternated with small golden arches. The edge of the brooch is now damaged, but it would once have been framed by pearls threaded onto a golden wire and interspersed with the golden loops still visible today. The back of the brooch is open and thus the pin for fixing it to the garment had to be moved to the upper edge of the frame. This feature is also characteristic of other late brooches (**72**).

Pyramidal or conical brooches consisting of a detailed gold body with pearl frames and a gem at the apex were popular during the early eleventh century. Fashions in elite circles were at this time as international as they are today. Some scholars have suggested that this piece was made in Germany. The Ottonian dynasty had close relationships with the Mediterranean, culminating in the marriage of Otto II (AD 973–83) to Theophanu (d. AD 991), a niece of the Byzantine emperor, in AD 972.

Yet many of the elements on this brooch are only found on jewellery produced in Constantinople itself or in the parts of Italy then under Byzantine control. Particularly characteristic components are the bands of looped, flat wire, rows of pyramids formed from gold granules and frames of pearls. The latter features are also found on Byzantine earrings (**37**).

An additional clue as to the provenance of the brooch may be that it came to the British Museum from the collection of Alessandro Castellani (1823–83; **94**), which is thought to have been composed exclusively of Mediterranean finds.

Byzantine, perhaps made in southern Italy

Unknown findspot

Early 11th century

Width 2.9 cm

1872,0604.761

104 THE TOWNLEY BROOCH

One of the most spectacular late disc brooches (**72**, **94**) in the British Museum is the Townley brooch. Early records are unclear, but it seems that it came to the Museum in 1814, when the Townley Collection of art and non-classical antiquities was acquired.

An intricate design unites a central dome of gold sheet with filigree work and a large cloisonné enamel medallion. The Townley brooch belongs to a group of pieces which are distinguished by an arrangement of circular drums around the edge of the central dome. There is no backplate, so as with other late brooches, the pin sits asymmetrically towards the top (**103**).

Apart from a comparable brooch fragment from Belgium, the closest parallel is one from the Mainz Treasure from Germany, which actually comprised a number of separate finds. This jewellery is thought to have been associated with Gisela (d. 1043), wife of the Holy Roman Emperor Conrad II (1027–39). In any case, there is no question that the workmanship of the Mainz and Townley brooches is among the best that could be obtained in eleventh-century Europe.

Both the location of the Townley brooch's manufacture, as well as its findspot, remain a mystery. Given the provenance of the other comparable pieces, it could have been found in Ottonian Germany, but even if this is the case, it is possible that it was made in Byzantine Italy or beyond. Details of the decoration, such as the large scrolls made from gold bands, hint at a Mediterranean origin. Moreover, similar examples of the enamel of the central field as well as its equal-armed cross formed of four heart-shaped volutes can be seen on jewellery from the eastern periphery of the Byzantine Empire.

During recent conservation work, it was discovered that some of the pearls had been replaced by white glass spheres. Accretions of perhaps dirt or corrosion products had built up around the glass spheres over time, suggesting that the replacement did not take place recently, although it is impossible to say when these repairs took place.

Mediterranean or Ottonian (?)
Unknown findspot
Middle third of the 11th century
Diameter 5.9 cm
OA.4821

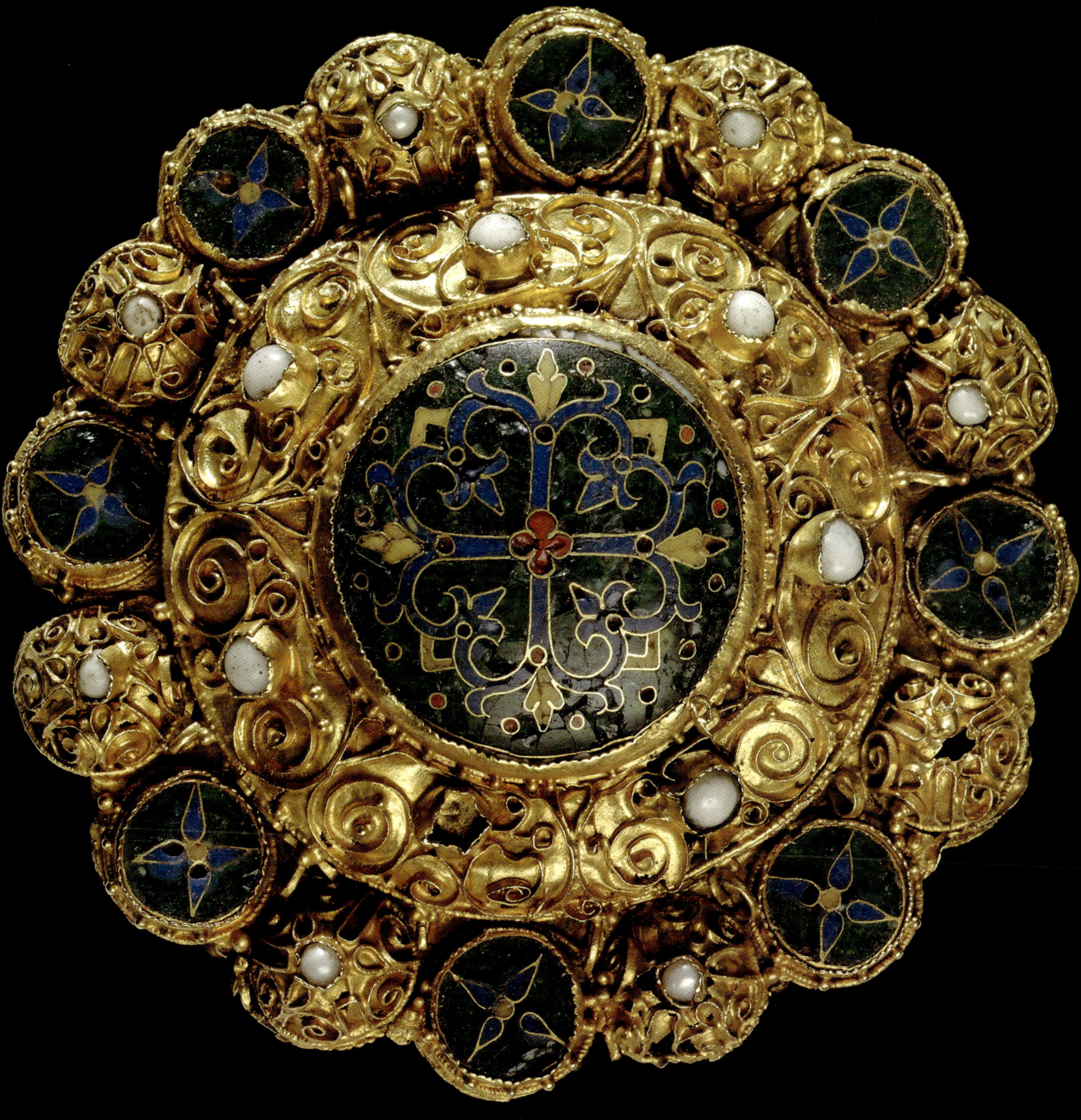

105 SILK TEXTILE

On a crimson background a repeating pattern in gold depicts rows of alternating paired birds, possibly falcons, and deer or, more likely, gazelles. Strands of stylized foliage separate the animal panels from each other. The gold thread is made from red silk yarn which was wrapped in the thinnest gold strips. The textile still has a very fine appearance due to the high number of threads used for both warp and weft.

A textile of this quality, made from such costly materials, was deemed fit for the emperor of the Holy Roman Empire (p. 167), just like the finest silks were the preserve of the Byzantine emperors, and was laid in the coffin of Henry VI. Henry had died in Sicily in 1197 and his body was later moved to Palermo Cathedral where a plot belonging to his family, the Hohenstaufen Dynasty, was established in 1215. When the graves were examined in the late eighteenth century, Henry's body was found to be covered with a plain yellow silk. The present textile was sewn to it, possibly as the upper border, which one bystander described as 'so lovely and delightful that it could not be made more beautifully today'.

The roots of the ornament go back to Sasanian silks, with their repeating patterns of decorative roundels which enclosed, for example, paired animals such as lions or griffins. Such motifs were still popular centuries later in Syria, and influential far beyond its borders (**133**). However, there is some debate as to whether this silk was woven in Syria, Egypt or Persia. Alternatively, it may have been made in Sicily, where silk embroidery was common, even though there is little evidence of silk weavers being present there.

It is likely that the grave cloth with the crimson border was placed in Henry's coffin when his body was moved by his son and successor Frederick II (1194–1250). The fact that Frederick established a family burial place in Palermo was a fundamental dynastic statement for the family who saw themselves as the successors of the Roman emperors: Frederick was king of Sicily and the German lands, later also king of Jerusalem and emperor of the Holy Roman Empire. An appreciation of this context emphasizes that this bird and gazelle silk must have been among the most precious textiles available at the time.

Mediterranean
From Palermo, Sicily, Italy
Early 13th century
Width 24.0 cm
1878,0907.4

5 THE VIKINGS AND THEIR NEIGHBOURS
(SIXTH TO ELEVENTH CENTURY)

Derived from the Scandinavian word for warrior, the term 'Viking' covers the diverse groups of people who came from Scandinavia, but whose penchant for long-distance travel and trade took them to places as far flung as North America, Russia, Byzantium, Sicily and even Baghdad between the eighth and eleventh century (**Map 4**). They were mostly feared as raiders, arriving across the sea without warning and intruding far inland to attack and plunder cities all across Europe. This was made possible by their sophisticated ship carpentry and the construction of boats that could be both rowed and sailed.

Copper alloy brooch from a grave at Tromsø, Norway, late 7th to early 8th century AD, 1900,0518.2 (see **106**)

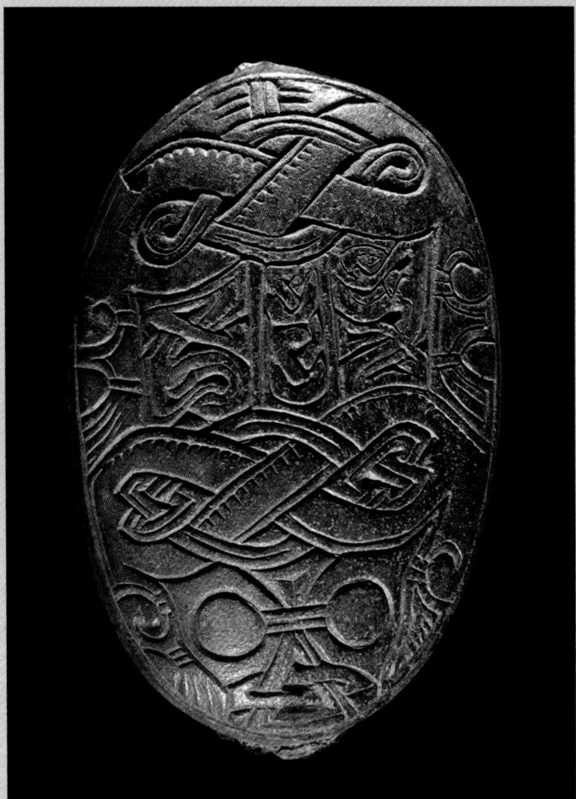

The Vikings made a brief appearance in Dorset in AD 789, before establishing themselves as a recurring affliction after they infamously raided the monastery at Lindisfarne off the coast of Northumbria in AD 793. Back in the Viking homelands, we find the spoils from their assaults on ecclesiastical establishments all over northern Europe, such as metal mounts torn from Christian shrines (**147**), Irish enamel work and Carolingian church vessels (**95, 111**). From the ninth century onwards, the Vikings also settled in the British Isles and the early urban centres of Ireland were founded by them. Viking kingdoms arose, for example around the cities of Dublin and York, and some of the eleventh-century kings of England were Danish. After Alfred the Great defeated the Vikings in AD 878, the region later known as the Danelaw was established, which was an independent part of northern and eastern England administered in accordance with Viking laws until the Norman Conquest. The events of 1066 themselves had a Viking root, as William the Conqueror (1066–87) was a descendant of Vikings who had settled in Normandy, named after the 'Northern Men'.

Close contact with the Irish and Anglo-Saxons, in addition to the large amounts of silver that the Vikings brought back from the Byzantine and Islamic worlds (**128**), led to a new flourishing in the arts. Viking ornament, characterized by sinuous animals (**107**, **126**) and enigmatic masks (see facing page), gained a new impetus, resulting in distinctly Irish- and Anglo-Viking metalwork and stone sculpture. Excavations in cities such as York and Dublin have also unearthed plenty of evidence for wood, stone and bone carving (**122–4**), as well as the working of iron, copper alloy and precious metals. Textile manufacture was far advanced with the production of a range of fine fabrics as well as the acres of cloth needed for the sails of their ships (**110**). The bloodthirsty invaders described in written accounts are in fact revealed as skilful and versatile craftsmen and women.

The Vikings also influenced their neighbours across the Baltic Sea where, for instance, highly skilled copper alloy casting following local traditions was combined with brooch forms adopted from Viking costume.

To the south, east and west of the Baltic and Finno-Ugrian peoples, Slavic speakers lived. Little is known about the early periods of the latter's history, but from the sixth century onwards they appeared regularly in Byzantine and Carolingian sources. They came into contact with Swedish Vikings who were exploring the river routes through Russia and settled, for example, around the areas of modern-day Novgorod and Kiev. Vikings were instrumental in the rise of the Kievan Rus', the precursor to both the Russian and Ukrainian states. They travelled all the way to Byzantium where they provided the mercenaries who formed the Varangian imperial guard, which was founded in the tenth century.

Waves of new protagonists from the East appeared on the European scene from the seventh century onwards and partly settled in formerly Byzantine territory or in its northern periphery (**Maps 3** and **5**). Among these peoples, the crucial importance of the horse found expression in elaborate riding gear worthy of great warriors (**132**). Some of these peoples, such as the Magyars and Bulgars, founded kingdoms whose successor states, Hungary and Bulgaria, are still part of contemporary Europe.

106 MILLEFIORI GLASS BEADS

Millefiori literally means 'a thousand flowers' and takes its name from glass decorations composed of very small sections. These could take the form of glass slips for inlays (**46**), whole millefiori vessels or beads. In order to produce the beads, thin rods of different coloured glass were fused together, producing chequerboard, floral or other types of patterns. Bundles of such rods were then merged to make the beads.

This style of bead emerged in the Roman Empire and examples such as those discovered in bog sacrifices at Nydam, Denmark, had already found their way to Scandinavia. These beads were large and much more complex than the local glass and amber examples, and must have been highly sought after. The yellow and purple bead from Gotland, shown here on the right, is thought to date from the Roman period. The fashion for large millefiori beads, however, had a renaissance in the Viking period, when they reappeared after an absence from the archaeological record. The blue bead with the yellow chequerboards, shown on the left, was found in a woman's grave at Tromsø in northern Norway, which also contained an oval brooch (p. 226). This type is more or less identical with the Gotland bead, but was buried some four hundred years later.

It appears that there were specialized glass bead makers, although their working areas in trading centres such as Ribe, Denmark, or Hedeby, northern Germany, are usually found among those of other craftsmen such as metalworkers or comb makers. At the important trading town of Kaupang, Norway, bead makers were among the first to set up their workshops. On occasions, it seems possible that they also carried out other crafts such as copper alloy working. While millefiori beads are among the most technically complex types, the process of making glass beads was still much simpler than the blowing of glass vessels.

Evidence of bead production in the form of unicoloured and millefiori glass rods, broken beads and glass melt has been found in a number of places in Scandinavia and it is likely that bead makers moved around to ply their trade.

LEFT:
Viking
From Tromsø, Norway
Late 7th to early 8th century AD
Diameter 3.3 cm
1900,0518.3-5

RIGHT:
Provincial Roman (?)
From Gotland, Sweden
3rd to 4th century AD (?)
Diameter 2.8 cm
1921,1101.59

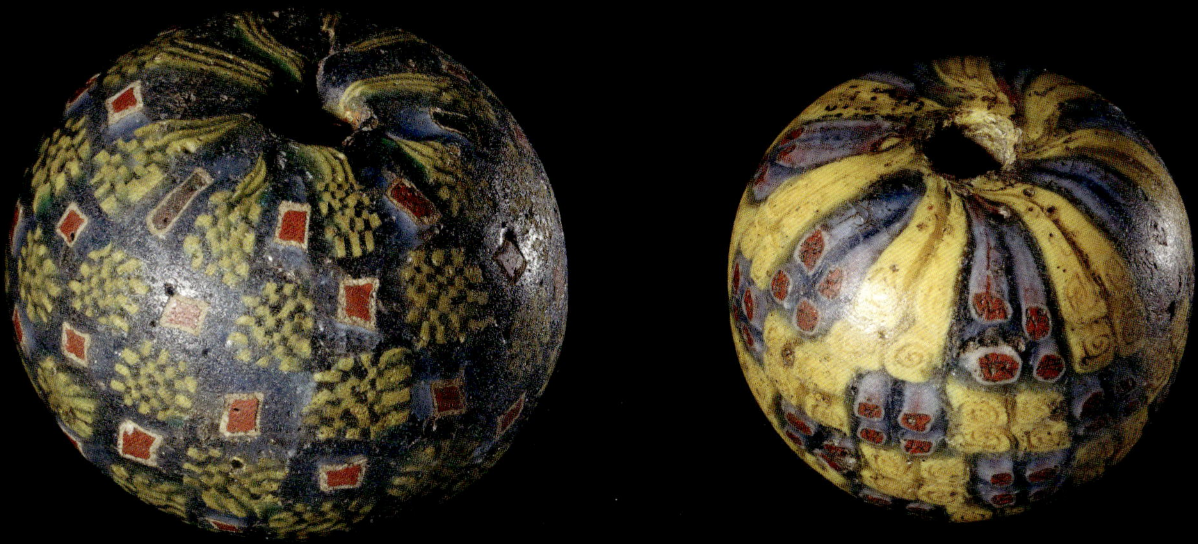

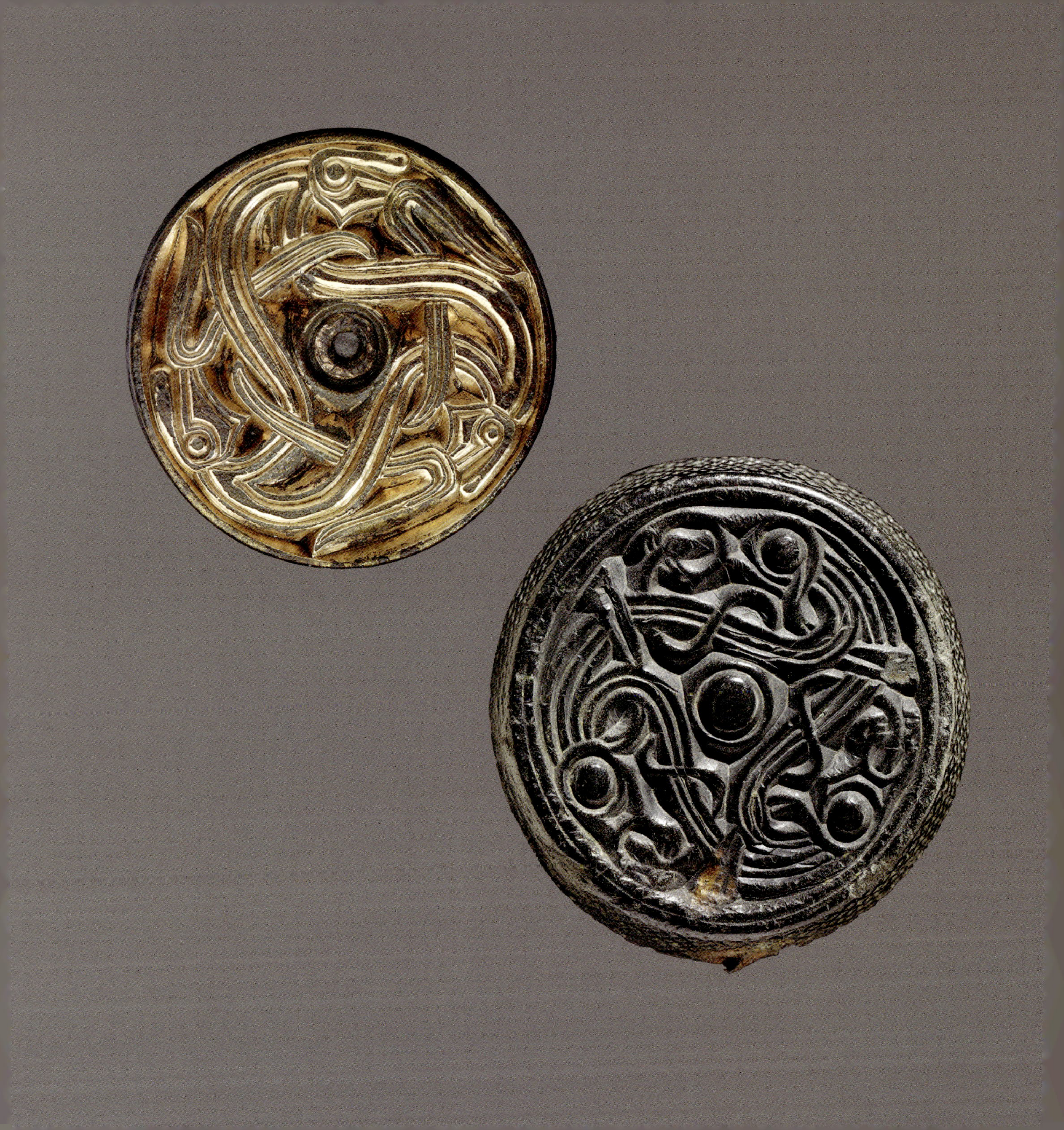

107 DISC BROOCHES

LEFT:
Vendel Period
From Nygårds, Gotland, Sweden
End of 6th to early 7th century AD
Diameter 3.8 cm
1921,1101.277

RIGHT:
Viking
From Gotland, Sweden
8th century AD
Diameter 4.3 cm
1921,1101.139

A whirling trio of animal heads is the feature which unites these two brooches. The gilt-bronze brooch on the left is in Animal Style II (**50**), with the eye of one of the animals seen towards the top. Its head is indicated by a frame ending in a forelock and long jaws which bite the outlines of the body linking this beast with one that follows it clockwise. The dark copper alloy brooch on the right shows the same motif, but in an anticlockwise arrangement. The animals on this brooch are less clearly delineated, and have more pronounced necks and pincer-like jaws, but the composition is the same, with each beast linked to the next and all rotating around a central boss.

More than a century may separate these two brooches and yet the designs are conservative enough to be still clearly related. Such disc brooches were common on Gotland and Bornholm, another island in the Baltic. They emerged in the early seventh century and over five or six generations were transformed into brooches with increasingly high, sloping sides, which were eventually superseded by even higher brooches with drum-shaped bodies (**116**).

Such uninterrupted developments are uncommon outside of Scandinavia during the early Middle Ages. Elsewhere in Germanic Europe, migrating populations, the arrival of new peoples from the eastern steppes and the rise and fall of kingdoms led to a much more fractured evolution of tastes and fashions. In addition, the closer proximity to the Mediterranean with the enduring allure of the Byzantine Empire (see p. 52), as well as the conversion to Christianity, which reached Scandinavia much later, influenced dress and jewellery styles.

It is no coincidence that the objects from Gotland in the British Museum illustrate the continuity of the island's artistic developments. In 1921 the Museum acquired the collection of James Curle (1860–1944), a noted lawyer, antiquarian and archaeologist. Curle had been interested in the development of different object types and indeed in 1891 he wrote in a letter: 'I also have a pretty complete series of the round box fibulae from the small flat brooch to the heavy ornament of the late iron age.'

108 WEIGHT

Viking commerce employed a bullion system, which meant that it was the weight of precious metals that counted. Even foreign coins were not used according to their denomination, but were considered to be just another form of silver. Consequently, it was extremely important to ascertain the exact weight of bullion, which might come in the form of silver jewellery such as armlets (**120**) or brooches (**113**, **115**, **150**), as well as coins, ingots or any of these chopped up into fragments. In parts of Scandinavia the bullion system lasted beyond the end of the eleventh century.

Small, portable balances were common and ingeniously designed. The beam could be folded and tucked inside one of the balance pans, which was then itself enclosed inside the other pan. Hemispherical copper alloy cases for such folded sets have been found. In addition, a calibrated set of weights was necessary. Simple lumps of lead were used, but highly elaborate lead weights also existed. They came in geometric shapes such as cubes, prisms or cones, and sometimes had pieces of Insular metalwork set into their tops. Whether gilt copper alloy or enamelled fragments, the Vikings clearly valued the aesthetic appeal that these recycled pieces of metalwork added to their weights.

This head of a religious figure of Celtic origin suffered such a fate. The fact that the crown of the head was left ungilt and is slightly recessed indicates that the head may have once been positioned within a niche or frame. It was removed from its original setting and the back was filled in with lead, thus converting it into a weight.

Parallels for the stern face, carefully modelled beard, curls and ears can be seen in small sculptures found on Irish reliquaries as well as in Insular manuscript illumination. The figure of St Mark in the Lichfield Gospels, for example, is not only similar in appearance, but also roughly contemporary with this head. The identity of the head remains uncertain, but it could well have been a saint or even Christ himself from an impressive piece of ecclesiastical metalwork made in Ireland or Northumbria.

Celtic, with Viking reuse

Found near the abbey at Furness, Cumbria, England

Made in the 8th century AD, modified in the 9th to 10th century AD

Height 3.9 cm, weight 126.3 g

1870,0609.1

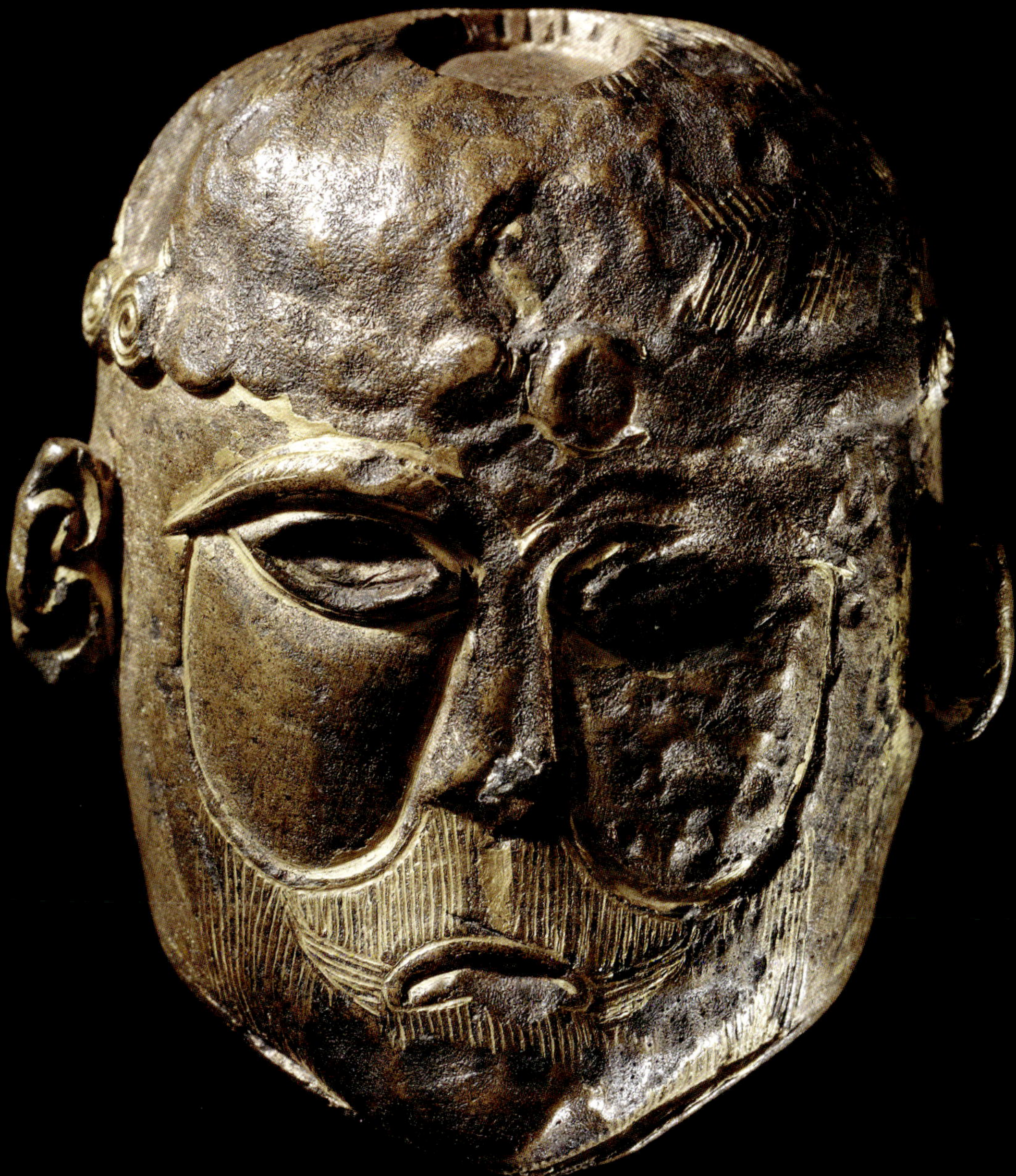

109 THE BALLYCOTTIN CROSS BROOCH

The donor of this brooch stated in a letter that it was 'said to have been found in or near Ballycottin Bog, Youghal, County Cork'. As provenances go, this is not unreasonable as Cork was one of the major Viking centres in eighth- and ninth-century Ireland, and could well have been the port at which the brooch arrived.

The brooch is of a well-known, Carolingian type which was popular in the Netherlands, the Rhineland and parts of northern Germany. It was cast from copper alloy and then gilt. The gilding as well as its ornament elevate the Ballycottin brooch over most of its contemporaries. A chip-carved and highly stylized animal in the Tassilo Chalice Style crouches inside a frame on each arm of the cross. This style is named after the famous chalice commissioned by Duke Tassilo III of Bavaria (AD 757–88), a contemporary, and sometime adversary, of Charlemagne (AD 768–814). It is the epitome of a highly distinctive ornament, originally derived from Insular art and subsequently developed in its own manner on the Continent.

The brooch was further embellished with twelve silver imitation studs at the end of each cross arm which surround the central setting. The latter is of special interest as it is an Islamic seal. Finger-rings with such seals have also been found in Russia, where Arab traders used them as gifts to offer their Viking hosts.

The Arabic inscription incised in the black glass may read 'We have repented to God'. While this would be an eminently suitable inscription for a Christian brooch, it is clear that the maker could not read it as it is unlikely that it would have been mounted on its side intentionally. For aesthetic reasons, he chose to set the oval gem so that it is standing on its side when the pin is horizontal, which is how the brooch would have been worn. Clearly what mattered to the craftsman and wearer was the presence of an exotic gem, but it is doubtful that its meaning was understood. The Vikings had connections to both the Islamic and Carolingian worlds, so they are a likely conduit for first the gem and then the finished brooch (**111**).

Carolingian, with an Islamic gem
From Ballycottin Bog, Co. Cork, Ireland
8th to 9th century AD
Width 4.4 cm
Donated by P.T. Gardner
1875,1211.1

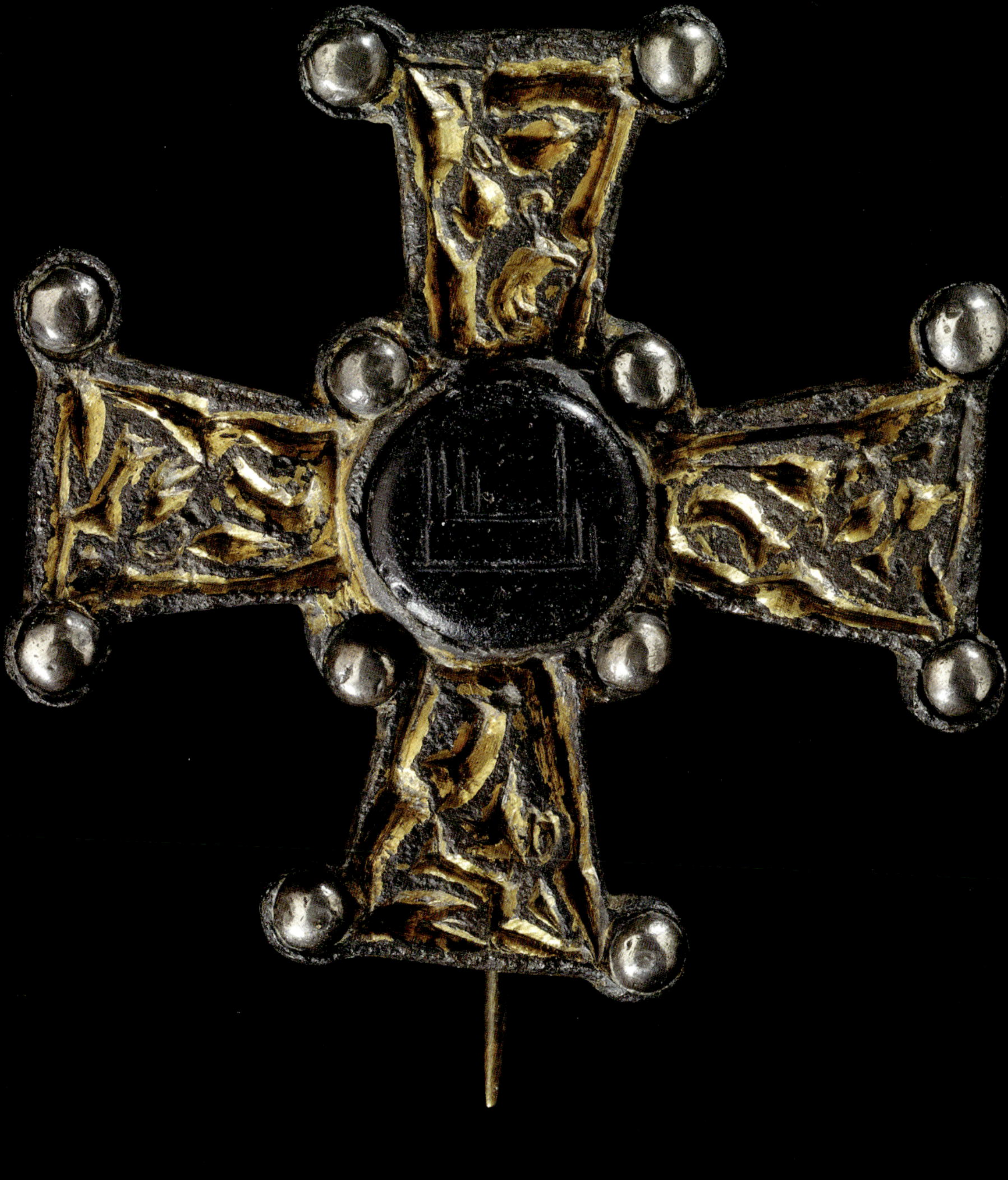

112 DISC BROOCH

Some of the most elaborate brooches of the Viking Age feature three-dimensional anthropomorphic and animal figures arranged on a gently curving disc. A common attribute of these silver and sometimes gilt brooches is that the figures are arranged around the rim and orientated towards the centre of the brooch. This is occupied by an openwork feature with a finial knob, though it remains unclear what this represents. The openwork is reminiscent of an architectural structure or sometimes a tree, with long-necked and often snake-like animals emerging from it.

The construction of these brooches is as complex as it looks. The disc was cast with some low relief in place and could be further textured by the application of punch tools, as on this brooch. If the disc was gilt, this process happened at this point before the separately cast, three-dimensional parts were riveted in place.

The meaning of these scenes is enigmatic. On the brooch pictured here two human-like figures are depicted pulling on their forked beards. This may be significant as it is a gesture seen, for example, in a bronze effigy thought to represent the fertility god Freyr from Lunda, Sweden. It also appears on some of the much earlier amuletic figurines from Anglo-Saxon England (**52**) and Scandinavia. Another representation of a forked beard being clutched by its owner is on an eleventh-century figure from Iceland, possibly representing the god Thor. The inclusion of goat-like animals on some of the brooches has led to suggestions that they were related to Thor, whose chariot was drawn by a pair of goats.

This brooch comes from the island of Gotland, although such pieces were mostly found in central Sweden. Some examples travelled much further, with one being discovered in the Viking Gnezdovo hoard in modern day Russia.

It seems that the brooch had an afterlife around the beginning of the twentieth century. One scholar recently noticed a goldsmith's mark on the modern brooch pin, probably standing for a jeweller who was active from 1893 onwards. He worked in Copenhagen, where the brooch was acquired for the British Museum.

Viking

Thought to have been found on Gotland, Sweden

Mid-9th to mid-10th century AD

Diameter 7.8 cm

Donated by the Friends of the British Museum

1901,0718.1

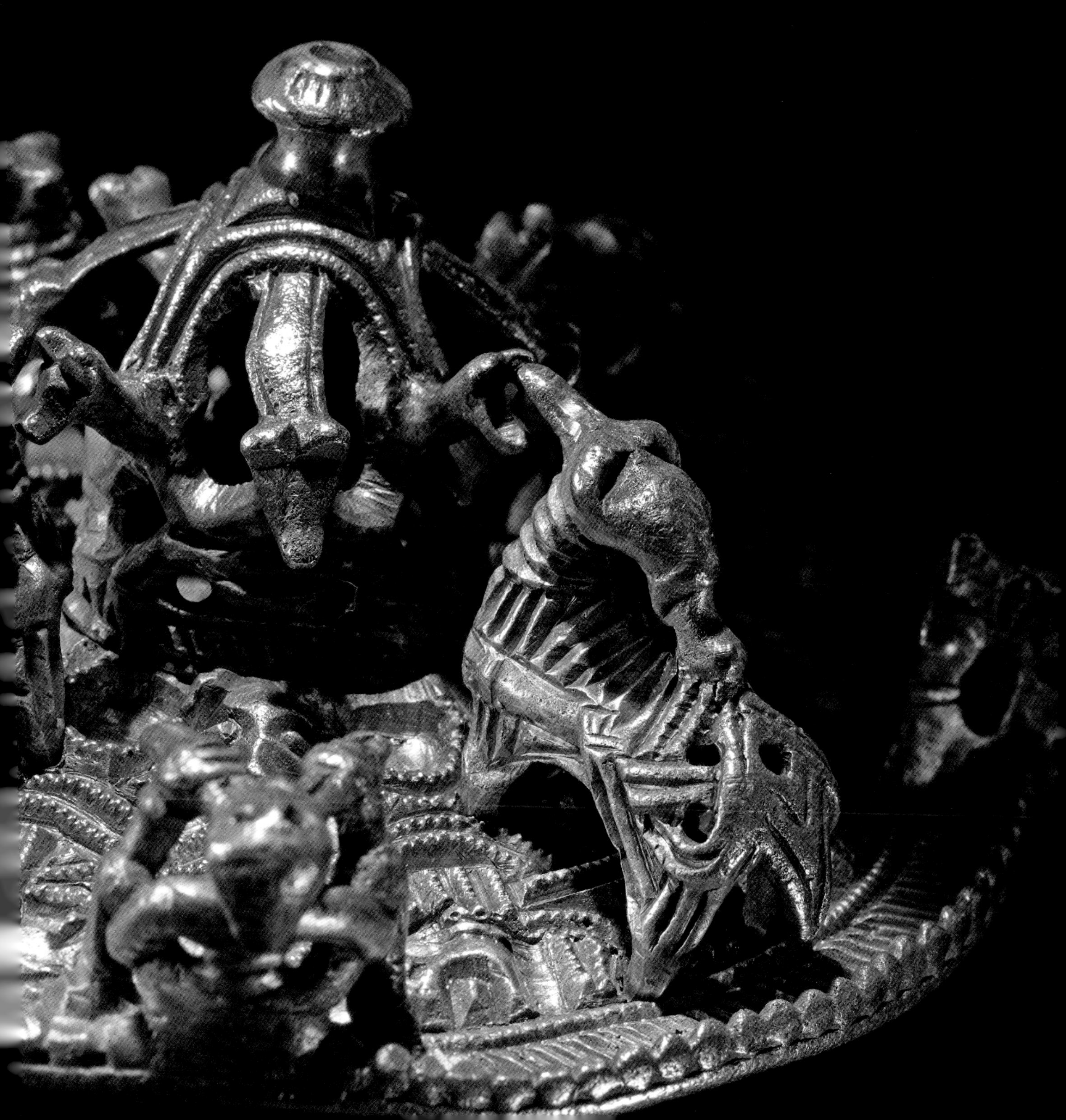

113 GALWAY BROOCH

Open-hooped brooches with unconnected terminals are described as penannular. They varied in size and shape, and were made in either silver or copper alloy (**115**, **139**, **150**).

The present brooch from Galway is characterized by its large, flat terminals, each of which were originally embellished with five conical bosses. One of these bosses has now been lost, leaving behind the rivet hole which shows how it was attached. The bosses are linked by cross-hatched bands which divide each terminal into four fields. These contain interlaced animals with small heads and three-toed feet. While the brooch form follows Irish traditions, the silversmiths who developed these dress fasteners were clearly aware of contemporary Anglo-Saxon metalwork with animal ornament in the Trewhiddle Style (**65**, **66**) as well as Viking animal art (**107**).

The decoration is distinct enough to have stood out to the vendor, Louisa Burdge, who believed the brooch to be Danish when it was in her possession in the late 1860s. Mrs Burdge ran a clock, watch and jewellery business in Galway, which she had taken over from her father. She may well have come into contact with archaeological material before, and therefore had an inkling of the brooch's Viking connections, even though she did not know that it was associated with both Irish and Norwegian-Viking fashions.

Businesses such as hers bought precious metals and were therefore occasionally offered archaeological finds. Another such example in the British Museum is a late Roman silver hoard from Coleraine, Northern Ireland, which had passed through the hands of a watchmaker after its discovery in the 1850s.

The brooch and pin weigh nearly 260 grams. The silver was recycled, perhaps from other jewellery (**120**), but ultimately melted-down coins would have been the source. Large amounts of silver coinage were brought back from Islamic lands by the Vikings (**128**), and this brooch alone equals the approximate weight of ninety *dirhams*.

Hiberno-Viking

From Galway, Ireland

Late 9th to first half of the 10th century AD

Length of pin 39.1 cm

1869,0301.1

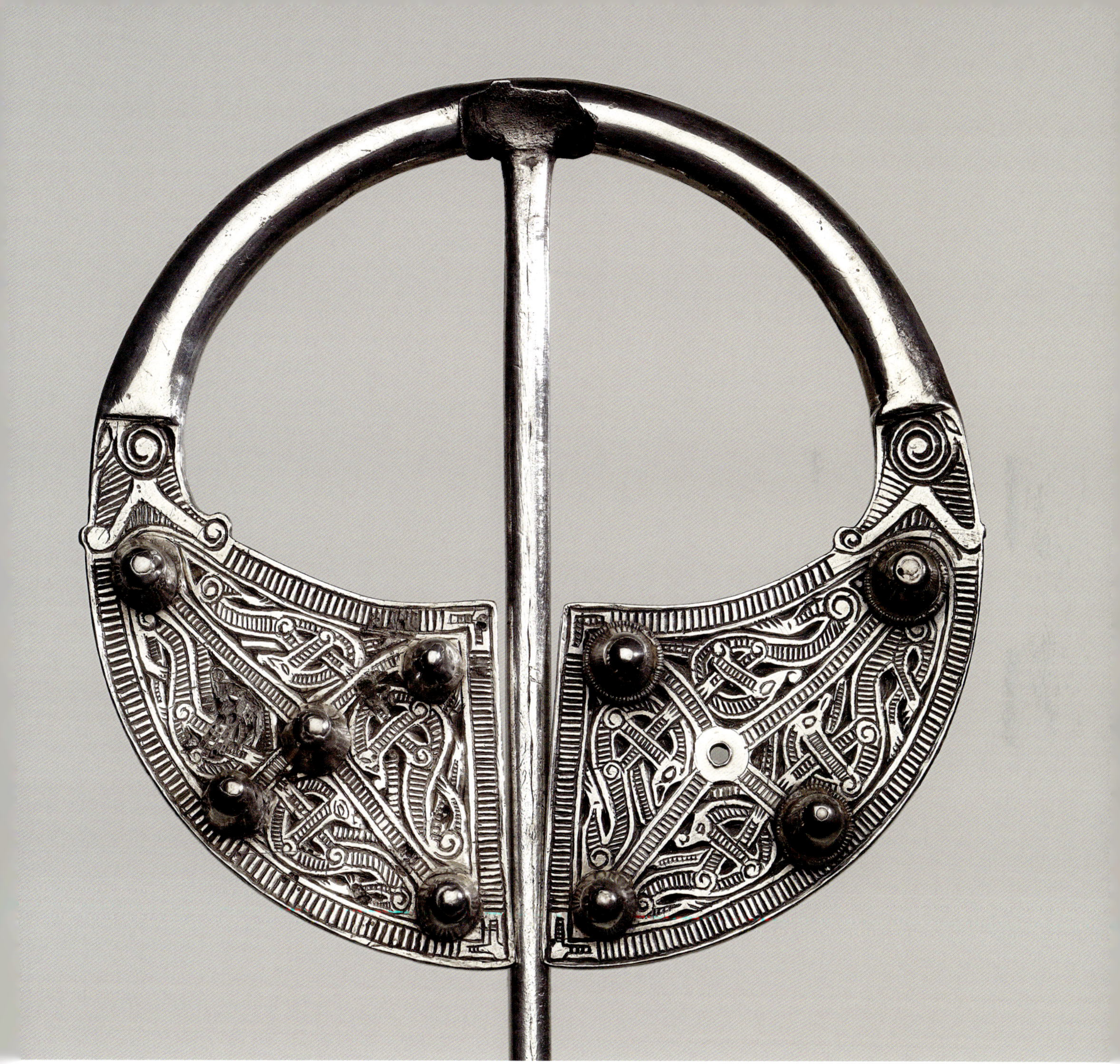

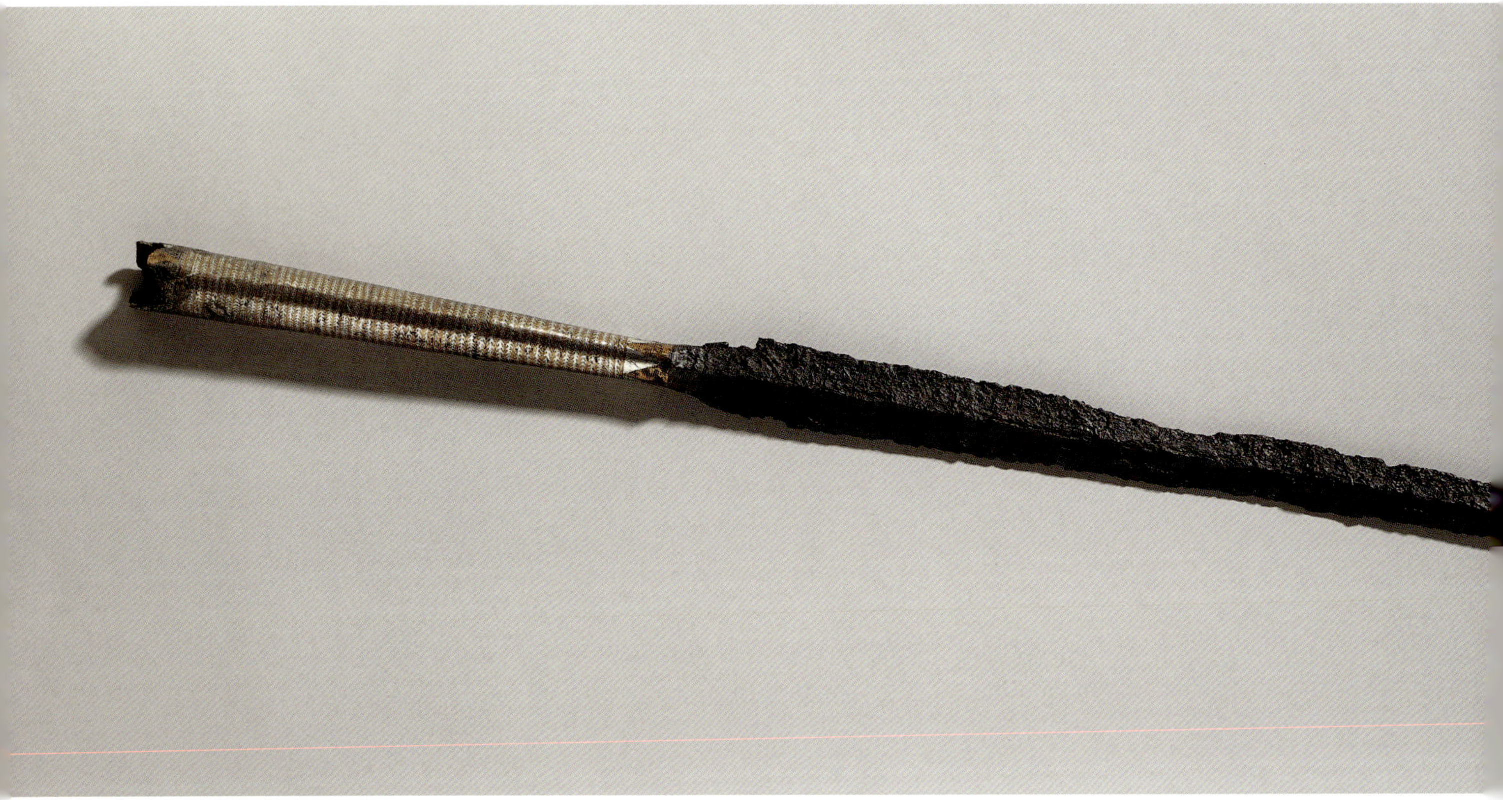

114 SPEARHEAD

Viking
From the River Thames, England
Late 9th–10th century AD
Length 54.6 cm
1893,0715.2

Martial prowess and courage were virtues considered by the Vikings to be as important as shrewdness and rhetorical skills (**127**). It was the prerogative of every free man to carry weapons, of which the sword was the most highly esteemed. Mail coats were rare and precious, while spears were the most common form of armament, possibly for economic reasons. While spears may have been the most affordable weapon, some were very elaborate. The blades could be pattern welded, just like the blades of swords (**117**). In some instances, complex metal inlays decorated the sockets.

Spears fell into two categories. Heavier ones were used for thrusting and lighter ones for throwing. Both types were employed for hunting as well as fighting, and are clearly distinguished, for instance, on the Bayeux Tapestry.

This British Museum spearhead is slender and the blade has the usual lozenge-shaped cross-section. The socket has been inlaid with twisted and plain silver and copper wires, forming a herringbone pattern. Examples of herringbone inlay on spears are also found in Norway, while interlace and animal patterns occur elsewhere in Scandinavia. The upper and lower edges of the socket have a fringe of silver and copper triangles composed from criss-crossing wires. This would have been a labour-intensive task. The intricacy of the design testifies to the skill of Viking weapon smiths, who enjoyed much prestige. Indeed, smithing was so highly regarded that in the Nordic myth about the creation of the world, the god Odin and his brothers began by processing iron ore and making tools.

This spearhead came from the River Thames, although it is not clear from exactly what point. Numerous weapons have been discovered in the river, particularly during the bridge-building activities of the nineteenth century. These weapons found in the River Thames may have been associated with Viking raiding or simply represent casual losses, but their numbers raise the possibility that at least some were purposely dedicated to the river, for example, after being seized from a defeated enemy (**61**).

115 THE PENRITH THISTLE BROOCH

The largest complete Viking-period brooch ever to have been found came to light in a field in Cumbria in 1785 and its discovery generated enough interest for it to be reported in *The Gentleman's Magazine* that year. The brooch appears to have entered into the possession of Sir Ashton Lever (1729–88), as it featured in a late eighteenth-century album illustrating his collection, which is now also in the British Museum.

The Penrith find belongs to the penannular type of brooch as the ring is not entirely closed. Unlike the other examples in this book (**113**, **139**, **148**, **150**), it does not have flat terminals, but ball ends. They are large, hollow-cast and covered with a deep-cut ornament described as 'brambling'. The effect is reminiscent of the head of a thistle flower, hence the name 'thistle brooches'.

Earlier variants were smaller and their balls were still solidly cast, but over time the fashion became more and more extravagant. The pin of the Penrith brooch is over half a metre long, and yet the brooch does appear to have been made for securing clothes. It would have fastened a heavy woollen cloak on one shoulder, and if the pin was pointing upwards and outwards, it could have been quite hazardous for passers-by. Indeed, written sources record the fine, which was payable in cattle, for poking out someone's eye with the pin of a brooch worn in a dangerous manner.

Like other penannular silver brooches, thistle brooches hark back to Celtic models. They are a development following Irish-Viking tastes, and types with ball ends spread as far as Norway and Sweden in the tenth century.

Up to this day, the findspot near Penrith is known as the 'Silver field' and as recently as 1989 and 2005, further brooches and a mixed silver hoard dated to the Viking Age have been found at this location.

Viking

Found near Flusco Pike and Penrith, Cumbria, England

Second quarter of the 10th century AD

Length of pin 51.1 cm

1909,0624.2

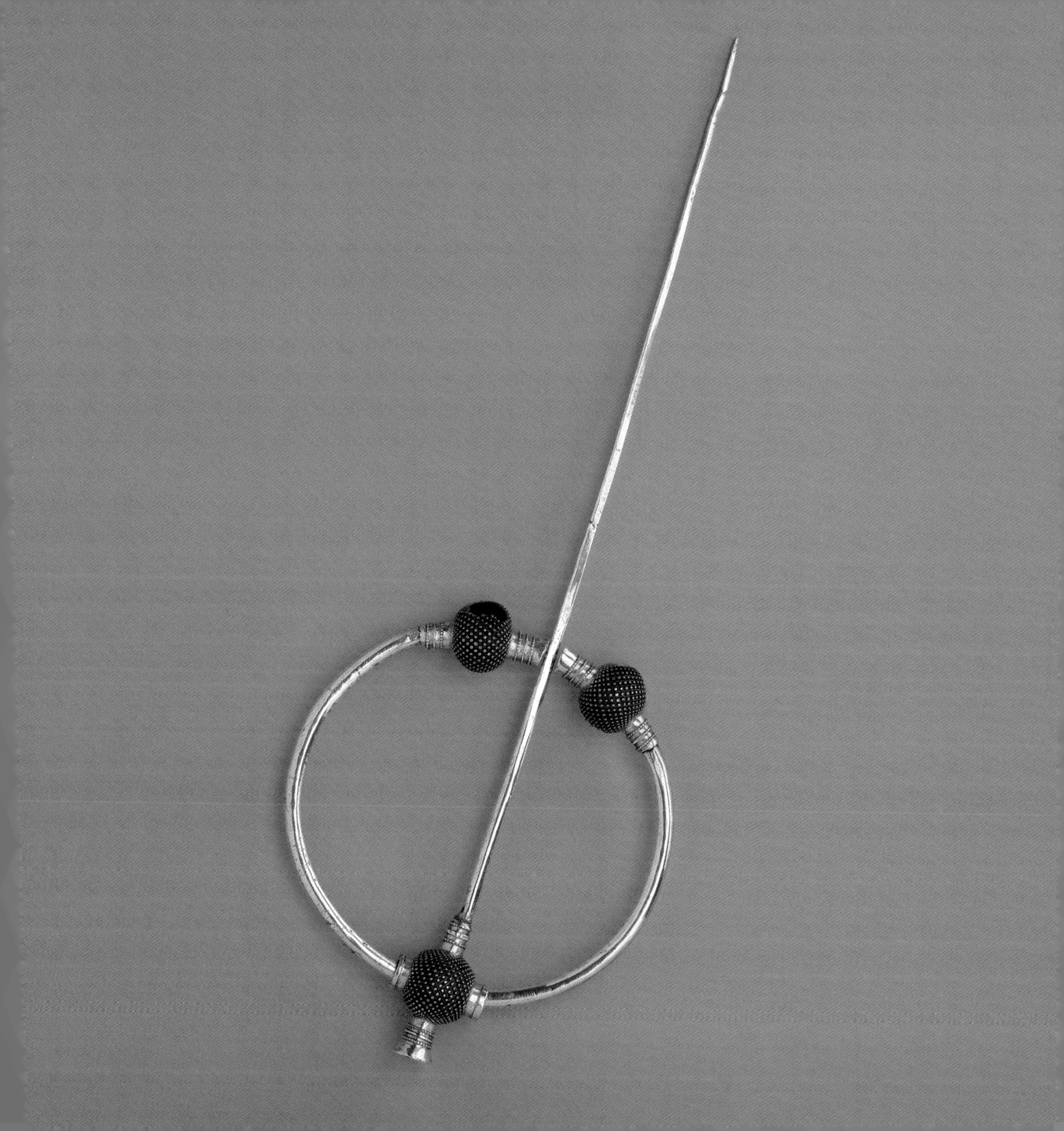

116 BOX BROOCH

Fashion in Gotland from the eighth century onwards necessitated a rather heavily cast box brooch for closing an overgarment. The type originated from more ordinary disc brooches (**107**), which over time became increasingly bulky. Box brooches are also similar to disc brooches with three-dimensional decoration (**112**), as both could carry moulded animals orientated towards a central device topped by a disc.

As with most box brooches, the top of this piece is divided into four fields. A less common feature are the masks set into the arches of the silver and niello rim. On the top, a regular openwork pattern is placed above a gilt background, a feature often found on tenth-century examples. Contrary to the type name, the top cannot actually be taken off, although their conical or cylindrical bodies are hollow.

These brooches occur in many well-furnished female burials from Gotland, but they are rarely found elsewhere. They were usually positioned on the centre of the chest holding a cloak, while large oval brooches at the shoulders would have fastened the shoulder straps of the dress underneath. While a similar costume was worn on the Swedish mainland, this used three-lobed trefoil or equal-armed brooches for the cloak instead.

As with other Scandinavian objects (**106**, **107**), long artistic continuities on the island of Gotland are notable. Box brooches were worn up to the end of the eleventh century, which means that they were popular for some four hundred years, albeit in varying decorative styles and techniques. Quite how common they were is illustrated by the fact that in the parish of Boge on the eastern coast of Gotland, where the British Museum piece originated, at least another fourteen box brooches have been discovered, with over eight hundred more known from elsewhere on the island.

This illustrates what an important hub of Baltic commerce the island was, as agriculture alone could not have allowed for the proliferation of metal jewellery on an island that had no ore deposits of its own.

Viking
From Gotland, Sweden
10th century AD
Diameter 5.7 cm
1921,1101.284

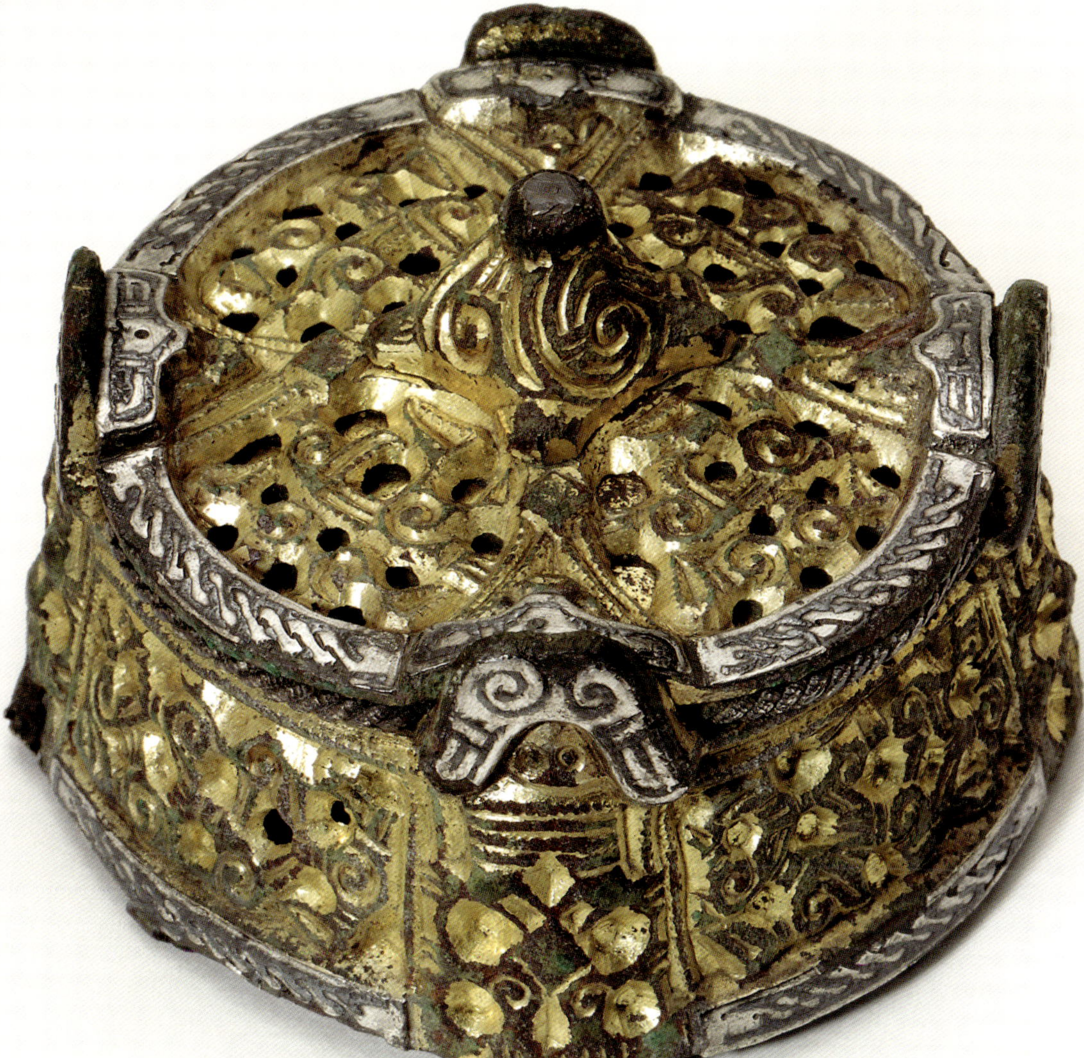

117 VIKING SWORD

A number of mysteries surround this fine sword. It is a Scandinavian type which also occurred in Viking-period England. According to a note in the British Museum archives, it was found in London, at the Temple. It was bought from a north London dealer in the nineteenth century, who claimed that it had come from the tomb of the Earl of Pembroke (d. 1148). Since there was no substance to this claim, it was then thought to be a river find, but the condition of the metal is unlike that of other objects found in wet conditions (**114**).

A further riddle is posed by the silver wire wrapped tightly around the grip and already shown this way in a publication from the late 1880s. New scientific analysis confirms that the wire is unlikely to be of nineteenth-century date, yet it shows much less wear than the inlay on the sword pommel. In its current configuration the grip would have been too narrow to hold securely and instead originally there was probably a grip pad made of horn or wood, perhaps clad in leather. As there are a small number of finds with gold or silver wire slung loosely around the grip, it is possible that this sword was tidied up at some point after it was found and before it was published. The fact that on close examination a probably modern, fibrous material is visible under the wire supports this idea. If the sword really came from the riverbed, it is possible to speculate that it was a sacrifice which either already had a wire-bound organic handle, or had been enhanced by the addition of the silver wire before it was deposited in the water.

The cross-guard, which separates the blade from the handle, was once inlaid with animal ornament in the Viking Mammen Style, which also covered the five-lobed pommel. Silver, copper and brass were used and would have provided a striking polychrome or multicoloured effect. As the blade was pattern welded from three bands with alternate straight and twisted sections, this would have been a very ostentatious weapon indeed.

Viking

Thought to be from London, England

10th century AD

Length 88.5 cm

Bequeathed by H. Dunbar Baines, through J.C. Jackson

1887,0209.1

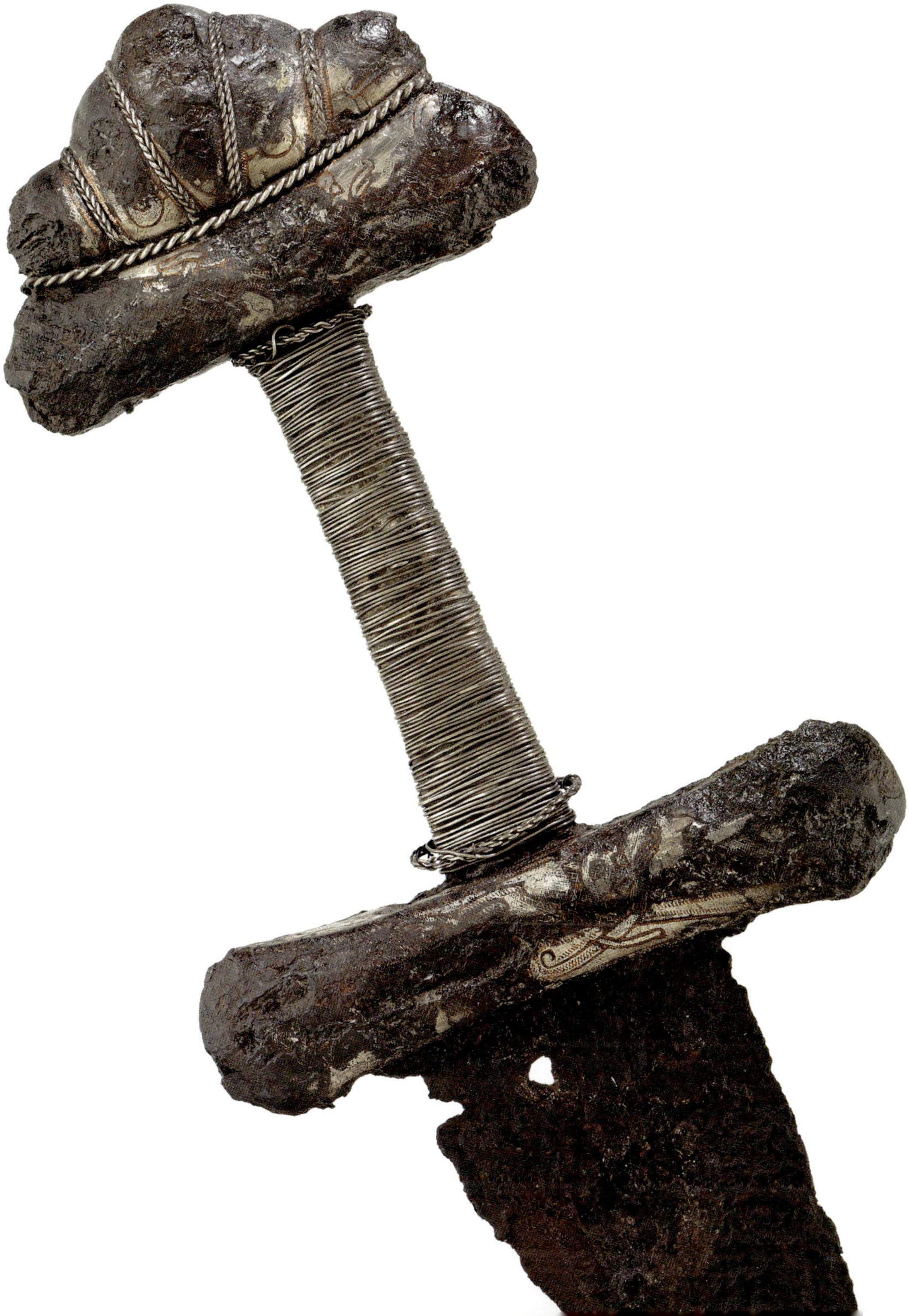

118 THE WENDOVER ARM-RING

A thick gold rod and a fine twisted wire have been twined together with beautiful regularity to make this heavy gold arm-ring.

While examples of silver jewellery, especially arm-rings, are common throughout the Viking world, gold is very rare. As opposed to the thousands of silver armlets (**120**), brooches (**113**, **115**, **150**), ingots, coins and indistinguishable fragments of silver, only some two hundred and ninety Viking gold rings are known from northern Europe. Most of these are arm- or finger-rings, as well as a small number of neck-rings. Apart from its rarity, there are two further, crucial differences that mark out gold from silver. Firstly, gold rings were not buried with the dead; instead, they are either single finds, like the Wendover arm-ring, or part of larger hoards. In the case of hoards, gold was exclusive, and only a few, including that from the Vale of York (**111**), contain both types of precious metal.

The second feature which sets gold apart from silver is that gold rings are nearly always complete. During the Viking period, many parts of northern Europe had a bullion economy, meaning that precious metals were valued by weight (**108**, **120**) and not by the denomination value of coins. Therefore jewellery represented portable wealth that could be exchanged for other goods. If small change was needed, bracelets, brooches and coins could simply be chopped up to achieve the desired weight. Thus hacksilver came into existence.

But gold apparently had significance beyond its bullion value. In Old Norse written sources, it is often associated with kings and the custom of giving gold rings as rewards. Furthermore, those who saw the rings were aware of their connotations, as one poem states: 'From their gear it is seen and their golden rings that they are close to the king'.

Both gold and silver rings are also mentioned in reference to sacred contexts, but it appears that gold had a special aura as it was often related to the king. Its restriction to very specific circumstances may also have suggested a connection with even higher powers.

Viking

Found at Wendover, Buckinghamshire, England

10th century AD

Diameter 8.8 cm

Donated by R.G. Fox

1849,0210.1

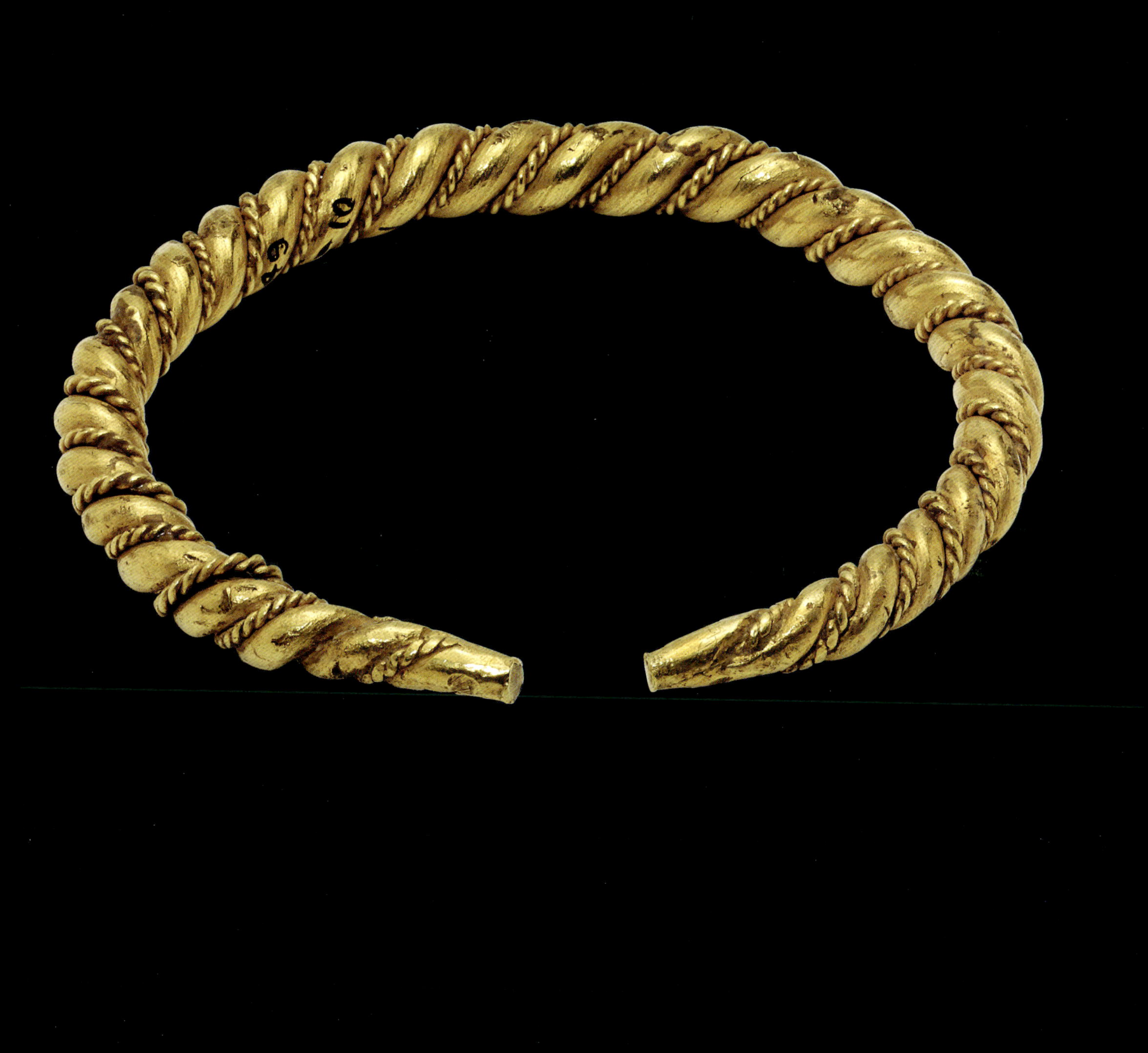

119 THE LITTLE SNORING PENDANT

The Viking 'Gripping Beast' is a veritable contortionist, so distinctive that it gave its name to a style element. On this pendant from East Anglia, the head of the beast, with its characteristic triangular shape and floppy ears, sits directly below the loop. From there, its speckled body curves to the right, from where its two front legs emerge. The body then thins dramatically and arches to the left, where the hindquarters of the beast meet the frame.

Here, the other two spindly legs are shown. One of them is turned upwards and seems to be strangling an animal whose head and neck are seen in profile on the outside of the pendant's frame. The other hindleg reaches underneath and reappears to grip its own body near the front quarter. Meanwhile, one of the front feet chokes another animal on the frame, whereas its last leg is just propped downwards against the frame, with its paw curled up.

So far, the Little Snoring find is the only such pendant known from the British Isles. Its strange subject matter and precious silver-gilt and nielloed appearance would have made it a notable piece of jewellery, even in the Viking milieu of the Danelaw. Fashions seem to have differed between the Danish settlers of eastern England and those who stayed in Scandinavia, as pendants are much rarer this side of the North Sea.

A hoard of six such pendants, albeit made from gilt copper alloy and less detailed in their execution, was found at Vårby in central Sweden. Deposited around AD 940, they are the closest parallels to this discovery from Norfolk. Another silver-gilt example and a casting mould from Hedeby, northern Germany, show that the pendants were not only popular, but also made in different parts of Viking Scandinavia. A Gripping Beast pendant was even found as far east as Russia in the Viking Gnezdovo hoard.

Viking

From Little Snoring, Norfolk, England

10th century AD

Height including loop 4.2 cm

1999,1001.1

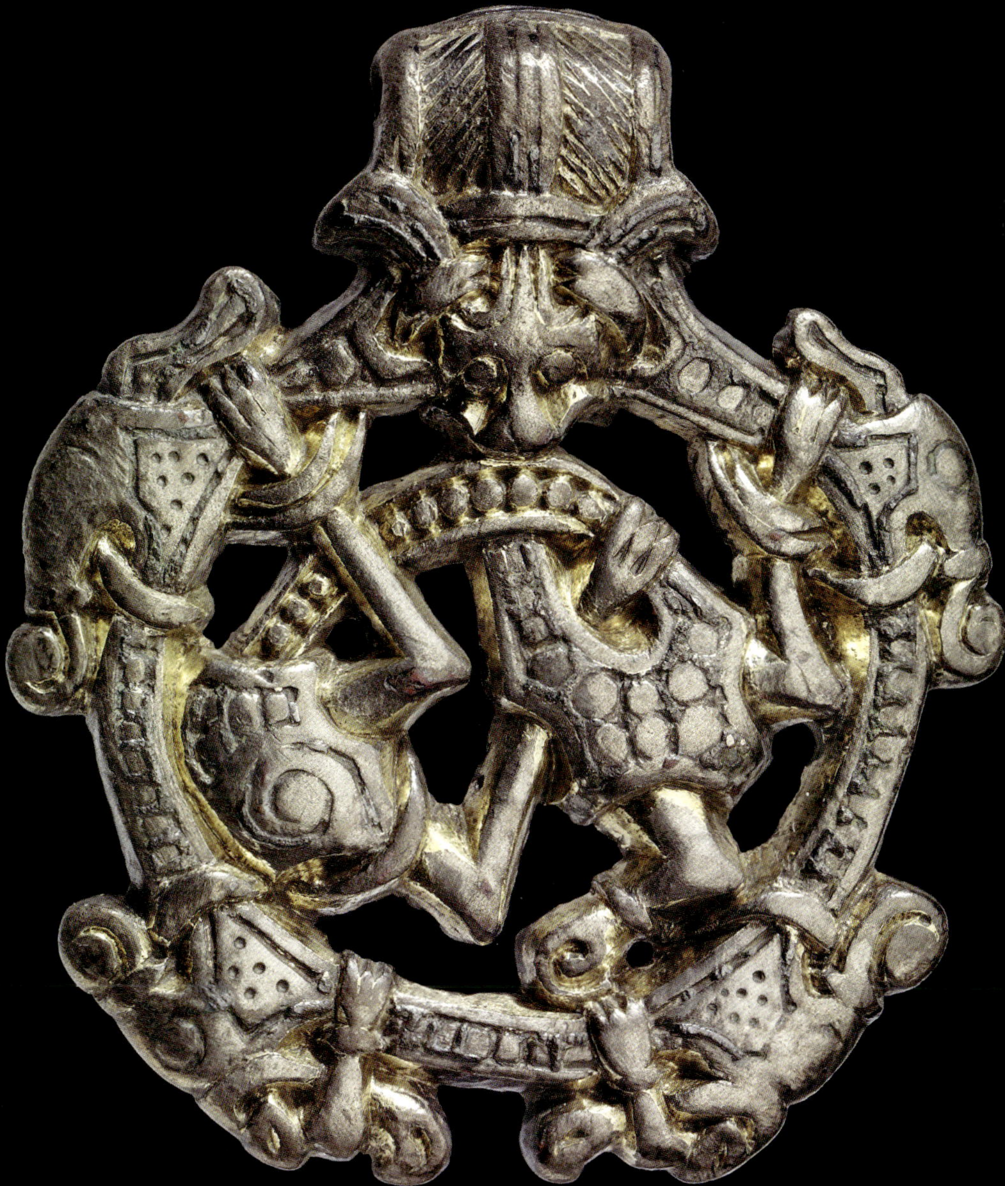

120 VIKING SILVER ARM-RINGS

LEFT:
Viking
From Gotland, Sweden
10th to 11th century AD
Diameter 7.1 cm
Acquired with a contribution by The Art Fund
1921,1101.304

CENTRE:
Viking
From Ireland
Late 9th to early 10th century AD
Diameter 6.7 cm
1854,1227.63

RIGHT:
Viking
From Gotland, Sweden
10th century AD
Diameter 5.8 cm
1921,1101.302

Viking silver arm-rings are found all over northern Europe. The image here unites two from Scandinavia with one from Ireland in the centre.

The two Scandinavian armlets were collected by James Curle, a Scottish antiquarian who visited Gotland from the late 1880s (**81**, **107**). This Swedish island was very prosperous throughout the late Roman and early medieval periods. It lay on trade routes across the Baltic and it was fertile, despite a scarcity of land. Even today Viking Age silver hoards are still discovered there on a regular basis during agricultural works.

The Irish arm-ring is of a Hiberno-Scandinavian type, which comprises over three hundred and fifty examples from the British Isles. In such armlets, a flat silver band widens towards the middle and the decoration, where present, consists of stamped rows and a cross, or in this case a star, at the centre and near the terminals. Their comparatively uniform appearance is reflected in their weight, which in many cases seems to conform to certain standards that can also be related to tenth-century weights from Viking Dublin. This may indicate that those arm-rings of Hiberno-Scandinavian type which fall into specific weight categories were purposely destined for economic transactions.

Arm-rings were worn by both men and women, but they had a significance beyond that of mere jewellery and display of status: they represented a convenient way of storing long-lasting wealth in a portable form. They could not only be exchanged as gifts or awarded to retainers, but also acted as bullion, which means that they were valued for their precious metal content (**108**). Indeed, the Gotlandic ring on the left has a small number of testing marks. These often come in the form of tiny nicks or pecks inflicted on a piece of Viking silver to check the softness, and consequently the purity of the metal.

Apart from ingots and coins, whole or fragmentary armlets are the most common components of Viking hacksilver hoards. This indicates that people had no compunction about chopping up an arm-ring to generate small change for their transactions. This is a significant distinction from gold rings, which are normally found intact (**118**).

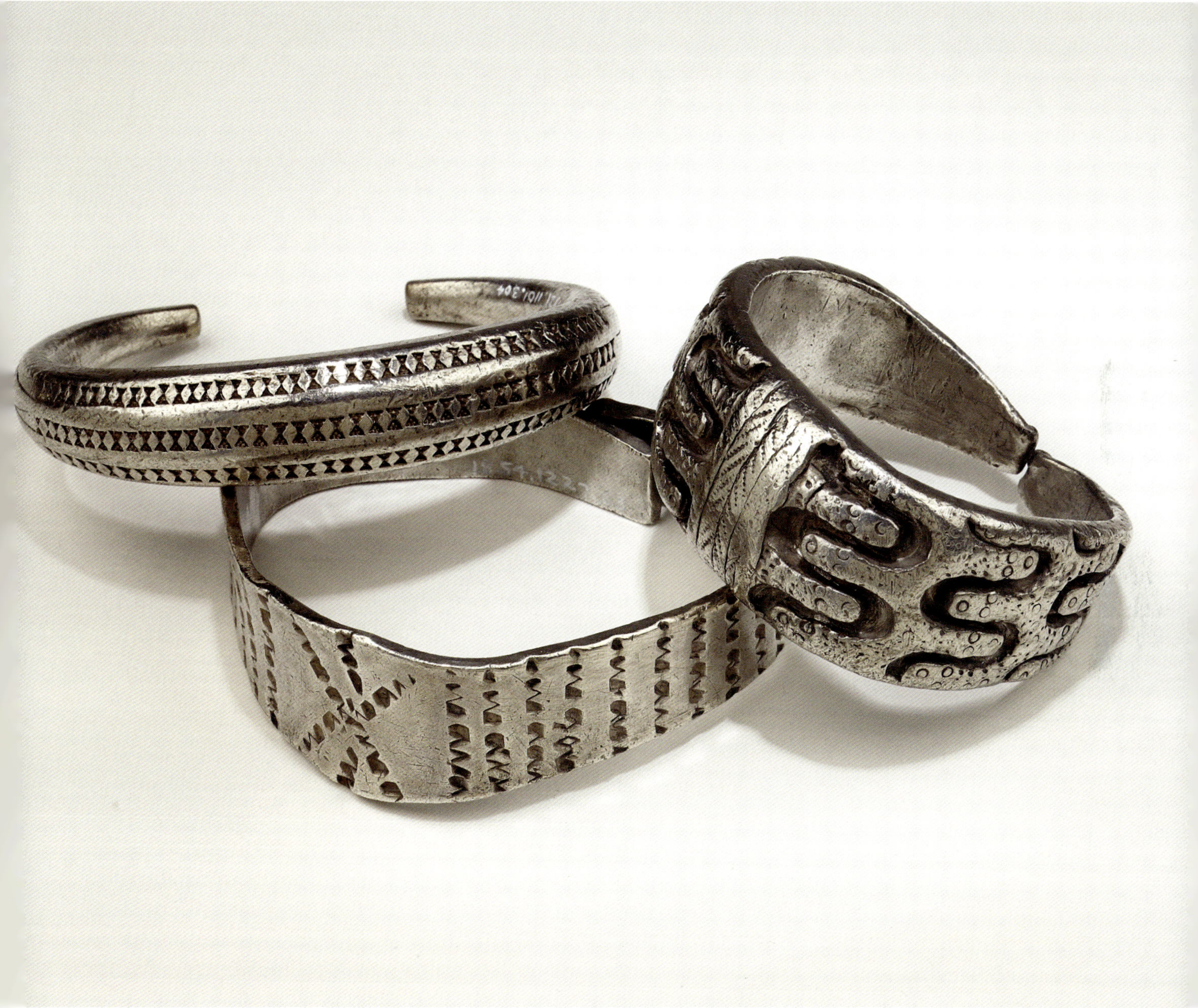

121 THE ÆDWEN BROOCH

The back of this disc brooch is even more notable than its ornate front. An inscription in clear Old English proclaims that a woman called 'Ædwen owns me, may the Lord own her. May the Lord curse him who takes me from her, unless she gives me of her own free will'. In addition, there are a number of rune-like ciphers on the fragments of a metal strip which are the only remains of the pin and catch. Perhaps these were torn off before the brooch was buried in a lead casket, together with around a hundred silver coins of William the Conqueror (1066–87), several gold rings and a silver dish or disc. This treasure came to light during ploughing on the Isle of Ely in 1694. All the other objects were lost soon after and even the brooch disappeared, before coming to light again in 1951. At this point it could be securely identified courtesy of a book published in 1705, which contained drawings of the Ædwen brooch.

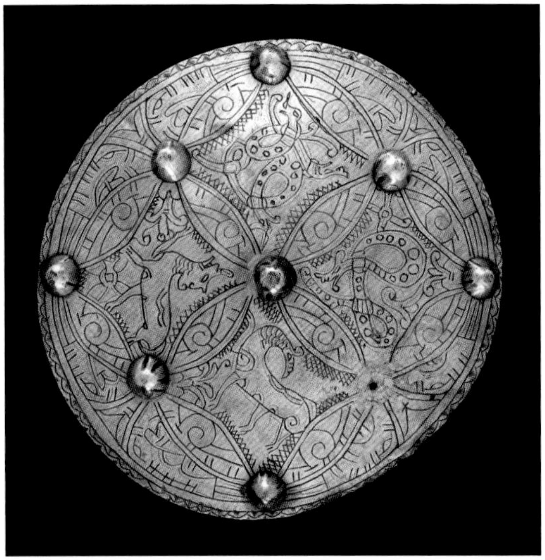

The brooch dates to the late Viking period, with its dual, Anglo-Viking pedigree clearly visible. Its construction from hammered silver sheet with applied conical silver bosses and the division of the surface into fields drawn by a compass reflects other Anglo-Saxon brooches, notably the larger one from the Beeston Tor hoard, Staffordshire, also in the British Museum, or the Strickland brooch (**65**). Moreover, the statement of ownership followed by a curse is included in a number of contemporary Anglo-Saxon wills. On the other hand, the niello-inlaid ornament is executed in a poorly implemented version of the Viking Ringerike Style (**122**). Four animals are shown in profile: two quadrupeds, possibly a horse and a wolf, and two interlaced snakes have the distinctive oval-shaped eye. In addition, they all sport characteristic snouts with grooves or extra lobes. The snail-like volutes framing each animal panel also occur sometimes in the Ringerike Style. Another large silver disc brooch with such animals was recently discovered near Bradfield in Suffolk, providing a further East Anglian parallel.

Anglo-Viking
From Sutton, Cambridgeshire, England
Early 11th century
Diameter 14.9–16.4 cm
1951,1011.1

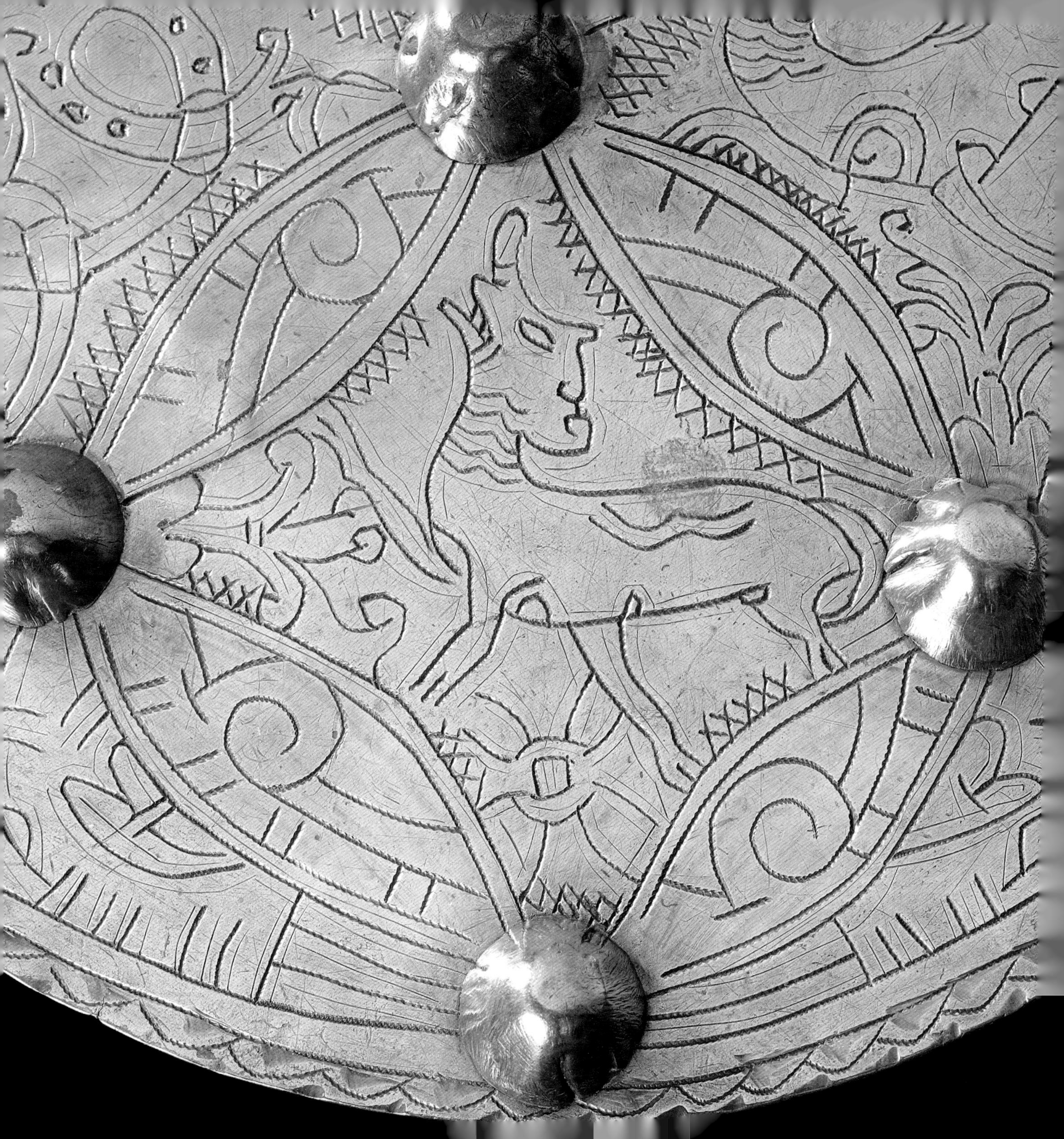

122 THE BIBURY STONE

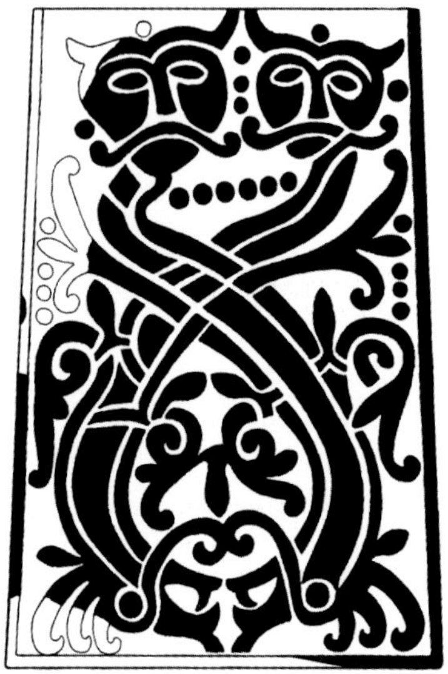

Anglo-Scandinavian

From Bibury, Gloucestershire, England

First half of the 11th century

Height 63.5 cm

Donated by the Revd F.G. Dutton

1913,0203.1

Only a few gravestones or, as in this case, grave covers from eleventh-century England are still preserved. This example is therefore a rarity, together with the three other sculpted gravestone fragments from Bibury, which are also in the British Museum.

In the tenth century, large parts of northern and eastern England were under Viking control, as the metalwork and sculpture from these areas clearly show. The latter is especially interesting insofar as stone sculpture was uncommon in Scandinavia. Outside Gotland, for example, rune stones were rarely set before the eleventh century. Once the Vikings were in England, this changed rapidly. Viking patrons dedicated standing crosses to commemorate the dead, in line with the practices of Anglo-Saxon high-status individuals. During the early and mid-tenth century a new Viking form of funerary sculpture, the curved hogback grave cover, evolved. By the early eleventh century, elements of Viking art had also spread through southern England. There was no major wave of Viking settlement here, but the striking fact that the Ringerike Style (**121**) was largely restricted to the south may be connected to the reign of Cnut (1016–35), who was also king of Denmark. Viking craftsmen were present in the south, at least in major cities such as London, as an exquisite sarcophagus panel from St Paul's churchyard, now in the Museum of London, demonstrates (**124**).

The Bibury stone represents a fusion of both Anglo-Saxon and Scandinavian stylistic traits. The leafy background from which two faces peer is inspired by acanthus foliage in the Winchester Style (**68**, **71**), which was common both in Anglo-Saxon manuscript illumination and on metalwork. The motif dominating the design is two S-shaped serpents of Scandinavian animal ancestry. Their dragon-like heads, shown upside down at the bottom of the stone, share a kinship with the Ringerike snakes on the Ædwen brooch (**121**). The two mustachioed faces towards the top remain enigmatic. Are they part of the dragonesque beasts? Or are they men, or lions, as has been suggested? The amalgamation of styles on this stone is of debatable success, but it clearly shows how new influences and fashions were being adopted by both craftspeople and customers.

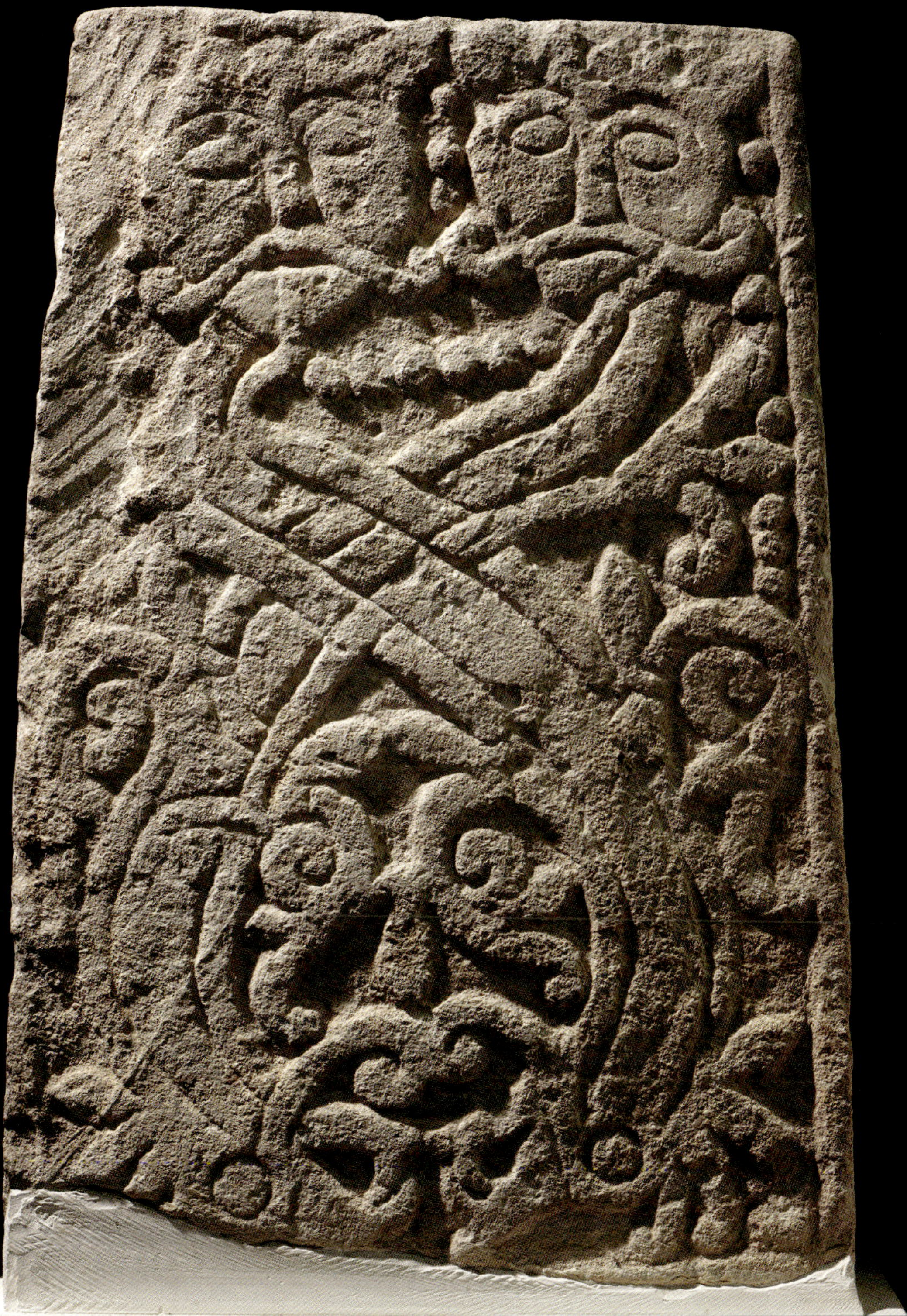

123 TRIAL PIECE

The British Museum's collection includes a number of trial pieces made from bone or, as in this case, stone, which represent the design stage of metalwork or large-scale decorative carvings. Viking craftsmen were not just highly skilled jewellery makers, but they also designed the pieces, perhaps to the customer's specifications. Paper was not yet available and the alternatives, vellum or parchment, were extremely expensive and difficult to come by. In addition, actually carving the patterns as opposed to sketching them would have helped the craftsman to work out the texture of complicated interlace and to align all the junctures properly. Such carvings were ways of developing new ideas, experimenting with designs and acting as practice pieces for those still in training.

As they were made from durable materials, trial pieces could be accumulated to form a stock of patterns which could be shown to customers and shared in a workshop. Thus they had a similar function to the pattern books of the late Roman and Byzantine periods (**16**, **33**). Trial pieces with fully finished designs could be impressed into wax in order to produce the casting moulds necessary for the lost-wax technique (**144**).

Both faces of this slab of slate are covered with carved interlace patterns forming discrete units of varying complexity. The focus is the large, circular design of a coiled animal. The bottom edge is missing, but towards the top of the spiralling body, a head with a drop-shaped eye is visible. Its jaws are curled and a lappet, an extension of the head, is interlaced with the ribbon-like contours of the beast's body.

The animal's appearance is rooted in Irish tradition, but small details, such as the shape of the eye and the curled lips, show the influence of the Viking Urnes Style (**125**, **126**), which became very popular in Ireland. This piece illustrates how the new hybrid Hiberno-Scandinavian styles spread from the Viking towns, where they probably emerged, to the rest of the country. Similar developments are also noticeable in Anglo-Scandinavian England (**121**, **122**).

Hiberno-Scandinavian
From Kilaloe, Co. Clare, Ireland
11th century
Height 8.9 cm
1858,0120.1

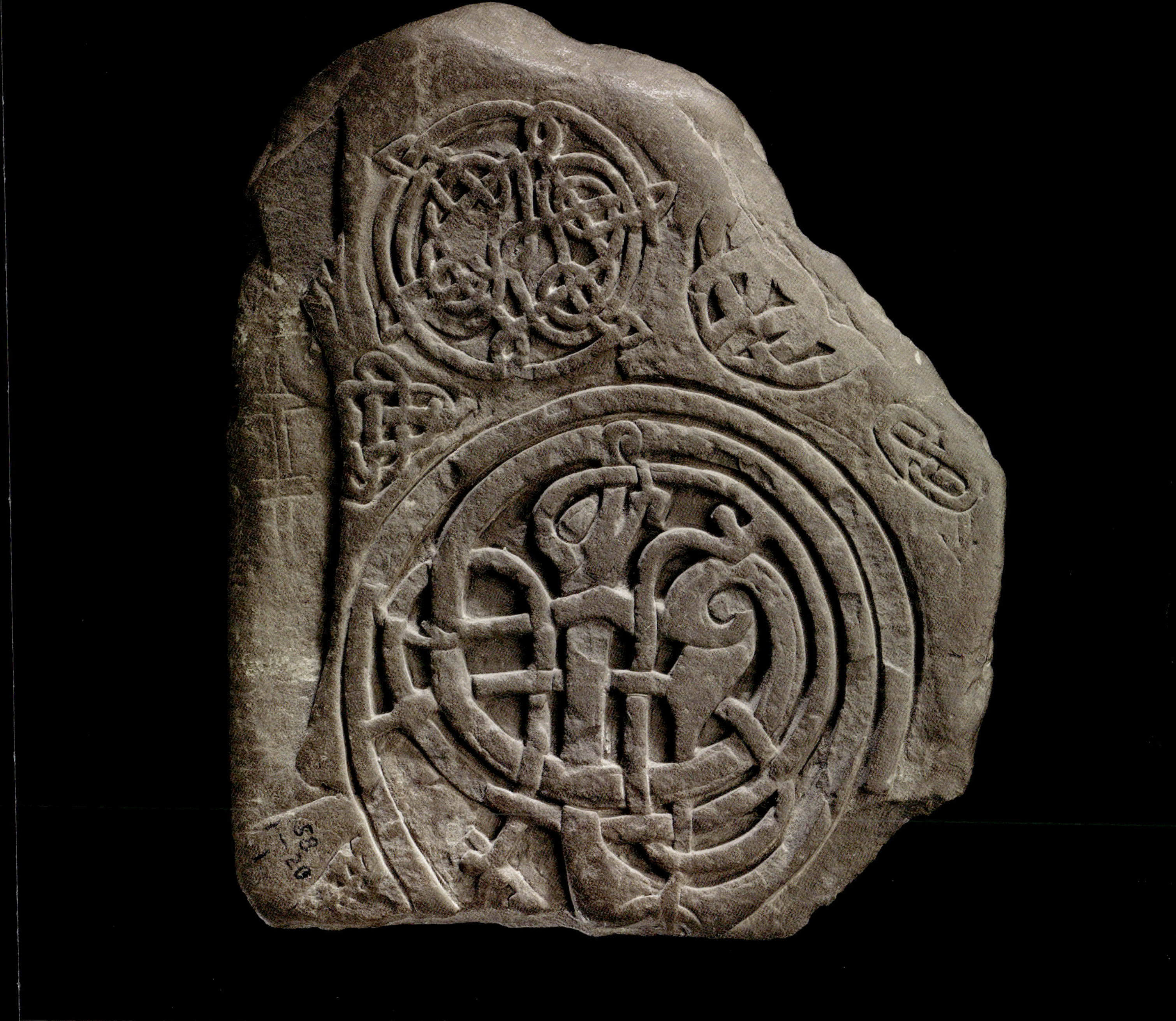

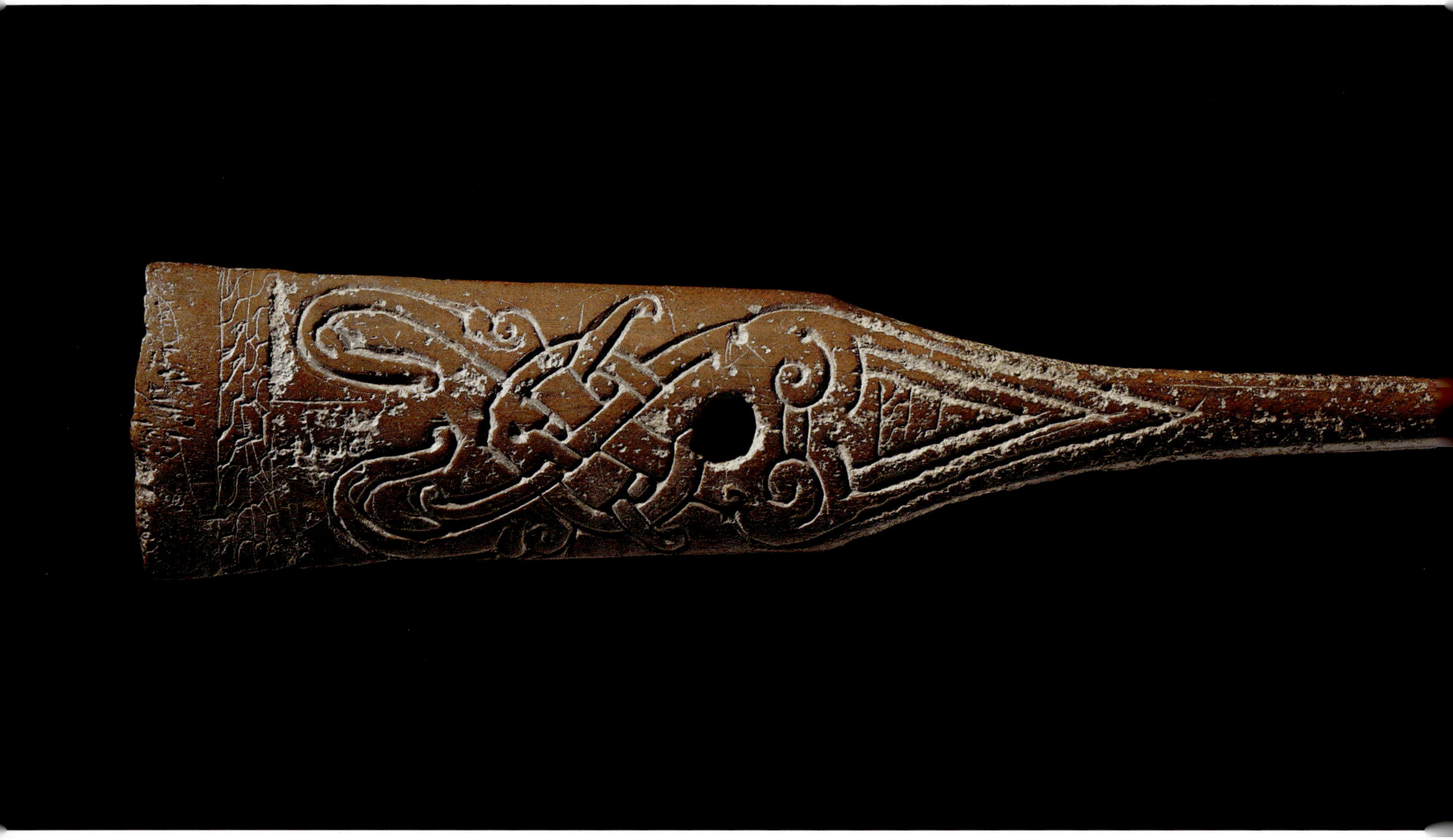

124 BONE PIN

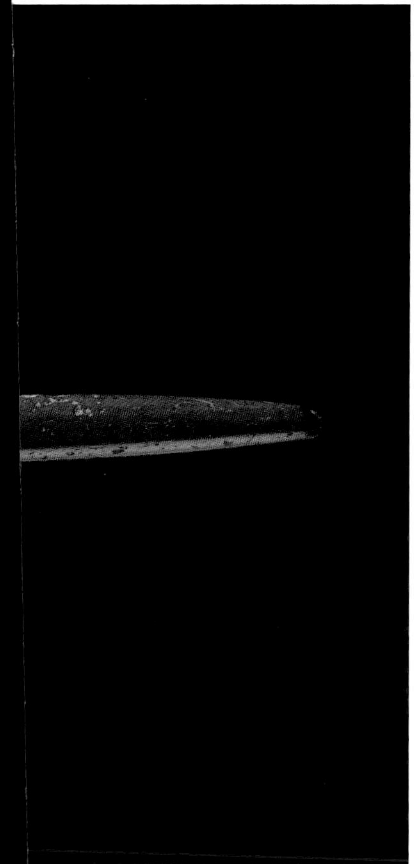

Viking

From the River Thames, London, England

11th century

Length 16.9 cm

1893,0618.72

Viking pins were worn by both men and women to fasten cloaks. Those who could afford it had the choice of a precious metal, but bronze, iron and bone, as in this case, were used as well. The metal types could have elaborate heads of various forms and in some cases were derived from Irish types of dress pins. Men wore pins just as flamboyant as those chosen by women, if not more so. After all, status and successful raiding or trading journeys were displayed through outward appearance, including fine clothes trimmed with exotic fabrics such as silk and precious metal dress accessories and jewellery.

Bone was a cheaper alternative for pins than metal and could still be decorated with attractive patterns. No zoological examination has taken place on this piece, but at Hedeby in northern Germany and elsewhere many pins were made from pigs' fibulae. These are naturally wider at the lower end and can easily be pierced at this point without splitting. Larger bones were less commonly used as raw material for pins.

The hole in the pinhead was meant for the attachment of a band or string, which would have helped to secure the pin after it was pushed through the fabric with the sharp end pointing upwards. With some of the metal variants a ring was an integral part of the pinhead and there are some rare finds with the cord still attached. This was a similar principle to the way in which pseudo-penannular brooches were prevented from slipping out of the cloth they held (**148**).

Ringerike Style ornament (**149**) in the form of elaborately knotted tendrils has been carved on the head of this pin found in the River Thames. Scandinavian in origin, this type of ornament also became popular in the British Isles. Craftsmen who were fluent in this style must have been present in London, as the remains of a stone sarcophagus with a beautiful relief from the vicinity of St Paul's Cathedral demonstrates (**122**).

125 THE PITNEY BROOCH

A ferocious battle is underway on this openwork disc brooch. An animal with a large, drop-shaped eye is being attacked by a snake, which is biting the animal's beaded body right behind its head.

The beast's body curves around and its shoulder, with a spiral joint, is clearly visible and set next to a three-toed foot. A spiral towards the bottom of the design represents its hip joint, but from there the body of the animal transforms into floral hooks with scrolled ends, and no other legs are visible. The skinny body of the snake dissolves into ornate spiralwork as well. The pin holder on the back of the brooch is broken, but it suggests that the animal's head would have pointed upwards when the brooch was worn, with the pin positioned horizontally, as was the usual custom.

The brooch is in the Urnes Style, the last phase of Viking art before it was superseded in the twelfth century by the Romanesque Style current throughout western Europe (**75**). The style is named after Urnes, once home to one of the most powerful families in western Norway, where a wooden stave church was carved with an intricate interlace showing a four-legged beast with a drop-shaped eye battling with serpentine monsters (**126**).

In keeping with the provenance of the brooch, it also displays clear Anglo-Saxon elements in its decoration. The beaded body of the beast is more characteristic of finds from England and the scalloped frame of the brooch is at home here as well. The fusion of different artistic currents is not unusual, but is exhibited in many pieces of metalwork and sculpture from the English and Irish regions where Vikings settled (**113**, **122**, **150**).

Its complex layout, precise workmanship and gilded front and back distinguish the Pitney brooch from a much simpler adaptation of the same design found at Wisbech, Cambridgeshire.

Anglo-Scandinavian
From Pitney, Dorset, England
Second half of the 11th century
Diameter 3.9 cm
1979,1101.1

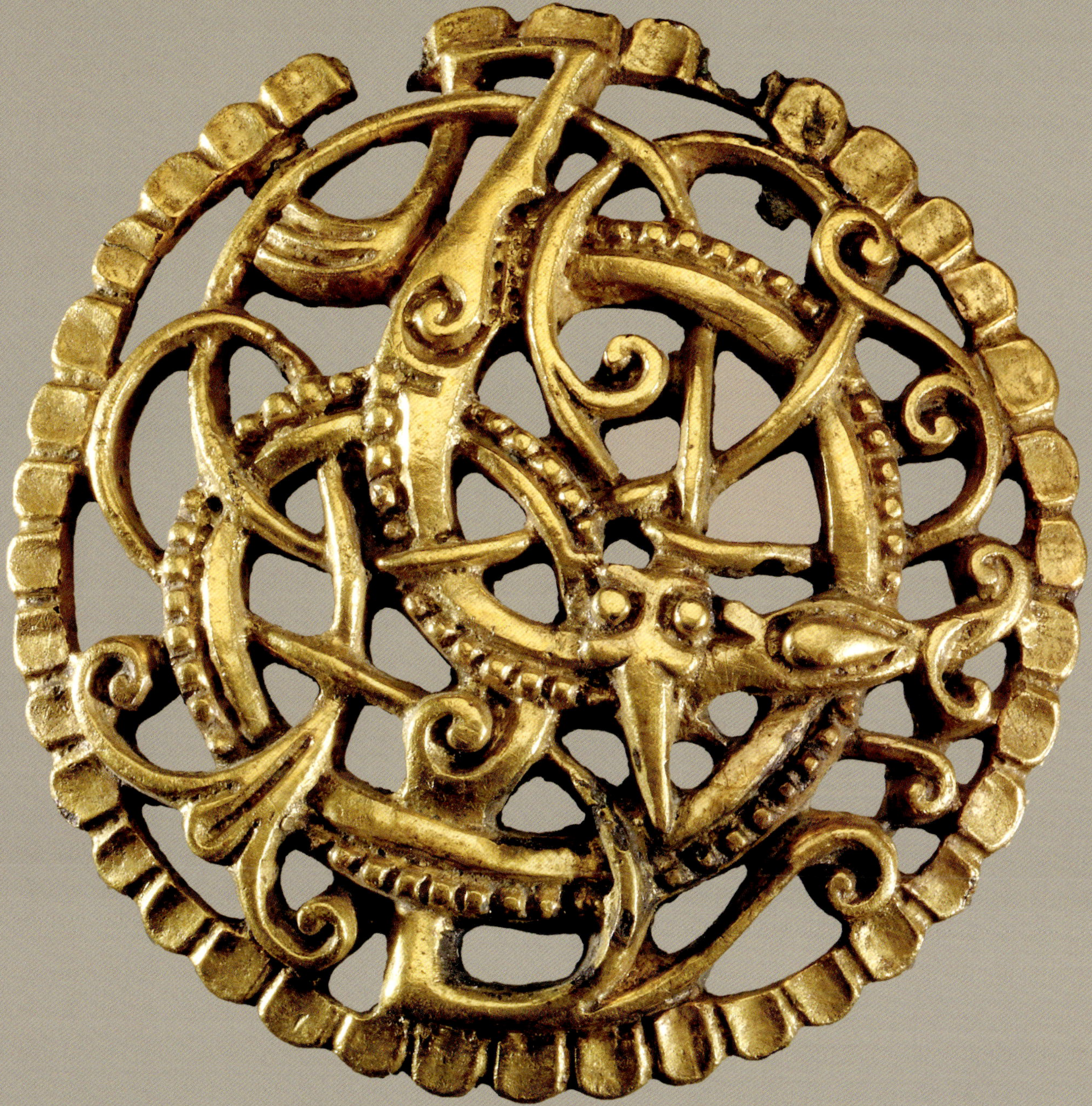

126 KIABY BROOCH

Like the Pitney brooch (**125**), this copper alloy cast was crafted in the late Viking Urnes Style. A standing beast with a proudly curved neck is entangled in an interlace mesh, which partly springs from its own body. With its large, pear-shaped eye and open, scrolled jaw it is similar to many other such beasts.

There are numerous examples of this brooch type, which all feature a delicate animal with at least one front leg and a hind body which splits into multiple strands of interlace. Such brooches were particularly popular in Scandinavia, where some of the best silver examples have been found, but stray pieces are also known, for instance, from Germany.

This brooch is from southern Sweden and there is indeed evidence of twelfth-century production in Lund, which was a major town and bishop's see at this time. It is, however, not one of the finest illustrations of this brooch type. The edges of the openwork are sharp and the relief is flat, without any of the moulded roundness of the best pieces. The body was originally enhanced with surface detail in the form of ribbing as well as a spiral representing the shoulder of the interlace beast. Much of this is now lost as the brooch is heavily worn.

It is debatable whether the design of such brooches carried any deeper meaning, but it has been suggested that the beast trapped in a web of tendrils may symbolize the struggle between good and evil. Support for this theory comes from the church at Urnes, Norway, from which the name of the style is derived. Here, a master carver created a wooden relief of a striding animal fighting with serpentine monsters. In contrast to the development of the Ringerike (**121**, **122**) and Mammen (**117**) Styles, Urnes Style does not reflect any Anglo-Continental influences, but grew out of purely Scandinavian traditions. Its association with Christianity is strong, not only at Urnes itself, but in fragments of wood carvings from early ecclesiastical buildings in Denmark, Norway and Sweden. As the most popular late Viking style, it also adorned a wide range of secular objects.

Viking
Found near Kiaby, Sweden
Late 11th century
Length 5.5 cm
1982,0602.1

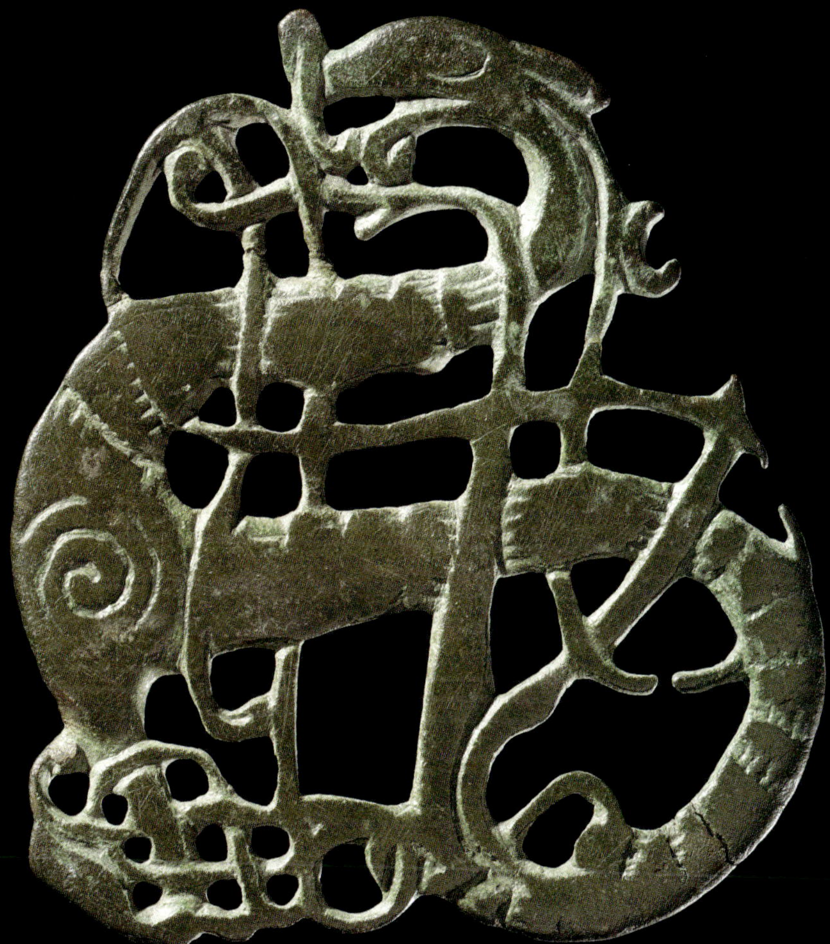

127 THE LEWIS CHESS FIGURES: THREE BERSERKERS

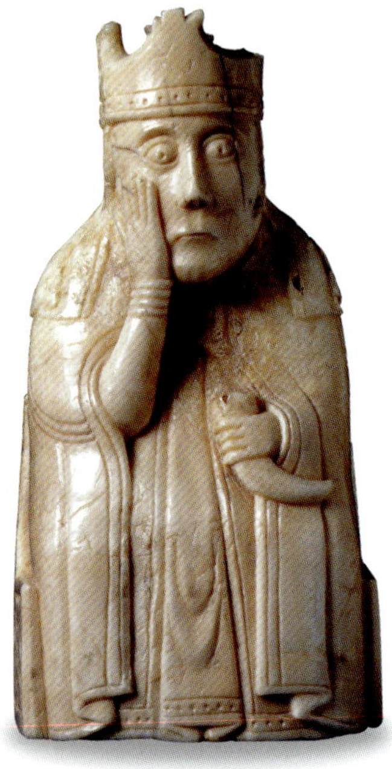

Viking

Found near Uig, Isle of Lewis, Scotland

c. AD 1150–75

Height of middle piece 9.2 cm

1831,1101.84 and 123–5

These Viking warrior chess pieces, clearly in the grip of *berserksgangr*, the state of battle ecstasy, form part of the cache of chess figures found in a sand dune on the Isle of Lewis in the Outer Hebrides. The three wild-eyed warriors opposite perfectly match the thirteenth-century Icelandic poet Snorri Sturluson's description of berserkers in the *Ynglinga Saga* as 'wild as dogs or wolves, they are biting their shields and are strong as bears or bulls; they kill men but neither fire nor iron could harm them'.

In their collective fury and matching postures, the berserkers are still subtly individualized. Each of their characteristic, pointed shields has a different design and their protective headgear varies from two different types of helmet to a mail hood.

Ninety-three chess figures are known from Lewis, enough to make up almost four complete sets. Many of the figures are carved from precious walrus ivory while others are made from whales' teeth. Moreover, the high-quality craftsmanship shows that they were destined for a prominent clientele. They seem to have been little used, if at all, and together with their large number, this indicates that they were most likely merchandise to be sold.

Stylistically, the ornament on some of the thrones for the seated kings, queens and bishops places them in the Romanesque Style (**75**). The shape of the thrones, reminiscent of a Norwegian type of chair, the general style of the chess pieces, the drinking horns held by the queens (**88**, **146**) and, of course, the presence of the berserkers suggests that they were carved in a Nordic cultural milieu.

Norway is a plausible place of production, as it had close ties with the Outer Hebrides which were a convenient stopping point on the way to Ireland. While they could have been made for a local Hebridean high-ranking noble or churchman, it is also possible that they were destined for one of the major Norse centres in Ireland such as Dublin, Waterford or Cork.

These were certainly places where such luxury goods would have been highly sought after. Chess was considered the 'kingly game' by the Norse and by then it was an important part of the education of any Viking noble.

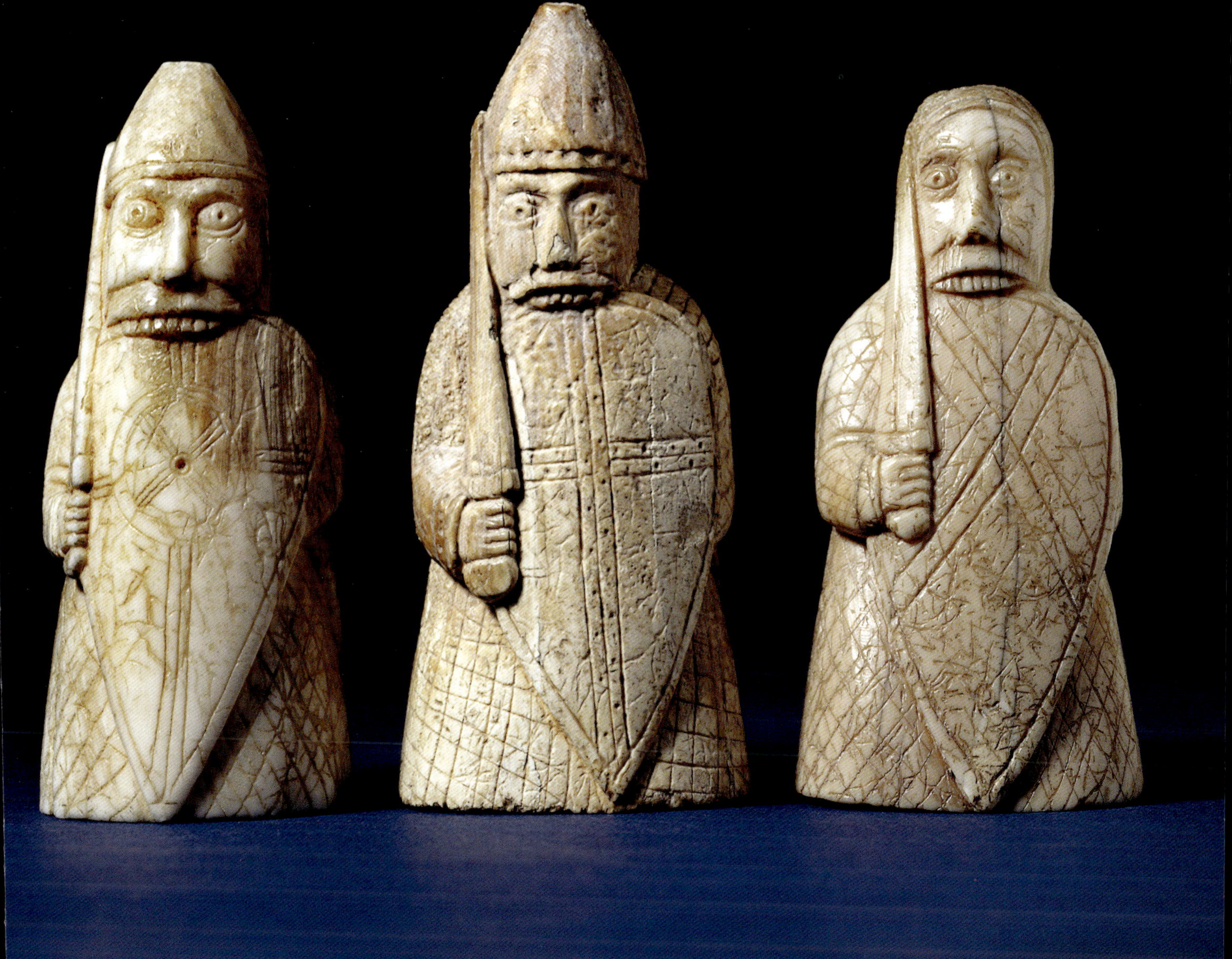

128 COIN PENDANT

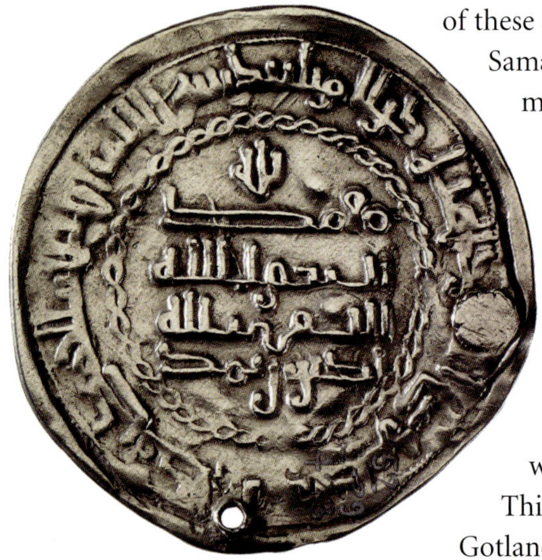

This small silver pendant is made from a pierced coin imitating Samanid silver *dirhams* minted during the reign of Nasr bin Ahmad (AD 913–42). The models for this coin are not surprising. It has been estimated that between 50 and 100 million *dirhams*, or up to 290 tonnes of silver, reached the countries around the Baltic from Islamic lands during the ninth and tenth century. Many of these coins were minted by the Samanid dynasty (AD 873–999). The Samanids ruled over parts of Central Asia, which were rich in silver mines, and at this time important mints were situated in the cities of Tashkent and Samarkand. The coins then travelled northwards, primarily by way of Viking and other trading networks along the Russian river systems.

The number of *dirhams* reaching the north dwindled from about AD 940 until they dried up completely in the early eleventh century. The Central Asian silver mines were exhausted, and in addition the arrival of horse nomadic peoples from further east led to the collapse of the Samanid Empire. Coins were occasionally hoarded for a long time in the Baltic Sea region. This is illustrated by the second hoard to be discovered at Spillings, Gotland, which contained more than 14,000 mainly Islamic silver coins accumulated from the seventh to ninth century.

A small number of exact parallels to the present medallion were found on Gotland, though not always with a hole for suspension. The cross and bird, perhaps a falcon, are never shown on Islamic coins, and neither is the twisted chain surrounding the inscription on the reverse. It is unlikely that these imitation coins were minted in Muslim terrorities due to the prohibition of the depiction of living beings and the association of the cross with Christianity. Furthermore, although the inscription is well cut, the Arabic is incorrect with letters sometimes the wrong way around. This seems to be another example of a well-respected currency being copied to inspire confidence in a different type of coinage (**60**, **84**).

Viking (?)
Thought to be from the Tartu area, Estonia
10th century AD
Diameter 3.0 cm
1852,0329.423

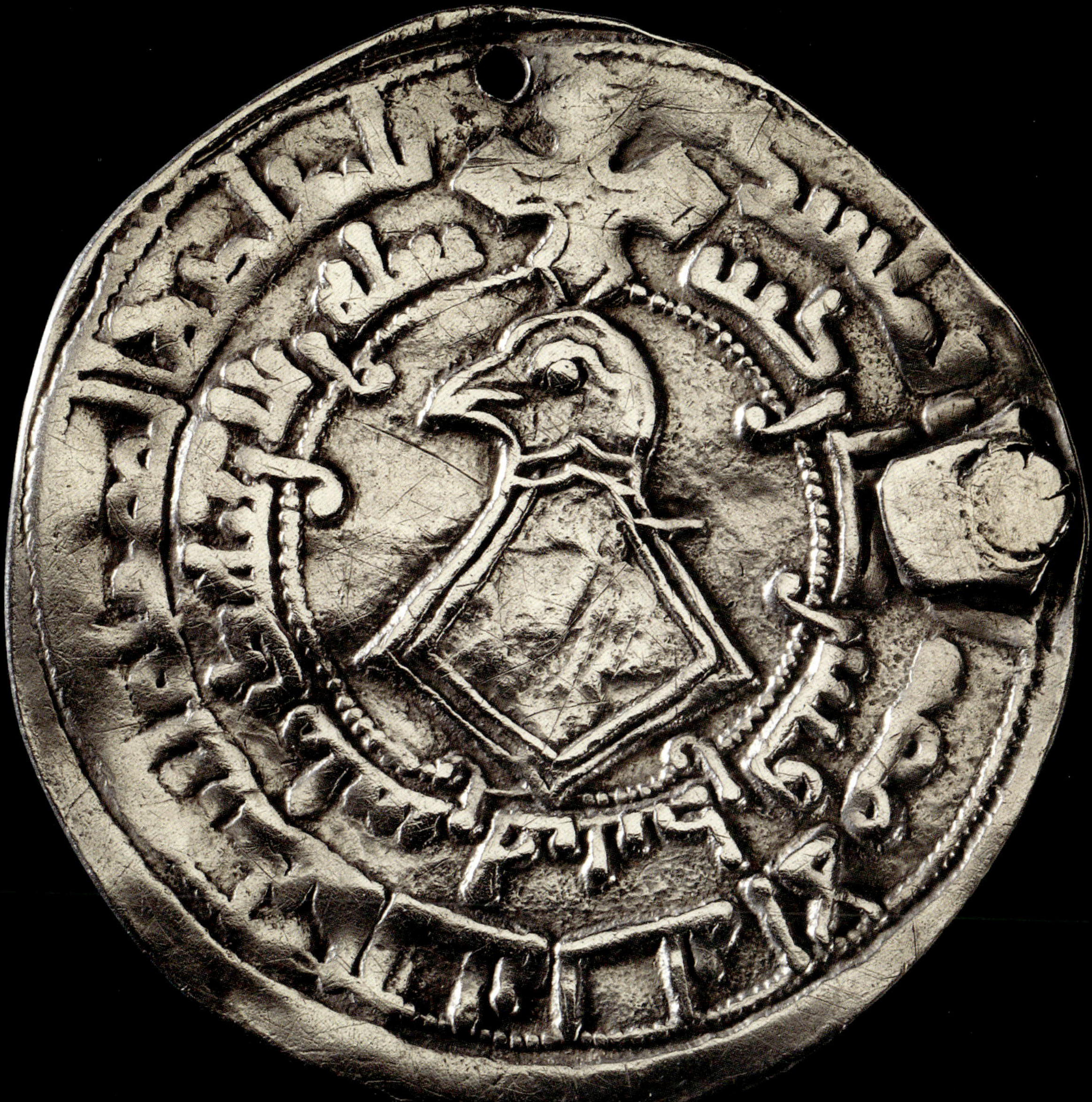

129 BALT ARM-RING

The British Museum's holdings of Baltic antiquities are among the most significant outside the Baltic states. They are largely based on the private collection of Professor Johann Karl Bähr (1801–69), who was a professor at the Riga Academy of Art. He became interested in the subject when archaeological material was exposed after a river near Riga flooded. The British Museum purchased his collection in 1852 as it was seen to complement some of its own Viking material.

The southern Baltic coast in the areas of modern-day Lithuania, Latvia and parts of Estonia was home to an assortment of Balt tribes. Their neighbours to the west and south were Slavs, while the Finno-Ugrians lived along the coast to their east (**130**, **131**). Some of these divisions were already mentioned by Greek and Roman writers who knew of the distant shores of the Baltic Sea, from where amber was traded to the Mediterranean.

Silver was rare, but the Balts were accomplished copper alloy casters, which requires much skill as bronze is a brittle material. A great deal of practice and experience would have been necessary to cast complex forms, filling all the crevices of a mould quickly before the molten metal cooled down.

They produced a variety of ornate armlets, and ring-shaped jewellery worn on wrists, arms and necks was popular. During the early Middle Ages this was partly inspired by late Roman and Germanic types, but many indigenous forms also existed. Later, the ninth to eleventh century saw close contacts with the Vikings. Heavy castings became fashionable and were not only worn by women but by men as well.

This penannular (**113**) arm-ring appears to have come from a male grave. After casting, it was embellished with geometric decoration. In its originally golden appearance it would have been a fine piece of jewellery. It seems that it has a pair, as an exact match for the British Museum armlet was exhibited in Riga by the Lettland Club in 1930. Its findspot was only given as 'Latvia', and therefore it is unclear whether it may also have come from the cemetery at Aizkraukle.

Balt
From Aizkraukle, Latvia
11th century
Maximum diameter 11.0 cm
1852,0329.194

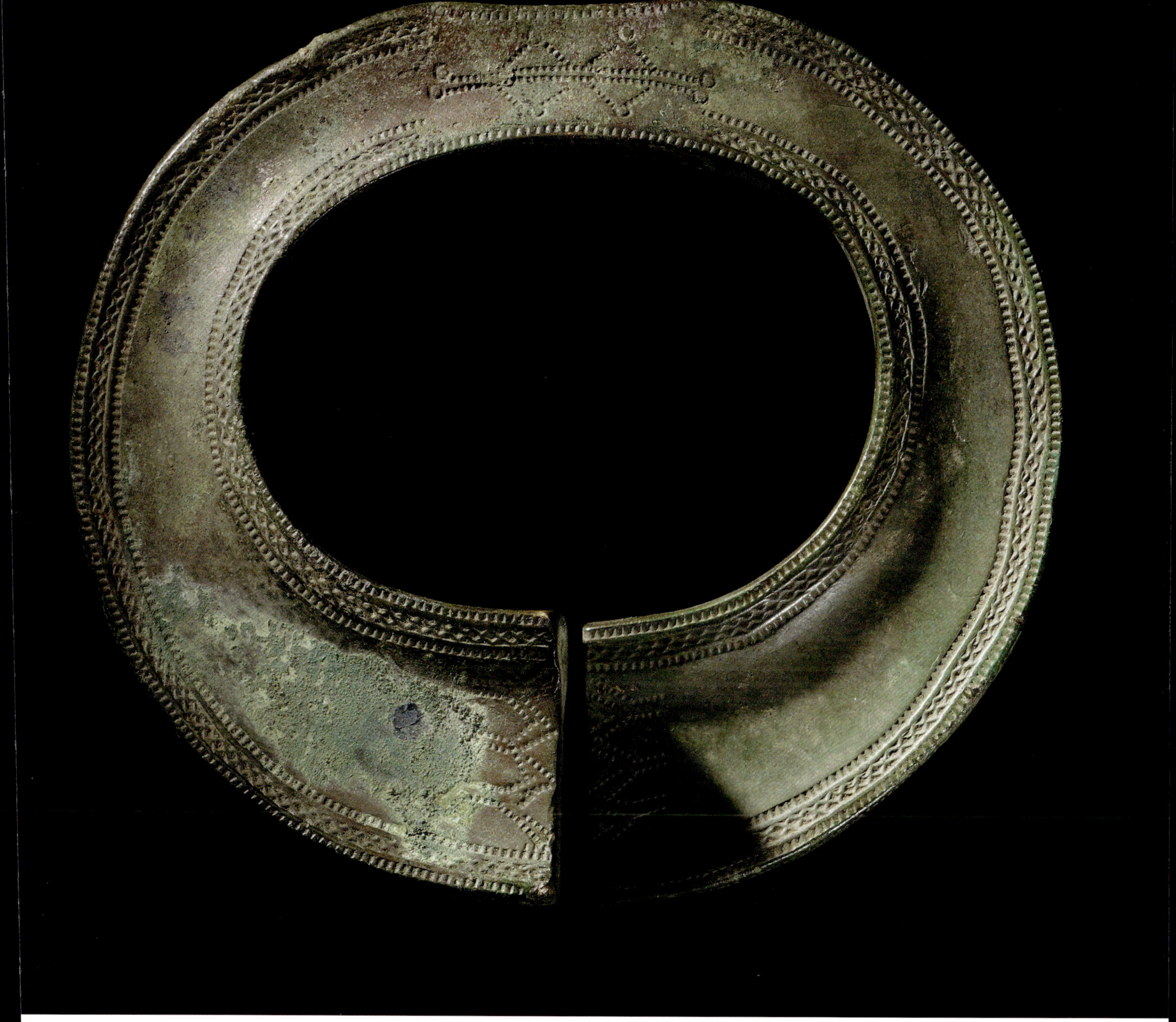

130 BROOCH AND BELT FITTING

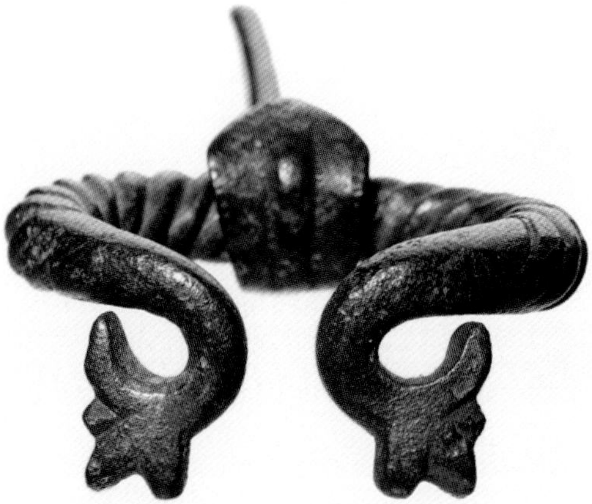

ABOVE:
Brooch
Balt
From Latvia
11th to 13th century
Diameter 4.0 cm
1852,0329.469

OPPOSITE:
Belt fitting
Finno-Ugrian
Found near Skjåk, Norway
11th to 12th century
Length 4.1 cm
1891,1021.108

Penannular brooches (**113**) became popular in the regions where the Balts lived in the seventh to eighth century, but they were still being worn as late as the seventeenth century. Inspiration may have come from Viking penannular copper alloy brooches, for example those from Gotland. Balt pieces often feature a twisted ring with two flat terminals, which are curled backwards. In early examples, these are clearly zoomorphic. Some of the animals resemble dogs or dragons, while others are more snake-like. An example of the latter was found in a tenth-century context at Hedeby, Germany. Over time, the animal heads became more stylized, until the open jaws and protruding tongue were transformed into a blossom resembling a lily, as on the brooch pictured here on the left. Dating is difficult, but silver versions of this type of brooch are thought to be from as late as the thirteenth or fourteenth century. In general, dress culture seems to have been much more conservative than in Scandinavia and some types, such as Balt versions of Viking oval brooches, were still worn a long time after they went out of fashion north of the Baltic coast.

However, influences between the two cultures did not only flow in one direction. The double-headed belt fitting illustrated on the right was found in central southern Norway. The hollow cast originally came from the Finno-Ugrian area, east of the lands where the Balts lived (**129**). When it was discovered, the little pendant still had a leather cord threaded through the ears of the animals as it would have been worn suspended from a belt (**131**). The back-to-back horses are embellished with cast ornament, seeming to imitate filigree and granulation, techniques which would have also decorated fine silver jewellery. The noise made by the little bells at the bottom of the pendant when the wearer was walking may have been intended to ward off evil, as was often the case with rattling jewellery. Perhaps a Viking traveller returning from Rus' (**128**) took a fancy to the pendant and brought it back to Scandinavia.

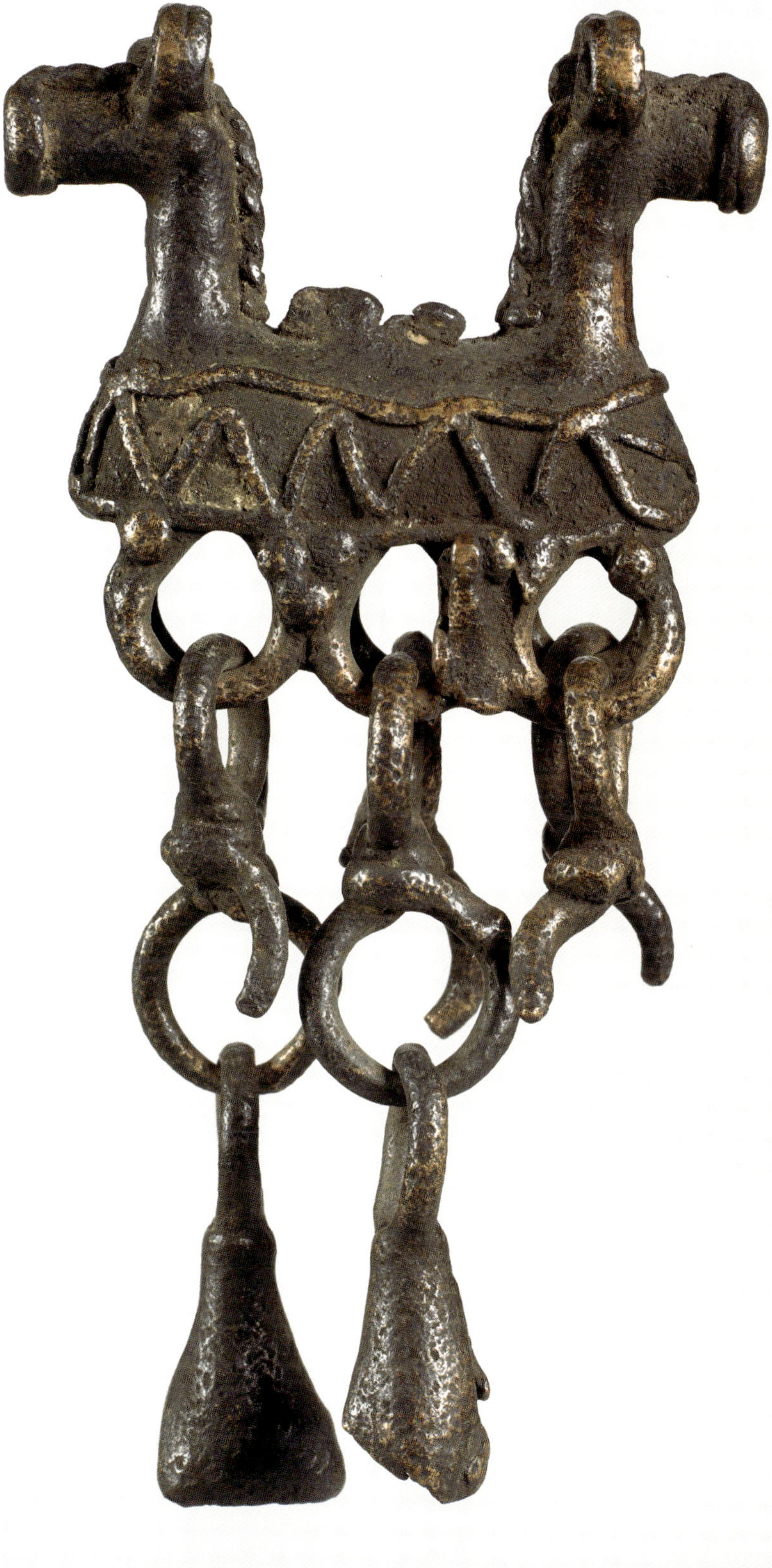

132 BRIDLE BIT

The Khazars were one of the many peoples who emerged during the early Middle Ages from the steppes of the East and moved westwards. Of Turkic stock, they founded a large kingdom, stretching from the north Caucasus and the northern shores of the Black Sea far into Russia, which lasted some three hundred years. The location of their dominions between eastern Europe, Central Asia and the Arabic domains south of the Caucasus placed them at a crossroads of trade routes. Unusually, the Khazar rulers and their subjects adopted the Jewish faith in the late eighth to ninth century. However, by about AD 970, their star had set as a result of the double assault of the Rus' and newly arrived steppe peoples.

Horses were of paramount importance to the Khazars, as they had been for the Huns and Avars (**92**), and would later prove to be for the Mongols. The success of their conquests was in part based on the speed with which their mounted warriors moved and attacked. Warfare was conducted on horseback and elaborate horse-gear as well as weaponry were a way of displaying status.

This iron bridle bit was sumptuously decorated with applied silver sheet (**91**). The ornament is based on the floral tendrils, especially vines, found on Byzantine and Slavic metalwork, reflecting the contacts of the Khazars with those to their south-west. The long side parts of the bit prevented it from slipping sideways out of the horse's mouth when the reins were pulled. They had already been used as obvious media for decoration in the late Roman period (**12**). This bit seems to have formed part of a larger set together with a pair of stirrups and a slender battle-axe, all displaying silver decoration.

Little is known about the provenance of this suite. It is thought to have come from the region of Perm in Russia, but nineteenth-century accounts are confused and contradict each other. The horse-gear and axe form part of a large group of objects acquired by the British Museum in 1878 (**131**), said to have come from Bielowodsk, Russia.

Khazar
Said to have been found near Bielowodsk, Russia
9th to 10th century AD
Width 22.9 cm
1878,0509.48

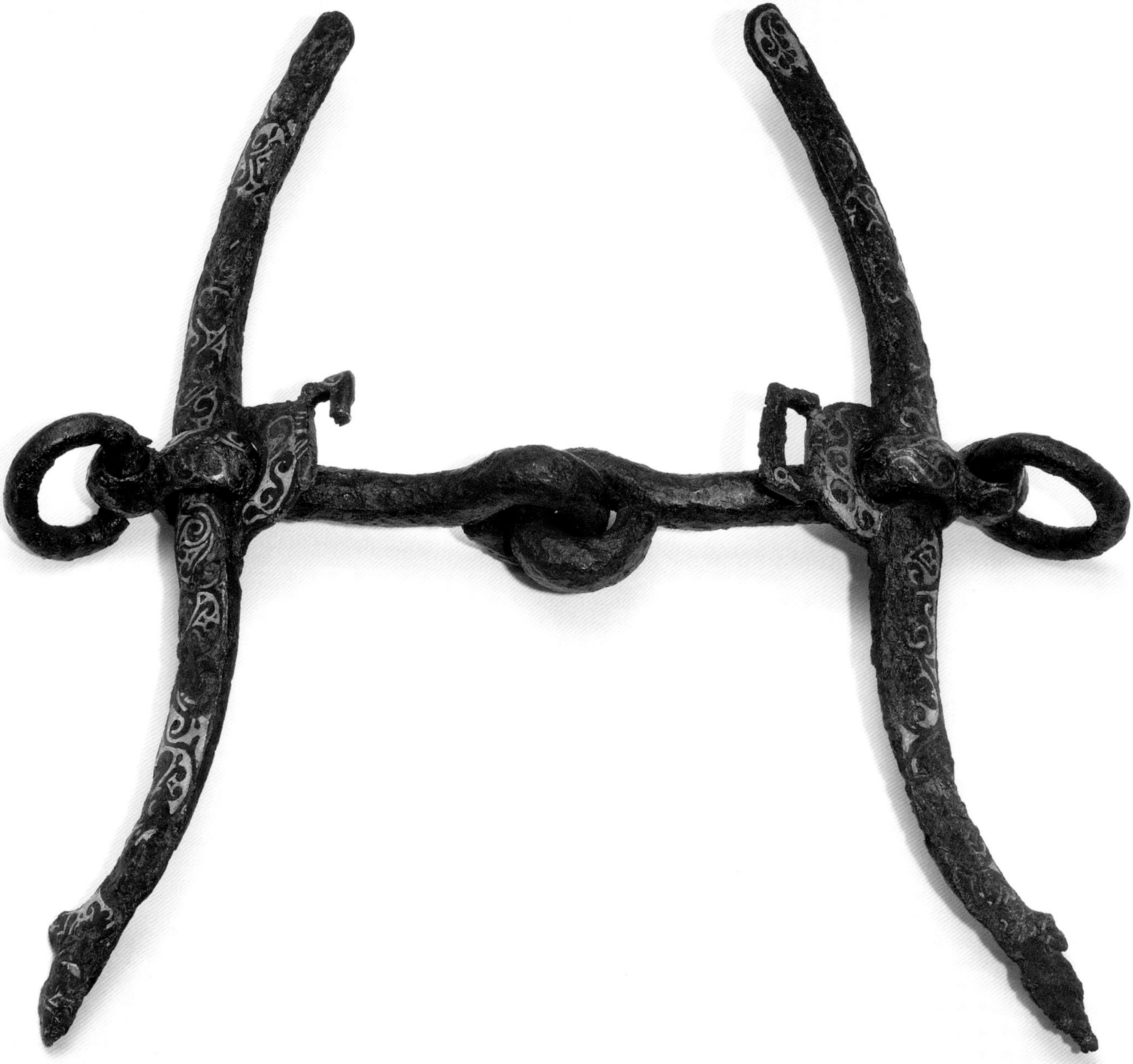

133 TEMPLE PENDANT

This hollow pendant belongs to a large and diverse group of objects called *kolty*, after the Old Slavonic word for earrings or ear ornaments. Many examples have been found in Slav territory. How they were used has been much discussed, but it is clear that they were items of women's jewellery and worn on the side of the head, down to the neck and frequently by the ears or temples, hence their name. No mention is made of *kolty* in written sources, nor are there any depictions from medieval Rus', where nonetheless many archaeological examples have been discovered in hoards or as stray finds. They do, however, feature in a number of Byzantine book illuminations and frescoes.

Recent excavations in Russia have shown that women in the tenth century and later were buried dressed in all their finery, which included various types of ornaments worn at the sides of the head. Copper alloy, silver and gold were used for these pendants, rings and spirals and sometimes they were also enamelled. They could be braided or twisted into the hair, or fixed to a veil or other headdress in many individual styles. Irrespective of their size and weight, many types of *kolt* were also used as earrings, threaded through the earlobe or upper ear.

For this example two gold sheets were impressed with designs of back-to-back birds, their heads turned towards one another, positioned either side of hanging foliage. The scene is enclosed in a heart-shaped frame with a scalloped edge, and many other *kolty* are decorated with the same motif. The birds often resemble doves, probably a Christian symbol for the Holy Spirit (**25**). The composition itself goes back to Syrian models (**105**), and from there the imagery spread throughout the Byzantine Empire and then northwards.

The plain rim surrounding the design has five loops. Originally further ornaments, such as pearl strings, would have been affixed to these. At the top of the *kolt* there are four larger hoops for a clasp. It has been suggested that the hollow bodies of *kolty* could be filled with small scented cloths, but there are no traces inside the current example.

Slav
Unknown findspot
11th to 12th century
Width 3.7 cm
Bequeathed by W. Burges
1881,0802.2

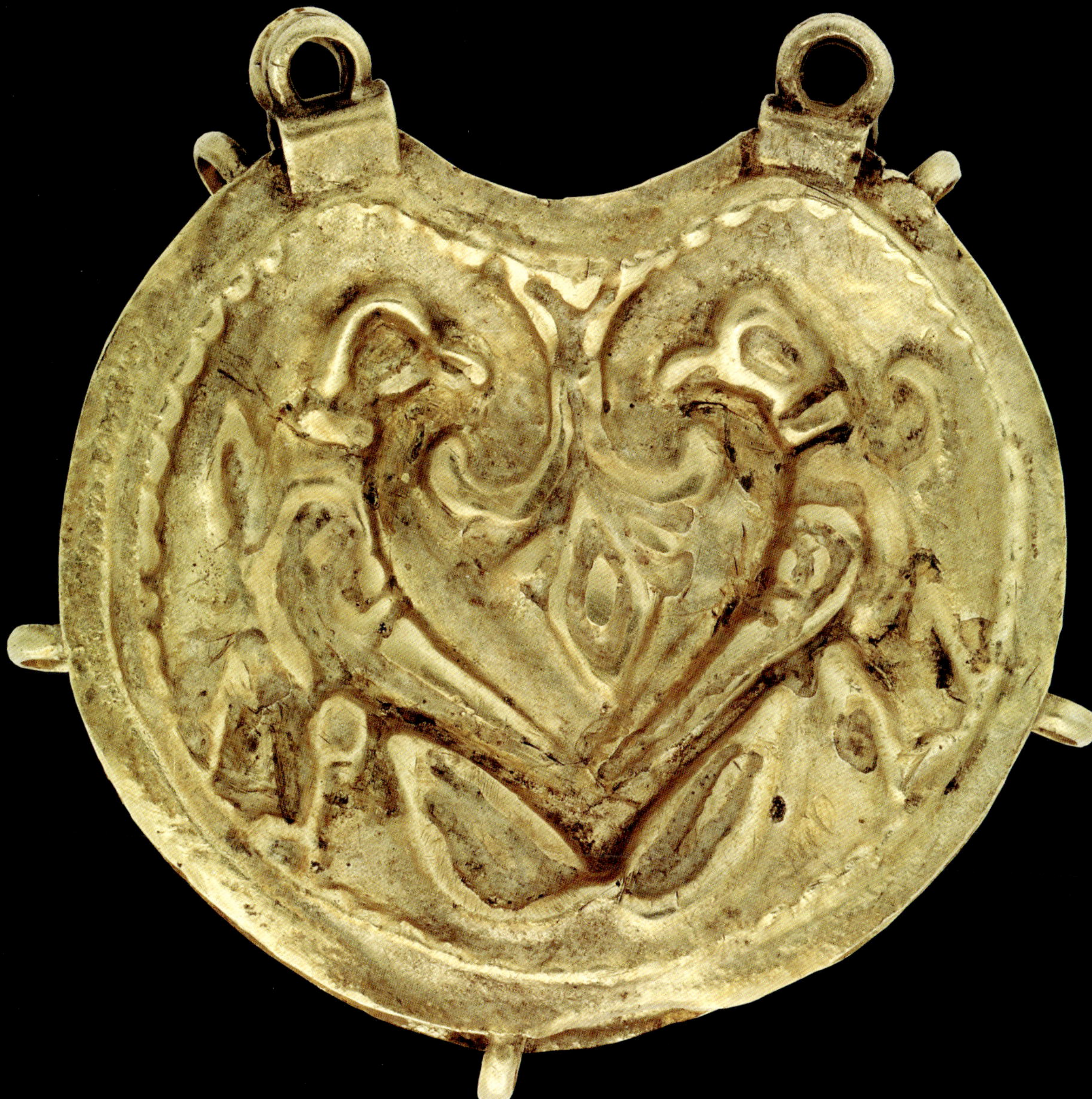

134 SILVER ARM-RING

The Banat region, where this heavy silver armlet is said to have been found, stretches from Romania through Hungary and into the north of Serbia. Metal rods of varying thickness were twisted together and the ends hammered out to form large, triangular terminals. These were then embellished with sizeable silver buttons, granules and grooved wires subdividing each triangle.

A handsome amount of silver would have been necessary to make this arm-ring. New ore deposits were discovered in Bohemia, Moravia and Silesia, roughly equivalent with modern-day Czech Republic, Slovakia and southern Poland, from the twelfth to thirteenth century onwards. The increase in mining activities led to a greater availability of silver, which was not only made into coin, but jewellery as well.

Two arm-rings identical to this one, which are said to come from the Banat and possibly Hungary, were in European museums by 1933. Eight further armlets are known from Serbia and four from Bulgaria. As all of these are old discoveries, there is no new information to provide a possible date. Similar arm-rings of slightly different construction can be dated to the late thirteenth or fourteenth century by coins issued by Byzantine, Serb and Bulgar rulers found with them.

Another parallel is a closely comparable arm-ring from the Balt settlement areas much further north. It came from a coin-dated hoard of about 1350 to 1450 from Šančiai, Lithuania. While it also has triangular terminals with large silver granules set inside a notched frame and a hoop made from twisted wires, it has a hinged closing mechanism. It is a unique find among Baltic jewellery of the period and as a Kievan silver-gilt armband was included in the hoard as well, it is certain that the bracelet is a Slavic piece. The prototypes for the Slav forms undoubtedly lie in twelfth-century Byzantine gold arm-rings.

With this arm-ring we have entered the high Middle Ages. By then, Slavic burials in the Balkans had long been without grave goods (**133**) or associated coins, so we know little about what people wore and when it was fashionable.

Slavic
Said to be from the Banat region
13th to 15th century
Maximum diameter 7.4 cm
1860,0609.7

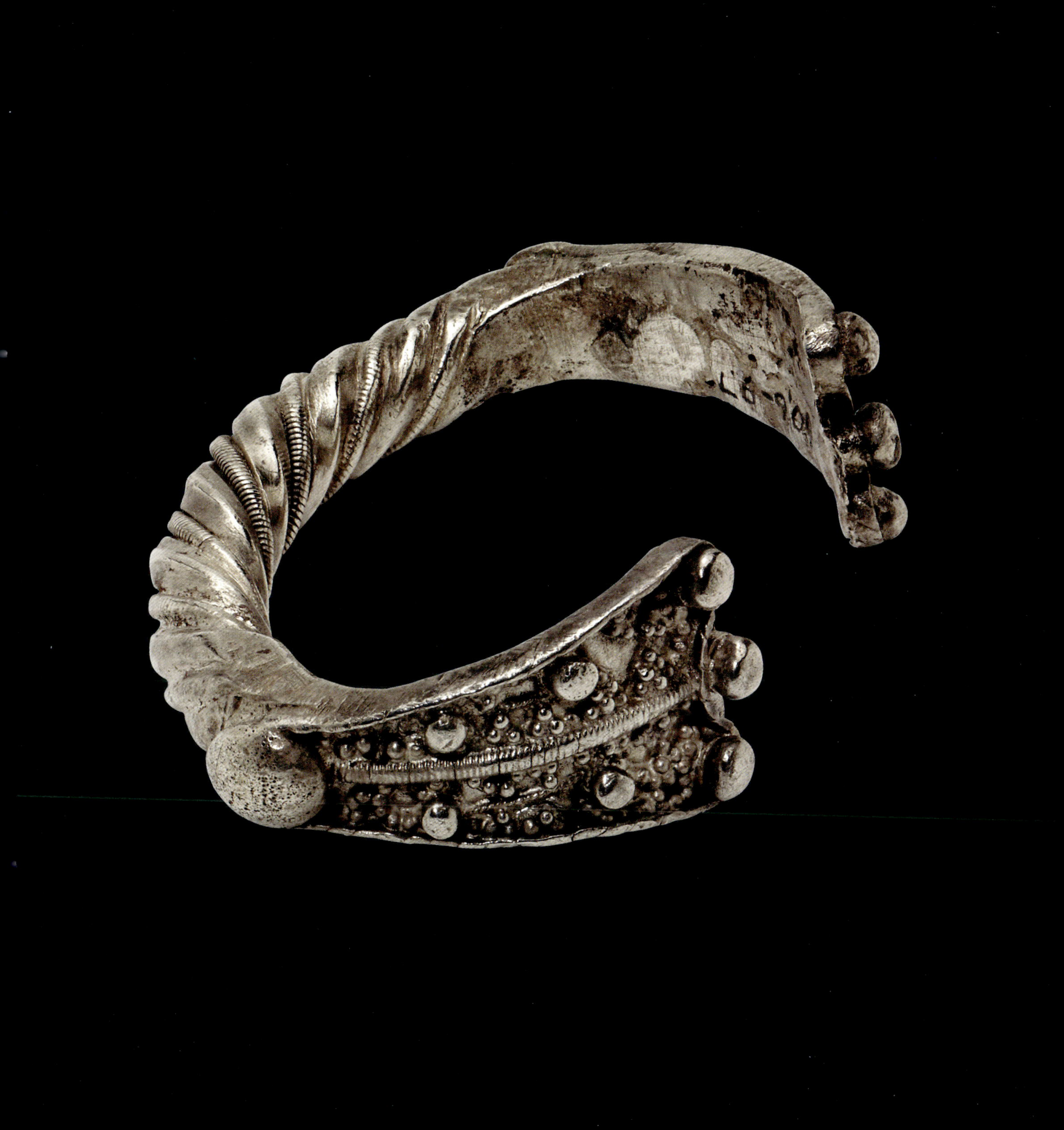

6 THE CELTIC SPHERE

(SEVENTH TO TWELFTH CENTURY)

The term 'Celts' encompasses a multitude of early medieval peoples who lived in Britain alongside the Anglo-Saxons, as well as in Ireland, Brittany and the Atlantic Isles (**Map 3**). While they spoke related languages and, judging from their art, may have had commonalities in their beliefs and mythology, it is doubtful whether there was ever one shared 'Celtic' identity. While large parts of their territories had previously remained outside of the Roman Empire, this had not prevented contact with their Roman neighbours. Although some late Roman written sources described the Irish as raiders and pirates, Celts also served in the Roman army. As a result of these connections, silver and the influence of Roman styles started to make an appearance in Celtic art (**19**).

Cornish, Welsh, western Scottish and Irish princes of the late fifth and sixth century had access to fine Roman pottery and amphorae, probably filled with wine and occasionally even olive oil, as well as to other luxuries such as glass. Unlike their Anglo-Saxon neighbours, the Celtic nobles seemed to be able to maintain direct, if infrequent, contact with the Mediterranean. As late as the seventh century, a bishop in Alexandria, Egypt, is reported to have sent a ship with grain to Cornwall with instructions for it to return laden with tin, which was necessary for the production of bronze. The recent discovery in an Irish bog of the papyrus-lined Faddan More Psalter from around AD 800 corroborates such links since papyrus only came from Egypt.

Gilt copper alloy brooch with glass settings, from Ireland, 8th century AD (1922,0510.1)

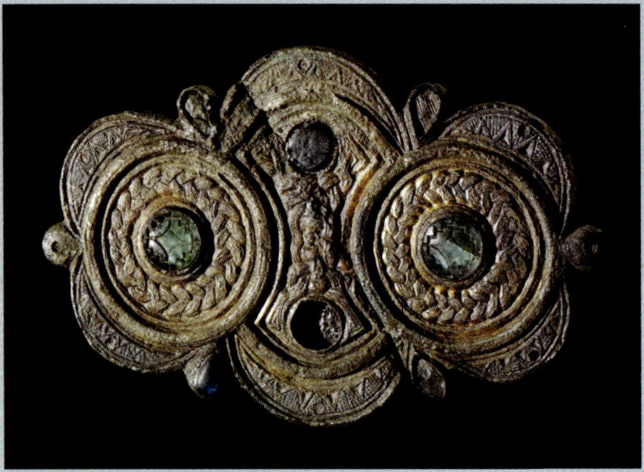

Indeed, religion may have been a crucial element in maintaining such relations. The Irish were converted to Christianity by British missionaries, most famously through the legendary efforts of St Patrick, in the fifth century. Many monasteries were founded, which later became instrumental in spreading the Gospel. St Columba (AD 521–97), for instance, established the monastery at Iona, Scotland, from where the Picts were converted. The monastery at Lindisfarne, Northumberland, had connections with Iona and was famed for its scriptorium where important manuscripts such as the Lindisfarne Gospels were written, copied and illuminated (**137**). Irish and Anglo-Saxon missionaries went on to preach among the Germanic peoples on the Continent, and founded monasteries as far away as France and northern Italy. Thus, Insular art styles spread to the Continent as well (**109**, **151**).

In Wales and Cornwall, large stones were set up and inscribed in the Roman tradition to commemorate the dead (**136**), while in Scotland, the Picts produced enigmatic carvings of exquisite quality (**143**). Together with the monumental stone crosses dominating the landscape in many parts of the Celtic world, they are among the finest pieces of sculpture to have been produced in the British Isles.

A rich spiritual culture developed which also found its physical expression in metalwork and book illumination. These forms innovatively united stylistic and technological traits passed down from the prehistoric La Tène Celtic period (**144**) with new developments and combined them with Germanic and Mediterranean influences. The outcome was a vast array of highly distinctive artworks. For example, precious jewellery delighted in the contrast of colours, textures and materials through a combination of various metalworking techniques, different metals and vibrant inlays or appliqués (**148**). Lavishly adorned reliquaries (**141–2**), book covers (**145**), illuminated manuscripts and ecclesiastical plate came to be focal points of Irish art, often produced in monasteries, and were revered by the faithful.

From the ninth century, the Vikings introduced their own distinctive material and visual culture (**Map 4**), and brought large amounts of silver to Ireland in particular. Their relationship with the Irish was not always easy and while the Norse founded towns and at times held kingdoms in Ireland, they were on occasion defeated and temporarily expelled.

Yet in the tenth and and eleventh century these different elements blended into characteristic Irish-Viking styles which were again employed to embellish relics (**149**) and new forms of dress accessories (**113**, **150**).

135 HANDPIN

The term 'handpin' is somewhat misleading, as it is a modern name which may not necessarily have had any significance during the early Middle Ages. But the label has stuck, as it is an apt description of the semicircular pinhead which has three to five perpendicular tubes emerging from its top, just like fingers on a hand. The pinhead itself protrudes forwards from the shank of the pin, a feature also seen on large dress pins with round heads, such as that from the Londesborough collection (**19**).

The heavy bronze casting on this example has been embellished with red opaque enamel, which is the colour most commonly used. It was employed to decorate brooches (**139**) and is also found on silver pins (**19**). Scientific analysis of Celtic enamels from the sixth to tenth century was carried out at the British Museum. This indicated that the predominance of red on Celtic metalwork is possibly a result of the enamels being produced from slag left over from silver recycling, which is likely to have resulted in red colourants. The scratches in the centre of the pinhead are keying marks to help hold in the enamel.

It was once thought that these pins developed in Ireland, but it now seems more likely that they evolved in Britain. Their origins reach back to late Roman times, and earlier models were particularly common in the north of Britain. Irish handpins were popular during at least the fifth to the seventh century, but unfortunately comparatively little is still known of Irish dress and jewellery in this period. Late examples seem to have lasted into the eighth century. The dating of the type is strongly based on stylistic criteria and, as one scholar put it, 'to a large extent speculative'.

The central hole in this pinhead would have been threaded with a cord, which was used to keep the pin in place after it was pushed through the fabric, most probably a woollen cloak. While this principle may seem unusual, it was a typical feature of both brooches and pins in the Viking period (**124**, **148**). The pin probably stayed in the cape-like cloak, which was simply pulled over the wearer's head.

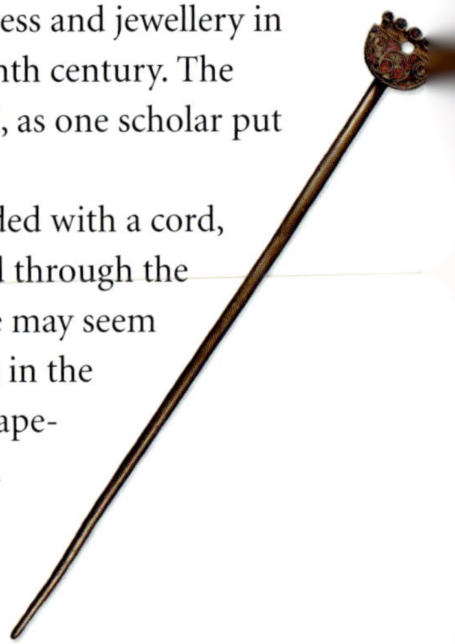

Irish

From Craigiwarren Bog,
Co. Antrim, Northern Ireland

5th century AD (?)

Length of pin 23.4 cm

1880,0802.132

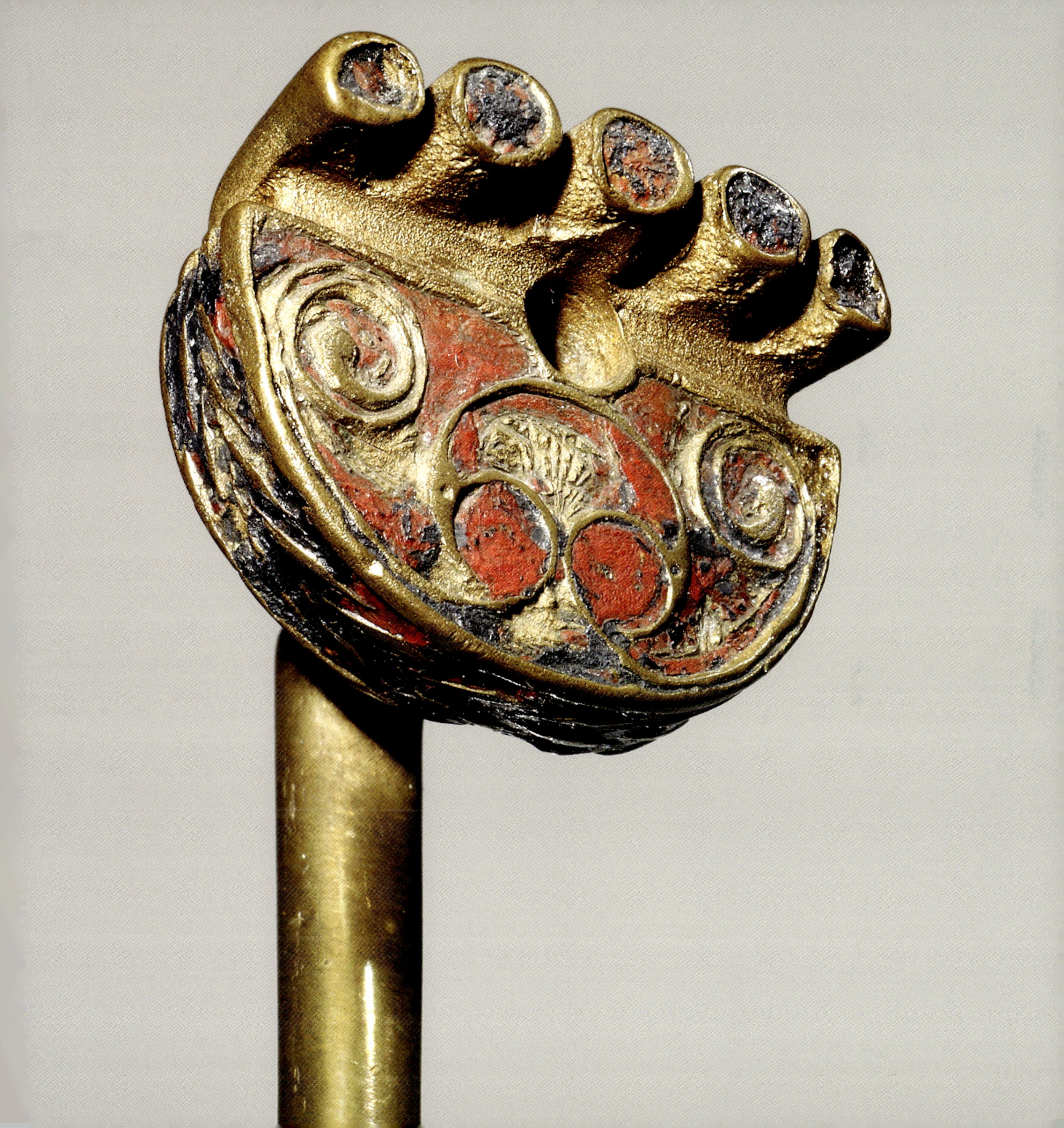

136 THE FARDEL STONE

This red sandstone memorial from Fardel may not be a masterpiece of sculpture in the same way as the Sheffield cross shaft (**63**) or the Burghead bull (**143**), but it is of paramount importance in telling us about the preservation of Roman customs, commemoration of the dead and conspicuous displays of status in early medieval Devon. At this time, the area belonged to the British kingdom of Dumnonia, and it also saw the settlement of Irish groups from both southern Wales and Ireland itself. The custom of setting up these memorial markers is likely to have come from Wales.

Latin letters have been employed together with the native ogam script which runs around the edge of the stone. Ogam was a way of recording the early Irish language and consists of short lines meeting or cutting across a base line, such as the edge of a stone, at a particular angle. Ogam was developed in southern Ireland, but its inspirations are unclear and it does not work in the same way as an alphabet, but rather more like a code.

Both the Latin and ogam inscriptions include personal names, as is typical for these stones. The Latin reads 'FANONI MAQUIRINI', dedicating the stone to a man called Fanonus. The 'Maqui' element of the inscription indicates that he was the son of someone called Rinus. While the ogam spells a different text, it is thought to be a rendition of the Latin. The Latin inscription on the back of the Fardel stone mentions a man by the name of Sagranuus, which appears to have been a later addition.

The individuals commemorated on ogam stones were aristocrats or clerics from the highest levels of society. Occasionally, a woman's name with the addendum 'daughter of' occurs. The tradition of erecting memorials follows Roman models, which is also reflected in the use of Latin and the shape of the lettering.

During the nineteenth century, this stone served as a bridge across a stream before it was moved to Fardel House. There it was used as a support for a shed before the lord of the manor donated it to the British Museum.

Celtic
From Fardel, Devon, England
Late 5th to early 6th century AD
Height 173.0 cm
Donated by Captain Pode of Slade
1861,0209.1

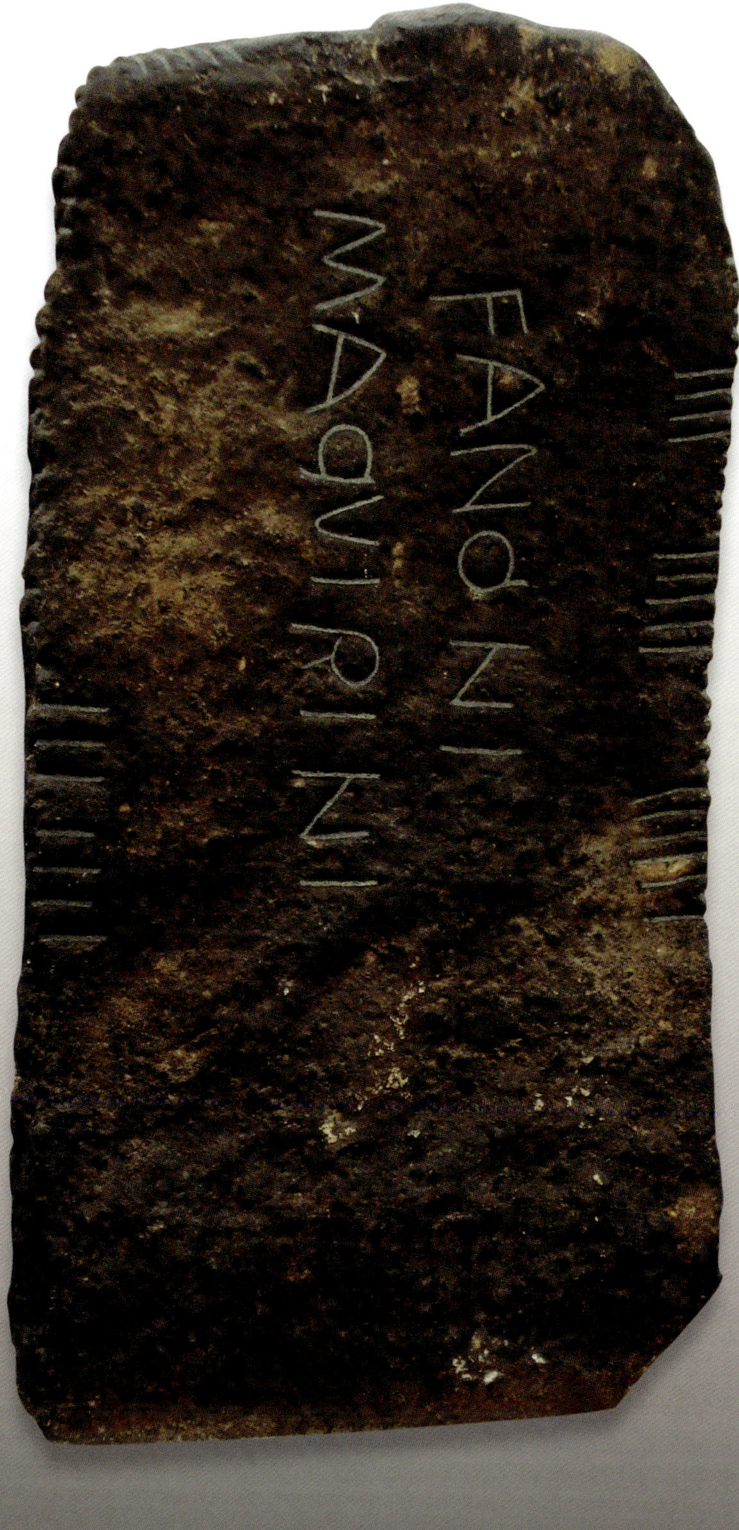
FANONI
MAQVIRINI

137 SEMICIRCULAR MOUNT

The curvilinear patterns of Celtic and Insular art from the fifth to seventh century are distinct from any other ornament in this book. Its repertoire of building blocks could be combined in inventive ways. What unified them was that the ornament formed a coherent whole, which was based on compositions designed using a pair of dividers. Characteristically, a frame of any shape was filled with interlocking elements, such as coils, spiral hooks and triskeles. These could be integrated with motifs inspired by Anglo-Saxon interlace patterns which were often 'animated' in the literal sense by adding the heads and limbs of birds, monsters or animals (**144**). It has been suggested that the juxtaposition of order and chaos may be a reference to the struggle of good and evil, or else represent the ordering hand of God.

The decoration on this cast copper alloy plaque is restricted to a range of geometric arrangements. Inside the flat rim a field displays two whirled triskeles above a pair of medium-sized scrolls which swing outwards towards either side, forming trumpet-like shapes. Their lower edges in turn interlock with a pair of coiled hooks and the upper ends of both the trumpets as well as the coiled hooks merge with the triskeles at the top. The recessed parts of the ornament would originally have been enamelled. This may have been the red commonly found on other artefacts (**19**, **135**, **139**), but instances of yellow, green and blue enamel are also known.

Metalwork such as this influenced book art. Similar patterns in an even more colourful palette distinguish the outstanding illuminated manuscripts of the period, such as the Lindisfarne Gospels. The detail on the left, for example, features the same interlocking curled hook and trumpet.

The monastery at Lindisfarne was founded by Aidan, an Irish bishop, in AD 635. A monastic setting could explain the connections between metalwork and book illumination, as major ecclesiastical centres would have had both scribes and fine smiths.

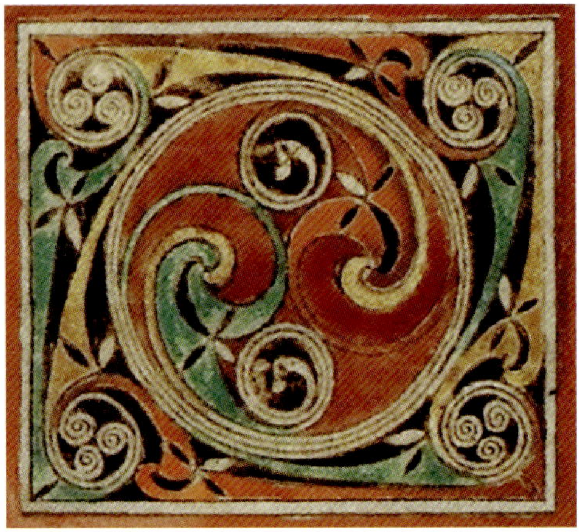

ABOVE:

Detail from the Lindisfarne Gospels

Late 7th or early 8th century AD

British Library Cotton MS Nero D.iv, folio 94v

OPPOSITE:

Celtic

Unknown findspot

6th to 7th century AD

Width 3.5 cm

1995,0905.1

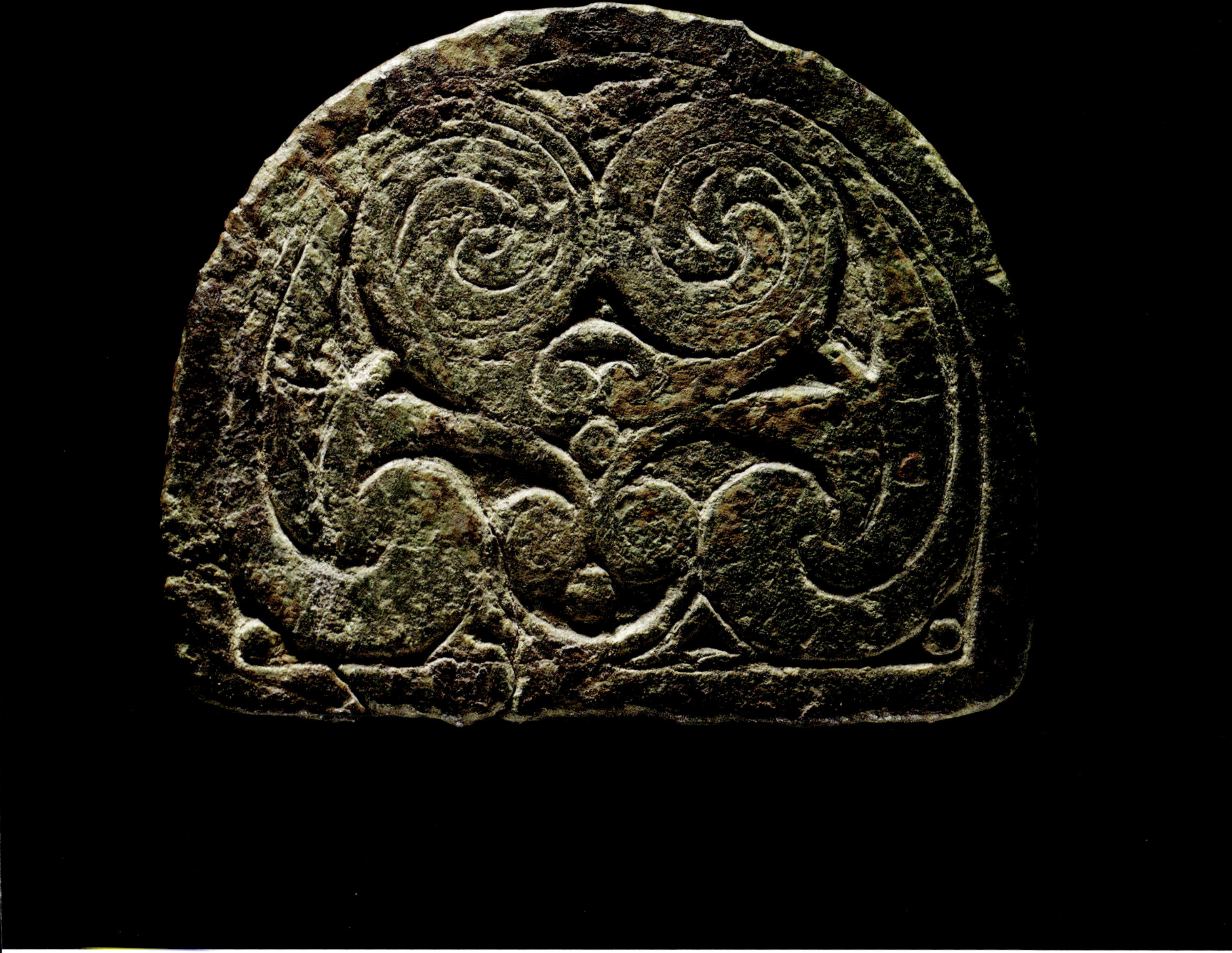

138 GLASS BEADS

Irish

6th to 9th century AD (?)

LEFT:

From Dungiven, Co. Londonderry, Northern Ireland

Height 1.5 cm

1890,0215.9

CENTRE:

From Antrim, Co. Antrim, Ireland

Height 2.0 cm

1862,0701.1

RIGHT:

From Ireland

Height 1.6 cm

Donated by the executors of F. Slade

1871,1210.17

Many Celtic glass beads from Ireland are entirely different from the early medieval beads discovered elsewhere in Europe. They stand out on account of their complex shapes, translucent colours and surface applications, the latter of which may have come in the form of glass bosses or applied, bicoloured cables. To produce the cable effect two glass rods of different colours were heated and then twisted together.

Such rods have been found in Ireland, the most common combination being translucent blue with opaque white. Twisted cables could have been imported from the Continent or the Mediterranean. It is clear that Ireland had direct links to the Mediterranean in the early Middle Ages, as the Faddan More Psalter and North African and eastern Mediterranean pottery finds demonstrate (see p. 286). Yet, there are also indications of the production of cable-twisted rods in Ireland, for instance from Dunmisk, County Tyrone. Glass may even have been made there from the basic ingredients of soda, lime and silica. However, the evidence is feeble and it is clear that raw glass was imported. Complex glass patterns were also created from millefiori glass rods. The Irish did not make millefiori beads (**106**), but they did produce an array of inlay slips. The blue-and-white chequerboard pattern of the slips from Sutton Hoo (**46**), for example, has parallels with those from Dunmisk. There is no evidence that the Irish made glass vessels, which instead were imported from the Continent.

As in Anglo-Saxon England, the hubs of artistic production in Ireland were not only the secular power centres, but also monasteries, both of which cultivated the working of glass and enamels. Both skills were closely linked and also had an affinity with metal craft, as colourful studs were common on both the highest quality secular jewellery (**147**, **148**; see p. 286) and outstanding church plate, such as that from Derrynaflan or Ardagh.

As the dead were not buried in full dress at this time, we do not know what necklaces looked like, whether beads may have also been worn with belts, as in Anglo-Saxon areas, or if men wore beads as well. Dating is complicated, as most finds come from old collections or poorly understood contexts.

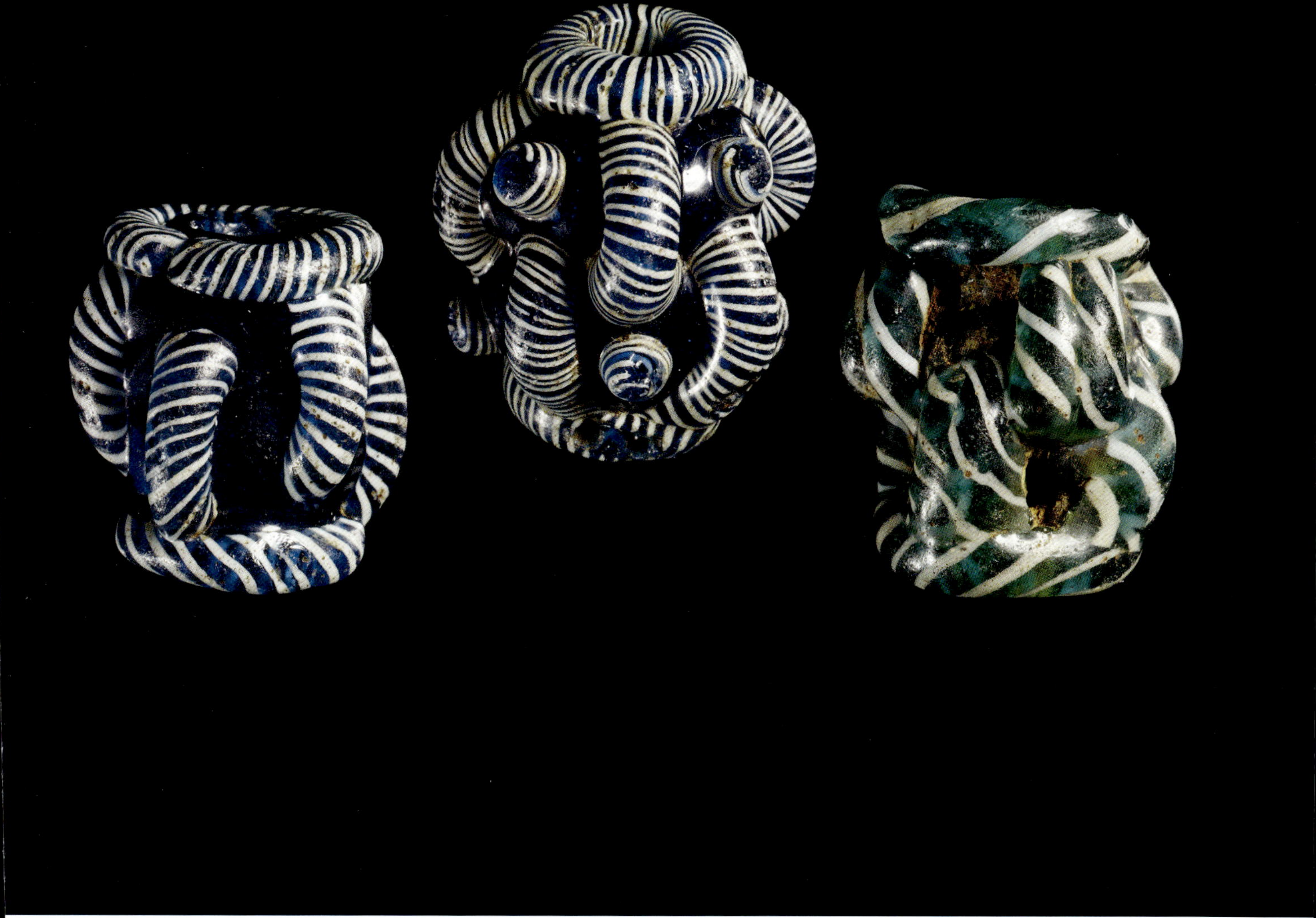

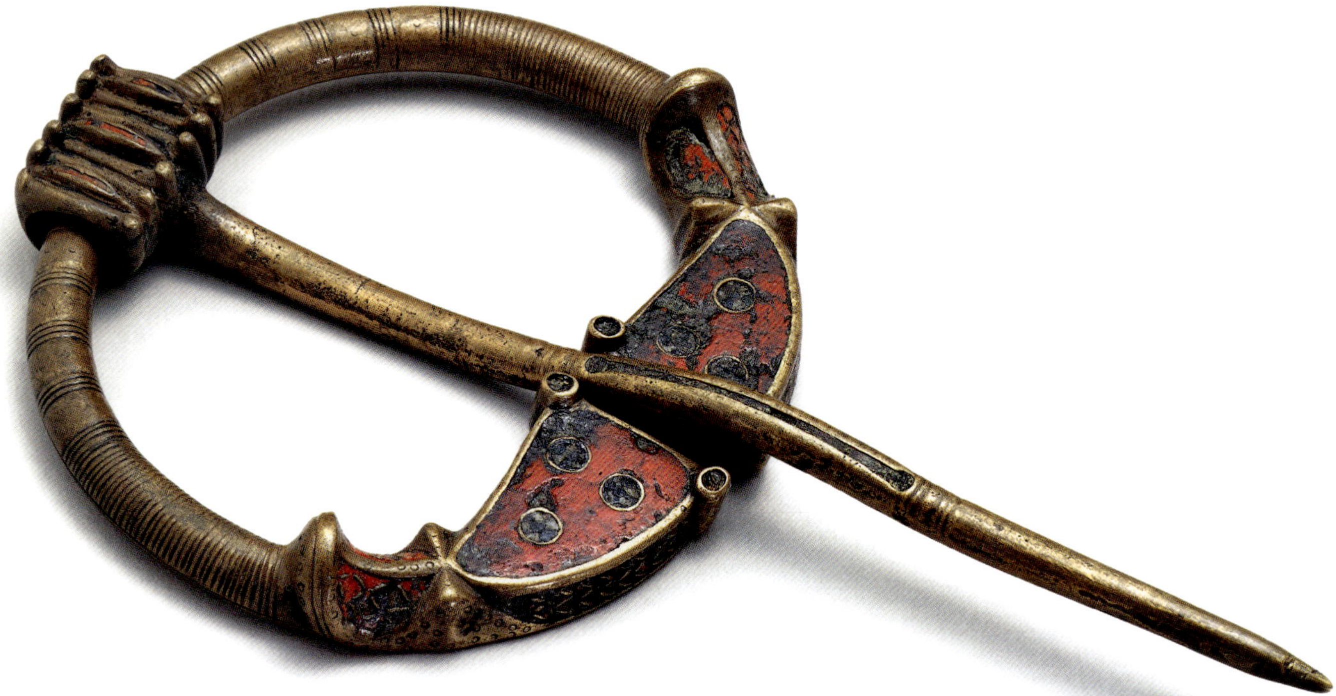

139 COPPER ALLOY BROOCH

This enamelled copper alloy brooch stands in a long tradition of Celtic penannular brooches. The pin would have been passed through the fabric it was meant to fasten. It was then slotted between the two open terminals and the ring of the brooch rotated, so that it could not slip out again. Brooches such as this one were worn by both men and women to hold cloaks in position. The type remained popular for a long time, and inspired both Irish and Viking silver versions (**113**, **115**, **148**, **150**).

This brooch is one of the more ornate pieces known. Its cast body displays narrow grooves and punched rings, while the base of the pin is decorated with cast bosses and heavy ridges. The brooch's most eye-catching feature, however, is the red enamel inlaid into the ridges and the terminals. As opposed to the enamelling techniques of the high Middle Ages, Celtic early medieval enamel is not fired onto the metal base. Instead, the molten glass mass, which was viscous rather than liquid, was pressed into recessed fields and then left to cool. This allowed for further embellishment through the use of inlays, which were pushed into the hot glass mass. On this brooch white and blue millefiori glass slips fill metal circlets on the terminals. Although they have deteriorated, these small roundels would once have given a gem-like impression.

Millefiori slips were made from fused glass rods of different colours (**46**, **106**), from which slices were cut. They were employed to great effect as contrasting glass inlays and were also used on some of the foremost metalwork from Anglo-Saxon England, such as that from Sutton Hoo, which is broadly contemporary with this brooch (**46**).

The enlarged ends of this brooch still preserve echoes of the animal-head terminals which featured on the earliest prototypes. By this time, brooch ends had simply become surfaces on which to display ornament, although it has recently been argued that some of the inlay patterns could have had a deeper, Christian, significance.

Celtic
From Co. Cavan, Ireland
Early 7th century AD
Width of hoop 7.0 cm
1856,0320.1

140 THE DOWRIS LATCHET

The British Museum's Celtic collection contains six objects known as latchets. They appear to have been used as dress fasteners to close an overgarment such as a cloak. Latchets always have a large, circular head, which is sometimes beautifully decorated, and a thin, snaking body. In the case of later pieces, such as this example from central Ireland, the body has eyelets, which hint at the way that a latchet must have been used. Wire spirals were pushed first through the fabric and then through the openings on the latchet. It would thus have worked like a clasp and on some pieces those spirals are indeed still preserved. Large and elaborate latchets such as this one have only been found in Ireland and it is possible that they were worn in pairs.

The Dowris latchet is the most ornate example known and its quality would have been a visual manifestation of its owner's status. It is distinguished by both the well-preserved red enamel and the extremely fine inlay of copper alloy wires in spiral and lozenge patterns. Like on many other examples of early medieval Celtic jewellery, the vibrant opaque enamel is the feature that dominates its appearance (**19**, **139**). The fields for the enamel were carved out of the cast copper alloy base and the recesses were then filled with the heated, viscous glass mass.

We can only speculate as to whether the lozenges on the middle section and the herringbone arrangement towards the smaller end of this latchet could have been inspired by Anglo-Saxon cloisonné patterns (**46**, **51**). It is clear, however, that the spiral ornament of the large roundel has close parallels elsewhere, notably on the round decorative plaques of the largest and most sumptuous of the three hanging bowls from Sutton Hoo. This, together with its first-class workmanship, has led to the suggestion that the bowl could have been a gift from a Celtic to an Anglo-Saxon ruler, setting the craftsmanship of the Dowris latchet in context.

Celtic
From Dowris, Co. Offaly, Ireland
7th century AD
Length 7.6 cm
1854,0714.97

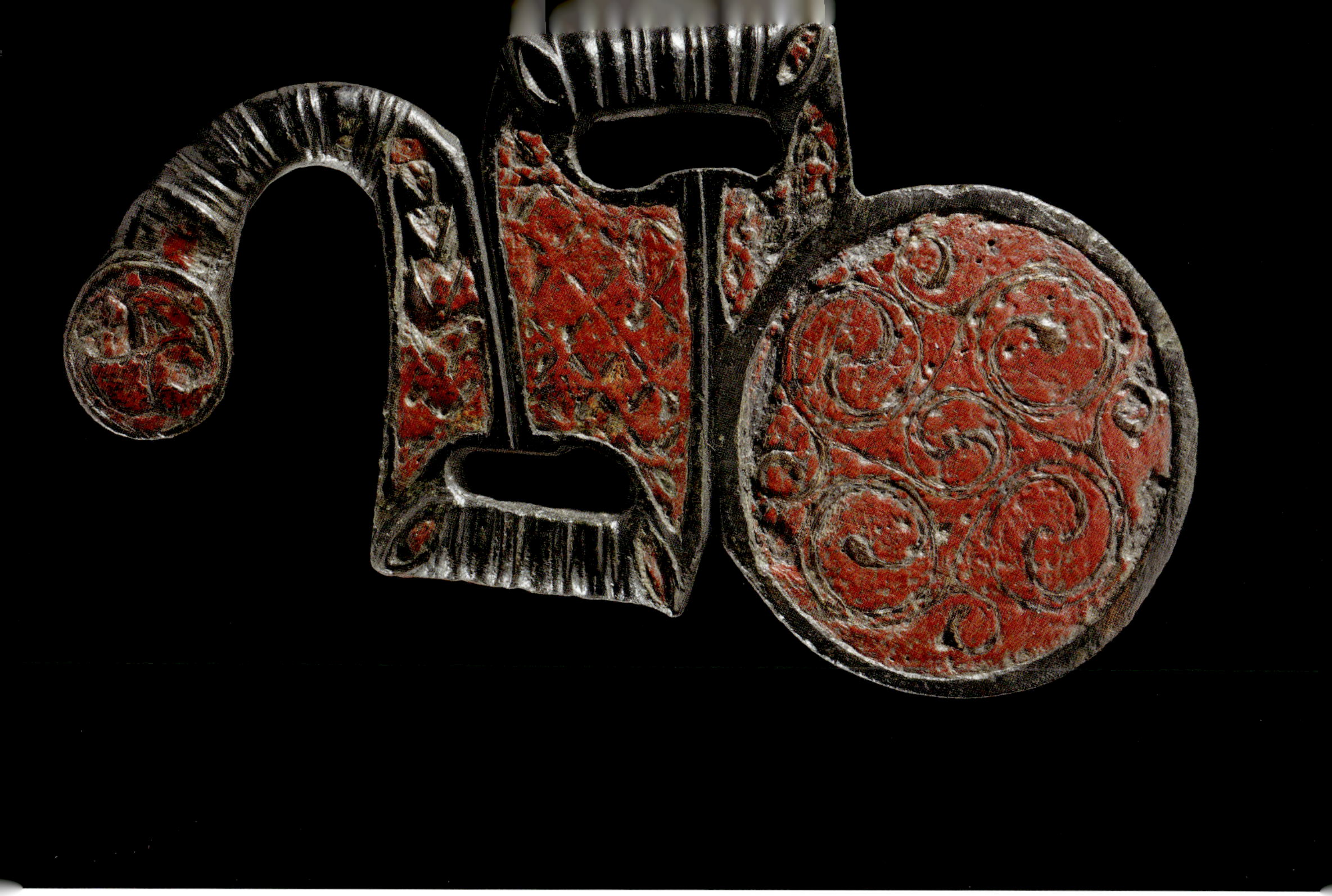

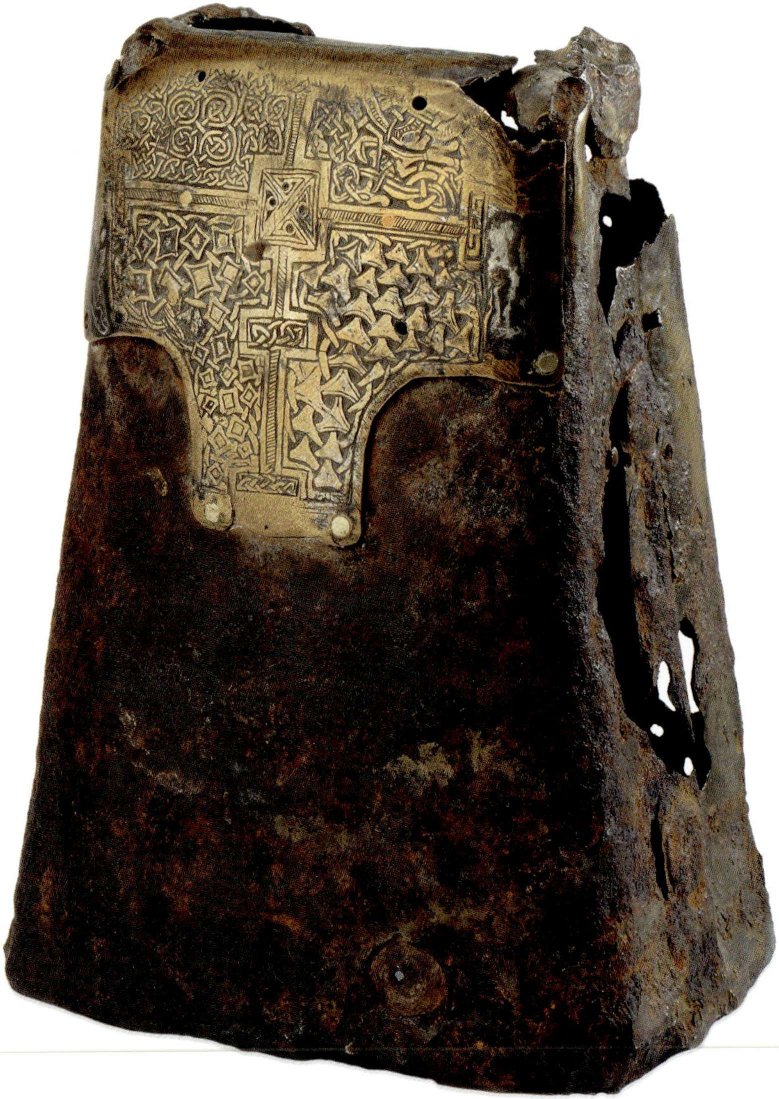

141 CONALL CAEL'S BELL

Bell reliquaries are some of the most unusual testimonies to early Irish Christianity. They are handbells that were believed to have been associated with particular saints during the sixth to eighth century. Once these bells would have been used to call the faithful to Mass, but over time they became objects of veneration. The oldest type are those riveted together from iron sheet, which were later often enclosed in highly ornate shrines, as were other associative relics such as crosiers (**149**) and books.

Conall Cael's bell, named Bearnán Conaill in Irish, was kept on the Island of Inishkeel, where it was visited by pilgrims to St Conall's well. Conall had been an abbot there in the sixth century and this bell, which is said to have belonged to him, went through several stages of embellishment. Firstly, a brass plate with Irish and Viking ornament was attached to the iron body. The type of decoration, which includes interlace patterns and triangular ring-chain shapes, suggests that this happened around AD 1000. During the medieval period a precious shrine of gold, silver and copper alloy completely enclosed the bell, both to honour and protect it.

Reliquaries were not only shown to the faithful, they were also used by them (**142**). Water drunk from bells was believed to cure illness, and from the seventh century onwards all kinds of relics were taken around the country and even carried into battle to ensure victory.

Hereditary keeper families, in this case the O'Breslens, looked after shrines and relics. During the nineteenth century many of these were sold to collectors. This may not only have been motivated by economic strictures as the Church at this time may have discouraged certain practices surrounding relics in an attempt to abolish superstitious customs.

It is said that the aged, last-surviving member of the O'Breslen family sold Conall Cael's bell in exchange for three young cows and an annuity. After that the bell changed hands repeatedly before it was acquired by Augustus Wollaston Franks (**58**), who donated it to the British Museum.

Irish

From Inishkeel, Co. Donegal, Ireland

Bell 7th to 8th century AD

Brass mount late 10th to early 11th century

Shrine 15th century

Height of bell 17.0 cm

Donated by A.W. Franks

1889,0902.22, 22A and .23

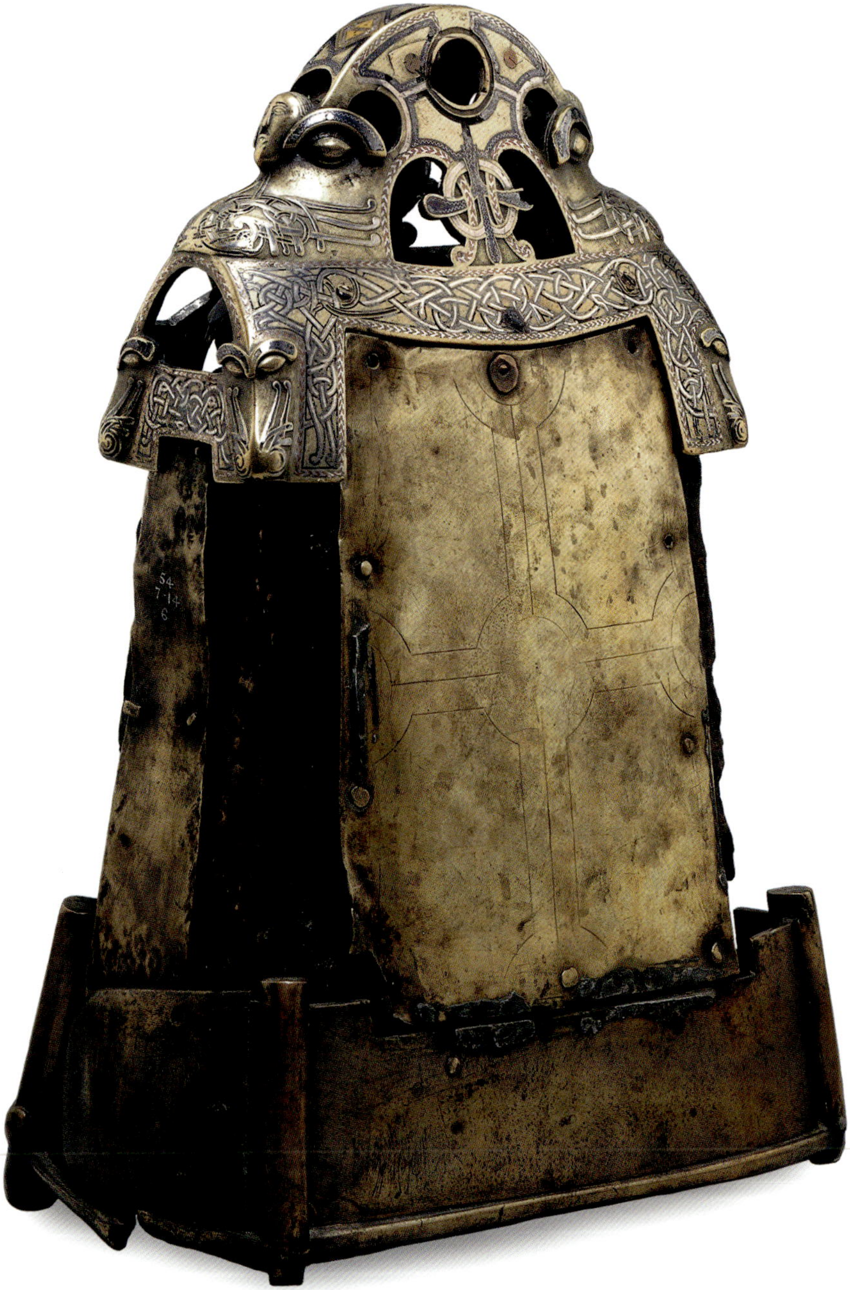
54
7-14
6

142 ST CUILEÁIN'S BELL SHRINE

In the seventh century St Cuileáin founded a monastery at Glankeen and therefore the bell, which is traditionally said to have been his, is known as either the Bearnán Cuileáin or the Glankeen bell. Like many important clerics in early medieval Europe, St Cuileáin came from an influential family. His brother Cormac was the king-bishop at Cashel, the stronghold of the rulers of Munster.

During the twelfth century the Glankeen bell was completely encased in a brass shrine made from individual sections. Several of these, including the original front plate, are now missing, revealing the iron underneath. The back plate is engraved with a large cross design and the front would have featured an applied jewelled cross. The top is intricately inlaid with silver and niello, which outline interlace patterns and highlight the contours of three-dimensional animal and human heads (see p. 4). The ornament is an Irish adaptation of the Viking Ringerike style (**121**). This is seen, for example, in the stylized knot forming the focus of the openwork top which would have accommodated the handle of the bell.

Numerous reliquaries were made or embellished during this time of significant changes in Ireland (**151**), when far-reaching reforms were introduced in the organization and structure of the Church. Meanwhile, several powerful families were competing for political supremacy. In the struggle for prestige, secular patrons commissioned artists to enhance the shrines of local saints. At the same time, the rivalry between churches to become the centres of the newly established dioceses meant that the presence of a powerful saint could tip the decision in their favour.

Little is known about the early history of the Glankeen bell, but it was supposedly discovered in a hollow tree at Kilcuilawn in the early seventeenth century. Thereafter it was used for the swearing of oaths and those who lied were said to suffer immediate convulsions. The bell eventually passed into the collection of antiquities belonging to the Irish historian and collector, T.L. Cooke, which also included the Dowris latchet (**140**).

Irish
Said to be from Kilcuilawn, Co. Tipperary, Ireland
Bell 7th to 8th century AD
Shrine early 12th century
Height of shrine 30.0 cm
1854,0714.6A & B

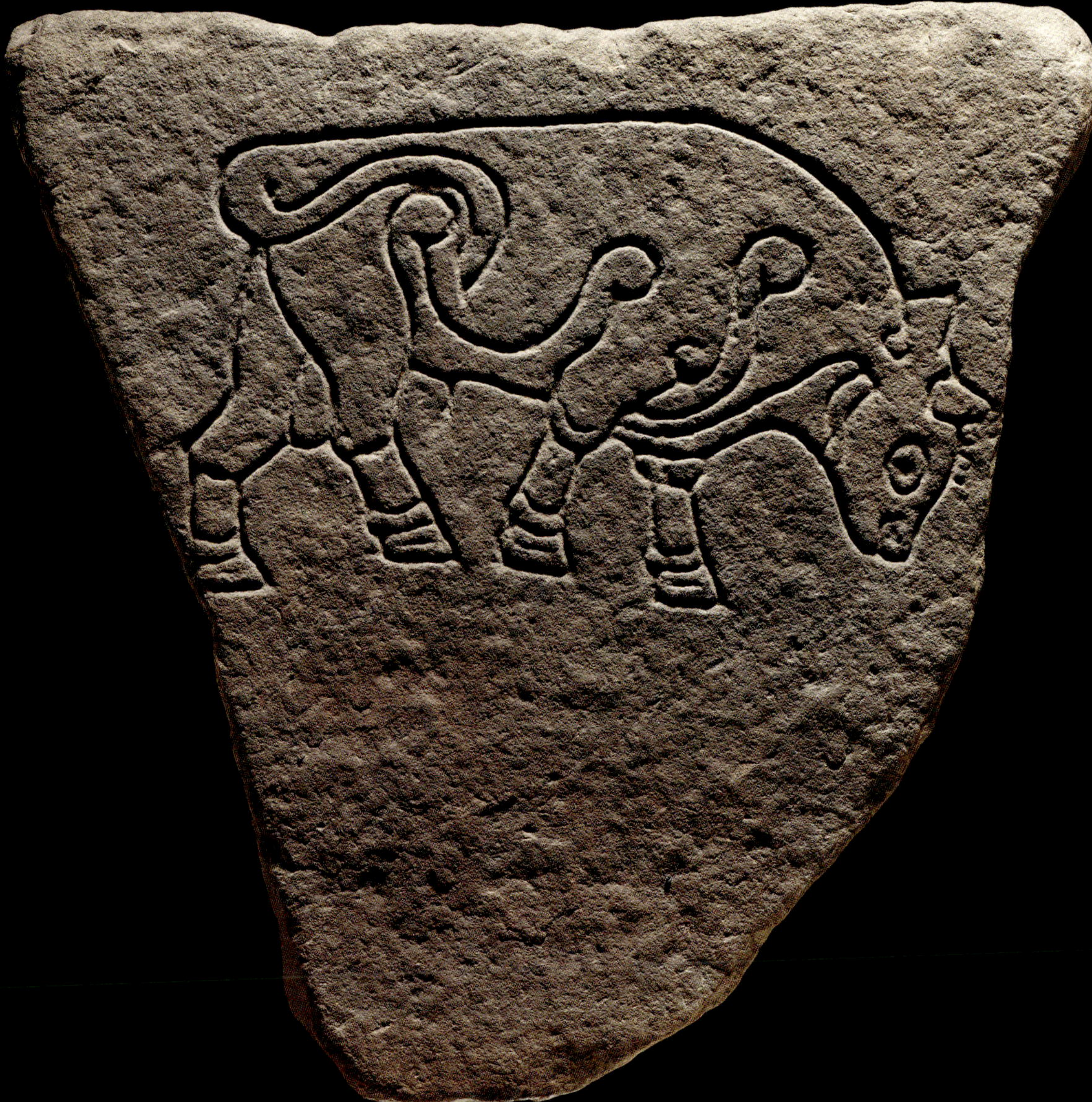

143 THE BURGHEAD BULL

The surface of a water-worn boulder has been evened out and then engraved with this impressive figure of a bull. He is one of about thirty that are said to have been situated around the fort at Burghead, northern Scotland. They were discovered in the nineteenth century during building works, but only six are still preserved.

The bulls are parading to the right, their heads lowered, and it is possible that they were once painted. The lifelike form of the present animal is combined with stylized scrolls to indicate its joints and muscles. Close parallels are known from early illuminated manuscripts, such as the Book of Durrow (folio 124v) from around the 670s or 680s, or the early eighth-century Echternach Gospels (folio 115v). The bull was the symbol of St Luke the Evangelist (**102**) and in both of these manuscripts it has the same curled hips as illustrated here.

Standing stones carved with either naturalistic designs of people and animals, or with an enigmatic set of symbols, were characteristic of the north-east of Scotland where the Picts lived. Little is known about their kingdom, but Pictish sculpture is some of the finest produced in the early medieval world. Earlier pieces such as the Burghead bulls were engraved with the outlines of the designs pecked into the stone. From about the eighth century, the Picts excelled at relief carving and from then onwards, Christian topics on both standing crosses and stone slabs were the most prevalent.

The meaning of the Burghead carvings is unknown, but as bulls are associated with notions of strength and aggression, they may have been linked to a warrior cult. The number of carvings, which must have been visible from a distance, was a statement of power as well as economic potency by whoever had them made and set into the walls of the fortress.

Pictish

From Burghead, Morayshire, Scotland

7th to 8th century AD (?)

Height 53.0 cm

Donated by J. De Carle Sowerby

1861,1024.1

144 THE STEEPLE BUMPSTEAD BOSS

Named after the church in north Essex where it was kept in the nineteenth century, this domed boss is one of the finest pieces in the British Museum's collection of Celtic metalwork. It seems that the boss served as the back plate for the knocker of the church door, although this was by no means its original function. Instead, sets of ornate bosses occur in Irish ecclesiastical contexts, for example, on the book shrine from Lough Kinale or the Tully Lough cross.

The ornament is divided into three tiers, all of which are cross-cut by three-dimensional animals. These are likely to be stylized lions, intended to act as fearsomely toothed guardians against evil. The flange or rim of the boss comprises a ring of spirals derived from the prehistoric La Tène Style (see p. 287). Next is a zone of interlaced animals, from where the detail on the right is drawn. The top tier is filled with whirling triskele panels.

The boss was hollow-cast using the lost-wax method. This process began with a detailed model being made from wax, with the ridges and low-relief ornament already in place. The four large beasts which divide the boss into quadrants were sculpted separately and then applied to the wax body of the dome. Next, the model was covered in clay and the wax was melted out, leaving behind the casting mould which was filled with copper alloy.

A band of niello surrounding the upper plane of the boss was inlaid with silver wires. This is very unusual, as substantial amounts of niello with silver inlay are rarely found on Insular metalwork. Lastly, the boss was gilded. But not everything went as the craftsman planned: some of the gilding has bled over the niello and in the lowest section of ornament the gilding has washed over the relief, partly obscuring the patterns. Comparable contexts for decorative bosses, as well as technological and decorative similarities with some of the foremost pieces of Insular art such as the 'Tara' brooch (National Museum of Ireland, Dublin), indicate that the boss was made in Ireland. How it came to Essex remains a mystery.

Irish

From Steeple Bumpstead, Essex, England

First half of the 8th century AD

Diameter 12.8 cm

1916,0705.1

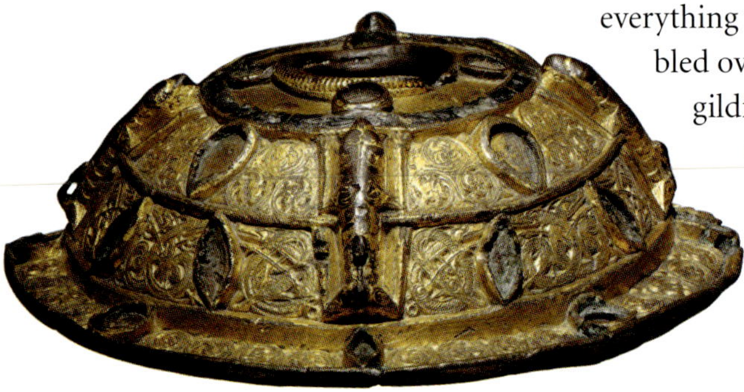

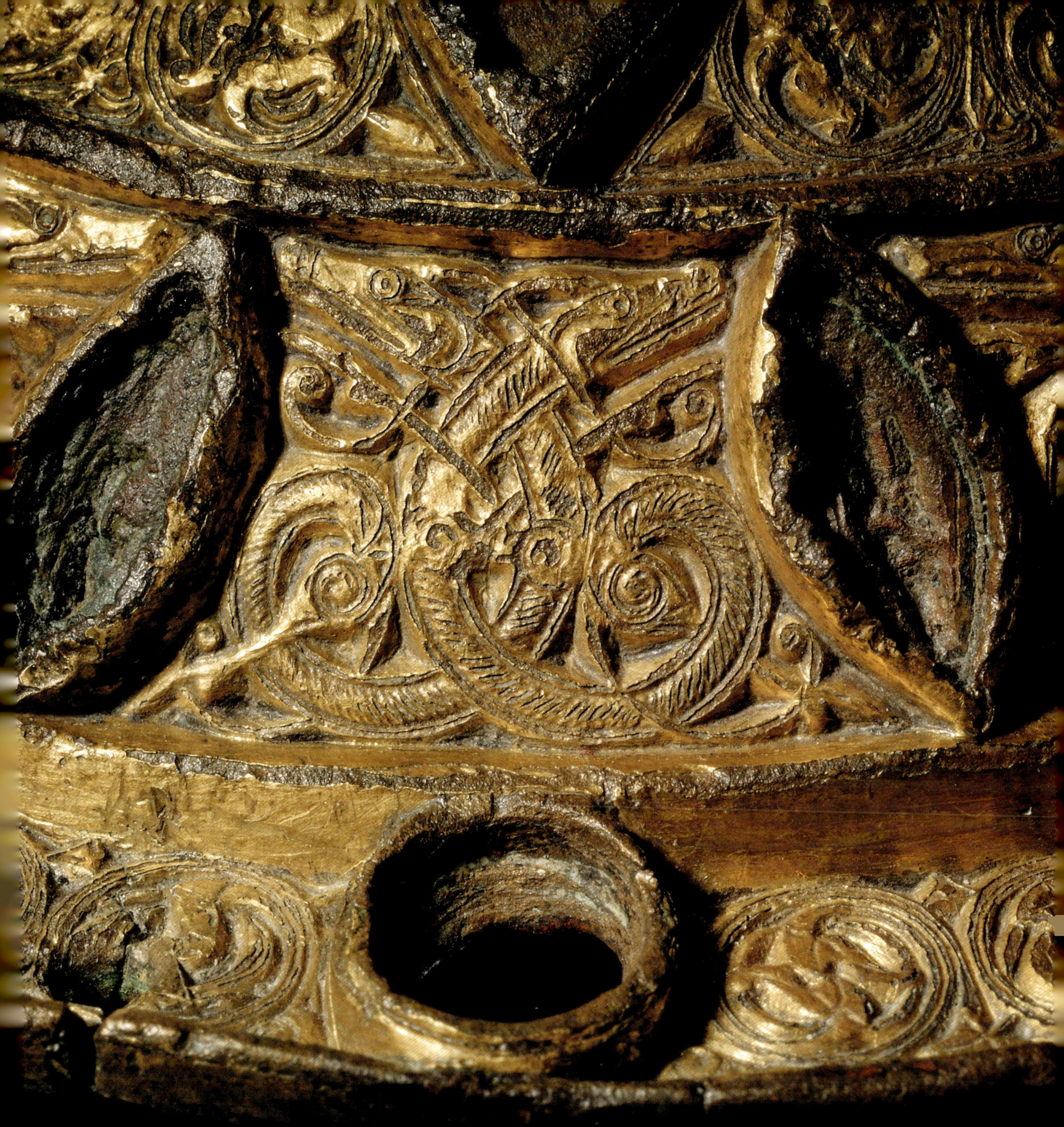

145 MOUNT

Dublin was the most important of the towns founded by Norwegian Vikings in Ireland. Some of the largest urban excavations in Europe have been carried out here, revealing a picture of a thriving settlement with commercial areas where many different crafts were practised.

A number of cemeteries sprang up around the settlement, one of which was in the area of modern-day Phoenix Park. In 1854 the British Museum bought the present gilded copper alloy mount from J. Smith Huband, an Irish antiquary, together with a typical Viking oval brooch. The latter's pair had been donated by Smith Huband to the National Museum in Copenhagen, so there is a possibility that all three pieces may have come from a Viking woman's grave.

The present mount is, however, a reused piece of Irish metalwork (**108**). The copper-gilt casting is decorated with two paired animals, their front legs crossed. The mount's apex is filled with an interlace knot. On either side of it a long-snouted beast with gaping jaws is looking back over its elongated and sinuous body, with spirals used to designate its hip and shoulder joints.

At some point in its history the mount was modified by the addition of two iron nails. As one of them pierces the body of the right-hand animal, it is likely that they were not there originally. It is conceivable that the mount was reworked into a Viking brooch, as there are a number of such finds from both Ireland and Norway.

There are various depictions of animals paired across a tree or similar device in this book (**30**, **34**, **95**, **105**, **133**). Arguably, the Phoenix Park beasts and their relatives on metalwork and in book illumination are a late incarnation of a motif which started out as birds flanking a Tree of Life (**34**). A deeper meaning would be in keeping with the original function of this object as it may have been a mount from a religious book. A second triangular fitting, also from Phoenix Park, possibly came from a wooden shrine (**147**), which would present an alternative ecclesiastical use.

Celtic
From Dublin, Ireland
8th century AD
Length of straight sides 4.9 cm
1854,0307.3

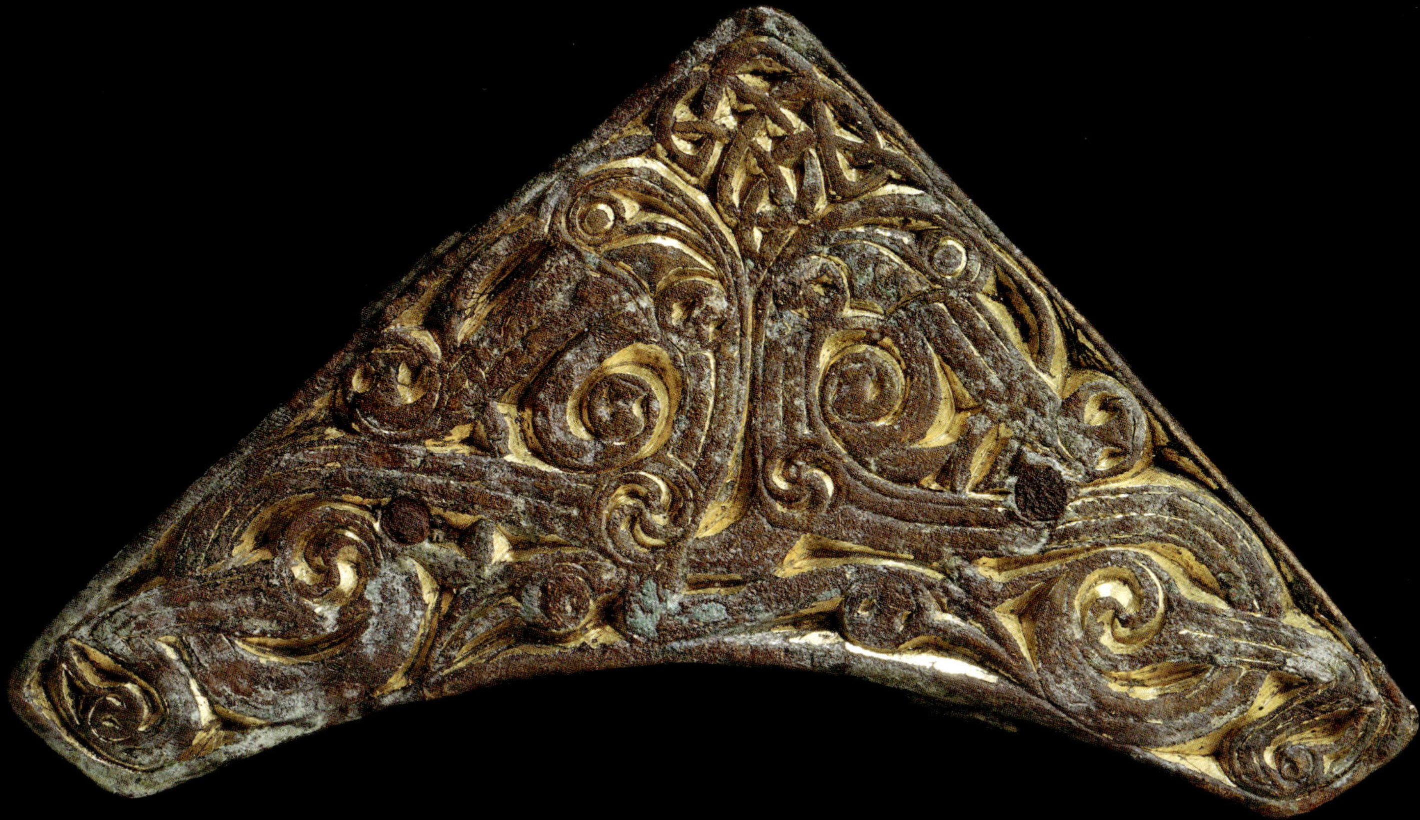

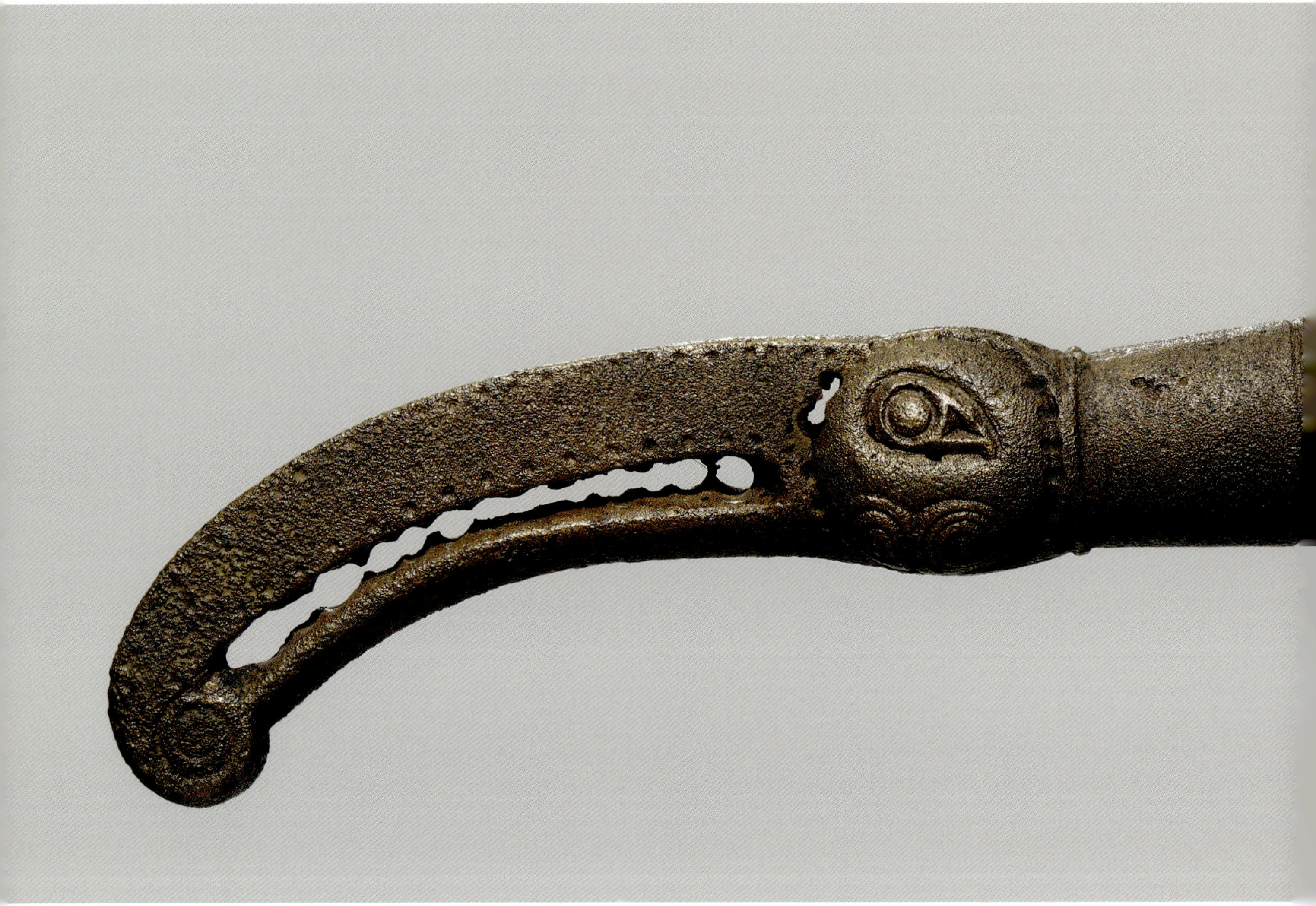

Celtic

From Lismore, Co. Waterford, Ireland

8th century AD

Length 9.0 cm

1853,1013.3

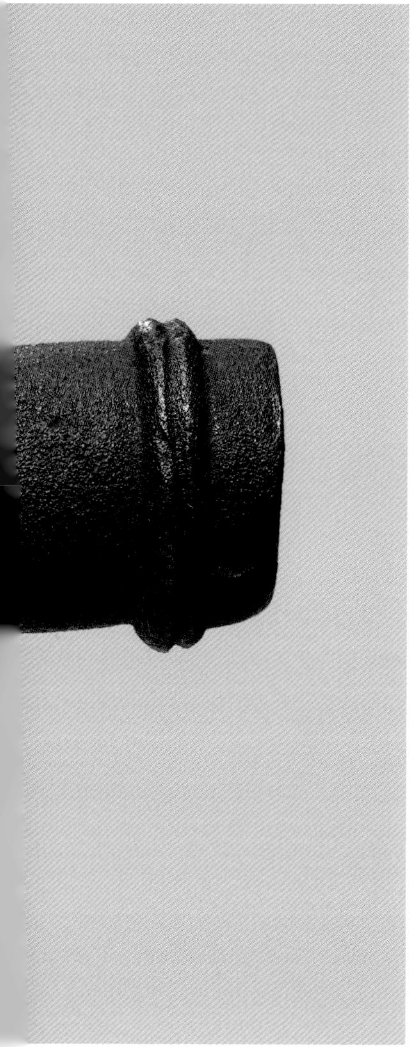

146 DRINKING HORN TERMINAL

Drinking horns were widely used throughout the Germanic world, even though the evidence for examples with metal mounts or those made from glass (**88**) is rare. These vessels were also used by the nearest neighbours of the Anglo-Saxons, although archaeological evidence is equally scarce here. A stone relief from Pictish Scotland in the National Museum of Scotland, Edinburgh, depicts a warrior riding along on his horse while drinking from a horn with a large bird-headed terminal.

The Pictish carving closely resembles this copper alloy terminal from south-eastern Ireland. The long jaws of the animal are slightly parted and its beak is strongly curved. The casting residues between the jaws have not been entirely removed, giving the impression of jagged teeth. The bird's head is modelled in fine detail, with each eye in a drop-shaped frame and two spirals decorating its cheek. The outline has been carefully picked out in dots, which is sometimes also seen in illuminated manuscripts.

The bird-headed terminal is clearly derived from Anglo-Saxon models such as the silver-gilt drinking horn birds in the princely burials at Sutton Hoo (**46**) and Taplow (**43**). The auroch horns in these graves were very large, but the size of the horns carried by some of the Lewis chess figures (**127**) seems to confirm that smaller cow's horns were also used as vessels.

Only a few examples of related drinking horn terminals are known from Ireland or from graves in Norway, where they had travelled with Viking raiders. These also feature the head of either an animal or bird. However, a wooden terminal of a drinking horn was preserved in the waterlogged conditions at the site of Ballinderry Crannóg 1, Westmeath, which is a rare reminder that in the archaeological record in northern Europe normally only non-organic materials are preserved.

Feasting and the hosting of guests were important aspects of the social fabric of early medieval societies. Such drinking horns were perhaps not only for personal use, but may also have been formally passed around the table. This example from Lismore would have reflected well on its owner at any gathering.

147 INTERLACE MOUNT

A common feature of Celtic metalwork of the eighth and ninth century was polychromy. On a gilt ground, glass and amber settings (**148**), as well as niello inlays (**144**), provided striking contrasts of colour. In addition, the rich texturing of the surface through the use of filigree, repoussé or chip-carved ornament enhanced the shimmering appearance of jewellery and ecclesiastical plate.

This mount combines dark blue glass gems with pale glass inlays. The oval shape of the latter is also seen on the Steeple Bumpstead boss (**144**), which has unfortunately lost all of its inlays. Perhaps the light glass lenses were meant to represent rock crystal, which was rare and difficult to work as it is very hard. Its attractive appearance as well as its purity made it eminently suitable for religious objects, such as the St Denis and Lothair Crystals (**97**, **98**), which both date to the ninth century. It is unclear where the crystals used on later medieval Irish metalwork came from, but there are deposits in Scotland and Wales, areas which Ireland had close contact with at the time.

The blue glass gems here are inspired by Anglo-Saxon metalwork. Round gold and garnet cloisonné bosses graced jewellery and dress accessories such as the Taplow buckle (**43**) and Kentish disc brooches. To imitate them, cabochons of glass were cast in a mould with a grid pattern. This grid was then inlaid with metal wires, imitating the metal cells of cloisonné. Remains of a poor-quality silver inlay are still visible in the recesses of the central blue glass setting of this mount. Some of the glass cabochons were fully translucent, as the light green settings on a brooch from Ireland shows (see p. 286). Most glass gems have been found without metal grids, although they do occasionally survive, for instance on a blue glass stud from the site of an early medieval monastery at Portmahomack, Scotland.

On the back of the present mount there is a thick shaft, constructed so that the fitting could be affixed to and removed from a substantial wooden backing, for example during cleaning. Some Celtic house-shaped reliquaries are decorated with ornamental discs, so this is one possible use of the mount illustrated here.

Celtic
From Ireland
8th to 9th century AD
Width including lobes 5.3 cm
1920,1022.1

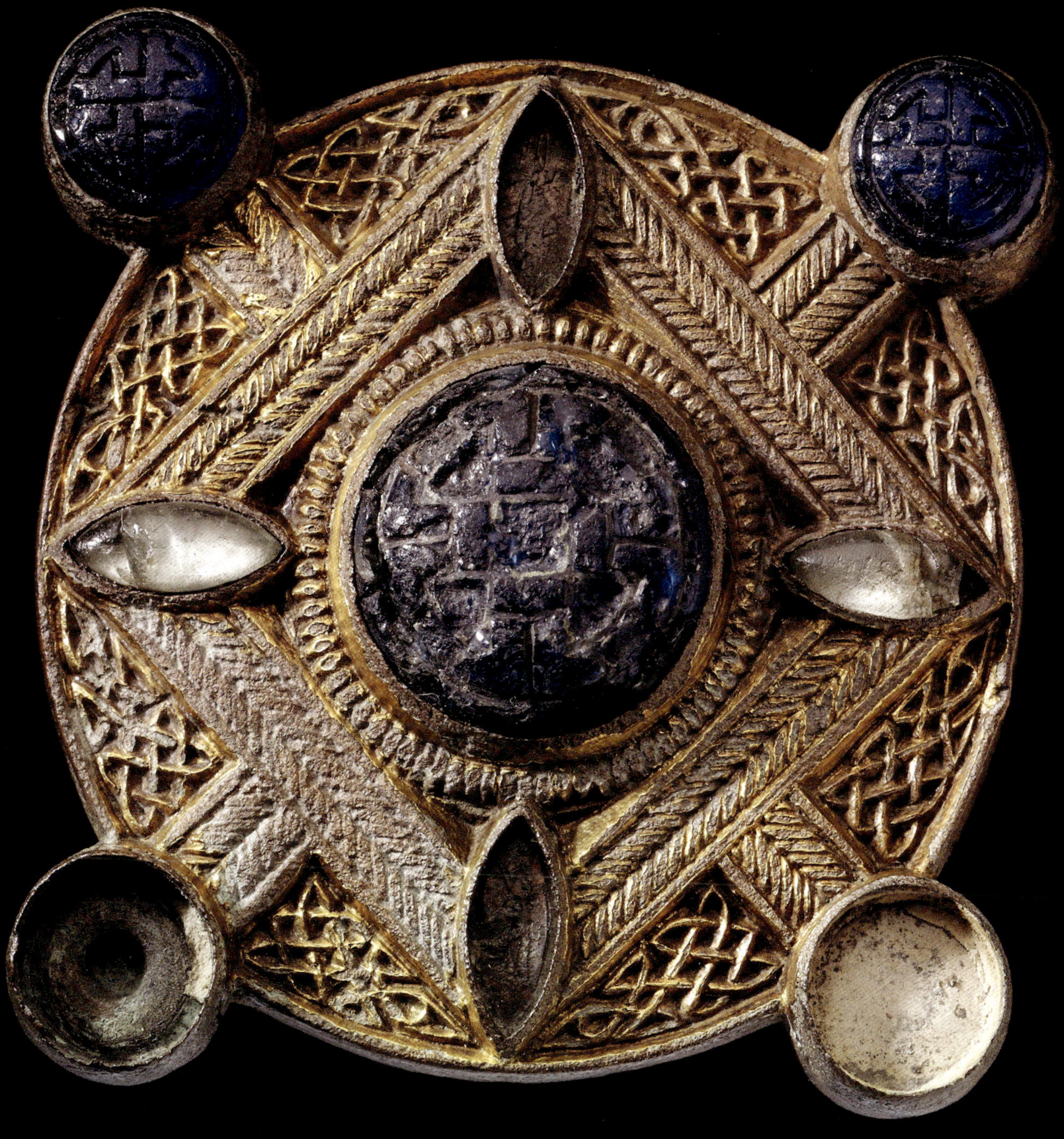

148 THE LONDESBOROUGH BROOCH

Like the previously discussed large silver pin (**19**), this brooch was formerly in the collection of Albert Denison, 1st Baron Londesborough (1805–60), a politician and collector of antiquities. It is unknown where and when the brooch was found, but by around 1871 Dublin jewellers were producing approximately half-sized replicas to meet the demand for historical jewellery.

The original illustrated here is a sumptuous example of an Irish brooch made in the penannular tradition (**139**). Being a late piece, the terminals of the brooch are linked rather than separate, and it would have been fastened to a garment with the aid of a cord or metal chain. Although the alloy from which it was cast is poor, composed of only about one third of silver, the front was thickly gilt. The ornamental bosses, which are clearly related to the much larger decorations found on shrines (**144**), had amber gems set into their tops. This is a rare material for inlays. It is also unusual that the complete texturing of the surface with interlace, spiral patterns and animal ornament is entirely executed in chip-carved and cast ornament, as opposed to filigree which was used on similar brooches. The corner frames set with blue glass inlays provide a further display of colour. The brooch is most probably an Irish piece, perhaps made for a prominent cleric, as a small number of stone sculptures show them wearing such cloak fasteners.

In some of the decorative panels on the brooch terminals and pinhead, there are writhing interlaced animals, some with open maws, and birds' heads flank the outer rim of the brooch terminals. It is accepted that in both technological and stylistic respects, such animal ornamentation on Celtic metalwork is heavily influenced by that of the Anglo-Saxons. And yet only a small quantity of Anglo-Saxon objects has actually been found in Ireland. Metalwork from Merovingian Francia and even Byzantium may have played a part as well. High-status centres in both western Scotland and Ireland played a pivotal role in the development of these new style elements. These sites would have brought secular patrons and excellent craftsmen together with imported goods and jewellery from the Anglo-Saxon regions, as well as from Francia and the Mediterranean.

Irish
Unknown findspot
Late 8th to early 9th century AD
Diameter including projections 10.6 cm
1888,0719.101

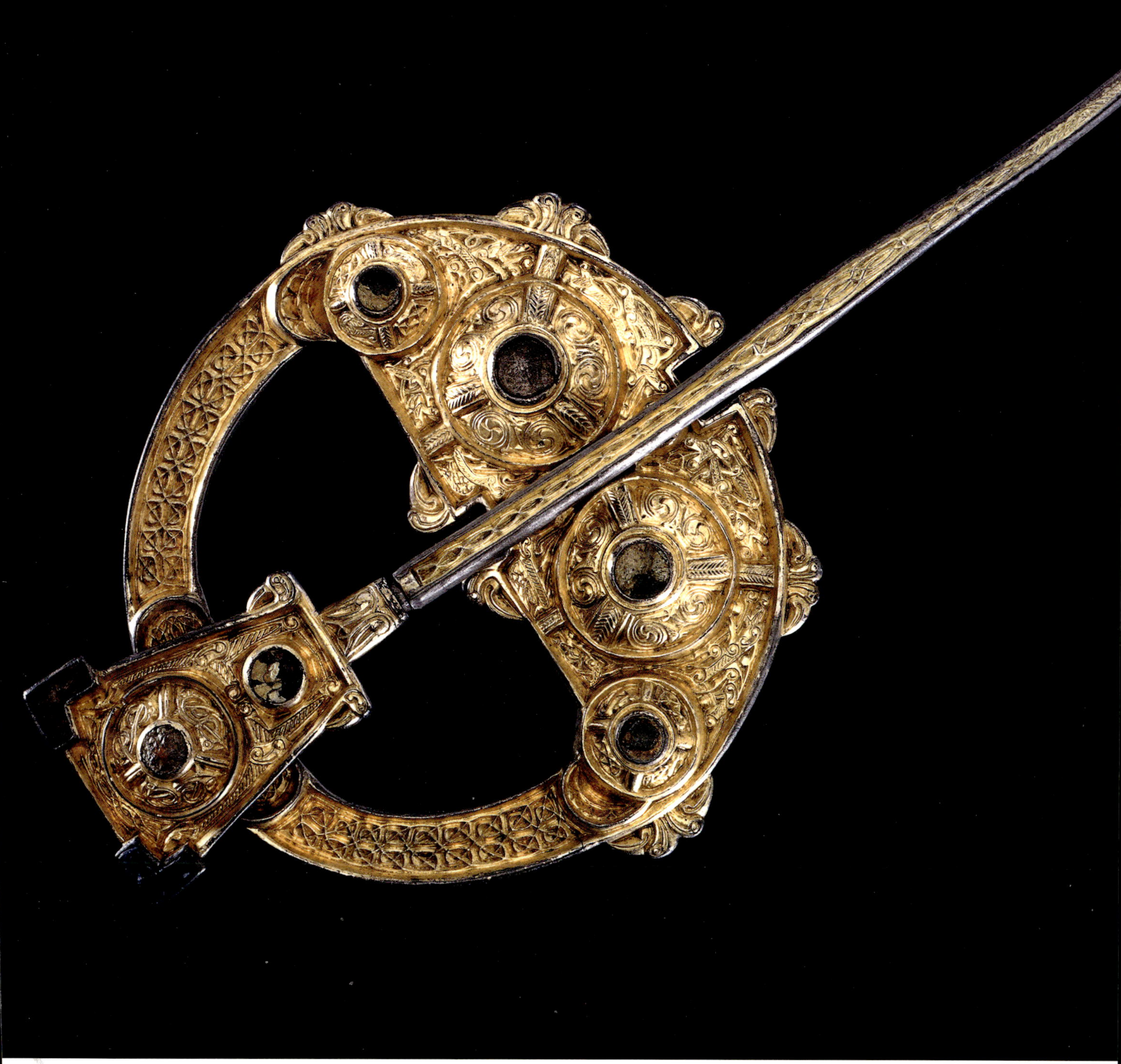

149 THE 'KELLS' CROSIER

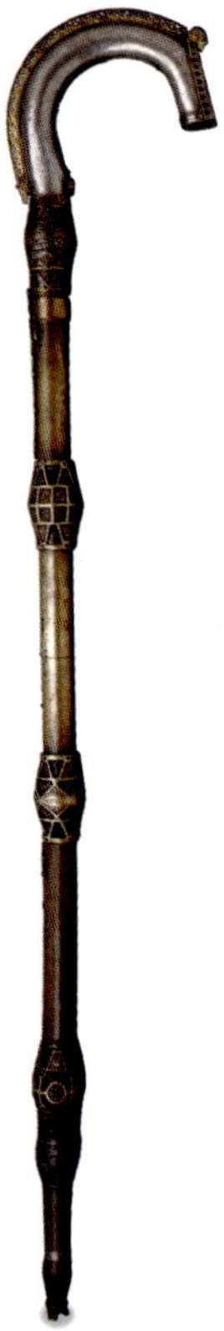

Irish

Unknown findspot

Wooden crosier 8th to 10th century AD

Mounts second half of the 10th, 11th and 14th century

Height 133.0 cm

1859,0221.1

This crosier was sold at the auction of the estate of a London solicitor in 1850. It had been discovered behind a cupboard at his chambers without any further information. From the names in an inscription on the crook, scholars have argued that the crosier had been refurbished at a monastery at Kells, County Meath, but this association has since been seriously questioned.

Crosiers and handbells are shown on contemporary Irish sculpture and both were venerated as holy relics and enshrined (**144**, **147**). Like other such relics, this crosier is therefore multi-layered (**141**, **142**).

The underlying crooked staff was made from yew wood. It is undated, but is a type of crosier found in Ireland from the eighth century onwards. This wooden core was given a brass casing with enlarged, ornamented collars called knops in the tenth century. The crook casing displayed panels of interlaced and animal ornament, but this became worn, perhaps by the hands of the faithful touching it, and was then partly filed down. Repairs and refurbishment may have followed a violent episode when the crook was cut off the staff.

In the eleventh century a new silver cover with a crest of gilded openwork was positioned over the brass casing for the crook. A sculpted head crowns the end of the crook and below there is a hollow box designed to hold relics. Its original lid was replaced during the later Middle Ages. In the late eleventh century the uppermost knop was replaced with another one featuring fine Viking-period Ringerike foliate ornament (**121**, **122**) in niello and silver wire.

During conservation work at the British Museum, red wool felt was found wrapped around the upper end of the wooden shaft, as well as red and blue pieces of felt which were located inside one of the knops, but their significance is as of yet unknown.

The splendid appearance of this crosier, with its animal, plant and anthropomorphic ornament executed in silver, gilding, niello and brass, demonstrates the esteem in which it was held for generations. Moreover, it splendidly illustrates the synthesis of Irish and Viking art styles through the medium of the finest Irish metalwork.

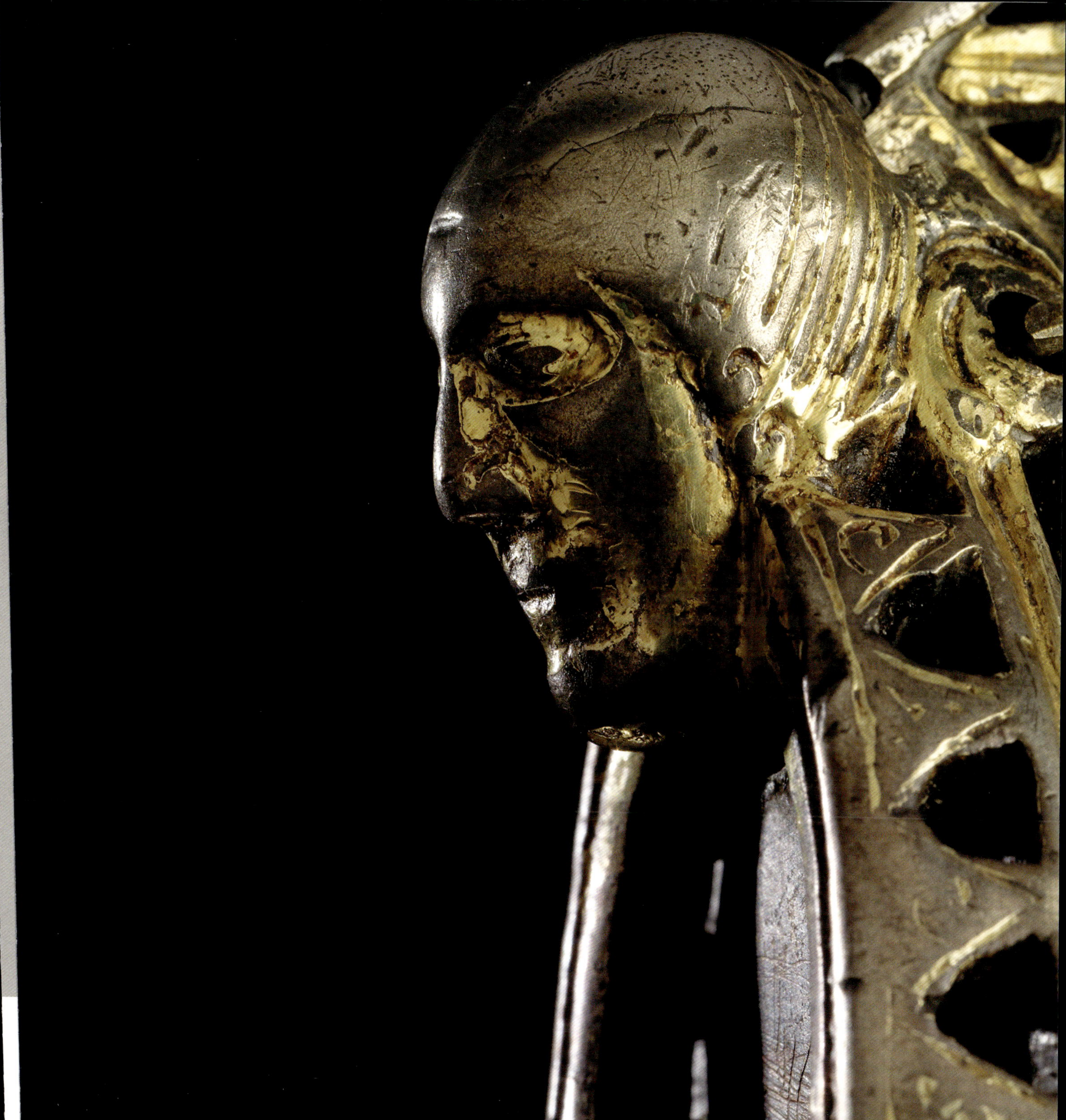

151 CRUCIFIXION PLAQUE

A crucified Christ is depicted on this cast copper alloy plaque, although the cross itself is not visible. His body is stocky and his eyes are wide open, mirroring the theological principle of Christ as the victor, triumphing over death, which was also followed on a late antique crucifixion ivory (**15**). Longinus pierces Christ's side with a lance, while another soldier Stephaton raises the staff with a sponge dipped in vinegar to his mouth. Above, two angels are seen in flight. The strictly symmetrical arrangement of the scene is accentuated by the geometrical treatment of Christ's hair, beard and loincloth, as well as the hair and tunics of the two soldiers.

This plaque is one of eight very similar examples, all from Ireland, and their function has been much debated. They could possibly be book cover mounts, which would have been applied in a similar way to the ivory carving (**15**). However, new research favours the suggestion that they were fixed to wooden crosses. Earlier examples of such altar or processional crosses are known from Tully Lough, Ireland, as well as Bischofshofen in Austria. The latter was made by an Anglo-Saxon craftsman for a monastery which had an Irish abbot. Furthermore, Crucifixion plaques were carved onto several Irish stone crosses, a practice which is thought to have been inspired by wooden crosses with metal mounts.

The introduction of crosses, with dimensions of a size suitable for the application of openwork plaques like this one here, may be related to the ecclesiastical changes in Ireland in the early twelfth century (**142**). These included modifications to the way in which the liturgy was conducted and to the layout of churches. All of this may well have precipitated the development of new forms of altar and processional equipment.

The British Museum plaque is damaged and heavily worn. The yellow sheen on the brass is caused by a lack of patina, which is in keeping with the idea that the plaque was regularly touched and kissed by the faithful.

Irish

Found near Kells, Co. Meath, Ireland

11th to first half of the 12th century

Height 8.2 cm

1983,0701.1

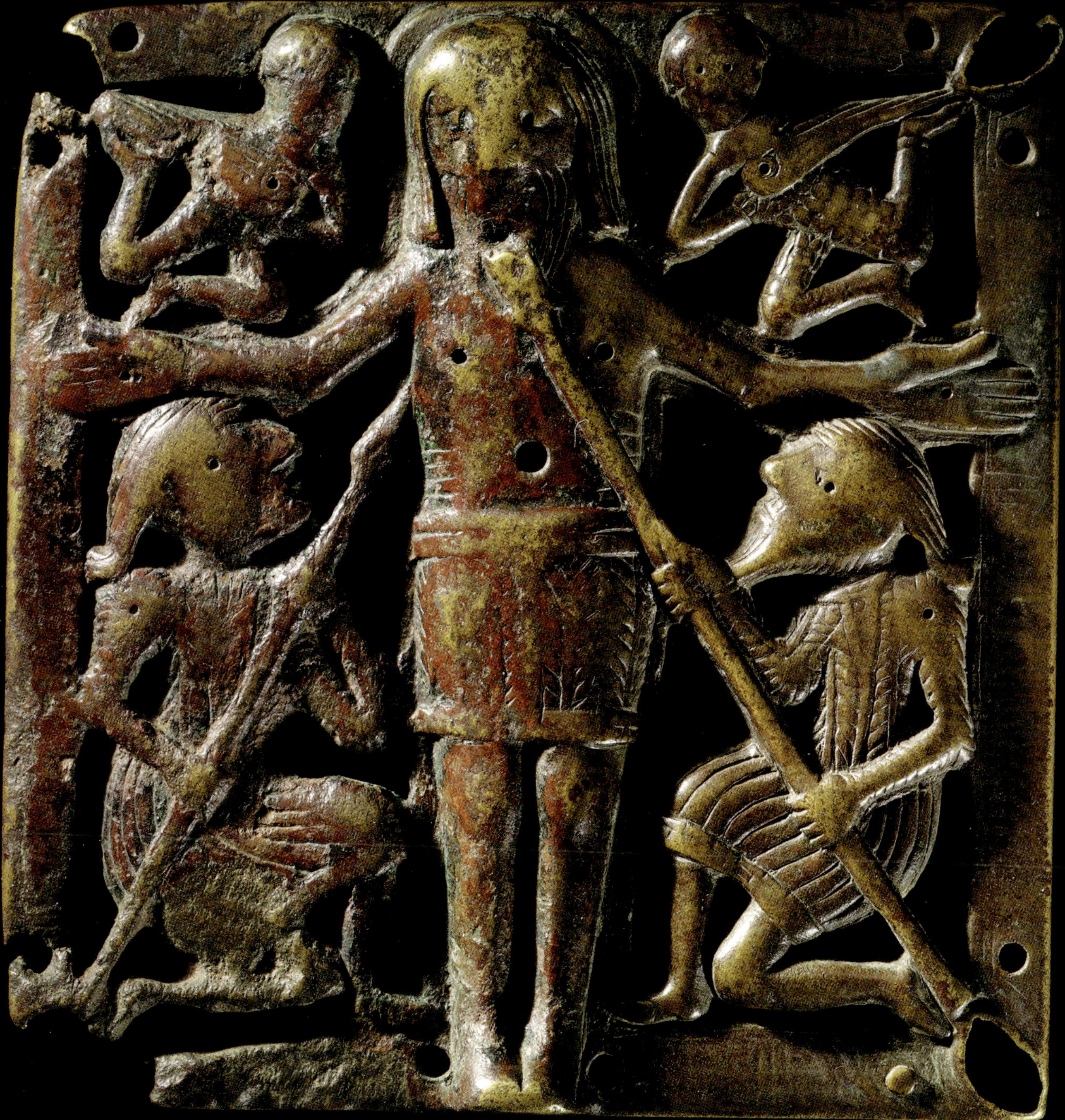

MAPS

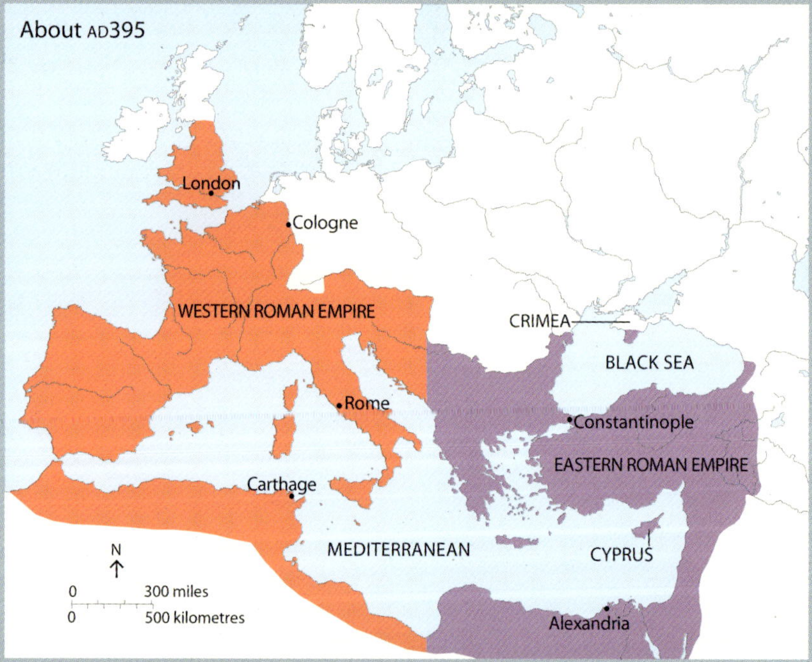

About AD395
London
Cologne
WESTERN ROMAN EMPIRE
CRIMEA
BLACK SEA
Rome
Constantinople
EASTERN ROMAN EMPIRE
Carthage
MEDITERRANEAN
CYPRUS
Alexandria
N
0 300 miles
0 500 kilometres

Map 1

Map 2

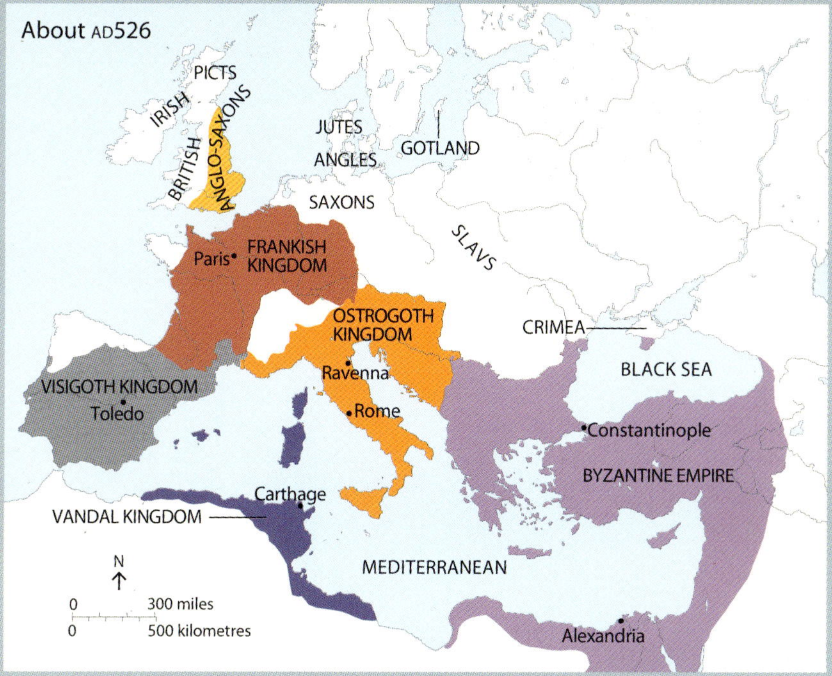
About AD526
PICTS
IRISH
BRITISH
ANGLO-SAXONS
JUTES
ANGLES
GOTLAND
SAXONS
SLAVS
Paris
FRANKISH KINGDOM
OSTROGOTH KINGDOM
CRIMEA
BLACK SEA
Ravenna
VISIGOTH KINGDOM
Toledo
Rome
Constantinople
BYZANTINE EMPIRE
Carthage
VANDAL KINGDOM
N
MEDITERRANEAN
0 300 miles
0 500 kilometres
Alexandria

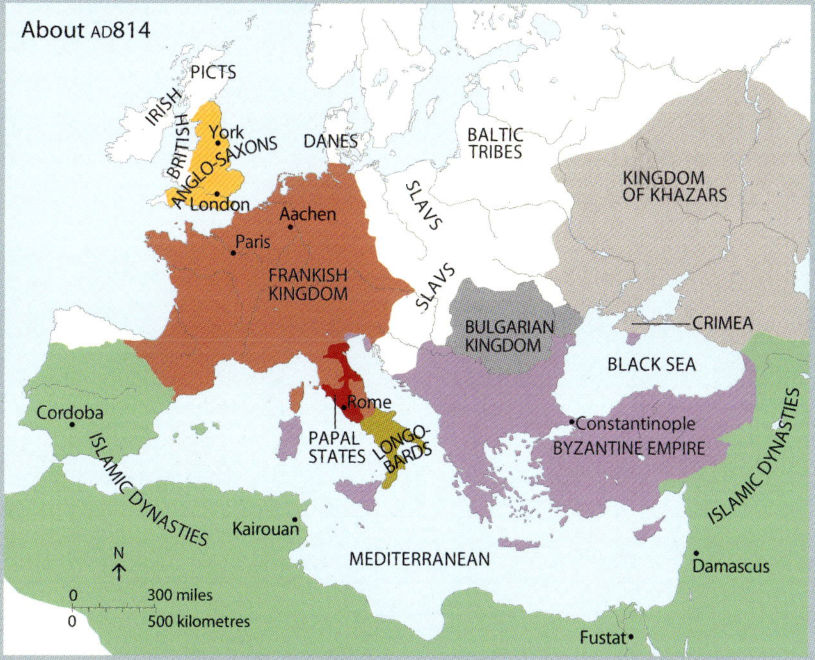
About AD814
PICTS
IRISH
BRITISH
York
ANGLO-SAXONS
DANES
BALTIC TRIBES
KINGDOM OF KHAZARS
London
SLAVS
Aachen
Paris
FRANKISH KINGDOM
SLAVS
BULGARIAN KINGDOM
CRIMEA
BLACK SEA
Rome
Cordoba
PAPAL STATES
LONGO-BARDS
Constantinople
BYZANTINE EMPIRE
ISLAMIC DYNASTIES
ISLAMIC DYNASTIES
Kairouan
N
MEDITERRANEAN
Damascus
0 300 miles
0 500 kilometres
Fustat

Map 3

Map 4

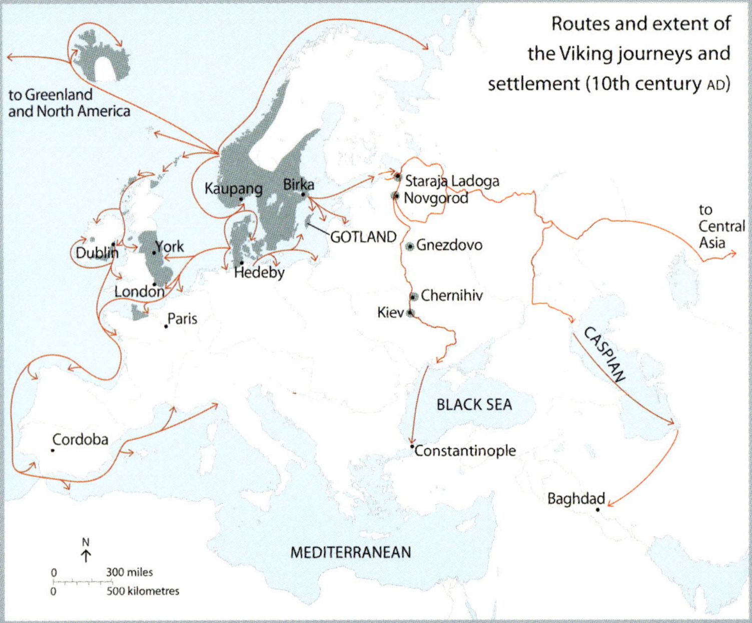
Routes and extent of
the Viking journeys and
settlement (10th century AD)
to Greenland
and North America
Kaupang
Birka
Staraja Ladoga
Novgorod
to
Central
Asia
GOTLAND
Dublin
York
Gnezdovo
Hedeby
London
Chernihiv
Paris
Kiev
CASPIAN
BLACK SEA
Cordoba
Constantinople
Baghdad
N
0
300 miles
0
500 kilometres
MEDITERRANEAN

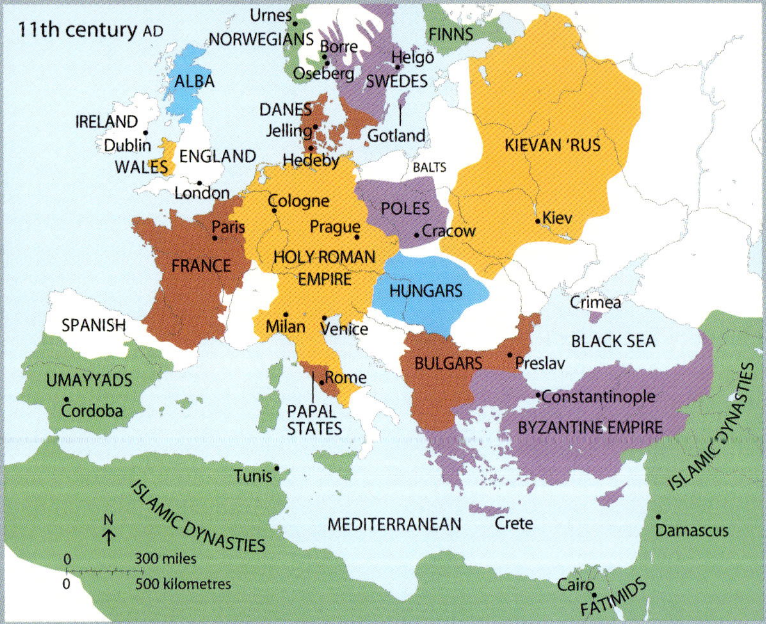
11th century AD
Urnes
NORWEGIANS
Borre
FINNS
Helgö
Oseberg
SWEDES
ALBA
DANES
IRELAND
Jelling
Gotland
Dublin
KIEVAN 'RUS
WALES
ENGLAND
Hedeby
BALTS
London
Cologne
POLES
Paris
Prague
Cracow
Kiev
FRANCE
HOLY ROMAN
EMPIRE
HUNGARS
Crimea
SPANISH
Milan
Venice
BLACK SEA
BULGARS
Preslav
UMAYYADS
Rome
Constantinople
Cordoba
PAPAL
STATES
BYZANTINE EMPIRE
ISLAMIC DYNASTIES
Tunis
ISLAMIC DYNASTIES
N
MEDITERRANEAN
Crete
Damascus
0
300 miles
0
500 kilometres
Cairo
FATIMIDS

Map 5

FURTHER READING

The literature recommended for each introductory essay will also be relevant to many of the objects in the chapter. Further information and images are available through the British Museum's Collections Online facility at www.britishmuseum.org. Unless otherwise stated, the objects fall under the care of the Department of Prehistory and Europe. The publications suggested for each entry will also provide information on the objects discussed but not illustrated in this book.

Some of the objects featured in the book (**41**, **52**, **59**, **68**, **111** and **119**) were acquired under the Treasure Act. For more information about this and the Portable Antiquities Scheme, please go to finds.org.uk.

PREFACE

The quote by Isidore is taken from his *Etymologies*, Book VI, viii.1–2, in a translation following that published by Barney S.A., Lewis W.J., Beach J.A. and Berghof O., *The Etymologies of Isidore of Seville* (Cambridge 2006), 139.

CHAPTER 1

Ward-Perkins B., *The Fall of Rome and the End of Civilization* (Oxford 2005).

1. Freestone I., Meeks N., Sax M. and Higgitt C., 'The Lycurgus Cup – a Roman Nanotechnology'. *Gold Bulletin* 40.4, 2007, 270–7.
2. Spier J., *Late Antique and Early Christian Gems* (Wiesbaden 2007), 53–4, cat. no. X66.
3. Elsner J., *Roman Eyes: Visuality and Subjectivity in Art and Text* (Princeton 2007), 200–24.
4. *Byzantium, Treasures of Byzantine Art and Culture from British Collections.* Exhibition, London (1994), cat. nos 13 and 14.
5. Toth B.L., 'The Six Techniques of Pierced Jewellery in Late Antiquity and their Evolution'. In: Entwistle C. and Adams N. (eds), *'Intelligible Beauty': Recent Research on Byzantine Jewellery.* British Museum Research Publications 178 (London 2010), 1–12.
6. Kaufmann-Heiniman A., contributions in: Guggisberg M.A., *Der spätrömische Silberschatz von Kaiseraugst: Die neuen Funde* (August 2003), 149–64 and cat. no. HF.92.
7. Nüsse H.-J., 'Römische Goldgläser – alte und neue Ansätze zu Werkstattfragen'. In: *Prähistorische Zeitschrift* 83, 2008, 222–56, esp. 249, 253–4 and ill. Abb. 27.
8. *Otto der Gosse und das Römische Reich.* Exhibition, Magdeburg (2012), cat. no. II.8.
9. *Saved! 100 Years of the National Art Collections Fund.* Exhibition, London (2003), cat. no. 56.
10. Baratte F., Lang J., La Niece S. and Metzger C., *Le trésor de Carthage: contribution à l'étude de l'orfèvrerie de l'Antiquité tardive* (Paris 2002).
11. Bisconti F., 'Primi passi di un'arte cristiana'. In: *Antiquité Tardive* 19, 2011, 35–46, esp. 39–40.
12. Aurrecoechea J. and Ager B., 'Late Roman Iconongraphic Representations of Hispano-Roman Bridle Cheek-pieces'. In: *Bonner Jahrbücher* 200, 2000, 275–92.
13. Kiilerich B., 'Symmachus, Boethius and the Consecratio Ivory Diptych.' In: *Antiquité Tardive* 20, 2012, 205–15.
14. Swift E., *Style and Function in Roman Decoration* (Farnham 2009), 155–7.
15. *Picturing the Bible: The Earliest Christian Art.* Exhibition, Fort Worth, Texas (2007), cat. no. 57.
16. *Corpus der römischen Funde im europäischen Barbaricum, Deutschland Band 6: Land Sachsen-Anhalt* (Bonn 2006), cat. no. VIII, 10–12/1.21 and pl. Taf. 86a, b.
17. Hunter F., 'Beyond the Frontier: Interpreting Late Roman Iron Age Indigenous and Imported Material Culture'. In: Collins R. and Allason-Jones L. (eds), *Material Culture in the 4th–5th Centuries.* CBA Research Report 162 (York 2012), 96–109, esp. 98–100.
18. Marzinzik S., *Early Anglo-Saxon Belt Buckles (Late 5th to Early 8th Centuries AD): Their Classification and Context.* BAR British Series 357 (Oxford 2003), Type II.3.
19. Gavin F., 'Insular Military-Style Silver Pins in Late Iron Age Ireland'. In: Hunter F. and Painter K. (eds), *Late Roman Silver Within and Beyond the Frontier: The Traprain Treasure in Context* (Edinburgh 2013), 427–39.
20. Hirst S.M. and Clark D., *Excavations at Mucking, vol. 3: The Anglo-Saxon Cemeteries* (London 2009), part i 146–7, part ii 551–3.
21. Inker P., 'Technology as Active Material Culture: The Quoit-brooch Style'. In: *Medieval Archaeology* 44, 2000, 25–52.

CHAPTER 4
Wickham C., *The Inheritance of Rome: A History of Europe from 400 to 1000* (London 2009).

77. Miks C., *Studien zur Römischen Schwertbewaffnung in der Kaiserzeit.* Kölner Studien zur Archäologie der römischen Provinzen 8 (Rahden/Westfalen 2007), vol. 1, 308–13.
78. Andrási J., *The Berthier-Delagarde Collection of Crimean Jewellery in the British Museum and Related Material.* British Museum Research Publications 166 (London 2008), cat. no. 15.
79. Eger C., *Spätantikes Kleidungszubehör aus Nordafrika I: Trägerkreis, Mobilität und Ethnos im Spiegel der Funde der spätesten römischen Kaiserzeit und der Vandalischen Zeit.* Münchner Beiträge zur Provinzialrömischen Archäologie 5 (Wiesbaden 2012), 227–30, Taf. 13, 21.
80. *Tesoro de las Culturas del Mundo.* Exhibition, Madrid (2009), 284.
81. Ljungkvist J., 'Continental Imports to Scandinavia'. In: Quast D. and Böhme H.W. (eds), *Foreigners in Early Medieval Europe.* RGZM Monographs 78 (Mainz 2009), 27–49, esp. 31–3, 44–7.
82. Kazanski M., Mastykova A. and Périn P., 'Die Archäologie der Westgoten in Nordgallien: Zum Stand der Forschung'. In: *Zwischen Spätantike und Frühmittelalter.* Reallexikon der Germanischen Altertumskunde Ergänzungsbände 57 (Berlin and New York 2008), 149–92, esp. 163–8 and ill. Abb. 14.
83. Böhner K., 'Die frühmittelalterlichen Spangenhelme und die nordischen Helme der Vendelzeit'. In: *Jahrbuch des Römisch-Germanischen Zentralmuseums* 41.2, 1994, 471–549, esp. 547–9.
84. Eagleton C. and Williams J., *Money: A History* (London 2007), 63–4.
85. Nerman B., *Die Vendelzeit Gotlands*, vol. I.1 and II (Stockholm 1975 & 1969), 11, 13–4, ill. Taf. 9 no. 68.
86. Quast D., 'Schmuckstein- und Glasschnallen des 5. und frühen 6. Jahrhunderts aus dem östlichen Mittelmeergebiet und dem "Sasanidenreich"'. In: *Archäologisches Korrespondenzblatt* 26, 1996, 333–45.
87. Daim F., 'Pilgeramulette und Frauenschmuck? Zu den Scheibenfibeln der frühen Keszthely-Kultur'. In: *Zalai Múzeum* 11, 2002, 113–24.
88. Evison V.I., ed. Marzinzik S., *Catalogue of Anglo-Saxon Glass in the British Museum.* British Museum Research Publications 167 (London 2008), esp. 12–13 and cat. nos 47–48.
89. Pekarskaja L.V. and Kidd D., *Der Silberschatz von Martynovka (Ukraine) aus dem 6. und 7. Jahrhundert* (Innsbruck 1994).
90. Skre D. (ed.), *Things from the Town: Kaupang Excavation Project vol. 3.* Norske Oldfunn XXIV (Oslo 2011), 185–6, fig. 9.62ao–aq, bj–bo.
91. Menghin W., *Tauschierarbeiten der Merowingerzeit* (Berlin 1994).
92. Bálint C., 'Avar Goldsmiths' Work from the Perspective of Cultural History'. In: Entwistle C. and Adams N. (eds), *'Intelligible Beauty': Recent Research on Byzantine Jewellery.* British Museum Research Publications 178 (London 2010), 146–60.
93. Schulze-Dörrlamm M., B*yzantinische Gürtelschnallen und Gürtelbeschläge im Römisch-Germanischen Zentralmuseum Mainz, Teil II.* Kataloge Vor- und Frühgeschichtlicher Altertümer 30.2 (Mainz 2009), esp. forms E25, E26.
94. Riemer E., 'Byzantinische und romanisch-mediterrane Fibeln in der Forschung'. In: Daim F. and Drauschke J. (eds), *Byzanz – das Römerreich im Mittelalter, Teil 1: Welt der Ideen, Welt der Dinge.* RGZM Monographs 84.1 (Mainz 2010), 283–335, esp. 285–7, 308.
95. *799 – Kunst und Kultur der Karolingerzeit.* Exhibition, Paderborn (1999), vol. 2, cat. no. XI.11.
96. *The Grand Atelier.* Exhibition, Brussels (2007), cat. no. II.7.
97. MacGregor N., *A History of the World in 100 Objects* (London 2010), no. 53.
98. *Le trésor de Saint-Denis.* Exhibition, Paris (1991), cat. no. 17.
99. Tait H., *5000 Years of Glass* (London 1991), esp. 115–22.
100. *Glass of the Sultans.* Exhibition, Corning, NY, and Athens (2001), 3–7, cat. nos 43–5.
101. *Otto der Große und Magdeburg.* Exhibition, Magdeburg (2002), 363–73 and cat. no. V.35g.
102. *Treasures of Heaven.* Exhibition, Cleveland, Baltimore and London (2010–11), cat. no. 60.
103. Schulze-Dörrlamm M., *Die Kaiserkrone Kondrads II. (1024–1039).* RGZM Monographs 23 (Sigmaringen 1991), esp. 119–21.
104. *Das Reich der Salier.* Exhibition, Speyer (1992), 275–6 and cat. no. 5.
105. Muthesius A., *Byzantine Silk Weaving* AD *400–1200* (Vienna 1997), 115 and cat. no. M119, pl. 110B.

CHAPTER 5

Brink S. and Price N. (eds), *The Viking World* (Oxford 2008).

106. Callmer J., 'Beads and Bead Production in Scandinavia and the Baltic Region *c.* AD 600–1100: A General Outline'. In: Freeden U.von and Wieczorek A. (eds), *Perlen: Archäologie, Techniken, Analysen* (Bonn 1997), 197–202.
107. Clarke D.V., 'James Curle and Newstead'. In: Hunter F. and Keppie L. (eds), *A Roman Frontier Post and its People: Newstead 1911–2011* (Edinburgh 2012), 23–34.
108. Skre D. (ed.), *Means of Exchange. Kaupang Excavation Project vol. 2: Dealing with Silver in the Viking Age.* Norske Oldfunn XXIII (Oslo 2007), esp. 126–7, 159–78.
109. Porter V., *Arabic and Persian Seals and Amulets in the British Museum.* British Museum Research Publications 160 (London 2011), cat. no. 232.
110. Bender Jørgensen L., 'The Introduction of Sails to Scandinavia: Raw Materials, Labour and Land'. In: Berge R., Jasinski M.E. and Sognnes K. (eds), *N-Tag Ten: Proceedings of the 10th Nordic Tag Conference.* BAR International Series 2399 (Oxford 2012), 173–81.
111. Wamers E., 'The Vale of York Cup'. In: Graham-Campbell J., *The Cuerdale Hoard and Related Viking-Age Silver and Gold from Britain and Ireland in the British Museum.* British Museum Research Publications 185 (London 2011), 133–5.
112. *Die Wikinger.* Exhibition, Speyer (2008), 201, 283.
113. McEvansoneya P., 'The "Ardrahan" Brooch'. In *Journal of the Galway Archaeological and Historical Society* 62, 2010, 19–29.
114. Pedersen A., 'Viking Weaponry'. In: Brink S. and Price N. (eds), *The Viking World* (London 2008), 204–11.
115. Tsigaridas Glørstad Z., 'Sign of the Times? The Transfer and Transformation of Penannular Brooches in Viking-Age Norway'. In: *Norwegian Archaeological Review* 45.1, 2012, 30–51.
116. Thunmark-Nylén L., *Die Wikingerzeit Gotlands,* vol. III.1, 64–87 and vol. IV.1, 73 (Stockholm 2006, 2000).
117. Peirce I., *Swords of the Viking Age* (Woodbridge 2002), 104–5.
118. Wendt A., 'Viking Age Gold Rings and the Question of 'Gefolgschaft''. In: *Lund Archaeological Review* 13–14, 2007–8, 75–89.
119. Graham-Campbell J., *The Cuerdale Hoard and Related Viking-Age Silver and Gold from Britain and Ireland in the British Museum.* British Museum Research Publications 185 (London 2011), 126–7.
120. Sheehan J., 'Hiberno-Scandinavian Broad-band Arm-rings'. In: Graham-Campbell J., *The Cuerdale Hoard and Related Viking-Age Silver and Gold from Britain and Ireland in the British Museum.* British Museum Research Publications 185 (London 2011), 91–100.
121. Wilson, D.M., *Anglo-Saxon Ornamental Metalwork, 700–1100, in the British Museum* (London 1964), no. 83.
122. Richards J.D., 'Anglo-Scandinavian Identity'. In: Hamerow H., Hinton D. and Crawford S. (eds), *The Oxford Handbook of Anglo-Saxon Archaeology* (Oxford 2011), 46–61.
123. O'Meadhra U., *Motif Pieces from Ireland,* vols 1 and 2 (Stockholm 1979, 1987), cat. no. 114.
124. Gibbons Mi., Gibbons My. and Higgins J., 'Hiberno-Norse Ringed Pin from Omey Feichín, Connemara: Its Historical and Cultural Setting'. In: *Journal of the Galway Archaeological and Historical Society* 57, 2005, 151–65.
125. *Die Wikinger.* Exhibition, Speyer (2008), 284–5.
126. Fugelsang S.H., 'Animal Ornament: The Late Viking Period'. In: Müller-Wille M. and Larsson L.O. (eds), *Tiere, Menschen, Götter: Wikingerzeitliche Kunststile und ihre neuzeitliche Rezeption* (Göttingen 2001), 157–94, esp. 176–7, 193.
127. Caldwell D.H. *et al.*, 'The Lewis Hoard of Gaming Pieces: A Re-examination of their Context, Meanings, Discovery and Manufacture'. In: *Medieval Archaeology* 53, 2009, 155–203.
128. Rispling G., 'Coins with Crosses and Bird Heads: Christian Imitations of Islamic coins'. In: *Fornvännen* 82, 1987, 75–87.
129. *Katalog der Ausstellung zur Konferenz Baltischer Archäologen in Riga.* Exhibition, Riga (1930), 6, 123 no. 31, 173, pl. Taf 44.4.
130. *Baltų menas – Art of the Balts.* Exhibition, Vilnius (2009), esp. 159–65.
131. Arne T.J., *Västsibirisk Kultur för 1000 År Sedan* (Stockholm 1932), esp. 9 and figs 4, 18, 24, 42.
132. Golden P.B., *Turks and Khazars.* Variorum Collected Studies 952 (Farnham 2010).
133. Ristovska N., '"Temple Pendants" in Medieval Rus': How were they Worn?' In: Entwistle C. and Adams N. (eds), *'Intelligible Beauty': Recent Research on Byzantine Jewellery.* British Museum Research Publications 178 (London 2010), 203–11.
134. Bosselmann-Ruickbie A., *Byzantinischer Schmuck des 9. bis frühen 13. Jahrhunderts* (Wiesbaden 2011), esp. cat. nos 116a and b, and ill. Abb. 146, 147.

CHAPTER 6
Laing L.R., *The Archaeology of Celtic Britain and Ireland c.* AD *400–1200* (Cambridge 2006).

135. Gavin F., 'Insular Military-style Silver Pins in Late Iron Age Ireland'. In: Hunter F. and Painter K. (eds), *Late Roman Silver within and beyond the Frontier: The Traprain Treasure in Context* (Edinburgh 2013), 427–39.
136. Redknap M. and Lewis J.L. (eds), *A Corpus of Early Medieval Inscribed Stones and Stone Sculpture in Wales*, vol. I (Cardiff 2007), 131–6, 139–45.
137. Youngs S., 'From Metalwork to Manuscript: Some Observations on the Use of Celtic Art in Insular Manuscripts'. In: *Anglo-Saxon Studies in Archaeology and History* 16, 2009, 45–64.
138. Henderson J., 'The Production Technology of Irish Early Christian Glass with Specific Reference to Beads and Enamels'. In: Price J. (ed.), *Glass in Britain and Ireland* AD *350–1100*. British Museum Occasional Paper 127 (London 2000), 143–59.
139. Murray G., 'A Zoomorphic Penannular Brooch from Tullahennell North, Co. Kerry'. In: *North Munster Journal of Archaeology* 50, 2010, 15–27.
140. Haseloff G. and Roth U., *Penannular-Fibeln, Latches, Hand-pins und Hanging Bowls: Studien zur spätkeltischen Ornamentik*. Bonner Beiträge zur Vor- und Frühgeschichtlichen Archäologie 4 (Bonn 2005), 123–5, no. 98.
141. Bourke C., 'Early Irish Hand Bells'. In: *Journal of the Royal Society of Antiquaries of Ireland* 110, 1980, 52–66.
142. Ó Floinn R., *Irish Shrines and Reliquaries of the Middle Ages* (Dublin 1994).
143. Netzer N., 'New Finds Versus the Beginning of the Narrative on Insular Gospel Books'. In: Hourihane C. (ed.), *Insular and Anglo-Saxon Art and Thought in the Early Medieval Period*. Index of Christian Art Occasional Papers 11 (Princeton 2011), 3–13, esp. 11–13.
144. Youngs S., 'The Steeple Bumpstead Boss'. In: Spearman M.R. and Higgitt J. (eds), *The Age of Migrating Ideas* (Edinburgh 1993), 143–50.
145. Hall R.A., 'A Viking Grave in the Phoenix Park, Co. Dublin'. In: *Journal of the Royal Society of Antiquaries of Ireland* 104, 1974, 39–43.
146. *The Work of Angels*. Exhibition, London (1989), cat. no. 53.
147. *The Work of Angels*. Exhibition, London (1989), cat. no. 141.
148. Ó Floinn R., 'The Anglo-Saxon Connection: Irish Metalwork, AD 400–800'. In: Graham-Campbell J. and Ryan M. (eds), *Anglo-Saxon/Irish Relations before the Vikings*. Proceedings of the British Academy 157 (Oxford 2009), 231–51.
149. Johnson R., 'On the Dating of Some Early-Medieval Irish Crosiers'. In: *Medieval Archaeology* 44, 2000, 115–58.
150. Graham-Campbell J., *The Cuerdale Hoard and Related Viking-Age Silver and Gold from Britain and Ireland in the British Museum*. British Museum Research Publications 185 (London 2011), 111, 113–16.
151. Murray G., 'Irish Crucifixion Plaques: A Reassessment'. In: Mullins J., Ní Ghrádaigh J. and Hawtree R. (eds), *Envisioning Christ on the Cross in the Early Medieval West* (Dublin forthcoming).

GLOSSARY

abrasive paste: an abrasive (for example, particular types of sand or ground pumice), mixed with oil or water.
acanthus: an ornament based on the leaves of the acanthus plant, an evergreen shrub from the Mediterranean area. Seen in scrolling arrangements in Graeco-Roman art and much used from the Carolingian period onwards.
aedicula: a building depicted in a classical style, with columns supporting a gabled roof.
ampulla: a small container, often in the shape of a flask, for holding sacred oil or water.
animal interlace: geometric ornament made from intertwined strands which may have added animal heads or limbs; the interlace itself may have formed the animals' bodies.
Animal Style I: see Style I.
Animal Style II: see Style II.
annular: in the shape of a closed ring.
apotropaic: evil-averting.
apse: a semicircular and often domed niche at the eastern end of a church where the main altar is placed.
aurochs: a today extinct species of large, wild cattle from northern Europe.
Bacchus: see Dionysus.
Bede/the Venerable Bede: a monk and scholar (*c.* AD 673–735), whose most famous work was *The Ecclesiastical History of the English People*, written at the monastery of Jarrow in northern England.
benedictional: a book of blessings used by a bishop on feast days.
bezel: the enlarged, decorative part of a finger-ring.
billeted: filled with transverse ridges arranged in an ornamental band.
Borre Style: a Viking art style current from around the mid-ninth to late tenth century AD, characterized among other traits by the presence of Gripping Beasts.
bucolic: referring to an (idealized) rural idyll.
cable pattern: a twisted form of ornament resembling a cable.
cabochon: a gemstone or glass setting of a convex, rounded shape without facets.
cameo: a gem, for example made from precious stone or glass, with a design carved in high relief.
Carolingians: a Frankish dynasty (AD 751–887) not founded by Charlemagne (AD 768–814), but named after him.
Carpathian Basin: a region, most of which is in modern-day Hungary, partly bounded by the Carpathian Mountains.
Celtic: here referring to the non-Anglo-Saxon parts of the British Isles in the early Middle Ages – Ireland, western Britain, the Atlantic Isles and Scotland – and their material culture.
Charlemagne: a Frankish king (AD 768–814) and emperor from AD 800, after whom the term 'Carolingian' was coined.
chasing: decorating a metal surface with tools by moving and shaping the material (rather than removing it, as in engraving).
chip-carving: a metalworking technique derived from woodworking and characterized by deep-cut relief surfaces separated by sharp, narrow ridges.
cloisonné: a technique of inlaying slips, usually of garnet or glass, into upright metal frames set on a metal backing surface.
cloisonné enamel: a technique of pouring molten enamel into upright metal frames set on a metal backing surface and allowing it to harden.
Coptic: here used as a chronological term describing textiles from Egypt which date from the late antique to early Islamic periods.
cuirass: a piece of armour protecting the torso.
cullet: broken glass intended for recycling.
Danelaw: the part of eastern and northern England later known by this name which was controlled by the Vikings from the late ninth century AD and administered according to Danish law until the Norman Conquest (AD 1066).
Dionysus: Graeco-Roman god of wine and fertility, called Bacchus in Latin. Also venerated in Egypt during late antiquity.
diptych: a pair of panels made from wood, ivory or metal, joined with hinges along their longer sides.
dirham: an Islamic silver coin.
dowel: a small peg or pin without a head used for fastening metal or wooden pieces together.
encolpion: a Byzantine piece of religious jewellery worn on the chest.
erots: often chubby, winged male children who represent Eros, the god of love, in late Roman and Byzantine art.
Evangelist symbols: the figures used to represent the four Evangelists and their Gospels: a man or angel for St Matthew, a lion for St Mark, a bull for St Luke and an eagle for St John.
filigree: decoration formed from fine wires, which are often twisted, plaited or beaded and applied to a metal background.
flange: a horizontal, broad rim.
floriate: a floral type of ornament which resembles flowers or foliage.
fresco: a painting executed on plaster which is still wet. Once the plaster has dried, such images are particularly durable.
garnet: a red gemstone.

INDEX

First published in 2013 by The British Museum Press
A division of The British Museum Company Ltd
38 Russell Square, London WC1B 3QQ
britishmuseum.org/publishing

A catalogue record for this book is available from the British Library

ISBN: 978-0-7141-2320-2

Designed by Andrew Shoolbred

Printed and bound in China by C&C Offset Printing Ltd

Papers used by The British Museum Press are recyclable products made from wood grown in well-managed forests and other controlled sources. The manufacturing processes conform to the environmental regulations of the country of origin

p. 1: Curtain (detail), Coptic, *c.* AD 600 (?) (**32**)
pp. 2–3: Disc brooch, Viking, mid-9th to mid-10th century AD (**112**)
p. 4: St Cuileáin's bell shrine (detail of the crest), early 12th century (**142**)
p. 5: Marriage ring, late Roman or early Byzantine, late 4th to early 5th century AD (**14**)
p. 340: The Mucking belt set (detail), first half of the 5th century AD (**18**)

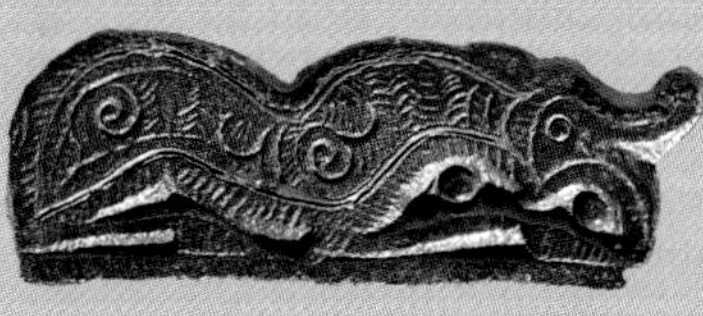